SUDAN IN TURMOIL

Memorial

Robert O. Collins, 1933-2008

More than a colleague
A close friend

Sudan in Turmoil

Hasan al-Turabi and the Islamist State,
1989-2003

J. Millard Burr
and
Robert O. Collins

Markus Wiener Publishers
Princeton

For information, write to Markus Wiener Publishers,
231 Nassau Street, Princeton, NJ 08542
www.markuswiener.com

Library of Congress Cataloging-in-Publication Data

Burr, Millard.
  Sudan in turmoil : Hasan al-Turabi and the Islamist state, 1989-2003 /
J. Millard Burr and Robert O. Collins. — 1st American ed.
   p. cm.
   Rev. ed. of: Revolutionary Sudan. 2003.
   Includes bibliographical references and index.
   ISBN 978-1-55876-509-2 (hardcover : alk. paper)
   ISBN 978-1-55876-510-8 (pbk. : alk. paper)
  1. Sudan—Politics and government—1985- 2. Turabi, Hasan. 3. Islam and
politics—Sudan. 4. Islam and state—Sudan. I. Collins, Robert O., 1933-
II. Burr, Millard. Revolutionary Sudan. III. Title.
   DT157.673.B867 2009
   962.404'3—dc22
                            2009025237

CONTENTS

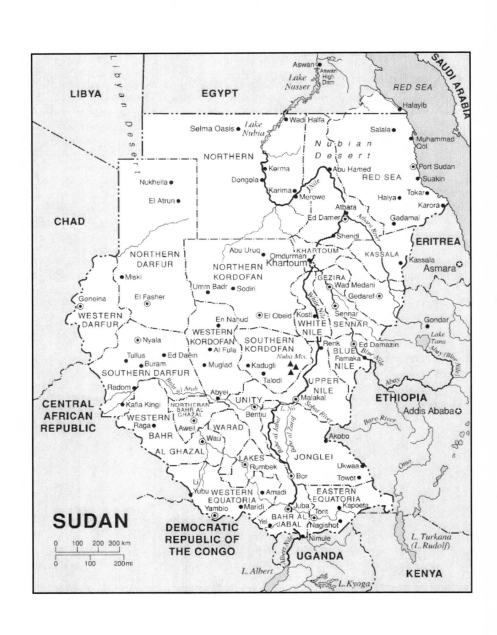

ABBREVIATIONS

AFP	Agence France Presse.
AGI	Arab Group International.
AID	United States Agency for International Development.
AIM	Armed Islamist Movement.
AKSEF	Call sign for Arakis Energy on the NASDAQ Stock Exchange.
BBC	British Broadcasting Corporation.
BND	Bundesnachrichtendienst (German Federal Intelligence Service).
bopd	barrels of oil per day.
CAIM	Council of Arab Interior Ministers.
CCI	Compagnie de Constructions Internationales.
CDLR	Committee for the Defense of Legitimate Rights.
CIA	Central Intelligence Agency (United States).
CIPF	Council for International People's Friendship.
CNODC	Chinese National Oil Development Corporation.
CNPC	China National Petroleum Corporation.
COPI	Chevron Overseas Petroleum Incorporated.
CSF	Central Security Force (Fgypt).
DFLP	Democratic Front for the Liberation of Palestine.
DGSE	Direction Générale de la Sécurité Extérieure.
EC	European Community.
EIJ	Eritrean Islamic Jihad.
ELF	Eritrean Liberation Front.
ELF-RC	Eritrean Liberation Front— Revolutionary Council.
EPLF	Eritrean People's Liberation Front.
EPRDF	Ethiopian People's Revolutionary Democratic Front.
FBI	Federal Bureau of Investigation (United States).
FBIS	Foreign Broadcast Information Service.
FIS	Islamic Salvation Front (Algerian).
GIA	Armed Islamic Group (Algerian).
GMT	Greenwich Mean Time.

GNPC   Greater Nile Petroleum Corporation.

GOS   Government of Sudan.

IARA   Islamic African Relief Agency.

ICF   Islamic Charter Front.

ICP   Islamic Committee for Palestine.

IGADD, IGAD   Originally Inter-Governmental Authority on Drought
            and Development (IGADD), which became the Inter-
            Government Authority on Development (IGAD).

IMF   International Monetary Fund.

INCB   International Narcotics Board (United Nations).

IOA   Islamic Organization in Africa.

IPC   Independent Petroleum Corporation.

IPK   Islamic Party of Kenya.

IPS   Inter-Press Services.

IPSL   International Petroleum Sudan Limited.

IRNA   Islamic Republic News Agency.

ISI   Inter-Service Intelligence Agency (Pakistan).

ISRA   Islamic Relief Agency.

IS-SOR   Originally Revolution/Revolutionary Intelligence Agency,
            later shortened to Internal-Security— Security of the
            Revolution.

IWR   Information World Review.

LMC   Legitimate Military Command.

LRA   Lord's Resistance Army.

MAK   The Mujahideen Services Bureau (*Maktab al-Khidamat
            al-Mujahideen al-Arab*).

ME   Middle East.

MENA   Middle East News Agency.

MSF   Médicins sans Frontières.

MWL   Muslim World League.

NDA   National Democratic Alliance.

NDG   National Democratic Grouping.

NGO   Non-Governmental Organization.

NIF   National Islamic Front.

NSRCC   National Salvation Revolutionary Command Council.

OAU	Organization of African Unity.
OIC	Organization of the Islamic Conference.
OLF	Oromo Liberation Front.
OPEC	Organization of Petroleum Exporting Countries.
PAIC	Popular Arab and Islamic Congress.
PANA	Pan-African News Agency.
PCP	Popular Congress Party.
PDF	People's Defense Force.
PFLG-GC	Popular Front for the Liberation of Palestine—General Command.
PFLP	Popular Front for the Liberation of Palestine.
PLO	Palestine Liberation Organization.
PNC	Popular National Congress.
PRC	People's Republic of China.
PSA	Production Sharing Agreement.
RCC	Revolutionary Command Council.
SAF	Sudanese Allied Forces.
SPAF	Sudan People's Armed Forces.
SPCC	State Petroleum Corporation of Canada.
SPDF	Sudan People's Democratic Front.
SPLA	Sudan People's Liberation Army.
SPLM	Sudan People's Liberation Movement.
SSB	Sudan Security Bureau.
SSIM	South Sudan Independence Movement.
TNA	Transitional National Assembly.
TNC	Transitional National Council.
TPLF	Tigre People's Liberation Front.
TWRA	Third World Relief Agency.
UN/DHA	United Nations Department of Humanitarian Affairs.
USC	United Somali Congress.
WBNF	West Nile Bank Front.
WIL	Originally the Muslim World League, now called the World Islamic League or Islamic World League.
WMD	Weapons of Mass Destruction.
YSP	Yemen Socialist Party.

PREFACE

This book investigates the objectives, activities, and a decade of success and failure by Islamist military officers and civilians to create the first Islamic government in Africa after the coup d'état by Brigadier Omar Hasan Ahmad al-Bashir on 30 June 1989. It is not a study of the internal political dynamics of the Sudan during the ten years after June 1989. Much has been written and more has been discussed accompanied by rhetoric and speculation about the Islamist revolutionary government that followed, but there has been little of substance about those who participated in this revolution. Nor does this volume focus on the multitude of and egregious human rights violations by a notoriously cruel government. It is not a biography of Hasan al-Turabi, the Sudanese intellectual and internationally known Islamist, a task begun by Abd al-Wahab al-Affendi in 1991. It is not a continuation of the historical narrative of the Sudan begun by the authors in *Requiem for the Sudan: War, Drought, and Disaster Relief on the Nile* (Boulder: Westview Press, 1995). Our intention is to delineate, describe, and analyze the role played by Hasan al-Turabi in the Sudan, the world, and the revolutionary government from its relative isolation at the confluence of the Blue and White Niles on the frontiers of Islam and the margins of the Arab World. *Revolutionary Sudan* follows the activities of this ideological and activist leader of the revolution as he is moved from a courtesy jail cell in Kobar prison in 1989 to the height of his authority in the 1990s and his return to imprisonment in Kober and then to house arrest in 2000. It describes how he used his influence as a charismatic Muslim scholar to precipitate an Islamist revolution whose precepts he had helped to fashion over three decades of political involvement in the Sudan. This study concludes with the downfall of Hasan al-Turabi, his expulsion from government, and his imprisonment by those followers he had hoped to mold to his Islamist ideologies. Today Hasan al-Turabi remains in house arrest, in ill health, and his vision of an Islamist state fading with his life.

Hasan al-Turabi himself demonstrates the dichotomy of Islam in the Sudan. Reared in a orthodox family and educated in the legal tradition of the Quran, Shari'a, and scholastic theology, he was not

immune to popular Islam, Sufism, its appeal to the mass of Sudanese
Muslims, and its tradition of Islamic radicalism. He did not share,
however, the enthusiasm of the Sudanese for the *tariqa* (Sufi brotherhood), but he recognized that they represented the driving force
of Islam in the Sudan. His theological conservatism embodied in the
National Islamic Front had little appeal for the Muslim Sudanese and
none for the non-Muslims. His definition of Islam could not embrace
either popular or secular Islam, for they were not committed to the
fixed doctrines of the past practiced by the keepers of traditional
Islam, the *ʿulama*. Thus his following in the Sudan has always been
small, and the intolerance of the Islamist state enforced by his supporters in the army, the security service, and the urban middle class
was unpopular with a vast number of the Sudanese. The totalitarian
character of the Sudanese Islamist theocratic state insisted that it be
the only authority to rule the Sudan by a constitutional government
based on the consent of the believers, the *umma*, and governed by
the divine law of the Shariʿa.

Hasan al-Turabi regarded his followers as members of the *umma*,
the historic community of Muslims ruled by the Shariʿa, whose political identity in the Sudan was personified in the National Islamic
Front protected by their members in the military. The mass of Sudanese Muslims who belonged to the Sufi brotherhoods (*turuq*) not
to mention a third of the Sudanese who were non-Muslims remained
without effective representation in the revolutionary government.
There was persecution of non-conforming Muslims in the notorious
ghost houses of Khartoum, armed suppression of most brotherhoods,
and twenty years of violent civil war against the *kafirin*, the unbeliev-
ing Africans in the southern Sudan. The Prophet Muhammad did
not create Islamic law or doctrine, but during the centuries which
followed his death Muslim scholars and theologians defined the state
as an integral part of divine revelation where the theocratic state was
the only legitimate authority to rule the world. Hasan al-Turabi conceived of himself as the heir to that historic, religious tradition that
was not confined to the Sudan on the frontiers of Islam, but to the
umma of the world who needed to be aroused by his learning, his Islamist message, and his charisma.

During his efforts to impose the Islamist state on all Sudanese
Turabi had to confront the formidable acceptance of Sufism and the
traditional and Christian religions of its Sudanese. Popular Islam is
deeply rooted in the rural regions of the Sudan where the holy man,

the *faqih* (pl. *fuquha*), has been venerated and many regarded as saints, intermediaries between Allah and man, the Creator and the created. He is to work miracles, convert sinners, advise on all domestic matters, and exude *baraka*, saintliness. Indeed, these *fuquha* are revered today in the Sudan, and the tombs of these saints, the *qubab*, are still places of pilgrimage. The practices of saint worship varied from one region and ethnic group to another in the vast hinterland of the Sudan. The *fuquha* in the Sudan were invariably associated with a Sufi brotherhood, the *tariqa*. Sufism is Islamic mysticism whereby a Muslim can submit to the oneness of Allah through practices of ritual and asceticism that appeal to the vast majority of illiterate Sudanese who have no knowledge or interest in the scholastic, legal traditions of the *ulama*. Sufi orders first came to the Sudan in the fifteenth century, and thereafter proliferated. The Qadiriyya was the oldest of the brotherhoods, but others followed inspired by holy men: the Shadhiliyya, Majdhubiyya, Sammaniyya, Idrisiyya, Rashidiyya, Khatmiyya, Isma'iliyya, and the Tijaniyya and a host of other minor orders.

Hasan al-Turabi was not of the Sufi or *tariqa* religious tradition. His brotherhood was originally the Muslim Brothers from whom he defected to establish the Islamic Charter Front that later became the National Islamic Front, a modern political party committed to orthodox Islam. Yet the return of the Islamist state to the Sudan by a military coup d'état of his followers was as revolutionary as that of Muhammad Ahmad al Mahdi a hundred years before the Islamist revolution at the end of the twentieth century. At the end of the thirteenth Muslim century Muhammad Ahmad declared himself to be the Mahdi who was to bring the messianic doctrine of Islam to the political and religious community of the Muslim Sudanese. Despite its defeat and suppression by the Anglo-Egyptian conquest of the Sudan in 1898, Mahdism has remained one of the most powerful political and religious forces in the Sudan in the twentieth century. The great grandson of Muhammad Ahmad al-Mahdi, Sadiq al- Mahdi, is the brother-in law of Hasan al-Turabi, and despite their differences the revolutionary spirit of Mahdism obviously influenced his followers in the National Islamic Front. The division between the brotherhoods and Mahdism and the Islamist revolutionary government of the Sudan is very deep, but their own rivalries have enabled Hasan al-Turabi, the National Islamic Front, and its military to impose the revolutionary Islamist experience on the Sudan that will ultimately fail as did the religious revolution of Muhammad Ahmad al-Mahdi.

We are deeply indebted to Alan Goulty who took time out from his demanding diplomatic duties to read the manuscript and to provide his perceptive comments that have made *Revolutionary Sudan* a much better book.

J. Millard Burr, Rio Rico, Arizona
Robert O. Collins, Santa Barbara, California

PREFACE TO THE AMERICAN EDITION

In 2003, *Revolutionary Sudan: Hasan al-Turabi and the Islamist State, 1989-2000*, was published in The Netherlands by Brill NV. Because the one and only print run was small, the book was sold at a price beyond the means of most readers. Nonetheless, it was favorably received by the circle of Sudanese scholars who were able to obtain a copy, and, among other periodicals, it secured an especially friendly review in the Spring 2004 issue of *Middle East Quarterly*.

Having completed *Revolutionary Sudan*, the authors needed to choose for their next project among three manuscripts either nearing completion or completed in first draft. The first concerned the history of the Popular Arab and Islamic Conference movement. The second dealt with post-1989 Darfur, where the budding civil war involved Western nations and threatened the stability of the Khartoum government. The third concerned the worldwide activity of Islamic charities. The first was set aside. Regarding the second, in 1999 the authors had published *Africa's Thirty Years' War: Libya, Chad, and the Sudan, 1963-1993*, and, given a succession of tragic events involving Darfur, a revised edition was badly needed. Despite this, the attacks of September 11, 2001, influenced our decision to instead move forward on a new book. The result was the ill-fated *Alms for Jihad*, published by Cambridge University Press in 2007; its distribution was halted shortly thereafter as the result of a charge of libel initiated by a Saudi family. The authors did not join Cambridge University Press in its capitulation to the family and strongly objected to it.

The Darfur issue would later receive our attention in an "Epilogue" that was added to *Africa's Thirty Years' War*, which was reissued in 2008 as *Darfur: The Long Road to Disaster* (Markus Wiener Publishers, Princeton, NJ, pp. 305-317). As with that book, we received numerous requests from friends and colleagues for copies of *Revolutionary Sudan* but were unable to comply. Thus, when the copyright reverted to the authors, we once again approached Markus Wiener Publishers to inquire as to whether it would be interested in reprinting the book. The publisher agreed, and it has reissued the book under a slightly modified title.

In this updated edition, a new final chapter, entitled "The Murshid Forsaken," brings the story of Hasan al-Turabi—the Sudanese intellectual and eminence grise of the Sudanese Islamist movement, and its political guide (*murshid*)—through 2003. In this final chapter, the recent history of Darfur is told from the perspective of Turabi's involvement in that region. It serves as an addition to and not a repetition of material the authors have published elsewhere. In concluding at the point in history that we have, the book has followed the Sudanese leader through fifteen years of turmoil. It ends with the murshid's suffering a political quarantine from which he has never really recovered.

CHAPTER ONE

THE ISLAMIST REVOLUTION

On the night of 30 June 1989 a select group of Sudanese army officers led by Brigadier Omar Hassan Ahmad al-Bashir overthrew the civilian government of the Sudan led by Prime Minister Sadiq al-Mahdi. Their coup appeared to be yet another of the many that have afflicted post-colonial Africa when the politicians had failed or military governance had not been fulfilled. There was, however, much more intellectual and political ideology behind the 30 June Revolution than just another circle of discontented junior officers seizing the government. For more than three years the coalition governments of Sadiq al-Mahdi had been unable to govern effectively. The civil war in the southern Sudan, precipitated in 1983 by the Sudan People's Liberation Army (SPLA) led by Colonel John Garang, continued to drain the human and limited material resources of the government, and those in the urban areas of the northern Sudan were bitterly discontented by the deteriorating economy plagued by inflation and the dearth of accustomed staples. Nevertheless, the Sudanese electorate was free in press, free in dissent, and free of fear of covert repression by the state. The Sudanese were historically survivors in a hostile natural environment. They valued education, whether traditional or academic. They were preternaturally optimistic that something good was bound to happen. As the burning heat of the Sudan settled over Khartoum in June 1989 Sadiq, as he was universally known, appeared to some about to resolve the civil war between the Arab North and the African South. The Sudanese of the southern Sudan had been devastated by war, drought, famine, and had lost more than a million lives. The Sudanese of the northern Sudan had experienced the loss of capital and goods by inflation and a war economy in ruins. Most Sudanese wanted peace.

In the past the ship of peace negotiations had been regularly wrecked on the rock of the Shari'a, known in the Sudan as the September Laws promulgated by President Jaafar Numayri in 1983. After years of deliberations and negotiations the Democratic Unionist Party (DUP) and the Sudan People's Libration Movement (SPLM) signed the Sudanese Peace Initiative on 16 November 1988 that would freeze the September Laws. It embodied the principles of the Koka Dam Declaration agreed in 1986 by all the unions and Sudanese political parties except the DUP that now accepted the suspension of the September Laws. Hasan al-Turabi and the National Islamic Front (NIF) denounced the peace initiative, for they perceived that once frozen the September Laws would never melt. Meanwhile the senior military officers with the support of the trade unions, students, and professional organizations convinced Prime Minister Sadiq to form a new cabinet that excluded NIF. On 3 April the assembly endorsed the peace initiative and on April 10th voted to table any further debate on the September Laws. NIF members of parliament stormed out from the assembly in protest, and their followers were soon engaged in violent street demonstrations. After his usual period of irresolution Sadiq initialed the draft legislation to suspend the September Laws on 19 June that was endorsed by the council of ministers on June 30th for presentation and enactment by parliament on 1 July. Sadiq al-Mahdi had scheduled a flight to Addis Ababa on July 4th where he was to confirm with John Garang the final arrangement for a conference in October to amend the constitution to include the enacted legislation. The delay between 10 April and 29 June enabled NIF and Brigadier Bashir the opportunity to plan and execute their coup d'état during the night of 30 June before the prime minister could place the "freezing" of the September Laws before the assembly.[1]

Calling themselves the National Salvation Revolutionary Command Council (NSRCC soon shortened to Revolutionary Command Council, RCC), the six brigadiers, six colonels, two lieutenant colonels, and a major who seized the government of the Sudan on 30 June were not an impressive lot. Presumably accomplished in combat they were politically naïve. The sophisticated, professional, educated Sudanese assumed that these inexperienced officers could not govern without them. Many of the Sudanese elite who had lived with twenty three years of military rule in the thirty three years of an independent Sudan and had overthrown two military dictators, Ibrahim Abboud and Jaafar Numayri, looked benignly on this latest exuberance by junior officers that would pass with their coup d'état. The NSRCC

[1] Steven Wöndu and Ann Lesch, *Battle for Peace in Sudan*, Lanham, MD: University Press of America, 2000, pp. 11–12.

did receive grudging admiration for carrying-out a bloodless seizure of power in the Sudanese tradition, but the populace waited to see how they would confront a bloody civil war that had divided them.

Unlike Sadiq al-Mahdi, Omar Hassan Ahmad al-Bashir was an enigma. He was born in 1945 in the rural town of Hoshe Bannaga sixty miles northeast of Khartoum. His parents were working class Ja'aliyyin Muslim Arabs but had sufficient means to educate him at the Ahlia Middle School in nearby Shendi. Upon his graduation he accompanied his parents to Khartoum and worked in a auto repair shop to supplement his secondary school education. Upon graduation he was admitted to the prestigious military academy where he earned his wings in the Airborne Forces before transferring to the Infantry. He was bright, determined, and encouraged to continue his military training holding two masters degrees from the Sudanese College of Commanders and the Malaysian military institute. In 1988 he had been promoted to brigadier and commanded the 8th Infantry Brigade which he led against the insurgency of the SPLA in the southern Sudan civil conflict, and the following year he was selected to attend a class at the G.A. Nasser Military Academy in Cairo when he led the coup d'état of 30 June.

An unknown brigadier who had been admitted and supported at the Sudan military academy by NIF and certainly knew of Dr. Hasan al-Turabi, Sudanese intellectual, politician, and a leading member (za'im) of the emerging world-wide "Islamic movement" (al-Haraka al-Islamiya). In the spring of 1989 he had met with Ali Osman Mohamad Taha, second in command of NIF, and had spent the two weeks before the coup ostensibly preparing for his study-program at the Nasser Military Academy but in fact planning to seize the government. Like Turabi, Bashir had no use for the sectarian parties (taifiya), the Umma and the DUP of the Mirghani family and their Khatmiyya supporters. Consequently, in the aftermath of the 30 June coup the two most powerful political parties and the two most significant religious sects were pushed to the periphery in the emerging revolutionary Sudan. Within hours twenty leading Sudanese politicians were arrested and incarcerated in Kobar prison across the Blue Nile in Khartoum North. Prime Minister Sadiq al-Mahdi was captured a few days later to be jailed with other Umma Party leaders, Idris al-Banna, Taj al-Din, and Ali Hassan, all members of the governing state council. Not surprisingly the RCC also imprisoned the leaders of the DUP, Mohamad Osman al-Mirghani and his former Minister of Foreign Affairs Sid Ahmad al-Hussein. One of the presidents of the Sudan and leader of the Khatmiyya, Ahmad Ali al-Mirghani, was on holiday outside Sudan, but other Sudanese political notables were jailed including Muhammad Ibrahim Nugud, the Communist leader, and al-Tigani al-Tayib, editor of *Al-Meidan*, the Communist newspaper.

To demonstrate their impartiality the RCC sent their ideological patron, Dr. Hasan al-Turabi, to a minimal security cell in Kobar prison, while his associates in NIF, Ibrahim al-Sanoussi, Ahmad Abd al-Rahman Muhammad, and Al-Fatih Abdoun were confined to more restricted quarters. Turabi's incarceration was not easily understood at the time. In 1985 he had founded the National Islamic Front (*Al-Jabhah al-Islamiyah al-Qawmiya*, NIF) that had financed the education and careers of selected young members of NIF, the *jabha*, some now members of the RCC who had jailed Turabi and his lieutenants. Given his accommodating imprisonment, however, rumors circulated widely through the streets of Omdurman and Khartoum that the military junta was receiving the unequivocal support of NIF and other Islamic fundamentalists.

Although the term "Islamic Fundamentalist" was popular in Khartoum and has become common currency in the Western media, the membership of NIF and other Islamists throughout the Muslim world strongly objected to this descriptive and, to them, a demeaning appellation. Hasan al-Turabi would use it on occasion, but he much preferred "Islamist," for the taxonomy (*al-Islamiyun*) could be traced to the "true believers" of al-Ashari (b. 873 CE) and his *Maqalat al-Islameen* (*Theses of the Islamists*), a classic polemic of its day. Thus Turabi and other modern Muslim leaders described themselves as "Islamists" to distinguish themselves and their followers from "other" Muslims and to differentiate their politics and theology from the secular political parties, Communists, Baathists, and democrats. The Orientalist, Bernard Lewis, considered "Islamist" a most unfortunate term. He defined its practitioners as "Muslim fundamentalists and those who feel that the troubles of the Muslim world at the present time are the result not of insufficient modernization but of excessive modernization." Their struggle was to "depose and remove" those "infidel rulers" who allowed the destruction of Islamic traditional laws, customs and institutions.[2]

---

[2] Bernard Lewis, "The Revolt of Islam", *The New Yorker*, 19 November 2001, p. 60.

Hasan al-Turabi was born in 1932 at Kassala near the Ethiopian border. The son of an Islamic judge (*qadi*), he was influenced at an early age by members of the Society of Muslim Brothers (*Jamiat al-Ikhwan al-Muslimin*) who had fled persecution in Egypt to the more tolerant Sudan. Known as the *Ikhwan* they were devoted to the restoration of Islamic law, the Shari'a, and Quranic values in the secular and morally corrupt Islamic world of the twentieth century now served by Western educated Muslims. In 1949 the Muslim Brothers founded a branch at the Gordon Memorial College that became the University College of Khartoum affiliated with the University of London where the Muslim Brothers had a profound influence among the students and the young Hasan al-Turabi. He graduated in 1952 and received a masters degree in law in 1961 from the London School of Economics. He then crossed the channel to Paris for study and a doctorate in law from the Sorbonne in 1964. His dissertation condemned the emergency powers employed by liberal democracies.

Turabi returned to the Sudan in 1965, the brilliant prodigal son, conciliatory, tendentious, and to lead, theologically and politically, his Islamist peers. Returning to the University of Khartoum with impeccable academic credentials he was appointed Dean of the Law School and, not surprisingly, became the secretary-general of the Sudan branch of the Muslim Brotherhood. Thereafter he served as the spiritual director to a generation of university students whose beliefs were under attack by Western secularists and Communist collectivists. A charismatic lecturer he used his political and organizational abilities to stimulate what he himself called a Muslim renaissance, and soon acquired converts through logic and learning and the sobriquet *'alim* (theologian). Although uncompromising in his Islamic convictions, Turabi impressed foreigners by his animation and sense of humor and the respect of his enemies for his personal magnetism and learning.[3]

Turabi argued that *Shari'a* was the essence of Islam: it "doesn't mean law" but "a way of life." "The closer you are to God the more civilised you are," and although in most modern nations the

---

[3] Hasan al-Turabi, "Principles of Governance, Freedom, and Responsibility in Islam," *American Journal of Islamic Social Sciences*, vol. 4, no. 1, September 1987; P.M. Holt and M.W. Daly, *A History of the Sudan: From the Coming of Islam to the Present Day*, London: Longman, 1988, p. 176; Concerning the Muslim Brotherhood see, "A Row in the Family," *Le Monde diplomatique*, April 2000.

Shari'a had become "only a legacy," it should be the foundation of the Sudanese state.[4] By his charismatic teaching and position as Dean of the Law School he restored and revived hundreds of Khartoum University students to believe in Islam through the rigor of Islamic law, the Shari'a, in distinction to Sufi mysticism widely practiced in the Sudan and throughout the Islamic world by Muslim brotherhoods, the *tariqa*, or the formalism of the Muslim Shiites and the Ayatollah Khomeini (1902–1989) of Iran. From a backwater on the frontiers of Islam more African than Arab, Turabi visualized a community of Islam without borders founded on the Quran and the Shari'a. By his knowledge of the Quran, legal training, personality, and the recordings of his lectures, he soon became widely known in the Arab world.

Turabi did not confine his beliefs to the lecture hall and the tape recorder. Soon after his return from Paris he became the ideological patron of the Islamic Charter Front (ICF). The Front was established as a legally chartered political party in 1964 and owed its inspiration to the Muslim Brotherhood, the *Ikhwan*. Composed generally of Muslim Brothers and Khartoum University graduates, the ICF emerged as a small but influential political movement that soon disturbed the powerful Mahdist and Mirghani brotherhoods and their respective political parties, the Umma and the DUP. Hasan al-Turabi provided the intellectual and legal foundations for the ICF, arguing that the separation of State and Mosque was heretical at best and not Islamic (*jahili*) at worst. Muslim Brothers believed that the Quran (God's revealed word), the Sunnah (the righteous existence manifested by the sayings of the Prophet Muhammad), the Shari'a (Islamic law), and jihad (the struggle against secularists and non-believers) were the four cornerstones of the Islamic community. He was determined to separate his position in the ICF from the authority of the Executive Office of the Muslim Brothers in Jordan by his proposal for "international obligation and territorial independence" that freed him from the influence of Egyptian and Palestinian brothers in exile.

Although Hasan al-Turabi was a religious adviser ('*alim*) to the Muslim Brothers in the Sudan and at one time its secretary-general, he began to distance himself from the Brotherhood in order to use his position to achieve the aims of the ICF. The Muslim Brotherhood

---

[4] "Islamic Fundamentalism In The Sunna and Shia World," address given by Dr. Hasan al-Turabi at a conference on Islamism held in Madrid, Spain, 2 August 1994.

had been founded in Egypt in 1929 by a youthful, Hasan al-Banna (1903–1948) who became its *murshid* (Supreme Guide). He owed much of his ideology and program to the reformist movement of the scholar from Afghanistan, Sayyid Jamal al-Din al-Afghani (1838–1897) who had preached that the time had come to restore Islam as the central core of life and, like Muslim prophets of the past, envisioned a world-wide Islamic revolution. The numerous religious and political writings by Hasan al-Banna have secured his place as one of the important Islamist intellectuals, but his efforts to revive and purify Islam could only be achieved through the organization of the Muslim Brotherhood. Its members preached the message of a strong, unified, puritanical Islam devoted to jihad, the "struggle" against the evil of Western cultural imperialism, rather than its more common interpretation of "holy war."[5] After Nasser expelled the Muslim Brothers from Egypt, they found a home in the Sudan where in 1954 Turabi attended its first public congress in Khartoum. He made a profound impression on the Brothers to become its most eloquent spokesman.

His political agenda founded on the Shari'a became abundantly clear in 1968 when he submitted to the Sudan Constituent Assembly a draft constitution (The Islamic Constitution Project) on behalf of the ICF that would have prohibited a non-Muslim from becoming president of the Sudan. Turabi himself was a member of the Sudanese elite and an intellectual snob. He believed that the people should be led by the learned, and they should be those in the ICF. "In order to retain the intellectual quality of the movement" the ICF was limited during its initial stage to students and recent university graduates.[6] Since most university graduates became government bureaucrats, he was able to infiltrate the civil service with his protégés. The two other institutions of importance to the Sudanese elite were the secondary school teachers, who had great influence on youth, and those young Sudanese admitted to the military academy. By the 1970s the Front was actively promoting their followers to be teachers and officers by influence, advice, and cash. Its task was to

---

[5] Jihad is a controversial issue. T.P. Hughes in the *Dictionary of Islam*, London: W.H. Allen, 1885, defines jihad as "a religious war with those who are unbelievers." John Esposito in *The Islamic Threat: Myth or Reality*, New York: Oxford University Press, 1995, p. 33, notes that Muslim jurists argue that *jihad* is a duty distinguished by the heart, tongue, hands, and "by the sword."

[6] Peter Bechtold, *Politics in Sudan: Parliamentary and Military Rule in an Emerging African Nation*, New York: Praeger, 1976, p. 89.

take control of student activity within the University of Khartoum, the teacher training colleges, and the military academy. Elitist it began, and elitist the ICF would remain until incorporated into NIF in 1985. It never deviated from its determined purpose to revoke what they called the secular "Transitional" Constitution under which Sudan was governed and replace it with one that would "clearly and specifically state that 'the Sudan is an Islamic Republic.'"[7]

After sixteen years (1969–1985) in power President Numayri had managed to alienate the powerful political parties, the Umma and DUP, *and* the military. Consequently, during a visit to Washington in 1985 he was overthrown by massive popular demonstrations that convinced his senior generals to take control of the government promising that their tenure would be transitional. Three months later Turabi founded NIF, a political party, that would appeal to a larger constituency than the restrictive membership of the ICF. There was little difference in the political and theological ideology between the ICF and NIF, and during its political campaign in the national elections of 1986 NIF insisted that religion and state were inseparable and Shari'a the legal foundation of the government. NIF attracted few voters. Turabi's advocacy for universal national conscription to win the war against the African insurgency in the southern Sudan alienated the voters. Although NIF demonstrated a modest showing among urban Sudanese professionals in the capital and the military, to his embarrassment he lost his own constituency in Omdurman. In the past Turabi had preached against "chauvinist nationalism," and after Sadiq al-Mahdi was elected prime minister, he preached to his followers that their highest loyalty was not to the Sudan but the ideal of a *Dar al-Islam* (the Muslim commonwealth) and to the *umma*, the Muslim community. The *umma* of Turabi would be led by its leaders to support legislative and administrative decentralization and create "basic units" of government in the countryside that would send their most dependable Islamists to the government in Khartoum.

During the year (1985–1986) of the Transitional Military Council Turabi had used his influence to continue Shari'a as the law of the land, and when Sadiq al-Mahdi formed his first government after

[7] Mohamad Omer Beshir, *The Southern Sudan: From Conflict to Peace*, London: C. Hurst, 1975, p. 33.

the elections of 1986, the prime minister could not ignore Turabi, his brother-in-law, or his NIF. In 1988 he was appointed attorney-general and used his position to frustrate Sadiq's ambivalent efforts to seek a peace agreement with John Garang and his SPLA. A supposed plot by Numayri's former security officers to assassinate Sadiq gave Turabi the opportunity as attorney-general to prohibit public demonstrations by the populist National Alliance for the Salvation of the Sudan. The National Alliance was the same broad base of Sudanese interest groups—professionals, unions, communists, socialists, students, and urban members of the Umma and DUP parties who had gathered together for the public good to overthrow Ibrahim Abboud in 1964 and Jaafar Numaryi in 1985. The National Alliance demanded peace for the Sudan and acceptance of the agreement, the peace initiative, that Mohamad Osman al-Mirghani had concluded with John Garang and the SPLA in November 1988. Turabi ominously predicted the fall of the government. Sadiq sought his own salvation by forming a new coalition on 1 February 1989 in which Turabi was appointed deputy prime minister and foreign minister. Members of the National Islamic Front were given several important ministries. Hafiz al-Shaykh Zaki, a protégé of Turabi, was made attorney-general. During the winter of 1989 NIF had become an unwelcome rival in the government of Sadiq al-Mahdi and his Umma. The southerners had no doubts that Hasan al-Turabi and the political philosophy of NIF were no different than the ICF and the Muslim Brotherhood, and crucial to that philosophy was their insistence the Shari'a should be the law of the land for all Sudanese.[8]

The National Salvation RCC Confirms Its Authority

When the NSRCC had rounded up and imprisoned most Sudanese political leaders including Hasan al-Turabi, he was given preferential treatment, even allowed, "to go home to pack a suitcase."[9] He

---

[8] See documents submitted to the House Foreign Affairs Africa Subcommittee Hearing on the Sudan 20 May 1992; for Turabi's political views see "Principles of Governance, Freedom, and Responsibility in Islam," *Journal of Islamic Social Sciences*, vol. 4, no. 1, Sept. 1987.

[9] "Fundamentalists Disavow New Cabinet," *The New York Times*, 15 March 1989, p. 5; United Press International, "*Sudanese Leaders Set to form New Cabinet*," 15 March 1989.

was not mistreated unlike his brother-in-law Sadiq al-Mahdi who was subjected to a mock execution. Having spent seven years in jail and preventive detention during the early years of the Numayri regime, Turabi was an old hand at making the best of time behind bars. He was allowed to meet freely with high-ranking NIF officials, including Ali Osman Mohamad Taha and Ali al-Haj Muhammad. The courtesy shown Turabi produced rumors and aroused speculation among the urban Sudanese of Khartoum and Omdurman that Bashir must be a Muslim Brother or a sympathizer to NIF, yet Bashir was not disposed to hand over his coup d'état to NIF. A parade organized by the Front on 1 July to support the RCC failed miserably and to avoid further embarrassment street demonstrations were banned. In Kobar prison with his characteristic aplomb Turabi remained patient predicting to fellow prisoners that a new chapter in Sudanese history was about to be written. The Shari'a would remain the law of the land, and an Islamic state would be created despite the protestations of southern Sudanese and Muslim unbelievers (*kafirun*).

Within a week after the coup d'état the RCC had successfully discouraged any protest. Demonstrations were prohibited throughout the country and a campaign was launched to assure the Sudanese that its members were committed to orthodox Islam, Islamic law, and Islamic dress. In public discourse, the press, and television the cultural identity of the Sudanese was defined as the struggle between the sacred and profane, religious and secular, and Islamic-Arabs and Western Christians. The Sudanese were called upon to gather with the faithful, the *umma*, to confront the Neo-Crusaders from the West. Omdurman television, which was generally secular, now proclaimed the virtues of a government founded on the Quran. By demonstrating their allegiance to it the true Muslim could become a part of a new pan-Islamic society. The violent civil war in the South and the deteriorating economy, which that were the dominant issues in the everyday life of the Sudanese, were ignored by the call to the Faith.

Not surprisingly the RCC always met in camera and little substantive information leaked from their closed sessions. Dismissed by many as just another coup d'état by colonels, within thirty days it became increasingly clear that a new Sudan was being born. At first the mass of Sudanese were amazed, confused, and then afraid. In Khartoum and Omdurman the public, who were accustomed to open discourse, ceased to argue politics in open forums and, as more

Sudanese intellectuals were arrested, rarely in private. The composition of the new cabinet made it quite clear the road to be taken by the revolutionary Islamist state. The Minister of Information and Culture Ali Mohammed Shummo was a well-known political opportunist with close ties to NIF. The Attorney-General Hassan Ismail al-Beili, Finance Minister Dr. Sayed Ali Zaki, Agriculture Minister Professor Ali Ahmad Ginais, Industry Minister Dr. Muhammad Omar Abdalla, and Commerce and Supply Minister Faruk al-Bushra were all close friends of Hasan al-Turabi. Housing Minister Major General Muhammad al-Hadi Mamoun al-Mardi (retired) was an engineer with profound religious convictions and sympathetic to NIF. While Turabi was languishing in Kobar Prison, the RCC was using his followers to run the government bureaucracy. It was a riddle not easily resolved. He received special treatment in prison and when released confined to a comfortable house arrest leaving his contacts with the command council to his confidante, Ali Osman Mohamad Taha. The former deputy secretary-general of NIF, Taha was deeply distrusted particularly by members of the Umma Party. Before the 30 June coup d'état he had repeatedly attacked Sadiq al-Mahdi. After the revolution he advocated that Islamic aid agencies should replace Western humanitarian organizations. While Taha operated among the members of the RCC, Ali al-Haj Muhammad took charge of the Relief and Rehabilitation Commission to circumscribe the ongoing United Nations Operation Lifeline Sudan program for food shipments to the southern Sudanese.

Despite the apparent collegiality of the RCC, "Sudanese intellectuals and foreign diplomats" and well-informed international journalists were convinced that "major decisions" were not those of Bashir and the command council but a enigmatic council or *majlis* "dominated by the fundamentalist NIF."[10] This elusive "Council of Defenders of the Revolution," popularly known as the "Committee of Forty," had been formed a few weeks after the coup by the most influential Islamists in the Sudan. The members of the RCC denied its existence. The Sudanese in the *suq* (market), civil service, and the army were convinced that this shadowy and sinister civilian advisory council had been delegated by NIF to see that the soldiers of the RCC

---

[10] On the Council of Forty advising the Revolutionary Command Council see: *Al-Ingaz Al-Watani*, Khartoum, 14 March 1990.

would pursue the mission for an Islamic state in the Sudan. Suq rumors were commonplace that Hasan al-Turabi manipulated the council from Kobar prison. More likely The Council of Defenders, which included prominent members of the Islamic Front, young Islamist officers, and members of the command council who met after curfew in a new mosque in downtown Khartoum, needed little coaching from Hasan al-Turabi. The chairman of the council was none other than Ali Osman Mohamad Taha who presided over a phalanx of prominent members in NIF. There was Muhammad Osman Mahjoub, who was NIF adviser to the command council on security, Mahdi Ibrahim from its executive committee advising the ministry of information, and the Muslim Brother and ethnic Nuba, Ahmed al-Radi Jabr.[11] Brigadier Bashir, soon to become Lieutenant General, emphatically confirmed to a Saudi journalist that "we have repeatedly denied the rumor about its [Council of Defenders] existence."[12] The Sudanese did not believe him and neither did those Sudanese living outside the Sudan.

Securing the Revolution

The elusive council of forty appeared determined to demand political correctness, but they were hardly those equipped to use force to defend the revolution from Sudanese dissent. After all that was the duty of those soldiers who had carried out the coup d'état of 30 June, and they acted swiftly with a systematic ruthlessness unknown in Sudanese society. Jaafar Numayri had introduced an inflated security system whose large numbers of informants and agents were more troublesome than ideologically vindictive. His security services were officially dismantled after his downfall in 1985, but those who were not dismissed or retired were incorporated by Prime Minister Sadiq al-Mahdi into the civilian intelligence service that was controlled by the Sudan Security Bureau (SSB) and its benign director, Brigadier Al-Hadi Bushra. The determination of the RCC to suppress all opposition deeply disturbed many Sudanese, particularly the intelligentsia. There was a deep tradition of freedom of speech and tolerance in

---

[11] "The Junta Shows its True Face," March 1990, *Middle East*, p. 20; "Sudan: A Government Going Nowhere," *Africa Confidential*, 3 November 1989.
[12] *Ukaz*, Jiddah, 16 May 1990, p. 5.

public affairs that was a source of great national pride. In the past when an unpopular government was overthrown, the deposed rulers were pensioned or allowed to depart into exile. Bloodshed and revenge were not characteristic of political life in the Sudan. The day after his military government collapsed on 14 November 1964, "Papa" Abboud was buying oranges in the suq. Even after President Jaafar Numayri crushed the Ansar in March 1970, killing the Imam al-Hadi, grandson of the nineteenth century religious reformer and revolutionary Muhammad Ahmad ibn 'Abdallah, al-Mahdi, his great grandson and successor, Sadiq al-Mahdi, was allowed to go free into exile. After the bloody suppression of an attempted communist coup in July 1971, Numayri executed the leaders and purged the military and government of leftists, but there was no massive witch hunt by his security forces. Even after the failure of the more violent attempt by Sadiq al-Mahdi to overthrow Numayri in 1976 with the support of Mummar Qaddafi and his Libyans, more than a hundred insurgents were executed. A year later, however, Sadiq and Numayri were reconciled in 1977, and the leader of the Ansar and Umma returned to the Sudan. Numayri had his own pervasive intelligence service under Major General Umar Muhammad al-Tayib, first vice president, that employed ruthless techniques of interrogation but was never organized to crush all dissent against the regime. When President Numayri was deposed in April 1985 by popular demonstrations in the streets, he quietly returned from Washington to exile in Egypt.

The RCC dramatically changed the Sudanese way to contain dissent. Officially, Sudanese intelligence services were under the authority of the ministry of the interior, and all security agencies, whether military or civilian, were officially responsible to the minister. During the first week of July 1989 Colonel Faisal Ali Abu Salih, a close friend and collaborator of Bashir, became the first minister of interior in the revolutionary government. Abu Salih was an Islamist zealot whose success in protecting the revolution was soon rewarded. Within the year he was a major general. At the ministry of the interior he set out to reorganize the intelligence and security agencies of the Sudan government. The structure of these agencies had become rather convoluted during the Numayri years. Its officials were old and the organization had remained somnolent during the parliamentary government of Sadiq al-Mahdi. Minister Abu Salih had responsibility for intelligence concerning both external and internal security that included counter-espionage, espionage, protection of embassies and foreign missions, infiltrating Sudanese expatriate organizations not to mention tax evasion, smuggling, and narcotics. Salih was a very busy man. In addition he became the representative of the command council on foreign tours and was given a number of idiosyncratic assignments that included combating banditry in Darfur and liaison with French intelligence officers in the French Embassy working to destabilize the government of President Hissene Habre in Chad. There were also time consuming excursions to Somali warlords and Libyan generals. The demands upon Abu Salih led to speculation as to his ability to reorganize the intelligence and security agencies of the RCC. In fact he soon turned over much of the internal security operations to his subordinates.[13]

A month after 30 June Abu Salih appointed Brigadier Ibrahim Nial Adam of the RCC Counselor for National Security with orders to totally restructure the Sudan Security Bureau. Adam turned out to be a wretched administrator, and in December 1989 he was demoted to the minor ministry of youth and sports. His replacement was one of the original leaders of the coup d'état of 30 June, Colonel and later Major General Bakri Hassan Salih, a much more efficient and sinister defender of the revolution. Under Hassan Salih a new organization was created originally known as the Security of the Revolution-Revolutionary Intelligence Agency. Its convoluted Arabic name, however, was even too much for the command council that shortened it to *Al-Amn al-Dakhili*, the Internal Security-Security of the Revolution (IS-SOR). IS-SOR was composed of party members from the NIF who replaced the moribund agents of Jaafar Numayri. Opponents of the new regime accused Salih of employing Islamist fanatics from NIF in the intelligence apparatus in order to intimidate the civilian populace. Others argued that IS-SOR was the creation of Bashir at the prodding of Turabi and Ali Osman Mohamad Taha. Whoever made the decisions became irrelevant, for IS-SOR soon demonstrated its independent authority by the use of extreme brutality. Its detention centers, the infamous "Ghost Houses," acquired a fearsome reputation for ruthless interrogation, torture, and death. The Sudanese quickly learned that the minister of the interior and his ministry actually had little control over General Bakri Hassan

---

[13] Rory Nugent, "My Lunch with Osama bin Laden," RollingStone.com, 11 September 2001.

Salih and his IS-SOR, for its civilian leaders received their orders from NIF to pursue its policies and principles. By 1991 Sudanese living in the northern Sudan were more fearful of the IS-SOR than the soldiers of the command council.

In March 1990 Abu Salih had laid the foundation stone for the central library and mosque at Omdurman Islamic University and was an enthusiastic supporter of the African International University of Khartoum. It was described by a visitor in 1994 as "the school of choice among radical Muslims looking for a career in terrorism."[14] The university was funded by the *Al-Da'awa al-Islamiyya* (the Islamic Call Society) founded by Muammar Qaddafi who established a Khartoum branch in 1980. Islamic Da'awa was an outreach organization funded by Libya to proselytize for Islam with offices in some forty Muslim nations and missions in a score of African states. Its chairman in Khartoum was General Abd al-Rahman Muhammad Siwar al-Dahab, who had been army chief of staff and minister of defense to President Numayri and having failed to support him during his overthrow in April 1985, became president of the Transitional Military Council until the parliamentary elections of 1986. Its executive director was another Sudanese Islamist, Abd al-Salaam Sulayman Saad. The Da'awa "worked to maintain Islamic identity" and to protect the "existence of Islam in Africa in particular" with "a view to fighting dangers of [European and American] colonization and Christian missionary activities which exploit conditions of poverty and ill health which prevail in a number of Muslim communities."[15]

Before and after the 30 June coup d'état the Da'awa had provided information to Sudanese intelligence as well as to other Islamic humanitarian aid agencies. A brother organization, the Islamic African Relief Agency (IARA), had been established in 1980 to assist Muslim Ethiopian and Eritrean refugees in the Sudan. It provided a humanitarian cover for Sudan intelligence agents to assist Muslim revolutionary movements in the Horn of Africa. These Sudanese initiatives

---

[14] *Al Da'awa Islamiyya* (Islamic Call Organization), Qatar News Agency, Khartoum, 24 April 1997.

[15] The responsibilities of the Intelligence agencies were institutionalized by the National Security Act of 1990 (amended in 1991 and 1992). The Minister of Interior had oversight for Internal or "Islamic" security (*Al-Amn al-Dakhili*) which Sudanese called IS-SOR, External Security (*Al-Amn al-Khariji*) that operated abroad, especially among exiled Sudanese, and Sudan Security "Military Intelligence" (often given the Egyptian title *Al-Mukhabarat al-'Ammah*).

were soon incorporated into a larger Islamic Relief Agency (ISRA) that was active in Pashawar, Pakistan. Here the ISRA joined the Islamic Coordination Council, a coalition of Islamic relief agencies to provide food and military assistance to the mujahideen fighting the forces from the Soviet Union in Afghanistan. Hasan al-Turabi had many friends and close contacts in the council.

The PDF

In 1956 the independent Sudan had the finest fighting army in the Middle East equal to the Arab Legion of Jordan. The officer corps had remained a solid professional group at their expansive club near the Khartoum airport during the military coups of Abboud and Numayri interspersed by parliamentary governments. In the 1980s the senior officers of the Sudan army were old, and the young junior officers, disillusioned with the past, were more susceptible to Islamist ideology than professional discipline. They despised the sectarian parties and their own military commanders who had failed to fulfil the promise and prosperity of the Sudan bequeathed to them by British, Christian imperialists. Hasan al-Turabi understood this discontent among junior officers as he understood it among undergraduates at the University of Khartoum. Young officers at the military academy, like those in the secondary schools and the university, were recruited into the Islamist world of the ICF that later became NIF. One of its exemplary graduates was, of course, Omar Hassan Ahmad al-Bashir.

When the RCC seized power on 30 June 1989, the army had become deeply demoralized after suffering severe defeats in the southern Sudan by the SPLA. At the time Prime Minister Sadiq al-Mahdi was about to conclude an agreement with the southern Sudanese insurgents that would "freeze" the Shari‘a, revoke its imposition on the non-Muslim southern Sudanese, and consider autonomy for the South, just as Jaafar Numayri had done in 1972. The prospects of abandoning the Shari‘a and an autonomous, non-Muslim southern Sudan was anathema to Turabi, Bashir, and the Islamists of NIF, but in the spring of 1989 the Sudan army was helpless to turn the tide of civil war in the southern Sudan. A year before the overthrow of Numayri Siwar al Dahab, his chief of staff, had equipped the Arab Baggara, the *murahileen* in South Kordofan on the frontier of

Islam, with automatic weapons to stem the advance of the SPLA. At the insistence of Minister of State for Defense Fadlallah Burma Nasr, a Baggara from Lagowa, Sadiq continued to arm the undisciplined *murahileen* to strengthen his negotiations with the SPLA. The result was massive devastation by the Baggara of the non-Muslim Dinka and Nuer in the northern Bahr al-Ghazal and western Upper Nile. The success of the *murahileen* confirmed the belief within the RCC that it must create a more organized militia, the People's Defense Force (PDF), to defend the State and spread the Faith when it could no longer rely on the army to defeat the southern Sudanese insurgents.

The paramilitary PDF was to protect the 30 June Revolution from armed opposition in the North and the suppression of the rebellion in the South. Its recruits were conscripted from a universal and very unpopular draft that numbered 150,000 by 1991. They were introduced to weaponry by instructors from the Sudan army, but their indoctrination was more religious than military including interminable lectures on Islam delivered by known members of NIF and Muslim Brothers. Hasan al-Turabi continued his role as ideological guide of NIF in the metamorphosis of the PDF. He had long argued in private and public that it would be impossible to "Islamize" the Sudanese army because its professional officers had been "secularized." In order to achieve "consensus," the Islamic Sudan should create "a small standing army and a large popular defense force" that would come from an "Islamized" society.[16] Prince Turki al-Faisal, a close observer of the Sudan and head of Saudi intelligence since 1977, believed that the PDF, supported and financed by *mujahideen* from the Islamic world, would serve a dual purpose. It would provide an organized militia to combat the insurrection by non-Muslims in the South, and if NIF and the RCC differed over policy and its practice, the PDF would protect the Sudanese Islamists and their friends.[17] The RCC was less than enthusiastic about the creation by NIF of a rival to its army, but it could hardly object given the success of the *murahileen* which perhaps they and the army could control if integrated into the PDF.

---

[16] "Islam, Democracy, the State and the West; Roundtable with Dr. Hassan Turabi," *Middle East Policy*, vol. 1, no. 3, 1992, pp. 49–61.

[17] "Al-Qaida estaria buscando armas de destruccion masiva", *N.C.O.*, Argentina, 20 November 2001, p. 14, from AP, dateline Manama, Bahrein.

The Islamic indoctrination of the PDF was entrusted to Ibrahim al-Sanoussi. He had been arrested with Turabi after the 30 June coup d'état and released from Kobar prison in November 1989. Thereafter the Egyptian newspaper *Al-Wafd* and others would refer to Sanoussi in their columns as the leader of the Islamic Front "military wing." He frequently lectured at the camps of the PDF, and his speeches and Islamist propaganda were widely distributed by the recruits. One of his more outrageous proposals during a polemic at Kosti in February 1994 advocated holding foreign ambassadors "hostages" in the interests of the Islamists. The speech precipitated a crisis within the RCC that was only resolved after the Minister of State for Presidential Affairs Ghazi Salah al-Din Atabani intervened to reassure the diplomatic community it was not in danger, but he did not reprimand Sanoussi.

The Egyptians, who had a historic concern about their Sudanese brothers to the south, were particularly alarmed by the rapid expansion of the PDF. The Egyptian government had bitter experiences with their own paramilitary organizations, and during the presidency of Gamal Abd al-Nasser the generals of the Egyptian army strongly resisted the formation of a "revolutionary guard" to protect his dictatorship. It was not until the reorganization of the military after its defeat in the 1967 war with Israel that Nasser created the Central Security Force (CSF) to deal with anti-government demonstrations. The CSF evolved into a neighborhood police and intelligence service, lightly armed, and used when the government needed to suppress dissent or demonstrations. Its role was expanded after the food riots of 1977, and by the mid-1980s it comprised a half-million conscripts many of whom were Muslim radical, Islamists, and sympathetic to the banned Muslim Brotherhood. Despised by the professionals in Egyptian security the CSF was gradually dismantled following their protests in 1986 when the tour of duty was extended to be from three to four years.

The few weeks of military training for recruits in the camps of the PDF consisted of many lectures on Islamist teaching and very few on how to become soldiers. It was no secret in the Sudan and the world intelligence community that the Sudanese PDF would become neither a revolutionary guard nor an efficient paramilitary organization. It was a rabble in arms, volunteers, used by the Sudan army in its southern civil war as cannon fodder whose depleted ranks had to be filled by forced and unpopular conscription. Even the warriors of the Baggara militia, the *murahileen*, who had been ravaging the Dinka of the Bahr al-Ghazal long before the revolution, did not improve their discipline or reliability when incorporated into the PDF. Other newer PDF units experienced their first test in combat in the Blue Nile province where they suffered heavy casualties from the SPLA to the consternation of many families in Khartoum and Omdurman. Thereafter the PDF was called upon only in times of severe military reverses. The most dependable units were eventually handed over to civilian control by members of NIF to become "Public Order Police," a NIF militia called Youth of the Home Land, considered more reliable than the police to suppress civilian or student demonstrations.

A Brave New Islamic World

On assuming power President Bashir appointed two vice presidents, a cabinet, the council of ministers, and the supreme commander of the Sudan's military forces. This was to be expected. His purge of the Sudan's judges was not. The Sudan Bar Association, its lawyers and judges, had a long and distinguished history of independence. It took great pride in its professionalism and had played an influential role in every government and its demise. As the Dean of the Khartoum University Law School at one time, Hasan al-Turabi himself was one of its most powerful members, and the Bar Association held a prestigious and respected position in Sudan society. No one was more aware of this than Brigadier Omar Hassan Ahmad al-Bashir. He could command the military. He could not control the Sudan Bar except by emasculating it, which he promptly did. The chief justice, formerly elected by sitting judges, was now appointed by the RCC who selected Chief Justice Jalal Ali Lutfi, an Islamist and stalwart member of NIF. Lutfi supported the Special Courts Act that provided sweeping powers to the appointed seventy-five new assistant magistrates chosen for their Islamist rather than their professional legal credentials. He then supervised the Special Courts, the Public Order Courts, and the Popular Defense Courts that had responsibility for narcotics, currency, and black marketeering cases. The Sudanese Bar Association was banned. Jalal Ali Lutfi imposed an Islamist judicial system on the Sudan that embraced criminal and civil courts, security courts for national security cases, and tribal courts that operated in isolated rural areas. It also had oversight responsibility for secretive military courts where legal counsel was not permitted.

Lutfi did not act on his own initiative. His family, legal education, Dean of the Khartoum University Law School, and Attorney-General of the Sudan had destined Hasan al-Turabi to be particularly concerned with the administration of justice. He would later argue that the "Islamic movement" did not necessarily require "the constitutional presence of jurists," but it must play an essential role in enlightening the public. Jurists were also required to be in the midst of the political and economic process, and they would "informally monitor" Islamic banking to determine whether the practices of Islamic banks were "in accordance with Islamic law, forbidden, desirable or not recommended." Jurists should review parliamentary laws to conform to their Islamic content. Shari'a must be the core of the legal system "to control government and guide it."[18] Lutfi and Turabi believed that justice must be Islamic and the legal system for the whole of the Sudan, Muslim and non-Muslim. Although there were three women and several Christians who were supreme court judges in 1995, the Islamists now controlled the military, the executive, and the judiciary.

Although the RCC swiftly took control of the constitutional institutions of government, they could not easily capture their political competitors. The leaders of the two great Sudanese political parties, the Umma and the DUP, and their followers refused to join the 30 June Revolution that deprived the country of a great pool of talented Sudanese. Many of them fled the excessive tyranny of the regime to become members of the global Sudanese Diaspora. There was no other option for the NIF and the RCC but to crush its political opposition. Their parties were regarded as redundant replicas of Western sectarian influence. They were banned and replaced by a transitional parliament in which the Muslim community (the *umma*) would prevail. Employing a strategy used by Muammar Qaddafi in Libya, the RCC appointed trusted, ideologically correct individuals to the Transitional National Council (TNC), a rump parliament, that would benignly and routinely approve its domestic policies. This transitional council would serve until the revolutionary government had

---

[18] "Al-Qaida estaria buscando armas de destruccion masiva."

the time to build a political structure in the vast Sudan countryside that would support the regime in the capital. In the provinces, districts, and villages people's assemblies (the Islamic *Majlis-as-Shura*, Consultative Assembly) would be created and like the transitional council in Khartoum eventually replaced by local Islamist leadership. The government subsequently held meetings throughout the Sudan to explain the revolutionary policy to the public and seek advice from civilians handpicked by NIF party leaders on pressing issues of peace, federalism, the economy, foreign investment, diplomacy, refugees, internally displaced persons, and local concerns of interest. The TNC and its numerous shura offspring in the provinces were to give popular legitimacy to the Islamist revolution in the Sudan and its government in Khartoum.

The RCC adopted an evolutionary approach to government that Hasan al-Turabi had advocated for many years as the essential condition to the establishment of an Islamist state "based on *shura* or consultation and *ijmaa* or consensus." Turabi argued that consensus by Muslims was essential for "the Quran emphasizes people and not government" and the Shari'a was "so all-encompassing" there was little need for legislation.[19] The concept of discussion arriving at consensus, he argued, was not to be confused with Western democracy. It was superior to Western parliamentary government, for only morally qualified individuals would act on behalf of the community. Although Turabi rhetorically respected all religions, his theology would require all people to accept Islam, sooner than later. Religious tolerance was acknowledged but ignored. The creation of his Islamic Republic in the Sudan would make Christians, not to mention Africans who adhered to their traditional religions, second class citizens. Arabic would replace English. Theocracy would determine gender roles, and to protect the honor (*ird*) of women. Prostitution, pornography, and exhibition of the female form for commercial purposes were proscribed. Sudanese women should wear their traditional garb, the *tobe*, and the progress they had made in the Sudan to achieve equality in the professions would be restrained despite the well-known views held by his wife, Wisal al-Mahdi, for greater emancipation of women.[20]

---

[19] "Show of Tolerance," *Middle East International*, 5 February 1993, p. 14.

[20] In 1973 Turabi wrote a pamphlet "On the Position of Women in Islam and in Islamic Society." An English translation can be found on the internet site, Islam For Today.com.

Whether influenced by his wife or more likely his personal views, Turabi reminded his critics that women were given full membership and privileges in the Muslim Brotherhood. From his residency in Kobar Prison, he played an influential role in the creation of the International Organization for Muslim Women, a progressive movement founded in Khartoum in November 1989. He had long been a champion of women's equality, for a woman's individuality was "a principle of religion" and female subservience was a contradiction of Islam as revealed both in the Quran and Hadith. Moreover equality and fairness in Muslim society were fundamentals of Shari'a law. His studies of early Islam convinced him that "a woman is an independent entity, and thus a fully responsible human being" entitled to "full freedom of expression". She could own property and dispose of it as she wished. Women were free to attend all public meetings and festivals and engage in business and commerce. While a strict sense of propriety was to be maintained between the sexes, a woman was responsible for her actions and no man could plead for or intercede on her behalf if she refused. Turabi argued that a revolution against the existing condition of women "in the traditional Muslim societies" was inevitable. However, some women were more equal than others. Non-Muslim African southern Sudanese women captured as the spoils of war did not have the right to equality of Muslim women and could be treated as property.[21]

As the days passed into months and years the RCC became more authoritarian, more ruthless. There was talk of peace, but the regime slowly and inexorably extended its repressive policies throughout the northern Sudan and in the southern Sudan garrison towns of Juba, Wau, and Malakal that the Sudan army occupied. Its proficiency at crushing internal dissent and opposition was driven by its ideology. The officers of the RCC were determined to reform the legislature to conform to Islam and to extirpate the legacy of parliamentary

---

[21] Hasan al-Turabi, "Women in Islam and Muslim Society, *The American Muslim*, vol. 2, no. 6, April–June 1993; also see, "Interview with Hassan Turabi: Women in Islam," *Koleksi Diskusi Isnet*, distributed by Asmawi Mohamad, Malaysian Islamic Study Group, 25 March 1995. For the relationship between a Muslim and a captured woman see Maati Kabbal, "L'islam, pile et face," see, Le Quotidien Liberation.com, 11 November 1997 and Alain Chevalerias, *Hassan al-Tourabi: Islam, avenir du monde*, Paris: J.C. Lattes, p. 314.

government that the British had left behind in 1956. Having banned Sudanese political parties and the Sudan Bar Association, the leaders of the revolution took control of the banks in order to impose the principles of Islamic banking.

The Faisal Islamic Bank had been chartered in Khartoum in 1983, and its first director, Abd al-Rahim Hamdi, was a good friend of Turabi and a Muslim Brother. Two months after President Numayri promulgated the September Laws in 1983 that applied the Shari'a to all Sudanese, Turabi and the leadership of NIF had sought to convert the Sudanese banking system "to an Islamic formula" based on the Quran. Turabi, himself, had been one of the founders of *Dar al Mal al Islami* in Geneva and the external holding company of the Faisal Islamic Banks. Islamic banking emphasized social development and sharing the profit and loss of its depositors and investors. Interest, usury, was forbidden by the Quran so that Islamic banks became the investors of capital for its depositors.

The need to modernize traditional Islamic financial institutions began in the 1970s and was stimulated by the Organization of the Islamic Conference movement. Saudi Arabia's conservative, self-effacing, and Western-educated Prince Muhammad al-Faisal, third son of King Faisal, played a central role in the development of Islamic Banking and the international Association of Islamic Banks. In 1975 the Dubai Islamic Bank became the first non-government bank to operate on Islamic principles, and Prince Muhammad's own Dar al-Maal al-Islami founded in 1981 soon opened offices in West Africa. Hasan al-Turabi, who often met with Faisal in Saudi Arabia, took advantage of his personal relationship with the prince. Although the Muslim Brotherhood was not allowed to organize in Saudi Arabia, its banking interests, with the support of Saudi investors, enabled the brotherhood to decide who would receive Saudi money in the Sudan. Concerned about his declining popularity Numayri had sought to "cultivate the allegiance of the Muslim Brothers," who were already entrenched in Sudanese financial and commercial circles. The Faisal Bank became the banker for NIF and Turabi. It supplied funds for the party, loans to its members to establish shops in the suq, a business in the cities and towns, and farms and livestock in the countryside. It provided the school fees for students of NIF members to attend the secondary schools, the military academy, and the university. It became the financial foundation of the Islamists and a source of capital in the Sudan hitherto controlled by banks in the Western tradition. Not long after its incorporation the Faisal Bank negotiated a soft loan that paid for the monthly shipment of 100,000 tons of oil from Saudi Arabia.[22] Later, the Islamic Baraka Bank, in which Hamdi was vice president, and the Shemal and Tadamon Banks opened in Khartoum, each capitalized by Saudi Arabian investors.[23]

After the consolidation of the RCC the Muslim Brothers and members of NIF would continue to dominate Sudanese banking and its economy. Bankers and currency traders like Shaykh Abd al-Basri, Tayib al-Nus, and Salah Karrar, a retired naval officer, were appointed to the command council's Economic Commission. They "speculated in grain deals, monopolized export licenses and hoarded commodities" to sequester scarce foreign exchange.[24] Hassan Ismail al-Bieli of the Faisal Bank, was named minister of justice, and the RCC optimistically predicted that the traditional institution of Muslim social welfare (*zakat*) would replace Western foreign aid agencies within ten years.

---

[22] "Sudan: Oil Spurs Investment," *Washington Report on Middle East Affairs*, 22 August 1983, p. 4.

[23] John K. Cooley, "Islamic Terrorists: Creature of the U.S. Taxpayer?", *The International Herald Tribune*, 13 March 1996.

[24] "Funding Fundamentalism," *Middle East Report*, September–October, 1991, pp. 16–17.

CHAPTER TWO

FOREIGN POLICY INITIATIVES

On the eve of the 30 June coup d'état the government of Sadiq al-Mahdi had few friends among the international community. The conflict in the southern Sudan with the SPLA had cooled relations with African states south of the Sahara. For many years Khartoum had provided aid and comfort to Islamic movements that sought to overthrow the Christian government in Uganda and the Marxist regime of Ethiopia. It had permitted and encouraged the Muslim rebels of Eritrea to live and organize in Sudan. Muammar Qaddafi and Sadiq al-Mahdi were barely on speaking terms. Libya used the western Sudan to overthrow the government of Chad and recruited, with the tacit consent of Hasan al-Turabi, agents from NIF to organize Islamist underground movements in Kenya, Tanzania, and Somalia. By 1989 these governments had few dealings with Khartoum, and they all provided the SPLA with either moral or military support.

The Arab countries were initially sympathetic to the government of the Sudan but soon became circumspect. Saudi Arabia and the Gulf States grudgingly provided economic aid. Libya would help as would Egypt, but their efforts were more self-serving than coordinated. The orthodox Mubarak was convinced that Qaddafi was mad and his Islamic theology bizarre even by the standards of Sufi mystics. Qaddafi rejected the Hadith (the collection of Muhammad's sayings), arguing that the Quran was the only single source for political and religious inspiration. His personal religious philosophy, expounded in his *Green Book*, was to awaken the Libyan people to the true Faith. Neither the Egyptian realist nor the Libyan mystic, however, had any illusions that they would crush any militant Islamists who sought to overthrow their governments. Paradoxically or perhaps in keeping with his personality Qaddafi was attracted to orthodox Islamist subversive movements whom he supported.

The Egyptian Reaction

The Egyptians were deeply perturbed when the Sudanese prime minister, Sadiq al-Mahdi, sought to resolve the civil war by giving greater autonomy, as Jaafar Numayri had done in 1972, to the southern Sudanese astride the waters of the upper Nile. Egyptian military intelligence (*Al-Mukhabarat al-Harbiya*) was in close consultation with their Sudanese counterparts prior to the 30 June coup d'état in order to obtain information on the Sadiq Peace Initiative. General Abd al-Atti, the Egyptian Military Attaché in the Khartoum embassy, was the first foreign official to learn of the successful coup, and Egypt was the first country to extend diplomatic recognition to the RCC. The Egyptian ambassador was the first member of the diplomatic corps to meet with Bashir, and an Egyptian journalist was the first to interview him. The Egyptian media supported the coup. Bashir was "moderate," and "pro-Egyptian." *Al-Ahram* proclaimed, rather disingenuously, that he was a leader of "tremendous popularity," and a soldier who had been decorated by Egypt as second in command of a Sudanese paratroop detachment sent to Egypt during the October 1973 war with Israel.[1] Egypt immediately provided 20,000 tons of oil for Sudanese civilians and a consignment of small arms for the Sudan army.

During his first month as ruler of the Sudan Bashir generally ignored the Western diplomatic community but immediately sent his emissaries to Egypt, Libya, and Saudi Arabia hopefully to return with their approval at best or neutrality at worst for his revolutionary government. The Interior Minister Colonel Faisal Ali Abu Salih arrived in Alexandria on 4 July to meet with President Mubarak. He was a curious choice. A Ja'ali Arab like Bashir, he was born in Shendi and associated with the Shadhiliyya *tariqa*, both town and brotherhood historically anti-Egyptian. A forty-five year old military officer Salih possessed few diplomatic skills to cover his Sudanese xenophobia and personal dislike for Egyptians. Egyptian military intelligence regarded Salih as a dangerous and potential rival to Bashir. He was a pan-Arabist and admirer of Gamal Abdel Nasser with close ties to Mubarak's antagonists including Muammar Qaddafi

---

[1] *UPI*, "Sudan Commander Leads Coup of 'National Salvation,'" 1 July 1989; *Los Angeles Times*, 1 July 1989.

of Libya, Idriss Deby seeking to overthrow President Hissene Habre of Chad, and pan-Arab friends in the Iraq military and the Palestine Liberation Organization (PLO).

Mubarak did not disguise his delight to be rid of Sadiq al-Mahdi, whom he regarded as an insufferable gadfly, but he was not impressed with Colonel Ali Abu Salih. Pan-Arab schemes were of no interest to the president of Egypt, but pragmatic, regional cooperation most certainly was, "provided that the policy and sovereignty of each of them remain unchanged."[2] Regional cooperation meant the end to the debilitating civil war in the southern Sudan through which flowed waters from the equatorial lakes that Egypt needed and had sought, by the aborted Jonglei Canal, to bring down through the Sudd of the southern Sudan to Aswan. Mubarak had never supported the SPLA. He was adamantly opposed to self-determination in the South that could lead to the secession of the southern Sudanese and would enormously complicate Egyptian efforts to acquire additional Nile waters. The meeting at Alexandria ended amicably with the accustomed formalities; Bashir was officially invited to Cairo. Mubarak soon had second thoughts. Colonel Salih continued on to Baghdad and his Iraqi friends where, to Mubarak's surprise, he signed a protocol of cooperation with the Iraq government in the "security field." The last thing that the Egyptian military intelligence service, *Mukhabarat al-Harbiya*, wanted was Iraqi competition in Khartoum. Mubarak had no illusions about President Saddam Hussein and his ambitions.

Pan-Islamic Sentiments

While Colonel Abu Salih was in Baghdad, Brigadier al-Tijani Adam al-Tahir from the RCC arrived in Libya to an enthusiastic welcome. Qaddafi was pleased to see Sadiq al-Mahdi replaced by junior officers, the Sudanese equivalent in 1989 of those who in the past had carried-out pan-Arab revolutions in Egypt and Libya. Bashir and his "RCC" was a replica of Gamal Abdel Nasser and his RCC in Egypt in 1952; their revolutionary rhetoric was the same. In Khartoum the command council immediately declared its commitment to promote

---

[2] *Reuters Library Report*, "Sudan's New Ruler Makes First Trip Abroad Since Military Coup", 12 July 1989.

pan-Arab and pan-Islamic ideology and practice. Islam and the Arabic language were to be the twin pillars on which the Sudanese Islamist state would be erected. Speeches were sprinkled with allusions to Arab unity, the universality of the Arabic language, and Islam as the central core of Sudanese political, economic, and social life. In his first speech on 1 July Bashir declared that the "armed forces motivation is a pan-Arab one," and he used a pan-Arab metaphor coined by Muammar Qaddafi that Arab unification was predestined because Egypt, Libya, and Sudan "represent the flanks for the Arab East and Arab Mahgreb."[3] Something, however, was missing in his speeches that perplexed many Sudanese and undoubtedly Hosni Mubarak and Muammar Qaddafi. There was no mention of Africa or pan-Africanism that had always been a third and important theme for the revolutionary rhetoric of Egypt and Libya. The absence was obvious and ominous, for a third of the Sudanese were African in culture, religion, and way of life, and many more were Muslims but not Arabs. The coup d'état and the Islamists revolution in the Sudan was not to follow the principles or practices of pan-Arabism in Egypt and Libya.

Three days after his speech on 1 July Bashir declared a unilateral cease-fire and offered an amnesty to anyone who had fought the government "for political reasons". The SPLA had heard similar pronouncements from Khartoum before and remained skeptical particularly when the 30 June coup d'état had abruptly terminated the peace initiative that appeared to have been a genuine commitment by Sadiq al-Mahdi for peace. Their suspicions were further aroused when the military newspaper, *Al-Quwat al-Musalaha*, published a bogus report that Bashir had approached the SPLA and its "influential friends" to begin "a "peace dialogue."[4] Their suspicions were confirmed when Bashir announced on national television his efforts to form a tripartite union with Egypt and Libya that would become "the heart of the Arab World."[5] He could not have done more damage to the peace process than to raise the issue of Arab unification at the same time the RCC claimed it wanted peace.

---

[3] Foreign Broadcast Information Service (FBIS), "Al-Bashir on Arrests, Unity With Libya, Egypt," FBIS-NES-89-132, 12 July 1989, p. 12.
[4] *Reuter Library Report*, "Sudanese Military Leader Declares Ceasefire In South," 4 July 1989.
[5] "Sudan—Al-Turabi Willing To Open Dialogue With Egypt" [translation], *Al-Quds al-Arabi* in Arabic, London, 20 July 1994.

Bashir next announced that he would approach the Ethiopian president, Mengistu Haile Miriam, to seek his good offices as a mediator between the government of the Sudan and the SPLA. This was as much a surprise as the offer of a unilateral cease-fire, for the RCC had not bothered to inform the Marxist president of Ethiopia of its intentions. The Ethiopian response from Addis Ababa was stony silence.

Within a month the citizens of Khartoum looked upon the change of government with increasing trepidation. The fuel lines were longer at the gas stations and the supply of electricity became more unpredictable. Air conditioning failed, and offices sweltered during the torrid heat of summer. Shops closed, buses stalled, water from the tap turned brown, and tempers became short. The Sudanese have always been great survivors in a hostile environment, but in the summer of 1989, it seemed that if anything could go wrong somewhere, it already had in Sudan. The new regime desperately requested Saudi Arabia, Libya, Egypt, and Iraq to provide oil and arms to save the revolution and the nation. The Arabs had plenty of oil and could be generous. Weapons were an entirely different matter. The Saudis did not have them and were not about to pay for them. Muammar Qaddafi had long, unhappy experiences providing arms to the Sudan. The Egyptians had a very low opinion of the Sudanese officer corps and, like the Saudis, were not prepared to provide military assistance that would be wasted by Sudanese technological ineptitude or captured and used by the SPLA. Bashir turned to Iraq. Within hours of the 30 June coup d'état a shipment of Iraqi arms was loaded at Aqaba, Jordan, and sent to Sudan as a token of Iraqi gratitude for the support Khartoum had given Baghdad during its long war with Iran.

The Iraqi arms were very little and almost too late. In October 1989 the SPLA overran the government's forces at Kurmuk on the Blue Nile at the Ethiopian frontier. This was a dramatic defeat that threatened the Roseires Dam which supplied most of the electricity for Khartoum, Omdurman, and Khartoum North. The prospect of the African SPLA marching on Khartoum created a frenzy in the capital and denial by the revolutionary government. The command council blamed its defeat at Kurmuk on external forces over which it had no control and called upon the faithful to a *jihad*, a holy war, to throw back the infidels of the SPLA. Government officials and military spokesmen began their reports on the fighting with

exhortations from the Quran against the SPLA unbelievers (*kafirun*).
Christian and atheist Ethiopia had provided the staging ground for
the attack on Kurmuk. After all President Mengistu had restored
Ethiopian diplomatic relations with Israel, and Khartoum now claimed
that the victory of the SPLA was only accomplished by their Israeli
military advisers and Israeli technical support through Ethiopia.[6] The
defeat—military, political, and propaganda—so alarmed Khartoum
that the RCC immediately sent its members on pilgrimages to friendly
nations seeking weapons, supplies, and moral support. Only Iraq and
Libya responded, but their aid was substantial. In November shiploads
of Iraqi military materiel were unloaded onto the docks at Port
Sudan. Libyan cargo aircraft were busy offloading military arms at
the Khartoum airport. The period of "no war, no peace" had ended.

In November former United States President Jimmy Carter convened a conference in Nairobi that failed to broker a peace between
Khartoum and the southern insurgents after which the SPLA launched
an offensive against the demoralized government forces. Casualties
were heavy particularly among the ill-trained paramilitary PDF who
had borne the brunt of the fighting at the battle for Kurmuk. The
Khartoum media extolled the courage of units called *mujahideen* (Islamic
warriors). They had only recently been formed, armed, and sent into
battle to die a hero's death in holy war, the *jihad*. The government
also waged a political and propaganda war against the West. The
BBC was particularly condemned for its reporting on the war, and
the term "Neo-Crusader" was commonly used in the Khartoum press
to describe Christian non-governmental organizations (NGOs) active
in Sudan. Ominously, government spokesmen and Bashir himself
raised the spurious claim that western relief agencies operating under
the aegis of Operation Lifeline Sudan were actually supplying arms
to the SPLA. Sudan airforce planes bombed a well-marked hospital
at Yirol staffed by the International Red Cross.

Revolutionary Connections: Iran and Libya

Seeking support for the revolution the command council in August
quietly sent two leading members of NIF to Teheran, the energetic

---

[6] U.S. Embassy Khartoum, Cable 3706, 5 April 1990; Xinhua GONS, 13 April 1990.

politician, Ali Osman Mohamad Taha, and the more intellectual Mahdi Ibrahim. Taha, the serious, studious former lawyer, judge, and the leader of NIF in parliament from 1986 to 1989. He had become an admirer of Hasan al-Turabi when he was president of the Khartoum University Student Union in the nineteen seventies. By 1988 he had become the deputy secretary-general of the Front and in December one of its most vocal opponents against Sadiq al-Mahdi's plan to make peace with the SPLA. His role in the 30 June coup d'état was "architect in-chief," and while Turabi was under arrest he served as his "homme de confiance."[7] Taha was later appointed minister of social planning to promote and presumably complete the conversion of the southern Sudanese to Islam. Mahdi Ibrahim was a former military officer educated in the United States at the University of California, Davis, and an influential member of the executive committee of NIF who edited the party's newspaper, *Al-Raya*. He had been a member of the Sudanese Constituent Assembly at the time of the 30 June coup and was soon made an adviser to the ministry of information and given the important post of director of the political department in the ministry of foreign affairs. He was the influential minister of state in the presidency during 1995 before being named ambassador to the United States in 1996.

The Sudanese emissaries had a difficult and sensitive mission. The members of the RCC were Sunni Muslims. Iran was predominately Shi'a, the historic religious rivals of the Sunni. The death of the Ayatollah Khomeini on 3 June 1989 and the election of Sayyid Ali Khamenei as the supreme spiritual guide of the Islamic Republic by the Assembly of Experts continued the dominant role of the conservative mullahs. They regarded the Sunni officers of the command council in Khartoum with suspicion if not disdain. Commentary on Iran television poured scorn on the "ambiguous" policies, political and religious, of the new Sudan revolutionary government and promptly recalled its ambassador. The Ayatollah Khamenei, the mullahs, and the new president Hashemi Rafsanjani were furious that the RCC did not immediately declare the Sudan an Islamic republic. They were also confused. Articles in the Western media indicated serious divisions within the command council. Who was in charge was debatable, for after all they had locked up Hasan

---

[7] *Jeune Afrique*, February and April 1993.

al-Turabi, the one Sudanese Islamic scholar and theoretician widely known in Iran. The command council was divided as to the implementation of the 1983 September Laws, the Shari'a. Turabi was adamant it should be the law of the land for all Sudanese. Tehran was indifferent to the fact that the Shari'a had been the rock upon which all peace negotiations to end the Sudanese civil war had foundered. It was the legal system of Iran and should be affirmed as the law in the new Islamic state of Sudan.

Unnoticed outside of Iran Ali Osman Mohamad Taha and Mahdi Ibrahim held secret discussions with Iranian President Hashemi Rafsanjani and the Iranian minister of interior. Taha worked assiduously in Teheran to consolidate his power as the principal Sudanese spokesman. Like Turabi, and undoubtedly coached by him, he was acutely aware of Iranian sensitivities. Unlike Turabi, he did not presume to be the Islamist theoretician and Islamic scholar. He worked easily with Rafsanjani and the Shiite hierarchy confirming what the Iranians wanted to hear. He argued that the time had arrived in the Sudan to revive the early and blessed epoch of the *ijtihad*, a conservative Islamic world view, and the military command council was following a path that would eventually lead to the Islamic Republic of Sudan. In Shi'a Iran Taha was wise enough not to discuss any of his own personal Islamic beliefs that might raise the specter of heterodoxy, confining himself to the theme that Islam was under attack by the Christian West. After the official Sudanese delegation returned to the Sudan Ali Osman took charge of relations between the Sudan and Iran by arranging personal meetings between President Rafsanjani and President Bashir.

In November 1989 a large Sudanese delegation arrived with little fanfare in Teheran led by President Bashir that included Taha, Major Ibrahim Shams al-Din, adviser to the president of the republic for security matters, and Colonel Al-Tayib Ibrahim Muhammad Khair, director of internal security, IS-SOR.[8] Cultural and religious differences were not the issues, but political differences were obvious. Sudan had supported Iraq during the long, bitter Iran-Iraq war (1980–1989) that had bled Iran in men and money. In their efforts to explain away the past the Sudanese argued that times had changed with the coup d'état of 30 June. A new Islamist revolutionary gov-

---

[8] *Middle East International*, 17 November 1989.

ernment was now in control at Khartoum and needed the support of the Islamic Republic of Iran to secure its own Islamic state. Iran, which had long sought to export its revolution to Africa, responded to Bashir's appeal. Personnel and heavy equipment from the Iranian ministry of construction jihad soon arrived in the Sudan with prospects that Iran would support a major road building program. Negotiations for a more comprehensive agreement of friendship dragged on during the next year as representatives shuttled back and forth between Khartoum and Teheran. Ali Fallahian, the Iranian minister for security, and Ali Menshawi, a leading commander in Pasdaran, the Iran Revolutionary Guard, arrived in Khartoum to discuss common concerns with Nafi Ali Nafi of Sudanese intelligence. Fallahian was a powerful member of the Supreme National Security Council chaired by President Rafsanjani, the Council that approved the "decision to assassinate opponents at home or abroad."[9] Neither Sudanese nor Iranians made any effort to disguise their discussions, and an Iran-Sudan rapprochement was evolving that the Sudanese, the West, or Egypt had not foreseen. President Mubarak was alarmed to learn that the Sudan and Iran had agreed to cooperate in matters of intelligence and security, and the appearance of Iranian agents in Khartoum convinced him that their presence could prove to be a threat to Bashir and therefore to Egypt.[10]

The Tripoli Relationship

Muammar Qaddafi had a long and frequently violent relationship with the Sudan. He had supported the overthrow of Numayri in 1976 and for years had created disruption on the Sudanese western frontier in Darfur. His policies and ambitions toward the Sudan were as ambiguous as his own erratic political and religious behavior. He had fallen out with Sadiq al-Mahdi and could not have been more

---

[9] For the Rafsanjani and the Khomeini succession see: "Iran: A Mullah for All Seasons," Newsweek, 16 February 1987; Bernard Poulet, "Rafsandjani, le requin de Khomaini," L'Express, Paris, 18–24 December 1987; on the power of the Pasdaran see "Iran's Armed Forces: The Battle Within," The Christian Science Monitor, 26 August 1987; on the Iran-Sudan relationship see: "Iran chief visits Sudan's radical leader," The Washington Times, 14 December 1991, page A2; Middle East Confidential, 18 December 1992; Jeune Afrique, 10 February 1993.

[10] Al-Safir, Beirut, 4 January 1990, p. 8.

pleased with his downfall, even at the hands of Islamists presumably determined to forge an Islamic state in the Sudan. Consequently, when a delegation led by Brigadier al-Tijani Adam al-Tahir of the command council arrived in Tripoli in July 1989, they were greeted by an outburst of staged enthusiasm, lavish hospitality, and an exuberant Qaddafi.

Tijani was forty-four and a member of a politically prominent family from Kutum in Darfur with whom Qaddafi had many dealings in the past. He was chairman of the RCC armed forces committee and the political supervisor for Darfur that Qaddafi was using as a sanctuary for Idriss Deby and his supporters to overthrow Hissene Habre in Chad. Sudanese rumors circulated in Khartoum that Tijani was already on the Libyan payroll when he met with Defense Minister Abu-Bakr Yunis Jabir on 8 July 1989. In August 440,000 tons of Libyan crude oil arrived at Port Sudan, a sufficient amount to meet the Sudan's needs until 1990, and Bashir was invited to Tripoli.[11] When President Bashir met with the Libyan media in Khartoum in August 1989 he pledged, to the delight of Qaddafi, that "Arab unity is our strategic goal," and "we have proposed [a unification] plan [with Libya] in principle, and when we put the Sudanese house in order, we will make this plan a reality, God willing."[12] Thereafter Brigadier al-Tijani, Major General Zubeir, and Major Shams al-Din were frequent visitors to the Libyan Embassy in Khartoum, the Brotherhood Office as it was known in the suq, and were suspected in some circles of forming a Sudanese-Libyan cabal. During his visit to Tripoli in early July Tijani had renegotiated a military compact with the Libyans similar to the one prepared in late 1988 by the government of Sadiq al-Mahdi but never ratified. In September he returned to Tripoli asking for more arms and oil and again in November as head of a Sudanese delegation to explain the government's National Dialogue Conference on Peace.

After his initial enthusiasm for the revolutionary Islamists in Sudan, Muammar Qaddafi began to respond with uncharacteristic caution to appeals from Bashir for Arab unification. He was suspicious of General Abd al-Rahman Swar Al-Dahab who was a Muslim Brother

---

[11] FBIS, Washington D.C., (FBIS-NES-89-132), 12 July 1989, pp. 13–15.
[12] Radio Omdurman, 1930 GMT, 25 August 1989; Tripoli JANA in English, Libya, 1656 GMT, 1 August 1989.

and close to Bashir. Qaddafi believed and preached his own autochthonous brand of Islam. His secular proclivities were well known and written in his *Green Book*, but he had, firmly, circumscribed his own Islamists and harshly suppressed Sufi sects in Libya particularly the Sanusiyya and their brotherhood whom he regarded as internal political rivals. He seemed baffled by colonels in Khartoum who were willing to share power with NIF and Islamic militants. As far as Qaddafi was concerned the Sudan was part of the Arab world, and it should merge with Libya as a single Arab state. To request arms from friendly Muslim states while seeking a peace agreement with the SPLA was an intolerable contradiction. "I believe that changing Sudan's Arab identity is a serious demand that should be rejected because [it] means the possibility of changing the identity of any Arab country where different races and sects live."[13]

Eventually, Tijani's diplomacy was able to win over Qaddafi. The Sudan needed weapons to halt the SPLA Bright Star offensive in the southern Sudan and to compensate for the arms given to the SPLA "from some neighboring countries," Ethiopia, Uganda, and Israel.[14] Qaddafi agreed to provide weapons, however, in return he demanded a free hand on Sudan's western frontier where his Islamic Legion and Libyan troops were supporting Idriss Deby's activity in Darfur and his efforts to overthrow the government of President Hissene Habre in Chad. Tijani also proposed, in the spirit of brotherhood, a Libyan-Sudan Joint Ministerial Committee as the first step toward future integration. Qaddafi responded with alacrity to precipitate a shuttle of delegations between Tripoli and Khartoum. By the New Year every member of the command council and most Sudanese ministers had visited Libya to be welcomed by Colonel Abu Bakr Yunis Jabir, one of a triumvirate that managed the Libyan state. To reward his success in Libya Tijani was promoted to Major General during the Sudan Independence Celebrations on 1 January 1990. The first meeting of the Libyan-Sudan Joint Ministerial Committee convened in Tripoli in November 1989, the delegations led by their respective foreign ministers. The committee reviewed all aspects of bilateral relations, and agreements were concluded for an exchange of $50 million in Sudanese meat for Libyan chemicals,

---

[13] *Al-Mussawar*, Cairo, 27 October 1989.
[14] *Al-Sudan Al-Hadith*, 31 January 1990.

cement, and fertilizers symbolized by a convoy of trucks crossing the
desert from Dongola on the Nile to the Kufra Oasis in Libya. By
1990, the joint ministerial committee had met three times with those
Libyans particularly interested in Sudanese agriculture, petroleum
exploration, and the civil war in the South. There was much commentary in the Sudanese media about an economic alliance between
Sudan, Libya, and Egypt, a proposition that had little appeal for
President Hosni Mubarak whose initial support for Bashir had begun
to cool as he sought to distance himself and Egyptian involvement
with Khartoum.[15]

War, the OAU, and President Mubarak

The greatest problem facing the new revolutionary regime had confounded every previous government of the independent Sudan. The
war was costing the treasury of the Sudan about $1 million a day
in one of the world's poorest countries resulting in the impoverish-
ment of its people, a huge national debt, and fiscal sanctions from
the international lending agencies. The government of Sadiq al-
Mahdi did not have the funds to purchase sufficient arms for the
Sudan People's Armed Forces (SPAF) and those donations from
friendly Arab states were more tokens than substance. The army in
the South had suffered serious reverses that had encouraged him to
seek a political solution in 1989 that was decisive in precipitating
the coup d'état of 30 June. Bashir and the command council realized it would take time to rearm and restructure the army with assistance from Arab states sympathetic to their Islamist revolution. Until
this could be accomplished it would be necessary to preach peace.
Bashir declared a unilateral cease-fire to forestall any further military reverses in the South.

Bashir made his first international appearance at the annual meeting of the Organization of African Unity (OAU) at Addis Ababa in
July. He impressed the African leaders with his plea to resume peace
negotiations with the SPLA, and following his speech he announced
at his press conference that his government would extend the cease-

---

[15] *Middle East International*, 17 November 1989; *Al-Safir*, Beirut, 4 January 1990,
p. 8.

fire in southern Sudan for another month. His claim, however, that the RCC was a government of "no party, no tribe and no grouping" seemed a bit disingenuous to the leaders from his Arab and African neighboring states.[16] He had conveniently forgotten to mention that the most powerful party, tribe, and grouping in Sudan were the officers of the RCC. They were committed to an Islamic state on the frontiers of Islam that would result in the continuing massive dislocation of African communities in southern Sudan which its neighboring African countries would have to absorb from war, disease, and famine. More than two million southerners had been displaced. Hundreds of thousands of Sudanese refugees were found dispersed in camps from Ethiopia to Uganda.

Nevertheless, Bashir had seemed reasonable and his extension of the cease-fire appeared a gesture that the new chairman of the OAU, Hosni Mubarak of Egypt, could seize to end a conflict that had divided its membership. The OAU looked to Mubarak to move the Sudan peace process forward, and presidents Museveni of Uganda, Moi of Kenya, and Vice President Desta of Ethiopia offered to mediate. Many "friends" of the Sudan, African and Arab, pestered the Egyptian president with their proposals to achieve peace. President Kenneth Kaunda of Zambia, twice chairman of the OAU, perhaps provided the most sage advice. Bashir "had made some very good noises" at the meeting, but Mubarak "should be patient because Garang has been suspicious of the [Khartoum] Government for a long time."[17] Behind the scenes Mubarak did confer with John Garang, who had left the bush to be present at the OAU summit, and urged him to be conciliatory for Bashir appeared willing to end the war in Sudan. Garang was concerned about the command council's search for new arms, and he made it clear that the SPLA was waiting for more concrete commitments to the peace process and fewer empty pronouncements at the OAU for domestic and foreign consumption. Unfortunately, Garang had come to enjoy his role as commander too much. He had alienated some of his chief lieutenants,

---

[16] AFP Radio, Addis Ababa, 25 July 1989, 1305 GMT.

[17] PANA Radio in English, Dakar, 1708 GMT, 25 July 1989; Reuters, "Sudanese Leader Extends Cease Fire," 25 July 1989; Associated Press, "Military Ruler Returns Home With Good News," 26 July 1989; Reuters, "Improved East-West Ties Prompt African States to Seek Peace," 27 July 1989; *The Daily Telegraph*, "Peace Hopes Grow As Sudanese Agree to Meet," 28 July 1989.

and he never gave the necessary time to raising funds to promote
the cause of the SPLA in the United States and Europe where there
was much sympathy for African, Nilotes, and Christians fighting the
forces of slavery and Islamic oppression. The SPLA never was able
to exploit these appealing themes in the West and secure funds to
promote their cause. In the southern Sudan the SPLA had no heavy
weapons, but it was still well armed and in 1989 was on the offensive.

Rejecting the Peace Process

By December Egyptian President Hosni Mubarak was disenchanted
by the cosmetic efforts of Bashir and his RCC to achieve peace in
the Sudan. He ignored the National Dialogue Conference on Peace
Issues, convened by the Sudan government in Khartoum, when it
conspicuously refused to invite the SPLA. He regarded the revolutionary government as a cabal of political neophytes unwilling to
compromise on fundamental issues. When they rejected the attempt
for conciliation by former President Carter late in November in
Nairobi, Mubarak became convinced that the southern Sudan quagmire was a war without end. Bashir bewildered him. The more interviews he gave, and there were many, the more he contradicted
himself. Neither Mubarak nor the SPLA were amused when he
insisted that his government was pursuing integration with Egypt
that would result in a "larger Arab grouping."[18] This infatuation with
pan-Arabism was promoted in Khartoum newspapers. Headlines
proclaimed that the government "aspired to set up an Arab State
from Morocco to Bahrain," and Bashir continued to emphasize in
his interviews that "Sudan is an Arab country which supports Arab
national unity" and that the revolutionary government "preferred"
an economic association that would include Egypt and Libya.[19]

Even worse, the revolutionary government displayed an egregious
lack of discipline. It did not speak with one voice. The military

---

[18] Radio Omdurman in Arabic, 1515 GMT, 26 October 1989; Catholic Archbishop
Zubayr finally met with lesser officials of the RCC in November when he complained that Christians were often accused without any reason and treated as "foreigners" in their own country. Radio Omdurman in English, 1530 GMT, 23
November 1989. See also *Al-Tadamun*, London, 30 October 1989, pp. 17–19.

[19] BBC, "Sudan Gen. Bashir Addresses Diplomats' Conference on Foreign Policy,
Peace Process, Relief Aid," ME/0636/A/1, 11 December 1989; BBC World Service,
0630 GMT, 7 December 1989.

officers would say one thing, their civilian advisers another. Even Bashir was ambivalent. He complained that under President Numayri the application of the September Laws, the Shariʿa, had been "revoltingly applied and their imposition on non-Moslems had created political strife," and the *hudud* punishments that included cross amputations of hand and foot "deviated from the essence of Islam which is justice and mercy." On other occasions he confidently proclaimed that, since Muslims were the predominant people in the Sudan, the Shariʿa was "the expression of the will of the democratic majority."[20] This view was shared by his attorney-general, the Islamist justice minister of the revolutionary government, Hassan Ismail al-Bieli, who was determined to strictly enforce Shariʿa as the legal code of the Sudan. The contradictory statements by the officers of the command council and the members of government from NIF were in reality not surprising. Without exception the civilians of the revolutionary government were members of NIF or sympathizers with the Muslim Brothers who had quietly become the bureaucracy upon which the hierarchy of the revolutionary government was dependent. At the end of the revolutionary year 1989 the foreign policy of the Sudan was now dominated by the Islamists from NIF at the ministry of foreign affairs. Equally disturbing was the capture of the government bureaucracy in the other ministries by Islamist ideologues from NIF and their allies in the Muslim Brotherhood.

Cairo had welcomed the military coup as a relief from the ambiguities of Sadiq al-Mahdi, but once the command council began to jail its enemies, intimidate Sudanese officers friendly to Egypt, frustrate Mubarak's peace proposals as chairman of the OAU to end the civil war, and employ Sudanese with personal ties to Egyptian Muslim Brothers, relations soon cooled and then turned hostile. MENA, the official Egyptian media agency, ceased referring to Bashir as "moderate" and "pro-Egyptian". Cairo newspapers that had compared the RCC to that of Gamal Abdel Nasser now began to report jailed politicians, military trials, and "Ghost Houses" for torture to extract confessions from unreliable civilian officials and military officers. Boutros Boutros Ghali, the Egyptian minister of state for foreign affairs, regarded the Islamist rhetoric of the command council as a greater threat to regional stability than the muddle of Sadiq

---

[20] F.M. Deng and P. Gifford, *The Search for Peace and Unity in Sudan*, Washington D.C.: Wilson Center Press, 1987, pp. 78–89.

al-Mahdi after the RCC held a Conference on Foreign Policy in
Khartoum attended by nearly all Sudanese diplomats. Bashir declared
that the revolutionary government would determine its own foreign
policy, choose its own friends, and its own diplomats should be prepared to follow without question the foreign policy directives of the
command council or seek employment elsewhere. The tentacles of
the revolutionary government had reached swiftly and ruthlessly to
choke dissent within the military and the civil service. It began to
dawn on those who had predicted a short life for these upstart
colonels that the government was unusually efficient, unusually dedicated, and unusually determined to impose their Islamist ideology
on the Sudanese.[21]

Islamists, Mubarak, and the Sudan

Hosni Mubarak's growing concerns about the Sudan precipitated his
whirlwind visit to Khartoum on New Year's Eve ostensibly to celebrate the 34th anniversary of the independence of the Sudan on 1
January 1956. He met with Bashir, but instead of the usual con-
gratulations on such an occasion, Mubarak minced no words about
his dissatisfaction as to the Sudan's rapprochement with Iran and
the agreement to establish a joint Islamic security apparatus. Egyptian
intelligence had concluded that the RCC was becoming hostage to
Islamist foreign policy schemes from Iran, Iraq, and Libya. Mubarak
distrusted the leadership in each of these countries, and he seized
the occasion to make their foreign policy misadventures the test of
the revolutionary government's commitment to maintain good relations with Egypt. To emphasize his displeasure Mubarak snubbed
the celebrations scheduled for the next day and promptly returned
to Cairo on New Year's Eve.

Mubarak had other reasons to worry about the Sudan. The end
of the war between Iraq and Iran had left both countries exhausted,
and the departure of Soviet forces from Afghanistan had led many
Egyptians indoctrinated with Islamist ideas to return from the Middle
East and Central Asia. Mubarak was particularly concerned about
those Egyptians who had fought alongside the Afghani mujahideen,

---

[21] *Al-Tadamun*, London, 18 December 1989.

the "Afghan-Arabs," and after the withdrawal of the Soviet Union they had found a temporary home in the Sudan from which to infiltrate back into Egypt where they joined radical Islamic groups. In Egypt there had been a resurgence of the Islamic Group (*Jama'at al-Islamiyah*) founded in 1970 as a radical offshoot of the more moderate Muslim Brotherhood. It had been responsible for the assassination of President Anwar al-Sadat in 1981, and one of its spiritual leaders was the blind mullah, Shaykh Omar Abd al-Rahman, a friend of Hasan al-Turabi.

Born in 1938 in Al Gamalia, a small town in the Nile Delta, Shaykh Omar suffered from diabetes and lost his sight at a very young age. As a youth he had assiduously studied the Quran achieving respect as a scholar and visibility within the growing community of radical Islamists including Hasan al-Turabi and Rashid al-Ghannushi of Tunisia. He served as adviser to the Guidance Office of the Muslim Brotherhood (*maktab-al-irshad*) to provide religious judgments (*fatwa*). Omar Abd al-Rahman was charged with providing the inspiration for the murder of President Sadat, arrested, and held in detention for three years until he was acquitted of the charges of abetting the assassination for lack of evidence. In 1985 Shaykh Omar had left Egypt for an Afghan-Arab training camp in Pakistan supported by the Pakistan Inter-Services Intelligence Agency (ISI) and its sinister chief, General Muhammad Aziz. There he served as spiritual adviser to Egyptians and other mujahideen led by Gulbaddin Hekmatyar the Afghan resistance leader and Islamic fundamentalist. Shaykh Omar was well-known in Peshawar where he often met with a young Saudi, Osama bin Laden. He also had a close association with the charismatic Palestinian Muslim Brother Shaykh Abdullah Azzam who had studied at Al-Azhar in Cairo and Muhammad Shawki al-Islambouli, a leader in the *Jama'at al-Islamiyah* whose former student at the University of Asyut had been one of President Sadat's assassins.

During the time that Shaykh Omar was active along the Afghanistan-Pakistan frontier, he issued a notorious *fatwa* permitting Afghan-Arab mujahideen to assassinate Muslims who had violated the Shari'a. It was a characteristic act for the blind cleric who had served for years as the spiritual adviser to Egyptian revolutionaries, and during his trial evidence from Egyptian intelligence claimed that he had issued a similar *fatwa* used by the Egyptian Islamic Jihad to justify the assassination of Sadat. By the time he left Afghanistan Shaykh Omar had established himself as one of the most important Islamist mujahideen.[22] Although a Sunni Muslim he was inspired by the Shi'a revolution in Iran and its universal message for a Muslim reformation. He traveled frequently seeking support for the mujahideen, preaching the Islamist message, and enlisting recruits for the mujahideen. He met Hasan al-Turabi in London, Khartoum, Afghanistan, and Saudi Arabia. Upon his return to Egypt he served as the spiritual adviser to the Islamists who in the elections held in May 1987 won 60 seats of the 458 in the Egyptian parliament. The Islamists were no political threat to Mubarak and his National Democratic Party, but the demonstrable impact they had at the polls could no longer be ignored by the Egyptian government.

Shaykh Omar symbolized the increasing alienation of radical religious Egyptians for the secular state precipitated by the Iraq-Iran war in 1980 and the Soviet invasion of Afghanistan in 1979. There were an unknown number of Egyptians who by choice or by conscription had joined the Iraqi army. Anwar al-Sadat had made no public objection when thousands of Egyptian expatriates were forcibly recruited into the Iraqi army, for the Egyptian community in Iraq at the outbreak of war in 1980 numbered more than 1.5 million. The war had been good for Egyptian business, and the economy profited from the sale of billions of dollars of arms to Iraq. Nonetheless, thousands of Egyptians had been captured, killed, or simply disappeared. Hundreds of these captured Egyptians had received Islamic "reeducation" in Iranian prisoner of war camps and returned home determined to overthrow Egypt's secular government.

Even more dangerous than the former Iranian prisoners-of-war were the Egyptian Afghan-Arabs who began to leave Afghanistan after the Soviet Union started to withdraw their troops in August 1988, and by 1989 a new and more dangerous organization of Egyptian Islamists had emerged from the veterans of Afghanistan. Called the Islamic Jihad, its members were the Afghan-Arabs, politicized Islamists, who regarded themselves as the heirs of the pure (salafi) tradition having fought the Soviet forces in Afghanistan. The irony that they would turn against Mubarak was not lost on the Egyptian president. After the Soviet invasion of Afghanistan in

---

[22] John Prados, *Presidents' Secret Wars*, New York: William Morrow and Company, 1986, p. 357.

December 1979 his predecessor, Anwar al-Sadat, had immediately provided "concrete assistance"—weapons, transport, and training— to the Afghan resistance. Sadat had personally "appealed to Egyptians to help buy arms for their Afghan brothers," and his government provided financial support for Egyptians who sought to join the Afghan rebels.[23] The funds collected for the Afghan rebels proved a bonanza for the Muslim Brotherhood. They received millions from the faithful and used the money to revive their moribund organization by laundering the remittances of hundreds of thousands of Egyptians working abroad through Islamic banks to finance clandestine activities to make Egypt Islamic.[24] Any sympathy among the Egyptian Islamic radicals for Sadat's efforts to assist the Afghans evaporated the day he signed the Camp David Accords that brought peace between Egypt and Israel. Considered a traitor to Islam, he was assassinated by the *al-Jamaʿat al-Islamiyah*.

Although Sunni Muslims the Egyptian Islamic radicals received their inspiration from the Islamic revolution in Shiʿa Iran and its "universal message" for all Muslims. It had an irresistible appeal to the underdog, the *mostazafin*, and the Muslim Brotherhood, for the Iranian Revolution represented to many Muslims a spiritual and universal regeneration against the parochialism of Arab Nationalism, the atheism of the Soviet Union, and the materialism of the United States. By the late 1980s a resurgent Islamic fundamentalism was preached from the pulpit (*minbar*) in the mosque and visible in the dress and appearance of hundreds of thousands of Egyptians. Those Egyptians who had been indoctrinated in clandestine camps located in Pakistan and Afghanistan returned to Egypt via the Sudan to destabilize the Mubarak government. They readily joined with other Egyptian Islamists against a government that had used coercion to force the theologians of Cairo's Al-Azhar University to issue judgements in support of the Egyptian military-secular administration. The central issue was the rule of law. The Islamists argued that the Shariʿa was paramount, and in the Muslim world only an "Islamic government" could be "the ultimate interpreter of the law." Egyptian radicals had begun a campaign opposing the sale of Egyptian arms

---

[23] "Islam: Seeking the Future in the Past," *U.S. News & World Report*, 6 July 1987.
[24] Mary Anne Weaver, "Blowback", *The Atlantic Monthly*, (digital edition), May 1996.

to Persian Gulf states that they felt would be used by Muslims against Muslims. They urged a rapprochement with Iran, claiming that Mubarak had become a tool of the West and Egypt was being used as a "demographic and military counterweight" to Iran.[25] Egypt could not tolerate the Sudan making common cause with Iran—a nation that Egypt refused to recognize—nor the possibility that Sudan would provide a sanctuary to his Islamist enemies and known Muslim Brothers in the Sudan government. He had no intention to improve Egyptian-Sudan relations when he refused Bashir's invitation to celebrate Independence Day in the Sudan.

After his confrontation in Khartoum, Mubarak was not prepared to become a mediator in the Sudan civil war, and when Bashir visited Cairo on 20–21 February 1990, there were more parochial issues than Islam and the state to discuss. Mubarak was particularly perturbed that the Sudanese ministry of foreign affairs had revived the old problem of sovereignty in the Halayib Triangle, a borderland province on the Red Sea that was subject to both an administrative boundary that favored Sudan and a recognized international boundary that favored Egypt. Egypt believed the Halayib boundary question had been settled by a previous agreement and was a dead issue and not one to be revived.[26] The Sudanese complained that Mubarak, the chairman of the OAU, had not been as sufficiently active as his position required to move forward the peace process in the Sudan. The Egyptian government had done little to support a brother Arab nation either militarily or economically. It had turned down requests for arms and had made no efforts to encourage Egyptian public or private investment in Sudan.[27] At the first session the hot-tempered Sudanese, Major Ibrahim Shams al-Din, complained about Egyptian paternalism toward the 30 June Revolution. Mubarak immediately terminated the meeting. Taking Bashir aside, Mubarak reiterated the warning he had given in December that the Sudanese leader was surrounding himself with Muslim fundamentalists and was thus risk-

---

[25] *Al-Mussawar*, Cairo, 4 December 1992; FBIS, "Near East and South Asia," 14 December 1992, p. 27.

[26] "Islamic Revolution Enters New Phase," *The Washington Post*, 3 April 1988.

[27] On the Egypt-Sudan boundary see Ian Brownlie, *African Boundaries*, Berkeley: University of California Press, 1979, pp. 110–120; "Egypt and Sudan Wrangle over Halayib," *Middle East Quarterly*, vol. 1, no. 1, 1994. MENA report, FBIS-NES-92–168, "Arab Africa," 28 August 1992, p. 10.

ing the support of potentially friendly Arab states. The talks were renewed only after Bashir promised to control his officers, but despite the usual praise for "Egypt's backing the revolution in Sudan," the meeting was a fiasco, receiving little attention in the Cairo and Khartoum media.[28]

The Sudanese delegation returned to Khartoum unhappy with Mubarak and unhappy with Bashir. The Deputy Chief of Military Intelligence Brigadier Kamal Mukhtar accused Egypt "of supporting the rebels in Southern Sudan" and permitting Sudanese students living in Egypt to protest against the RCC.[29] Members of NIF, particularly in the ministry of defense, criticized Bashir for being too deferential in his public and private discussions with Mubarak. Bashir appears to have assured Mubarak that he would distance himself from the fundamentalists, make peace with the SPLA, and take steps to improve the economy and consequently its strained relations with the International Monetary Fund (IMF). Reports of these "capitulations" to Mubarak preceded his return to Khartoum where he retired into seclusion for three days to emerge on 28 February to emphasize on behalf of the command council the historic relationship between the Sudan and Egypt and the "distinguished understanding" that presently existed.[30] There was no doubt that as the chairman of the OAU Mubarak was not about to expend his personal prestige on peace in the Sudan when neither the SPLA nor the RCC demonstrated any interest in negotiations.

The Consolidation of the Revolution

In April 1990 the RCC responded to yet another challenge to its Islamic mission. A group of disaffected officers, whom the council had retired because of their Baath Party affiliations, seized control of the airport but failed to take the Shaqqara military base and Radio Omdurman. It was the most significant threat to the revolutionary government since an abortive coup by seven former senior

---

[28] MENA report, FBIS-NES-92-168, "Arab Africa," 28 August 1992, p. 10.
[29] MENA Radio, Cairo, 1537 GMT, 21 February 1990; Radio Omdurman, Khartoum, 2145 GMT, 21 February 1990.
[30] Al-Nahar, Beirut, 23 February 1989, p. 1.

officers was crushed in November 1989. Within twenty-four hours twenty-eight senior Sudanese military officers were tried, blindfolded, shot, and buried in a common pit.[31] The commander of the Sudan air force, General Khalid al-Zain, and more than 200 enlisted men were executed. The drumhead trials and arbitrary executions were in violation of the Sudan Peoples Armed Forces Law of 1983. This savage suppression, especially at the close of Ramadan when leniency should have been expected, was unlike the Sudanese who tradition-ally would arrest those who challenged the government and promptly pardoned them on good behavior or sent them into exile. The RCC had crossed the line in the sand of the Sudan separating barbarous and civilized conduct. The mass executions of fellow officers appalled Mubarak; many had been trained in Egypt with close friendships in the Egyptian military. This cleansing of the Sudan military was soon followed by the arrival of more Egyptian Islamic radicals in the Sudan. Cairo claimed that Egyptian citizens were receiving training in secret camps near Khartoum and in "some areas under the con-trol" of NIF.[32] The RCC had agreed to provide a safe-haven for Egyptian radicals determined to overthrow the secular government of Hosni Mubarak.

Five months later General Fatih Ali Ahmad, General Abd al-Rahman Said, Sadiq al-Mahdi's former chief-of-staff, and Brigadier al-Hadi Bahri, former deputy director of Sudan security were given asylum in Addis Ababa where they announced the formation of the "Legitimate Military Command" (LMC). They exhorted their fellow officers and men in the Sudanese army to support their movement, "I, the Sudan" (*Ana al-Sudan*), which would one day "topple this mur-derous, corrupt, ugly and failed regime."[33] Three days later eighteen senior non-commissioned officers were executed followed by a purge of the ethnic Nuba who comprised a significant number of the non-

---

[31] MENA Radio, Cairo, 1605 GMT, 28 February 1990.

[32] Moscow International Service in Amharic to Ethiopia, 1530 GMT, 3 November 1989; AFP Radio in French 1432 GMT, 4 November 1989. Other attempted coups were reported in Juba in January and in Khartoum on 28 March 1990; "Life in Impoverished Sudan Grows Harsher After Failed Coup," *The Washington Post*, 24 May 1990, p. A45.

[33] "Sudanese grads may have won the battle but not the war," *Middle East Times*, 6–12, August, 1995.

commissioned officers in the Sudan army. The LMC was immediately incorporated into the conglomerate of political exiles in Egypt, Ethiopia, and Eritrea who were organizing themselves into the National Democratic Alliance (NDA) to oppose the new regime in Khartoum. The Alliance was long on rhetoric and short on action. It had few arms and little money. Its leadership, however, was determined to restore parliamentary government in Sudan united with the SPLA, for it was the only effective fighting force in opposition to the government. The historic political parties of the Sudan, the DUP and Umma, former enemies, and the SPLA exchanged political manifestos that invited "all the political parties and factions to agree and consult on a clearly defined framework for the downfall of the NIF military dictatorship and for the future governing of Sudan."[34] All the leaders of the NDA in exile were in agreement that the officers of the RCC were being manipulated by Islamic fundamentalists and to overthrow the military junta was to destroy NIF. United more by common fear than common interests the representatives of the alliance sought support from Arab and Western governments with little success. President Mubarak allowed General Fathi sanctuary in Egypt but refused to provide political or military aid. Fathi, Mubarak al-Mahdi, and the other Sudanese leaders of the Alliance were regarded as noisome mendicants rattling an ubiquitous begging bowl. They found no enthusiasm for their cause in London, Washington, or Riyadh. They were a useful, but often a misleading source of information on the government of the Sudan and the Afghan-Arabs training mujahideen in Sudanese camps.

After the meeting of the Arab League in May 1990 at Baghdad, the African Water Use Summit Conference in June at Cairo, and the annual meeting of the OAU in July at Addis Ababa, relations between Egypt and the Sudan had become sullenly hostile.[35] Mubarak passed legislation making it a crime for an Egyptian to receive unauthorized military training in a foreign country.

Some 2,000 Egyptians were reported to have received training "in fundamentalist concepts in camps in Sudan," four of which

---

[34] *Al-Qabas Al-Duwali*, London, 29 September 1990, p. 1.
[35] Democratic Unionist Party (Sudan), Secretary-General Office, London, 19 January 1991.

were administered by "Iranian and Arab" instructors trained by the Hizbollah, a Shiite terrorist organization founded in 1979 by Fathi Shqaqi and Bashir Musa in Lebanon and funded by Iran. It was allied with the Palestinian Islamic Jihad that also operated from Lebanon.[36] Hasan al-Turabi welcomed the leaders of Islamic Jihad and members of its Al-Aqsa battalions, including friends and family of its founder, Shaykh Assad Bayud al-Tamimi. Turabi also had allies in Hamas (*Harakat al-Muqawama al-Islamiya*, the Islamic Resistance Movement). Founded in August 1988, Hamas was a powerful force throughout the West Bank and Gaza in the expanding Palestinain *intifada*. Among the secular organizations, Turabi had extended his friendship to the Popular Front and the Democratic Front for the Liberation of Palestine (PFLB and DFLP) and to Yasser Arafat, leader of the PLO. After his expulsion from Egypt Arafat often visited the Sudan where he forged ties with the Egyptian Muslim Brothers in exile and their Sudanese friends, even serving in Sudanese delegations to international conferences.

The presence of Islamist revolutionaries in Sudan was ample evidence for President Mubarak to circumscribe the "Afghan-Arab" mujahideen returning from the war in Afghanistan and passing through the Sudan to Egypt.[37] By then Omar Abd al-Rahman, who was an adviser to Islamic Jihad, extended his influence to the New Jihad Group (*Tala'i' al-Fath*) and the dangerous Vanguards of Conquest (*Talaa' al Fateh*) led by Dr. Ayman al-Zawahiri who was regarded as a protégé of Hasan al-Turabi. Omar with his long and close ties to the Muslim Brotherhood and the Islamic Jihad became more than a radical preacher after he issued a *fatwa* that tourism in Egypt was "definitely not permitted by religion." His declaration precipitated a series of Islamic Group (*Jama'at al-Islamiyah*) assaults on foreign tourists

---

[36] Omdurman Domestic Service in Arabic, 1930 GMT, 14 November 1989; *Al-Safir*, Beirut, 25 January 1990, p. 6; Sudanese interest in reviving the Permanent Joint Technical Commission for Nile Waters was announced on Omdurman Domestic Service in Arabic, 1500 GMT, 25 September 1989; for a general review of this problem see: J. Bulloch and A. Darwish, *Water Wars: Coming Conflicts in the Middle East*, London: Victor Gollancz, 1993; Robert O. Collins, *The Nile*, New Haven: Yale University Press, 2002.

[37] "U.S. Fears Sudan Becoming Terorists 'New Lebanon,'" *The Washington Post*, 31 January 1992; Tarun Basu, "Pakistan Called an 'Incubator of Terrorism,'" 1 December 1995, India Abroad Publications, 1995.

justified by what Omar called "forbidding what is sinful."[38] Wanted by the Egyptian authorities for his *fatwa* Abd al-Rahman fled to the Sudan where he met with Hasan al-Turabi, Rashid al-Ghannushi from Tunisia of the proscribed *An-Nahda* (Renaissance) party, and 'Abbas (Abassi) Medani from Algeria, the leader of its Islamic Salvation Front. In Khartoum the Shaykh obtained a visa in the spring of 1990 to visit the United States despite the fact that he was on the State Department's "look-out" list that barred entry. Once in the United States he was issued in due course an immigrants "green card" which allowed him freedom of movement in and out of the country.

Iraq Invades Kuwait

After the invasion of Kuwait on 2 August 1990 and its subsequent occupation by Iraq, the relationship between the Sudan and much of the Arab world underwent a dramatic metamorphosis. At the emergency meeting of the Organization of the Islamic Conference (OIC) on 4 August Sudan made a host of enemies when it abstained during a crucial vote that urged an immediate Iraqi withdrawal from Kuwait. Sudan's vote was no trifling matter. The OIC was the successor to the Muslim World League (MWL) founded by King Faisal of Saudi Arabia to counter the pan-Arabism of Gamal Abd al-Nasser. The MWL envisaged a global *umma* designed to forge a working relationship with the Shi'a and Sunni *ulama*, and it soon became the forum for debate about issues confronting the Middle East. In 1990 the OIC received ample funding and strong political support from Saudi Arabia, and it was still the principal deliberative council for Islam. The willingness of the RCC to help Saddam Hussein by its abstention was a direct challenge to Saudi Arabia. Prince Naif, an important member of the Saudi ruling family, later expressed his disappointment with the Sudan in general and with Turabi in particular, for he had considered him a close personal friend "who had lived and studied in Saudi Arabia." When Turabi met with the king and crown prince after the Iraq invasion of Kuwait, the royal family was dismayed to learn that he along with other Islamists including Rashid al-Ghannushi from Tunisia, Abd al-Majid al-Zindani of

---

[38] *The Times*, London, 28 June 1990.

Yemen, and Necettin Erbakan in Turkey had issued a statement "backing Iraq's occupation of Kuwait."[39]

In contrast to the radical Islamists when the Arab League Heads of State met in Cairo on 10 August, twelve of twenty members voted to contribute forces to a multinational force to restore sovereignty to Kuwait. A majority of members demanded the immediate withdrawal of Iraq. The ill-will engendered by the vote of the Islamic Conference and the subsequent Sudanese moral support for Saddam Hussein would cost Sudan the friendship of many countries for many years to come. Egypt, Libya, Saudi Arabia, the Gulf Coast States, and the European Community "virtually washed their hands of Sudan."[40] The RCC suddenly found itself isolated in both the Arab League and the United Nations. The 92nd Session of the Arab League meeting in Cairo on 10 September 1990 voted to return the league headquarters from Tunis to Cairo to symbolize the return of Egypt to its former predominant position among the Arabs and the league in which the Sudan would now be a marginal player. Egypt expressed its "displeasure at Sudan's stance on the Gulf crisis," and Mubarak suspended his mediation effort to resolve the civil war in Sudan.[41] In October the speaker of the Egyptian parliament was assassinated. The assassin was arrested a year later. He was known to have close ties to Omar and had received his training in the Sudan.

During his visit to Tripoli in August 1989 Bashir had been impressed by the Libyan people's committees, and upon his return to Khartoum he established similar Sudanese popular committees as the eyes and ears of the government to warn of dissenters. The program was managed by the inept Yassin Omar al-Imam and made little political sense, for their interminable indoctrination and soporific instruction was guided by Sudanese Islamists of no particular merit. Muammar Qaddafi was not impressed. He had always kept a tight rein on the Muslim Brothers and Islamists in Libya and publicly chastised the RCC for its Islamist drift that was inimical to Qaddafi's grand design. He was convinced the Bashir government would soon implode because its military leadership had failed to blend together two historically

---

[39] "Naif says Muslim Brotherhood cause of Most Arab problems," *Arab News*, Riyadh, 28 November 2002.

[40] *Middle East International*, "Sudan: Unprecedented Isolation," 28 September 1990.

[41] *Sudan Update*, 7 September 1990, p. 2, from *Al-Sharq Al-Awsat*, Khartoum, 3 September 1990.

antagonistic forms of government. He believed that investing power in an improbable diarchy of a military command council and the theologically oriented NIF was bound to fail, and by late 1990 the Libya-Sudan Brotherhood Charter was a dead letter, an ephemeral proposition when the Sudan supported Iraq in the Gulf War. Qaddafi chided his Sudanese brethren for an unholy mix of religion and politics.

The RCC was also on a collision course with the United States. The State Department had quietly protested the Sudan government's statements, often ambivalent, that seemed to support Iraq, but after President George Bush declared the Iraq occupation of Kuwait unwarranted and unacceptable, the State Department, became "harshly critical of the Khartoum regime."[42] When the first American troops arrived in Saudi Arabia to prepare for war against Iraq, the RCC organized street demonstrations throwing rocks and burning American flags in front of the United States embassy in Khartoum. The United States protested quietly, then more strongly when the demonstrations continued. In September members of the command council argued that, given the Arab and international opposition, it should abandon its support of Iraq. The Minister of Finance Abd al-Rahim Hamdi feared that Saudi Arabia would impose sanctions on Khartoum's Islamic banks and force those in which the royal family had an interest to close their doors in Sudan.

Hamdi had close ties to Hasan al-Turabi since he helped to produce and publish Muslim Brotherhood pamphlets in the 1960s. Hamdi's enemies considered him an elitist first, a capitalist second, and an Islamist third because he claimed to have been influenced by the American economist Milton Freidman. He argued the loss of foreign banks would cause a mortal blow to the Sudanese economy. Thus the banks continued to operate, but the economy suffered. Remittances, crucial to the economic health of the Sudan, disappeared as tens of thousands of Sudanese expatriates were expelled from Kuwait, Egypt, Saudi Arabia, and the Gulf states. In October 1990 Hasan al-Turabi visited Saudi Arabia in a futile attempt to justify Sudan's support for Iraq. No explanation or rationalization was acceptable. Khartoum was fast running out of friends and sinking

---

[12] On the New World Order see: George Bush, "Facing New Challenges of Diplomacy," Naval Academy Commencement Speech, 27 May 1992; U.S. Department of State Dispatch, 1 June 1992; R. Winter and J. Prendergast, "An Embargo for the People of the Sudan," *The Washington Post*, 31 October 1990, p. A19.

into the pit of international isolation with no prospects of financial
or military assistance.

In December 1990 Bashir led the Sudan delegation to Iran and
returned bearing arms but his visit only aggravated relations with
Cairo. The Cairo airport was closed to Sudan Airways. The Sudan
responded by terminating financial assistance to Sudanese studying
in Egypt and ordered them home. The Egyptians retaliated by can-
celing 3,000 scholarships to Sudanese students studying in Egypt.
Those Sudanese who did not return lived off the meager charity
provided by Egyptian agencies and faced the growing hostility of
unemployed Egyptian youth. On 1 January 1990 at the celebration
of the 34th anniversary of independence from British and Egyptian
rule, President Bashir announced the command council's master plan
for government, a federal system with limited administrative powers
for nine states, six in the North, three in the South. The Shari'a
would be enforced as the law of the land. The devolution of federalism extended the distance—administrative, political, and ethnic—
between the periphery, Nubia, Equatoria, Darfur, the Red Sea hills,
and the center at the confluence of the Blue and the White Niles.
It symbolized and exacerbated the historic hostility between the rural
Sudanese and the *Awlad al-Bilad*, the more sophisticated towns people
by the Nile, and, of course, between the northern and southern
Sudanese. The South retained its three traditional provinces, now
states—Bahr al-Ghazal, Upper Nile, and Equatoria—but in each the
southern governor was a figurehead, for power resided in the northern Muslim deputy governor who had control of fiscal and economic
affairs, the Muslim minister for state government, and the Muslim
minister for education. The three regions were "in effect Islamic federal states" because political power in each resided in the "hands of
Muslims" who were members of NIF or their supporters.[43] NIF would
use all its resources—the government's Zakat Chamber, the Shari'a
Implementation Support Fund, the training of converts (*muhtadeen*),
and Islamic charities—to spread Islam throughout the southern Sudan.
It was a brave new world for the Sudan in which the southern
Sudanese had no influence and could expect to get none.

---

[43] *Sudan Update*, 8 October 1983, p. 3.

The Disintegration of Ethiopia

Just when relations with Mubarak and Egypt to the north were deteriorating, if not hostile, events in Ethiopia to the east worked to the advantage of the government in Khartoum. In 1991 the President of Ethiopia, Mengistu Haile Miriam, and his government fled from Addis Ababa overthrown by the Tigre People's Liberation Front (TPLF) led by Meles Zenawi. In the months that followed, there was anarchy in western Ethiopia, a political vacuum filled by the Muslim Oromo Liberation Front (OLF) opposed to the SPLA and its leader John Garang. The RCC had provided arms for the OLF who promptly assaulted the southern Sudanese refugee camps at Gambela and Asosa forcing the SPLA leadership to return to the southern Sudan followed by waves of desperate southern Sudanese refugees. At Nasir on the Ethiopian-Sudan frontier UN and international relief workers were overwhelmed by thousands of starving Sudanese in search of food. The OLF allowed two Sudanese army units to operate on both sides of the border and made no protest when the Sudanese air force bombed Sudanese refugees fleeing Ethiopian refugee camps. In Addis Ababa the SPLA office and its clandestine radio at Laris outside the capital were closed. The loss of their Ethiopian safe-havens was dramatically demonstrated by deep divisions within the SPLA leadership. Riak Machar Teny-Dhurgon, a PhD in engineering and the SPLA commander for western Upper Nile and a Nuer, Gordon Kong Chol also a Nuer, and Lam Akol, a prominent Shilluk and deputy to John Garang, agreed to defy him as leader of the SPLA. Their "Nasir Declaration" demanded the right of self-determination for the South. They accused John Garang of excessive authoritarianism and human rights violations. They argued that his "obsession with the military aspect of the civil war" prevented the development of a civilian administration or the creation of community organizations capable of providing health and education services or "leadership development" in the region under its control.[44]

Riak Machar and his colleagues sought to open talks with Khartoum to bring about a resolution to the civil war in which so many

---

[44] "Testimony of Moses Akol, Special Representative, SPLM/Nasir to the Subcommittee on Africa, House Foreign Affairs Committee," Washington D.C., 10 March 1993.

southern Sudanese had perished. Garang considered their actions treason and tribal, Nuer and Shilluk against his Dinka, seeking arms from the government to achieve their own personal and political objectives. What remained obscure was any difference in political philosophy that had led to this tragic division in the leadership of the SPLA. Yusuf Kuwa, third in the SPLA hierarchy, later claimed, without conviction, that it was the collapse of the Soviet Union and the disintegration of the "Socialist Bloc" that caused the rebellion of the Nasir Group in August 1991.[45] It remains doubtful that such a global event as the disintegration of the Soviet Union motivated Riak Machar's Nuer to attack and destroy Dinka villages killing thousands of Dinka men, women, and children in a resurrection of historic hostility over cattle and pastures that had been put to rest by British administrators during the Anglo-Egyptian Condominium. This traditional antagonism was now revived by Dinka loyal to John Garang and the SPLA. Provided with weapons from the Sudan government the Nuer and Shilluk militia enabled the Sudan People's Armed Forces (SPAF) to attack and retake much of the Upper Nile and halt the growing success of the SPLA to control the countryside since 1985.

The crisis within the SPLA was perceived, correctly, by the RCC as their opportunity to bring a military conclusion to eight years of civil war and the unity of an Islamic Sudan. In the southern Sudan the split within the SPLA was followed by years of internecine conflict "along tribal lines," and the Nasir Group soon matched the Sudan army in the ruthless extermination of its "enemies."[46] When Riak's Nuer attacked and pillaged Dinka villages in Kongor, and Dinka communities located within the traditional Nuer districts of Akobo, Waat, Bentiu, and Leer, UN Operation Lifeline Sudan personnel had to be evacuated from most of Upper Nile. By January 1992 the civil war within a civil war had generated an additional 270,000 displaced southerners. In October 1991 the Ethiopia-Sudan Treaty of Friendship and Cooperation ended all SPLA activity in Ethiopia. Without the SPLA's safe-havens in Ethiopia the SPAF were poised to sweep the SPLA from the southern Sudan.

---

[45] *Al-Arabi* in Arabic, Cairo, 25 July 1994.
[46] *Monthly Report October 1991*, Norwegian People's Aid, 4 November 1991; See Douglas H. Johnson, *The Root Causes of Sudan's Civil Wars*, The International African Institute with James Carrey (Oxford), Indiana University Press (Bloomington), and Fountain Publishers (Kampala), 2003, Chaps. 7–8.

CHAPTER THREE

THE RETURN OF HASAN AL-TURABI

During the first year of the 30 June Revolution Hasan al-Turabi was studiously ignored by the government press and spent six months in Kobar Prison followed by house arrest before being released at the end of the Gulf War. He used the time in detention to work with his colleagues in NIF and with his wife to promote the International Organization of Muslim Women founded at Khartoum in November 1989. Upon his release he became a travelling emissary for the revolutionary government as the most powerful Sudanese politician and Islamic theologian. He appealed to Islamists in Saudi Arabia disenchanted with the royal family because of its profligate lifestyle and corruption attributed to a half century of Western influence. Islamic radicals with long memories recalled the September 1967 Arab League meeting held in Khartoum during which Turabi supported their declaration to isolate Israel as an illegal state and reject any peace with the Zionists. Ironically, Turabi himself had been a cabinet member in the Numayri government that had accepted the Camp David Accords of September 1978 and the peace treaty in March 1979 to end the official state of war between Egypt and Israel. After the Gulf War there was a revival of Islamist sentiments in the Arabian Peninsula confirmed by the presence of Western, Christian troops in Saudi Arabia who had defeated and humiliated an Arab, Muslim state. Tapes of lectures by notable Islamists—Hasan al-Turabi, Shaykh Omar Abd Al-Rahman, and Osama bin Laden—condemning Western materialism were circulated widely in Riyadh and Jidda.

Almost unnoticed, Turabi arrived in Chicago in December 1990 to promote the Islamic Committee for Palestine (ICP) Conference, "Islam: The Road to Victory." The ICP described itself as a charitable organization that was, however, "identified by experts as part of a U.S. support network for terrorist groups."[1] Rashid al-Ghannushi

---

[1] "The Connection," *The Tampa Tribune*, 28–29 May 1995.

of Tunisia, Khalil Shqaqi of Al-Najah University in Nablus, Shaykh
Abd al-Aziz Odeh of the Palestinian Islamic Jihad, Shaykh Said
Shaban of Lebanon, and Muslim Brothers from Egypt and Jordan
were in Chicago to support the Palestinian *intifada* and the liberation of Palestine. A month later, January 1991, the five Abu Nidal
terrorists convicted in the 1988 attack on Khartoum's Acropole Hotel
that killed eight people five of whom British, were freed from prison.
The British embassy terminated economic aid to the Sudan and
advised British nationals to leave, but Hasan al-Turabi was more
concerned about the RCC than itinerant Brits. In 1991 Faisal Ali
Abu Salih, now Major General, had been unexpectedly fired as minister of interior. He had been a close friend of Bashir for many
years. As a trusted envoy he had negotiated an intelligence sharing
agreement with Libya, and in July 1990 he had appeared in Iraq
where he signed a cooperation protocol for mutual security. He had
complained in the past about interference in his ministry by civilians from NIF that had begun in October 1990 when police raided
a "farm" at Halfaya in Khartoum North. Here foreigners from "six
Arab and Islamic countries were covertly undergoing military training under the watchful eye of Sudanese security agencies, but without the knowledge of the police."[2] They possessed official passports
authorized by Hasan al-Turabi.

The Popular Arab and Islamic Congress

In April 1991 a State Department report on international terrorism
acknowledged that Hasan al-Turabi and NIF were the dominant
partners in the Government of the Sudan. Released from the shackles
imposed by Bashir he organized from Khartoum the Popular Arab
and Islamic Congress (*Al-Mutamar al-Arabi al-Shabi al-Islami*, PAIC).
The PAIC, or General Assembly as it was called by its delegates,
was the culmination of a quarter-century of study, political activity,
and international travels by Turabi during which he had met with
the Islamists of the Muslim world where his rhetoric and ability were
acknowledged in that exclusive fraternity. Turabi was determined

---

[2] *Behind the Red Line: Political Repression in Sudan*, Human Rights Watch, New York,
New York, 1995, p. 129.

that the PAIC General Assembly was not to degenerate into a debating society. It was a movement that would be the inspiration for the Islamic revolution and "coordinate the activities of the anti-Imperialist movement" in some fifty Muslim states.[3] His motives to found the PAIC in the Sudan in 1991 remain only to Turabi and his memory of those times, but he had certainly been disappointed by the response of the Saudi government to the Iraqi invasion of Kuwait that coincided with his long talks with other peripatetic and like-minded Islamists who denounced and were in turn opposed by the Arab League and the Organization of the Islamic Conference (OIC). After the disastrous defeat of Iraq in the Gulf War there was only one "free port" in the Arab world with an international airport and no visas required for Arabs, the Sudan. At the same time Turabi himself had emerged from detention as a domestic and international political personality whose arguments to the RCC to sponsor and provide a venue could not be denied.

With consummate enthusiasm the Sudan government described the first meeting of the PAIC General Assembly as "the most significant event since the collapse of the Caliphate," and the "first occasion where representatives from mass movements from all over the Muslim world came together in one place" to represent an alternative to the timidity and acrimonious backbiting between the Arab League and the OIC.[4] The PAIC General Assembly was to end "the splits among the Arab and Muslim governments," and in so doing it would not become a mirror image of the Arab League. Turabi believed that the PAIC would be successful because it was led by "intellectuals and not reactionary traditionalists."[5] He later explained that it was the Gulf War that decided him to establish this Islamic conference for the convergence of Arab and Islamic beliefs that the OIC and Arab nationalists had failed to accomplish by the personal greed of their leaders and their regional interests. He sought to provide "all

---

[3] "Islamic Mediator," *The Economist*, 11 December 1993, p. 48; *The Economist* also made the curious claim that the PAIC had been "set up by the Sudanese, with Yemeni help." Turabi's statement appeared in an interview with *Al-Shiraa*, Lebanon, October 1994, pp. 26–27.

[4] Tom Niblock, "Sanctions and Pariahhood: The Case of Sudan," Fifth International Conference on Sudan Studies, University of Durham, U.K., 30 August–1 September 2000.

[5] "Le sabre et le Coran," *Jeune Afrique*, 4 January–10 February 1993, p. 24.

of them, and behind them, all of the Islamic fronts, a forum together,"
and in so doing he would serve as the first secretary-general for the
renewal of Islam at his Islamic conference.[6]

It remains unclear who provided the funds for the initial gathering of the first PAIC General Assembly in Khartoum in April 1991.
Bashir was not about to spend money he did not have on Turabi's
project and remained aloof from its proceedings. It was Turabi's
instrument from the beginning, and so it would remain. Iran, always
determined to establish Shia Islam in Africa, was rumored to have
donated a $100 million to encourage Turabi's belief in the unity of
Islam by supporting his conference as a bond between Shia and
Sunni Islam. There were numerous individual patrons of the conference, like-minded Saudis including Osama bin Laden who had
recently begun to invest in the Sudan. During the deliberations of
the conference Turabi presented a foreign policy initiative to the
Sudan government based on an Islamist model of his own creation.
He argued that Khartoum should serve as an outpost, a meeting
place, and a training camp for Afghan-Arabs. Using the Sudan as
a safe-haven they could spread the Islamist message to Afghanistan,
Pakistan, Kashmir, and the former Soviet republics of Central Asia.
In return Iran, Iraq, and members of the conference would support
the Islamic revolutionary government of the Sudan and insure the
survival of NIF. Iran would provide funds for arms to Islamist movements in the Maghrib. In the Levant Turabi was well known in
both the secular and Islamist movements. Hamas opened an office
in Khartoum in 1991, and when Shaykh Muhammad Mahmud
Seyom, the former Imam of the Al-Aqsa mosque in Jerusalem and
the spiritual leader of Hamas, was exiled from Israel, he sought
refuge in the Sudan. Turabi was equally involved with the *Jama'at
al-Islamiyah*, the Islamic Jihad in Egypt. He arranged for their training in Sudan camps and mediated their internal differences.

The First Congress

The first PAIC General Assembly was held in Khartoum for three
days from April 25 to 28, 1991, and attended by 300 Sudanese and

---

[6] "Interview with Sudanese Leaders Al-Turabi and Al-Attabani, 11/1994," *Contemporary Islamic Political Views*, 14 November 1994.

200 delegates from forty-five states. Islamists from the Middle East were, of course, well represented, but there were exotic members such as the Abu Sayyaf movement from the Philippines. Among their leaders was Muhammad Jamal Khalifa, brother-in-law of Osama bin Laden. The Abu Sayyaf took their name from the Afghani intellectual Abdul Rasul Sayyaf, but their Islamic revolutionary zeal derived from the "puritanical vision" of the Filipino Adburajak Janjalani, trained in Libya who in the late nineteen eighties fought in Afghanistan with other Filipino mujahideen trained in Pashawar. In 1990 Janjalani returned to the Philippines and Mindanao to organize the Islamist Abu Sayyaf. They bombed a Christian relief ship off Zamboanga, several Catholic churches, and the Davao Catholic Cathedral killing seven and earning for Abu Sayyaf a blood-thirsty reputation. Abu Sayyaf received its financial support through Muhammad Jamal Khalifa who used the International Islamic Relief Organization and the Muslim World League to move funds to the Philippine Benevolence International, an Abu Sayyaf front.[7]

The first PAIC General Assembly oddly did not received much publicity, even in the Khartoum press. Only little by little did the sophisticated Sudanese of the capital learn through the network of rumor in the market, club, and office that the delegates had "set the foundations for the establishment of the Armed Islamist International—the umbrella organization of Sunni Islamist international terrorism affiliated with Tehran." Yassir Arafat, well aware of the emerging "predominance of the Islamist trend," played "a leading role" in the April conclave.[8] Founder of Al Fatah revolutionary movement in 1959, Arafat became leader of the PLO ten years later. In April 1991 he was at the nadir of his political career and under attack from Hamas, the emerging Palestinian terrorist organization. Many Hamas leaders had close ties with the Muslim Brotherhood and considered the organization the Islamist alternative to the secular PLO. It had only recently evolved from a social outreach program to armed opposition, and its Izzedin Kassam units in Gaza, the West Bank, and South Lebanon had received considerable publicity for their terrorist attacks against Israel. The RCC had allowed

---

[7] Dan Murphy, "The Philippine Branch of Terror, *The Christian Science Monitor*, 26 October 2001.

[8] Yossef Bodansky, "Arafat—Between Jihad and Survivalism," *The Maccabbean*, May 1997.

Hamas to open an office in Khartoum, and thereafter it used the
Sudan as a safe-haven. Arafat was forced to confront his growing
irrelevancy in the Palestinian movement, and he tried to convince
the PAIC that Khartoum would "become the springboard for the
liberation of Jerusalem."[9]

The congress established a permanent secretariat with Hasan al-
Turabi its secretary-general and Ibrahim al-Sanoussi, an Islamic
Front stalwart, as deputy secretary-general while retaining his position as director of Islamic indoctrination for the Sudanese PDF.
Turabi had no doubt that under his guidance the PAIC would be
a successful instrument of revolutionary Islam, for after all he had
led the Sudanese Muslim Brotherhood, the NIF, and was in large
part responsible for the administrative mechanism of the RCC that
"governed Islamically". He was a renowned spokesman for the Islamic
revival and leader of the Muslim intellectual renaissance who personally knew every prominent Islamists from the Muslim Brothers
in Senegal to the Islamic Student Association in the Philippines. The
PAIC General Assembly confirmed his preeminence, and he would
become head of an Islamist movement dedicated to the "resurgence
of new [political] action."[10] Pragmatic, ideological, jusrisprudential,
and theocratic Turabi believed that the Islamist movement, symbolized by PAIC, was born at a time when the Muslim world from
the Atlantic to the Pacific Ocean was in confusion. It sought to offer
an Islamic religious structure to that of the secular Muslim states.
Slogans that had moved the Arabs for more than a generation, "Arab
socialism for instance," no longer inspired much enthusiasm. Now,
after the war in Afghanistan, Islamists like Turabi had a new and
more universal message to revive Islam as a way of life as the Muslim
Brotherhood had sought to restore Islam earlier in the twentieth century. By 1991 Turabi's essays, tape recordings, videos, and radio
broadcasts had made him a popular 'alim whose name was esteemed
throughout the Muslim world. The Gulf War ensured the success of
his Islamic Conference. According to Turabi it turned limited "Islamist
movements into mass movements" taking control and "undermining"

---

[9] Yossef Bodansky, "Arafat's 'Peace Process'", Policy Paper No. 18, 1997, Ariel
Center for Policy Research, Shaarei Tikva, Israel.
[10] Turabi discussed the PAIC in *Al-Insan*, (in Arabic) *AMANE* editions, Paris, No.
5, July 1991. *Al-Insan*, No. 2, Paris, August 1990 published papers presented at the
Islamist symposium held in London, 4–7 May 1990.

conservative governments that would either "go popular or perish." He was navigating a "course of history" that made the establishment of Islamic states "almost inevitable" and as more states go Islamic, many in the West will realize that Islam cannot be stopped, "and they will cease interfering."[11]

Although the Sudan was a member of the larger and benign OIC, Turabi considered that organization devoid of intellectual merit and ineffectual in its program because it was "not representative" of Islam or of the Muslim *umma*, the Islamic community. In contrast, his PAIC was the very personification of the *umma* ideal—the community of Muslim leaders surrounded by Arabs and non-Arabs, Sunni and Shia. Turabi visualized that his conference would be unique. Islamists, like Rashid al-Ghannushi, and Arab nationalists, like Yassir Arafat and Abu Nidal, would always be welcome in Khartoum. He was proud that the PAIC General Assembly had "assembled Muslims from all over the world" to demonstrate that its participants were able to "overcome the internal divisions, Shia, Sunna, differences in jurisprudence or spiritual orders."[12] Turabi even briefly considered and promptly discarded the notion that PAIC might "drop the word" Arab from its title for it was unnecessary in the new world of the larger Islamic community, the *umma*. Shortly after the close of the PAIC convention a Transitional National Assembly was convened to determine the constitutional framework for the governance of the Sudan. Its members, carefully scrutinized by the RCC, carried out their deliberations with the speed of moving sands accompanied by much rhetoric to become more a consultative congress than a legislative body. Few were fooled. The assembly was little more than an appendage for discussion, the *shura* of NIF, in which Turabi served as the unofficial adviser to this unofficial parliament.

As Turabi moved slowly back into the mainstream of Sudanese politics, he assured his Islamist friends abroad that the Sudan would "develop relations with all Islamist movements in the world." He had used the PAIC to revive "the first meaningful contacts between Iran and Iraq" in more than a decade. Thanks to Turabi's intercession

---

[11] "Islam, Democracy, the State and the West; Roundtable with Dr. Hassan Turabi," *Middle East Policy*, Vol. 1, No. 3, 1992, pp. 49–61.

[12] "Islamic Fundamentalism In The Sunna and Shia World," Dr. Hassan al-Turabi address, Madrid, Spain, 2 August 1994; see SUNA, "Daily Bulletin," Khartoum, 19 November 1989.

Iraqi intelligence officials met with their Iranian counterparts at the conference. During those discussions Saad al-Takriti, an Iraqi friend who had used Turabi to provide funds for Egyptian mujahideen, became a "major figure" in later Sudan-Iran-Iraq negotiations. In December 1991 General Iyad Futayyih al-Rawi, the Iraq commander of the Republican Guard during the war in Kuwait and chief of staff of the Iraq army, used Khartoum as the place to negotiate with Iran the "transfer of Iraqi military assets already in Sudan to Sudanese and Iranian forces."[13] The negotiations exceeded all expectations when Iran announced it would lift its decade-old blockade of Iraq. As mediator or manipulator Turabi had indeed scored a diplomatic triumph to enhance his prestige.

With that success the PAIC General Assembly was no longer another manifestation of a nationalist phenomenon symbolized by Muslim institutes, the Muslim media, and Islamic aid agencies that served as the outreach units of the Islamist movement. It had become almost overnight a major institution in the Muslim world. The militant mujahideen from the *Jama'at al-Islami* of Pakistan and India, the *Hizb-i Islami* and *Jamiat-i Islami* of Afghanistan, and the *Hizb-ul Mujahideen* of Kashmir soon joined PAIC. They "provided assistance to" and closely cooperated with "Islamists from Egypt, the Hizbollah in Lebanon, FIS [Islamic Salvation Front] in Algeria, and NIF in Sudan." Eighteen Kashmiri Islamists would receive six months of "highly specialized terrorist training" in the Sudan that was personally supervised by "Sudanese leaders Turabi and Mustafa Osman [Ismail]." When Turabi visited Pakistan and Afghanistan in September 1991, his enemies claimed, he was there to "coordinate terrorist support activities" in South Asia. By December he had "consolidated arrangements for the exchange and dispatch of trainees" to camps in Peshawar, Pakistan.[14] As many as 300 Sudanese later "appeared in the ranks of the militant *Hizb-ul Mujahideen* in Kashmir."[15] More

---

[13] "Tehran, Baghdad & Damascus: The New Axis Pact," *Task Force on Terrorism & Unconventional Warfare*, Washington, D.C.: House Republican Research Committee, U.S. House of Representatives, 10 August 1992.

[14] "Current Affairs", www.tehelka.com, India, 18 December 2001. Data from report submitted to the House of Representatives, 1 February 1993. Turabi's visits to Afghanistan and Pakistan has not been verified by other reporting.

[15] "The New Islamist International," US House of Representatives, Task Force on Terrorism & Unconventional Warfare, House Republican Research Committee, February 1, 1993.

threatening, in 1992 the Pakistani Shaykh Mubarak Ali Shah Jilani had "started a camp in Sudan incorporating instruction in terrorist activities," after which a "cadre of about 3,000 such trainees was created."[16] Jilani had founded the Islamist terrorist group, *Jamaat-ul-Fuqra*, with the support of Pakistan's ISI.

It was to be many months after the delegates had returned to their homes that the West became aware of the significance the first PAIC General Assembly had in shaping the future course of the Islamist movement in the Muslim world. The United States and its allies were absorbed in the events leading up to the war in Kuwait and the defeat of the Iraqi military in May 1991. When the first PAIC General Assembly was held in April, the United States Embassy in Khartoum was without an intelligence presence, and European diplomatic representation, including that of the United Kingdom, was limited. Consequently, reporting on the PAIC was minimal at best, for the Egyptian Embassy and its military intelligence service, *Mukhabarat al-Harbiya*, had been greatly circumscribed since the rift between Egypt and the Sudan had become conspicuous early in 1990, and with the other Arab states—Saudi Arabia, Libya, Algeria, Tunisia—relations with the Sudan were strained. The Sudanese media itself provided no coverage of the PAIC General Assembly, and with the world's media concentrated in the Persian Gulf yet another Arab conference in the Sudan was neither worthy of news or of any significance. The Sudanese delegation was dominated by reliable riverain Arabs, and the marginalized peoples of the Sudan—southerners, Fur, Beja, Nuba, Funj—were few and inconsequential. The participants from other countries were either known to Turabi or approved by his NIF colleagues. The deliberations were not public. The participants were accustomed to secrecy and not likely to leak its deliberations since there was no one eager to receive them.

The Arrival of Osama bin Laden and Al Qaeda

Osama bin Laden, Sudan resident, engineer, son of a very wealthy Jidda-based Saudi construction magnate, was probably the first Saudi

---

[16] P.B. Sinha, "Pakistan—The Chief Patron-Promoter of Islamic Militancy and Terrorism," *Institute for Defense Studies and Analyses*, New Delhi, October 1997, pp. 1015–1029; Jalani's effort was cited in *Punjab Kesari*, Delhi, India, 28 February 1994.

mujahid to arrive in Afghanistan after the Soviet invasion in December 1979. He was born in 1957 the seventeenth son of Muhammad Awad bin Laden and a Syrian mother. His father had come from a poor family in the Hardramawt, Yemen, but at the time of his death in 1967 he had amassed a large fortune from his construction business in Saudi Arabia where he was well-known and close to the royal family. Osama himself was married at seventeen to a Syrian relative during his education at the King Abdul-Aziz University in Jidda where he attended courses by the renowned Pakistani Islamist educated in Egypt, Shaykh Abdullah Azzam. His visibility as the son of Muhammad Awad bin Laden and Islamist activities brought him to the attention of the Saudi minister of the interior, Prince Naif, whose agents kept him under surveillance until he eluded them and fled to Pakistan and Afghanistan in April 1991. Using his own personal wealth, that of his family, and other Saudi patrons, he built, roads, bunkers, and safe-houses for arriving Arab mujahideen to fight the Soviets. He soon established a reputation as a "freedom fighter" among the Afghan-Arabs, from the Middle East who were drawn to Afghanistan to do battle with the Soviet unbelievers, *kafirun*.

In Pakistan Bin Laden met his former teacher, Shaykh Abdullah Azzam, and together they founded The Mujahideen Services Bureau (*Maktab al-Khidamat al-Mujahideen al-Arab*, MAK) to provide food and shelter for Arab mujahideen. As he had been at the Abdul-Aziz University Professor Azzam was a popular and inspiring lecturer at the Islamic University in Islamabad whose students followed him to Peshawar after the Soviet invasion to enlist in the Afghan-Arab mujahideen. In Peshawar his pan-Islamic message and charismatic personality inspired thousands of mujahideen and with Bin Laden's resources, he constructed a dozen guesthouses in Peshawar where mujahideen recruits from more than fifty nations could rest and organize before entering or leaving Afghanistan. The American Central Intelligence Agency (CIA) could hardly ignore this conspicuous Professor Azzam, but its station chief in Peshawar from 1986 to 1989 claimed that no American official knew Bin Laden. "He wasn't on anybody's scope. He was just one of lots of guys with money out there." Perhaps because he was known to dine with Pakistan President Zia ul-Haq, he was not considered "a menacing figure."[17]

---

[17] Milton Bearden, "The Afghan Quagmire, *Foreign Affairs*, November/December 2001, pp. 17–30.

Bin Laden himself has always denied having any formal or informal contacts or arrangement with any United States officials in Pakistan or Afghanistan.[18]

In Peshawar Shaykh Abdullah Azzam, a mullah, became the spiritual leader for the first generation of Afghan-Arabs. Called the "King" of the Afghan-Arabs, he taught Bin Laden and his followers in Al Qaeda that against the infidel there was "Jihad and the rifle alone: no negotiations, no conferences and no dialogues." It was the responsibility of every Muslim "to accomplish his life's noble mission of restoring the *Khilafah*" (the office of the Khalifa). Like other modern Islamists, Azzam was consumed by the armed struggle to establish Islam not just in Afghanistan but throughout the world. He taught that Jihad would never end "until the *Khilafah* was established and the 'light of Islam' would shine on the whole world."[19] In 1988 Azzam was assassinated in Peshawar by a mysterious car bomb, a murder that was never solved. In the same year Bin Laden established a close relationship with Dr. Ayman al-Zawahiri, the leader of the Egyptian Islamic Jihad. Together they and other fellow Afghan-Arabs including Mamdouh Mahmud Salim, Abu Ubaidah al Banshiri, and Muhammad Atef (aka. Abu Hafs al-Misri, aka. Shaykh Taisir Abdallah) founded the Islamic Salvation Foundation. Universally known as Al Qaeda, "The Base," the Islamic Salvation Foundation united in a single cohesive clandestine operation hundreds of mujahideen. They became a global network of Afghan-Arab Muslims experienced in the battles of the Afghan war and now devoted to the struggle against Muslim states who had failed to follow the path of the true Faith. Like Turabi in the Sudan and Islamists elsewhere, Bin Laden was driven by the vision of a single Islam whose leader, the Khalifa, would one day serve as the vice regent of Allah on earth.

Osama Bin Laden, the leader of Al-Qaeda, surrounded himself with an advisory council of close friends that never exceeded five people. Beneath this leadership there was a council of consultation (*majlis al-shura*) of thirty-one; it approved military operations,

---

[18] "On Trail of the Real Osama bin Laden Profile," *The Los Angeles Times*, 15 September 2001; "Bin-Ladin denies any links with CIA in Afghanistan—98 Jazeera TV interview," Al-Jazeera TV, Doha, in Arabic, 20 September 2001. BBC Monitoring Service, United Kingdom, 22 September 2001.

[19] "The Striving Sheikh: Abdullah Azzam," *Nida'ul Islam*, Issue 14, July–September 1996.

commercial activity, and resolved theological issues. In addition committees were created to advise the council on various matters— financial, media, military, and the issuing of *fatwa*. The fatwa committee was the most unusual, if not important and played a central role in Al Qaeda. It issued rulings by those Al Qaeda members who were religious scholars of the Quran, the Shari'a, the Hadith, and the history of Islam to justify terrorism in pursuit of the revival of Islam defined by Al Qaeda. Its most important decisions were the *jihad fardh al-ein*, the duty for Muslims to fight against the enemies of Islam. One became a member of Al Qaeda only by taking the oath (*baya*) to accept the rules of the fraternity and by following them to achieve its objectives. When Soviet troops left Afghanistan in 1989, Al Qaeda continued to operate with funds from the ISI and Saudi Arabia. In its Farouq Camp at Khost in Afghanistan Al Qaeda planned and built a network of guest houses in Egypt, Saudi Arabia, and Pakistan that "enlisted and sheltered thousands of Arab recruits" to be indoctrinated in Islamist precepts and devoted to the overthrow of secular Muslim governments."[20] Business concerns were established to provide funds and cover for operations in Sudan, Pakistan, Yemen, Afghanistan, Malaysia, and the Philippines.

A few members of Al Qaeda remained in Afghanistan, but after 1988 the other mujahideen went home to confront their secular governments in the Islamic world. In 1989 President Hosni Mubarak of Egypt ruthlessly suppressed both the *Jama'at al-Islamiyah* (The Islamic Group of Shaykh Omar Abd al-Rahman) and the Islamic Jihad led by Dr. Ayman al-Zawahiri and Ibrahim Eidarous. Consequently the mujahideen had less opportunity to organize inside Egypt and became peripatetic. Zawahiri was reported to have a home in Yemen and Sudan. In 1990 he twice visited the United States in search of funds and was seen in Khartoum during the April 1991 PAIC General Assembly. Osama bin Laden was equally elusive. He returned to Saudi Arabia in 1989, ostensibly to become involved in the Bin Laden family construction business, but a hero "showered with praise and donations and was in demand as a speaker in mosques and homes. Over 250,000 cassettes of his fiery speeches

---

[20] "Usama Bin Ladin: Islamic Extremist Financier," *Factsheet*, U.S. Department of State, Washington D.C., August 14, 1996; "U.S. Says Bin Laden Sought Nuclear Arms, Complaint Cites Alliance With Sudan, Iran," *The Washington Post*, 26 September 1998, p. A19.

were distributed, selling out as soon as they appeared." Bin Laden "lashed out at U.S. foreign policy and called for a boycott of American goods." It was his first overt move to confront the presence of the United States in the Middle East.[21]

Osama Bin Laden next became deeply involved in the eternal civil wars in the Yemen, his father's birthplace. Prince Turki bin Faisal, the head of the Saudi intelligence service (*Istakhbarat*), had met with Bin Laden shortly after he visited Afghanistan in 1980 and thereafter used him to send Saudi money to the Arab-Afghan mujahideen. Turki then supplied funds to Bin Laden and Yemeni Afghan-Arabs returning from Afghanistan to support Tariq al-Fadli, the founder of South Yemen's Islamist movement, against the godless southern-based Yemeni Socialist party. But when Bin Laden began to support the Islamist Shaykh Abdallah al-Ahmar and his Islah Party in northern Yemen on the sensitive Saudi frontier, he had crossed the line. Saudi Arabia deeply distrusted Ahmar and his Islah movement, and Prince Turki warned Bin Laden that his plans for a unified Islamist Yemen were not in the interests of Saudi Arabia.

During his early days in Pakistan and discussions with his former teacher, Shaykh Abdullah Azzam, Bin Laden became convinced that the Afghan-Arab mujahideen could play a decisive role in a changing Middle East where the balance of power had shifted dramatically after the defeat of Soviet forces in Afghanistan. The growing presence of American unbelievers in Saudi Arabia in 1990 was as distasteful to him as the arrival of Soviet *kafirun* in Afghanistan in 1980. He had personally sought "to dissuade the Saudi government from allowing 'infidel' armies into Saudi Arabia, home of Islam's holiest sites," and he had discussed his concerns with Prince Turki. He also wrote a ten page report to Prince Sultan, the Saudi defense minister, "describing how he and colleagues could train Saudis to defend themselves and how equipment from his family's large construction firm could be used to dig trenches on the border with Iraq and lay sand traps against potential invaders."[22] His proposal was

---

[21] Faiza Saleh Ambah, "Bin Laden Wants to Die Fighting US," AP, Dubai, 29 August 1998.

[22] Jason Burke, "The making of the world's most wanted man: Part 2", *The Observer*, London, 28 October 2001.

refused, and when he preached sedition in the mosque and at private gatherings, he was put under house arrest in Jidda. In late 1990 "an escape route" was offered to Bin Laden when Hasan al-Turabi sent the Saudis a proposal guaranteeing him asylum in the Sudan. The two had first met in 1984 when Bin Laden visited the Sudan. Thereafter there had been several meetings between them in London and Afghanistan, and in 1988 Bin Laden had established an air charter company in Khartoum flying DC8 aircraft.

Bin Laden was convinced more than ever that both the American forces and a corrupt Saudi government had to be eliminated. In April 1991 "Saudi intelligence officers caught Bin Laden smuggling weapons from Yemen" and promptly appropriated his passport. Within days he disappeared, and Prince Turki was not sorry to see him go. He was next reported in Peshawar and then in Afghanistan where internecine warfare had erupted among the various Afghan mujahideen factions intent on destroying one another. Al Qaeda could clearly not function in the anarchy of factional strife in Afghanistan, and he himself was not safe from the Pakistan ISI. After a warning of a plot to assassinate him, Bin Laden once again sent emissaries to Khartoum to expand his established business interests but also to relocate Al Qaeda in the safe-haven of the Sudan. By July 1991 he had left Afghanistan in a private jet to the Sudan where "he was welcomed by NIF leader Hasan al-Turabi."[23] He stayed at the Green Village Hotel before renting a villa in Khartoum's fashionable Riyadh district near that of Ali Osman Muhammad Taha. Whether Bin Laden was a hardened, merciless mujahid when he arrived in Khartoum has been the subject of much debate. Essam Deraz, an Eyptian freelance photojournalist who spent three years with him in Afghanistan in 1986–1990, has revealed that by 1991 Bin Laden was ready to change his legal residence from Saudi Arabia to the Sudan. Deraz maintains that the move was a mistake because, "the people around him were very tough [Islamists] in Sudan, and they pushed him to be leader of a new Islamic revolution."[24] True

---

[23] Yunis Khalis, "An Appeal to support the Holy War in Sudan," United States District Court, Northern District of Illinois, Eastern Division, "United States of America v. Enaam Arnaout," February 2003, p. 42; "Usama Bin Ladin: Islamic Extremist Financier," Factsheet, U.S. Department of State, Washington D.C., 14 August 1996.

[24] "Osama is probably dead, says friend," *Dawn Internet Edition*, Karachi, www.dawn.com., 18 January 2002.

or false, Bin Laden was received with great deference, and only a few days after his arrival in Khartoum Hasan al-Turabi held a "lavish reception in his honor," during which Turabi announced that he would be a member and adviser to NIF. The London Arab daily, *Al-Quds Al Arabi*, reported that at the reception he had "announced a $5 million donation" to support Turabi and NIF.[25]

At Home in the Sudan

As early as 1983 Osama bin Laden had begun to explore investment opportunities in Sudan, and in the following year his interest was stimulated during a visit with Hasan al-Turabi. The two later met in London and Afghanistan, but it was not until after the 30 June Revolution that Bin Laden seriously began to contemplate relocating from Afghanistan to the Sudan. His war with the Soviets was over, and in September 1989 he sent Mamdouh Salim, a trusted lieutenant and member of Al Qaeda's Fatwa Council, to Khartoum to conduct a "feasibility study related to the movement of Bin Laden and his Al Qaeda friends from Afghanistan and Pakistan to Sudan."[26] Salim discovered in Khartoum Islamists, Hasan al-Turabi, members of NIF, and an insatiable thirst for international investment. On his return to Peshawar he recommended that Bin Laden increase his business interests and consider relocating Al Qaeda to the Sudan. Bin Laden followed this advice, and in late 1989 he established his Wadi al-Aqiq holding company in Khartoum, and shortly thereafter a Sudanese aide, Jamal Ahmad Muhammad al-Fadl, arrived in the capital to purchase property and rent office space. The Bin Laden commercial headquarters in Khartoum were located in a nondescript office on Mek Nimr Street, and he opened an account and deposited $50 million in the Al-Shamal Islamic Bank, a moribund institution where his transactions would go unnoticed. Al Shamal Islamic Bank had been founded in 1983 by the Saudi financier Saleh Abdullah Kamel, chairman of the powerful Dallah al Baraka Group, and

[25] "Part One of Series of Reports on Bin Ladin's Life in Sudan", FBIS-NES-2001–1124, Foreign Broadcast Information Service, Washington D.C., 24 November 2001 (from *Al-Quds Al-Arabi*, London, 24 November 2001).

[26] Gail Appleson, "Bin Laden aide reserves right to seek new venue," Reuters, New York, October 9, 2001.

Mutasim Abd al-Rahim, a close associate of Hasan al-Turabi. Shaykh Abdel Abdul Jalil Batterjee became its chairman. In 1987 he had founded the Muslim relief agency, Benevolence International Foundation (*Al-Birr al-Dawlia*), that supported Afghan-Arab mujahideen, and known to Al Qaeda as "Abu Sulafa" he facilitated its banking needs. Osama bin Laden later opened accounts in the Tadamun and Faisal Banks in Khartoum, London, Malaysia, and Hong Kong. In February 1990 the personal representative of Shaykh Omar Muhammad bin Laden of the Bin Ladin International Overseas Company, a major construction company with extensive projects throughout the Muslim world, arrived in Khartoum to meet with President Bashir. He was followed in March by the Shaykh himself with an entourage of Saudi business men that included Prince Faisal Muhammad al-Faisal al Saud, Chairman of the Faisal Islamic Bank, and Dr. Ahmad Muhammad Ali, Chairman of the Islamic Development Bank. Shortly thereafter the Bin Laden group under the supervision of Abu Bakr al-Humayd began construction of a new airport at Port Sudan. Osama bin Laden later offered $2.5 million to operate and maintain the facility through which arms shipments were later flown to mujahideen in Somalia and Yemen.

In the social life of Khartoum's fashionable suburb of Riyadh Bin Laden quickly established a close personal relationship with Hasan al-Turabi.[27] He married Turabi's niece as his third wife. In return Turabi arranged for Bin Laden to import construction equipment and vehicles free of duty. Bin Laden was accompanied to Khartoum by his family and the leadership of Al Qaeda in his guest house including Sudanese prominent in NIF.[28] They moved freely in and out of the Sudan, for the usual customs formalities were facilitated by a "delegation office" that also arranged meetings with Sudanese intelligence officials who appointed Colonel Abd al-Basit Hamza its liaison officer with Al Qaeda. Once established in Khartoum Al Qaeda obtained from the Sudan government a "couple of hundred" Sudanese passports, and some members were given Sudanese citi-

---

[27] Jim Landers, "Islamic unity, by any means," *The Dallas Morning News*, 21 October 2001.

[28] Data provided by Mamdouh Mahmud Salim a Bin Laden associate interrogated by German police after his arrest in September 1998; see "U.S. Case Against bin Laden in Embassy Blasts Seems to Rest on Ideas," *The New York Times*, 13 April 1999.

zenship. In return, members of Al Qaeda screened the credentials of Afghan-Arabs for Sudan state security.[29]

Bin Laden's commercial interests were conducted through the Islamic banks of the Sudan and the official government Bank of Sudan and the Sudanese Commerce Bank, all of which were "a closely-linked, Turabi-dominated business group known as *Al-Mahfazah* (the portfolio)" that controlled the marketing of cotton, sesame, and wheat. Bin Laden facilitated the exchange of Sudanese cotton to the Taliban in Afghanistan for "weapons captured from Soviet forces."[30] By 1992 Bin Laden had established two holding companies, Taba Investments, founded in 1990, and Laden International an umbrella operation that included Qudurat Transportation, a bakery, a furniture, fruit, and vegetable export companies, and the Al-Ikhlas Company which imported sweets and honey. His Al-Hijra Construction Company employed 600 people for the construction of a major arterial road from Khartoum to Port Sudan. He opened a company office at Port Sudan to handle imports of everything from arms to farm equipment and exports of Sudanese cotton, sesame, and wheat. When the government was unable to pay Bin Laden for his roadwork in cash, he was granted rights in perpetuity to a million acres of farmland in the Gash River Delta north of Kassala, an important provincial capital on the Eritrean frontier. In a region where the growing of food was unpredictable and land ownership in historic dispute, the grant gave rights to Bin Laden in direct conflict with those of the semi-nomadic and settled Hadendowa of the eastern Sudan. He soon made enemies among the poor farmers when he over planted his land to watermelons that depressed the price of melon and seed and among the wealthy farmers when the government granted him a monopoly for the export of sesame.

When not at his Mek Nimr office in downtown Khartoum, Bin Laden could most often be found at his second-floor office at the Al Qaeda guesthouse in Riyadh or on a large farm he purchased south of Khartoum on the Blue Nile. Here members of Al Qaeda,

---

[29] "Grand Jury Indictment Against Usama Bin Laden: United States of America v. Usama Bin Laden," U.S. District Court, Southern District of New York, 5 November 1998; "United States of America v. Usama bin Laden, et al.," Trial in the Southern District of New York. "Digital files from the Court Reporters Office," 10 July 2001.

[30] Peter C. Lyon, "Patronage and Politics in Islamic Banking," *LBJ Journal of Public Affairs*, Austin, Texas, 1998.

Egyptians from *Jama'at al-Islamiyah*, Algerians from FIS, Libyans opposed to Qaddafi, Eritrean and Yemeni insurgents, Hamas including the notorious Hassan Salami, known as Abu Ahmad, received training in weapons and explosives. On Thursday evening the Al Qaeda leadership met at the farm, but other members regularly attended lectures on Islamic and political issues delivered by Bin Laden and his associates, Abu Fadl al-Makki, Saad al-Sharif, and Mamdouh Mahmud Salim (Abu Hajer al-Iraqi). Construction equipment brought from Afghanistan was stored at the farm, but until Bin Laden began work on the Al-Tahaddi road from Khartoum to Atbara, it was used in the "building and furnishing of 23 camps for Afghanistan's Arab majahideen."[31] He supplied funds for three Al Qaeda training camps and financially supported the PDF and military training by NIF for secondary and university students.

Throughout his sojourn in the Sudan Bin Laden's presence in Khartoum was that of a wealthy businessman willing to invest in nation building. The construction of roads required strong men of which the Sudan had many unemployed who had to compete with tough, taciturn non-Sudanese Arabs who had served in the war in Afghanistan. He had paid to be "transported 480 Afghan veterans to the Sudan" after Pakistan officials threatened their expulsion from towns and villages strung along the Afghan border.[32] They arrived expecting his hospitality. Many were given employment in his Al-Hijra construction company. The RCC either gave its tacit support to its Afgan-Arab visitors, in customary Sudanese fashion, or ignored their presence, but they received opportunities most Sudanese could not imagine. Their symbiotic relationship with PAIC soon developed. The PAIC General Assembly fully supported Al Qaeda's revolutionary aims in more than a dozen nations. In turn, Al Qaeda supported Turabi's political objectives in the Sudan and used his PAIC as cover for its international operations. When President Bashir was questioned after Bin Laden was forced to leave the Sudan in 1996, he blandly replied with a straight face that Bin Laden never really

---

[31] "Part One of Series of Reports on Bin Ladin's Life in Sudan", FBIS-NES-2001-1124, Washington D.C., 24 November 2001 (from *Al-Quds Al-Arabi*, London, 1 November 2001, p. 13).
[32] Hasan al-Turabi, "The Islamic Awakening's New Wave," *New Perspectives Quarterly*, Vol. 10, No. 3, Summer 1993.

had partisans or a "network" in Sudan. He only had "a small group of assistants" who always "stayed far away from the media."[33]

Turabi Triumphant

Under the ideological and charismatic leadership of Hasan al-Turabi the Sudan, long perceived as a marginal state on the frontier of Islam, became an intellectual nexus for Islamist intellectuals and a sanctuary for the more militant Afghan-Arabs and other Islamic terrorists. By 1991 the RCC, which had originally maintained its distance, was now associated in the minds of the Sudanese with Turabi and NIF.[34] Like the great *habubs* (sandstorms) that periodically engulf Khartoum, Islamic dignitaries, mullahs, and intelligence agents from the Muslim world made their way to the office of Hasan al-Turabi. Here they met with young men captivated and aroused by a spiritual experience unknown since the early years of the Muslim Brotherhood who would serve to lead the revival of Islam. Some sought to eradicate all Western influence. Others were determined to destroy the state of Israel. There were intellectuals who argued that the insidious spread of Western secularism had corrupted the true meaning of Islam and the incontrovertible union between the mosque and the state. They all rallied around the PAIC General Assembly organized and led by Hasan al-Turabi, and they welcomed discussion and debate that urged Muslims to turn away from the secular, hedonistic, and selfish proclivities of the West. Although not as virulently anti-American as the Iranian revolution of the Ayatollah Khomeini, the PAIC General Assembly sternly rejected the morals and mores of the "Neo-Crusader" invasion that would continue to corrupt and erode the fundamental faith and meaning of Islamic culture.

As founder of the PAIC General Assembly Turabi soon became a commanding figure in "the rejectionist front" that consisted of individuals and organizations controlled by Islamists and funded by Muslims who endorsed his call for the regeneration of Islam. His

---

[33] "Bin Laden has no network in Sudan: president," *AFP*, Dubai, 28 September 1998.

[34] " 'Fundamentalist' Military Junta Pushing Sudan to Catastrophe," *Washington Report on Middle East Affairs*, August/September 1991, p. 48.

role as mediator in the Hamas-PLO peace talks demonstrated the power of his personality, ideology, and political presence. The Higher Liaison Committee of the General Assembly, dominated by Turabi, Shaykh Omar Abd al-Rahman from Egypt, Rashid al-Ghannushi of Tunisia, and Abbasi Madani from Algeria, drafted an "Islamic Plan" in support of radical Islamist movements—the Sudan NIF, Algeria's FIS, the Hamas and Fatah movements in Gaza and Palestine, Al Nahda in Tunisia, and representatives of various Islamist radical movements in Egypt.

Unlike Turabi, who needed no excuse to speak at length on Islam, most participants at the PAIC General Assembly were very circumspect. They left Khartoum without giving interviews so that it was frustrating for Western journalists to discern if the Islamists meant what they were reported to have said or said what they meant. They were equally perplexed to define or explain the Turabi phenomenon in the Sudan. The PAIC General Assembly provided Turabi with the instrument he needed to establish his political and religious influence throughout the Islamic world. He would proudly declare. "I am close to, I know every Islamic movement in the world, secret or public."[35] He was in contact with the *Ikhwan* and shaykhs active in Tadjikistan and the secretive Nahda parties in the other former Soviet republics of Central Asia and corresponded with the mujahideen in Afghanistan and Kashmir. Strange political and religious bedfellows would meet in Khartoum. Sunni Sudan would join Shiite Iran to spread the message of the Islamist revival from West Africa to Mindanao. Turabi would keep apprised of Islamic warriors—Nur Hashim in the Philippines, Abd al-Quddus, the Burmese leader of the Arakan Liberation Front, and Islamist friends in the disintegrating Socialist Federal Republic of Yugoslavia. In the Horn of Africa Hasan al-Turabi was the patron of the Islamic Ogaden Union which sought to overthrow the Christian Amhara-Tigrean Ethiopian government of Meles Zenawi that had seized power from the communist, Mengistu Haile Mariam, in 1991. He closely followed the activities of Shaykh Omar Abd al-Rahman in the United States and welcomed to Khartoum Louis Farrakhan, the American Black Muslim leader.

Members of the Sudanese Umma Party in exile were the first to report that Hasan al-Turabi was involved in an alliance between Al

---

[35] "Interview with Sudanese Leaders Al-Turabi and Al-Attabani," *Contemporary Islamic Political Views*, 14 November 1994.

Qaeda and Hizbollah. Curiously, Turabi had never met Shaykh Shaykh Muhammad Husayn Fadlallah of Lebanon, the Hizbollah spiritual leader born in 1936, but they had much in common because both sought to bridge the political and theological divide that confounded the Shia and Sunni Islamic worlds. Ironically, before relocating to the Sudan Al Qaeda had demonstrated little interest in continuing to cooperate with Shiite organizations operating in Afghanistan, but their relations with Iran improved immeasurably after a meeting between Osama bin Laden and Shaykh Nomani, the Iranian representative in Khartoum. Introduced by Ahmad Abd al-Rahman Hamadabi, a Sudanese Sunni and scholar close to Turabi, a Bin Laden aide arranged for Al Qaeda "militants" to receive "advanced explosives" training, for the destruction of large buildings in the Iranian-sponsored Hizbollah camps in Lebanon.[36]

The Sudan and the Arabs

Turabi had always maintained his connections with the Muslim Brotherhood and to its seventy country branches. He knew its leaders in Eritrea and Central Asia. He had many friends in Hamas and a gaggle of ineffectual Libyan Islamists who lived in Khartoum conspiring against Muammar Qaddafi. Qaddafi was a man of many contradictions. Sybarite at one moment, anchorite at another, he was a dictator who derived little inspiration from Turabi's pronouncements. He was not amused that Islamic governments should bring "all life back to the service of the One God." Neither was he interested "re-emphasizing the concept of *tawheed* [the omnipresence of Allah] in philosophy, economics, learning, culture, art, social life, and international affairs as a practical alternative to modern versions based on secularism, greed, materialism, titillation, convention, and injustice."[37] Qaddafi was very concerned that his Libyan enemies who had settled in the Sudan would one day return to threaten his government. Early in 1991 Qaddafi warned Bashir and his colleagues on the RCC that their Islamist advisers and administrators were

---

[36] *Al-Wasat*, London, 14–20 December 1992, pp. 22–25; on Hamas, Fatah, and the Khartoum connection, see *Al-Watan al-Arabi*, 30 October 1992, pp. 21–22.

[37] Mohamed Elhachmi Hamdi, *The Making of a Political Leader: Conversations with Hasan al-Turabi*, Boulder: Westview Press, 1998, p. 120.

leading the nation astray. He was particularly disturbed by reports of a "conspicuous influx" of Iranians who were "believed to be working in Islamist military training camps" in the Sudan.[38] Despite his suspicions the irrepressible Qaddafi arrived unannounced in Khartoum to celebrate with a few other foreign dignitaries the second anniversary of the 30 June Revolution.

His surprise appearance was motivated more by the fact that the UN was about to impose economic and diplomatic sanctions on Libya for the destruction by two Libyan agents of Pan American Airways Flight 103 over Lockerbie, Scotland, in December 1988. When Qaddafi refused to give up the two agents, he had sought to prevent the imposition of sanctions by containing the terrorist organizations operating from Libya. To demonstrate that Libya could change, "the Jamahiriya decided to sever ties with international liberation movements, including the Irish Republican Army." Qaddafi closed down Libya's *Al-Da'awa al-Islamiyya* (Islamic Call Society), and "froze all its activities within Arab and international revolutionary committees."[39] In Khartoum Qaddafi discovered that the training camps he had closed in Libya had reopened in Sudan where Islamists from Tripoli were plotting against him. He was exasperated that his proposals for a Libya-Sudan brotherhood were politely ignored and angered by public statements from Hasan al-Turabi about his attempts to improve ties with Egypt. Receiving no sympathy from the RCC he returned to Tripoli in a huff and promptly halted oil shipments to the Sudan and demanded repayment for the shipments he had sent during the past two years.

Qaddafi was not the only leader in the Maghib angry with the Islamists in Khartoum. Turabi was assisting members of the Algerian FIS to move freely in and out of the Sudan. During his first and only trip to Algeria to attend a conference in Algiers in May 1990 he had distributed a controversial paper in which his first priority of "Islamic movements" was "to change the oppressive secular regimes now ruling over Muslim societies." The pamphlet was not appreci-

---

[38] Yossef Bodansky and Vaughn S. Forrest, "Iran's European Springboard?" Congressional Task Force on Terrorism and Unconventional Warfare, U.S. House of Representatives, Washington D.C., 1 September 1992. Bodansky was Director of the Congressional Task Force.

[39] "Civilians Bear the Brunt," *Middle East International*, 20 December 1991, p. 11.

ated by the military rulers of Algeria whose government was under assault by Islamist insurgents.[40] By 1991 the Sudan was providing training camps and Iran the financial and military assistance to the Algerian FIS that was only frustrated from taking control of the government by the intervention of the Algerian military in January 1992. President Chadli Benjedid was deposed and parliamentary elections canceled precipitating a bloody civil war between the army and the Islamists that cost more than 75,000 Algerian lives.

The leaders of Tunisian were no more impressed with the revolutionary government of Sudan than Egypt, Libya, or Algeria. The Sudan had become the home for Tunisian Islamists in their training camps, and in October 1991 Tunisia recalled its ambassador after "a group of 16 Tunisian terrorists, a high quality assassination squad, left Khartoum for Paris and Tunis."[41] In November, diplomatic relations were broken when Tunisian revolutionary Islamists carrying Sudanese diplomatic passports attempted to cross the border from Algeria. Tunis newspapers reported that Fathi al-Daw, the secretary of Sudan Human Rights Organization, accused the PAIC of a plan to destabilize Tunisia, Algeria, and "a number of fraternal countries" and that Turabi was an adviser to Rashid al-Ghannushi, the Tunisian Islamist intellectual, and the Tunisian mujahideen.[42] Al-Ghannushi was the leader of the proscribed Tunisian Renaissance Party (*Hizb al-Nahda* or *Al-Nahda* for short). He traveled with a Sudanese diplomatic passport and declared that Turabi was "the leader of a generation of Islamists," a true "Reformer" (*mujaddid*) of Islam.[43] Like Turabi, Rashid al-Ghannushi had made the journey from Muslim Brother to pragmatic political philosopher. Although there were the usual disagreements between him and Turabi about interpretations

---

[40] Mohamed Elhachmi Hamdi, *The Making of a Political Leader: Conversations with Hasan al-Turabi*, pp. 115, 120.

[41] *Middle East Confidential*, 18 December 1992.

[42] "Sudan Is Seen as Safe Base for Mideast Terror Groups," *The New York Times*, 26 January 1992. On Islamists and Africa see: *Africa Insight*, vol. 22, no. 4, 1992; *Il Giornale* in Italian, Milan, Italy, August 1994.

[43] In 1987 al-Ghannushi was imprisoned for life at forced labor but was released the following year. He moved to Europe. In 1992 and again in 1996 the Tunisian government sentenced him in absentia to life imprisonment. On al-Ghannushi and Tunisia see: Francois Burgat and William Dowell, *The Islamic Movement in North Africa*, Austin: University of Texas Press, 1993, pp. 151, 182–246; also see FBIS-NES-92-173, "Arab Africa", 4 September 1992, pp. 17–18.

of Islamic theology, law, and revolution, in 1993 Turabi convinced Bashir to expel the Tunisian Salafiyah Movement and the Tunisian Jihad Movement from the Sudan after they criticized the *Al-Nahda* and al-Ghannushi for their hesitancy to employ violence to overthrow the Tunisian government.

Hasan al-Turabi had greater success and always a warmer reception from the states and rulers of the Persian Gulf than he ever had in North Africa. He was especially fond of Qatar. It was small enough to escape close scrutiny, and its government was the sinecure of the Al-Thani family. The emir Prince Khalifah bin Hamid al-Thani and his son, the crown Prince Hamad bin Khalifa Al-Thani, were conservative Wahhabis and strong supporters for the revival of Islam by the new Islamists. Qatar had grown wealthy from its major oil and gas fields, and to defend that resource from predatory neighbors the emir and his powerful Foreign Minister Hamad bin Jasim, energetically encouraged private Western oil companies to explore and extract petroleum for their mutual profit. In its dispute with Bahrain over the Hawar Islands, the United States had remained neutral, and Qatar was regarded as politically quixotic in the Gulf. Crown Prince Hamad was more friendly with Iraq than Saudi Arabia and had amicable relations with Iran with whom Qatar shared a large offshore gas field. The emir welcomed Islamist agitators and Muslim Brothers who sought refuge and homes in Doha that became the port for Islamists travelling east to Central Asia and Indonesia. Members of the PAIC, particularly Hasan al-Turabi, and officials from Qatar exchanged regular visits. He used his friendship with the emir and Foreign Minister Bin Jasim to move Afghan-Arabs by air from the Al Qaeda base in Pashawar to Doha and then to Khartoum without scrutiny from Qatar custom or security officials.

In the Yemen Turabi continued his close relationship with Shaykh Abdallah al-Ahmar, politician and leader of the Islamist Islah Party and met often with President Ali Abdallah Saleh. After South Yemen merged with the North in May 1990, the Marxist-dominated Yemeni Socialist Party of Ali Salem al-Baidh challenged President Saleh. The Sudan instantly offered Port Sudan and its airfield to Turabi's friends and would send Afghan-Arabs residing in Sudan to suppress the southern uprising.

Iran and the Sudan

Neither Bashir nor Turabi sought to disguise their friendship with Iran and a joint Iran-Sudan strategy to influence events in the Horn of Africa. There were many meetings and many promises in which each party sought to take advantage of the other. In December 1990 an Islamic conference on Palestine was convened at Tehran where for the first time Shiite Iran made a determined effort to reach out to the Sunni Palestinians involved in the Arab rebellion (*intifada*) against Israel. Iran would provide military assistance to Hamas and signed a secret agreement for cooperation between the Sudanese and Iranian intelligence services. By 1992 Iran had become the most dependable political partner of the Sudan that symbolized the success of Turabi to bridge the theological differences between Shi'a and Sunni by a close working relationship with the Iranian mullahs. Hasan al-Turabi was considered the architect of this "opening to the east," by his writings, peripatetic travels, and personal involvement in Islamist movements. Iran welcomed Turabi's initiatives and his determination to launch a "genuine effort to export its revolution to Sunni-populated areas, such as Sudan, Tunisia, Egypt and the Palestinian arena."[44] Bin Laden had not been idle. He was anxious to exploit the new relationship between Shiite Iran and Sunni Sudan in order for Al Qaeda to forge "an anti-American alliance with the governments of Iran and Sudan in the early 1990s." He had personally met with Iranian officials in Tehran and Khartoum to arrange for training in explosives for Iranian-sponsored Hizbollah in Lebanon and had met with Imad Mughniyah. One of the founders of Hizbollah and leader of the team that blew up the American Embassy in Beirut in April 1983, Mughniyah was the director of its terrorist operations and readily provided instructors to train Al Qaeda in the Sudan.[45]

Iran in return began construction of the "Peace Highway" with personnel from the Iran Ministry of Construction Jihad to link Rabak on the Blue Nile in the northern Sudan with Malakal, the capital of Upper Nile Province where Africa begins. Although the road was never completed, the construction crews were well-armed, and their

---

[44] Bruce Hoffman, *Holy Terror: The Implication of Terrorism Motivated by a Religious Imperative*, Santa Monica: RAND Corp., RAND Paper, 1993, p. 7834.

[45] "A Global, Pan-Islamic Network," *The Washington Post*, 23 August 1988, p. A01.

commitment to a strategic road to connect Arab and African produced bizarre rumors that thousands of Iranian soldiers would soon arrive in the Sudan. Other rumors flourished in the Omdurman suq that Iran had "begun active preparations for long-term terrorist operations in Western Europe" training "Islamists from Tunisia, Algeria, France, and Belgium in camps in Sudan." In May 1991 sixty-five mujahideen arrived from Iran to serve as the "nucleus for Islamic action in Europe" that was later to be known in Europe as "the Islamic Tide Brigade." Their training was "under the direct supervision of the newly promoted Brigadier General Bakri Hassan Salih," the director of the RCC's committee of security.[46] In October 1991 the Second International Conference on the Struggle for Palestine was convened in Tehran with representatives from the Sudan, Hamas, and Islamic Jihad.

Islamic Jihad was to play an important role in Iran's Pan-Islamic and ecumenical efforts to bring Shiite and Sunni together. Its leader, Fathi Shaqaqi, "saw Khomeini's greatness in his capacity to illuminate the great cultural clash between the Islamic nation with its historical tradition, faith, and civilization, and on the other hand the satanic forces of the West represented by Israel. Shaqaqi often quoted a fatwa issued by Khomeini which spoke of the religious duty of bringing about the elimination, *izala*, of the Zionist entity."[47] At the Palestine conference Ahmad Khomeini emphasized the Muslim world's inevitable and implacable struggle with the United States. At the end of the conference Tehran received the whole-hearted support of Islamists from Turabi in Sudan to Shaykh Muhammad Husayn Fadlallah in Lebanon. The Middle East would become the crucible for a New World Order. Turabi was said to have told the conferees that "those who cannot be convinced by the Quran will be convinced by power," confrontation was "inevitable," a statement he later denied.

The U.S. Department of State did not need to be convinced. It reported in 1991 that Sudan "continued a disturbing relationship with international terrorist groups." President Bashir had announced

---

[46] "U.S. Says Bin Laden Sought Nuclear Arms: Complaint Cites Alliance With Sudan, Iran," Michael Grunwald, *The Washington Post*, September 26, 1998, p. A19; "Excerpts From Guilty Plea in Terrorism Case," *The New York Times*, October 21, 2000, Section B, p. 2.

[47] See: "Soudan, Le Sabre et Le Coran," *Jeune Afrique*, 4 Jan.–10 Feb. 1993, p. 4.

at a meeting of Arab and Foreign Investors Symposium in Khartoum in March 1990 that henceforth all "Arab brothers" would be allowed to enter Sudan without a visa.[48] The doors were now open to legitimate visitors and terrorists alike whether the Sudanese leadership knew it or not. Mujahideen, whose fanaticism had been forged in the crucible of the Islamic Holy War against the Soviet invaders in Afghanistan were on the move from training camps at Qom in Iran and from Khost on the Afghanistan-Pakistan border. Once in Africa, "these terrorists, under the flag of the Islamic Peoples' Conference of Hassan al-Turabi of Sudan, established contacts with terrorist organizations in the Middle East, including groups in Egypt [where two million Sudanese resided], Algeria and Lebanon, and Kashmir." The Sudan, "backed" by $10–20 million "and expertise from Iran," was determined to "establish a beachhead for Islamic radicalism in Khartoum." The Sudan could emerge as a "new Lebanon."[49]

By 1992 the United States Department of State had become increasingly concerned about the PAIC and the Iranian presence in the Sudan. In December 1991, Deputy Assistant Secretary of State for Africa Robert G. Houdek, had expressed Washington's apprehensions about Iran in the Sudan and "the increasing numbers of people from organizations . . . considered to be terrorist." When the RCC denied any support for terrorism, Houdek replied. "Be careful. These people can violate your hospitality."[50] That same month a conspicuous influx of Iranians arrived in Khartoum many of whom were believed to be working in Islamist military training camps to be followed in December 1991 by the President of Iran, Hojdatoleslam Ali Akbar Hashemi Rafsanjani, on an official state visit to Sudan. A few days before his arrival in Khartoum Rafsanjani had attended the OIC annual meeting in Dakar, Senegal. After a decade of Iranian Shi'a isolation from the larger Muslim community, Rafsanjani at Dakar went out of his way to court African Sunni Muslim leaders and those in Khartoum where he received a warm welcome, the streets festooned with pictures of the Ayatollah Khomeini.

---

[48] E. Rekhess, "The Terrorist Connection . . ., Tel Aviv University, 3 April 1995.

[49] See U.S. House of Representatives, Committee on Foreign Affairs, Subcommittee on Africa Hearing, Washington D.C., 20 May 1992; N. Gardels, "The Islamic Awakening's Second Wave," *New Perspectives Quarterly*, Summer 1992; U.S. Department of State, *Patterns of Global Terrorism*, Washington D.C., 1992, p. 3.

[50] SUNA, "Daily Bulletin," Khartoum, 13 March 1993, p. 1.

Rafsanjani was the first head of state from Iran to visit the Sudan
since 1979, the year of the Iranian revolution. He was accompanied by a large delegation including Defense Minister Akbar Torkan,
commander of the Revolutionary Guards Major General Hussein
Radhair, and senior Iranian intelligence officers. He declared his
wholehearted support for the RCC and proclaimed the Sudanese
civil war a "jihad" to be prosecuted with all vigor as had Hasan al-
Turabi in April 1989. Rafsanjani signed a number of protocols,
including $300 million for Chinese military materiel paid by Teheran
for delivery at Port Sudan by March 1992. There also appears to
have been discussions between the chief of Iran intelligence, Ali
Fallahian, and his Sudanese counter parts to establish "terrorist bases
in Sudan from which groups like the Popular Front for the Liberation
of Palestine-General Command (PFLP-GC) and Abu Nidal could use
to strike out against Egypt and strategic Western interests in the
Horn of Africa."[51] After Rafsanjani's visit a "high-level military delegation [from Sudan]" visited Tehran "during the summer of 1992
to seek increased support" for its war with the SPLA and "to strengthen
its ties to Iran, a leading state sponsor of terrorism." The Iranian
Pasdaran was "training the NIF-controlled national militia" (the PDF)
in support of the Sudanese armed forces.[52] Arms from and through
Iran were sent to the Sudan and to revolutionary Islamist organizations in Algeria, Egypt, Tunisia, the West Bank, Gaza, and Jordan
where King Hussein "called Saudi Arabian leaders and 'our other
friends'" to warn them that Bin Laden was building a terrorist network in the Sudan. Despite his warnings, an aide to King Hussein
would later claim that, although Jordan took steps to counter the
Islamist invasion, "no one did anything at all."[53]

This new infusion of arms enabled the SPAF, now numbering
some 80,000, troops to launch a major offensive against the SPLA
to recover the territory in the southern Sudan they had lost during
the past three years. Iran also agreed to provide a million tons of
oil, technicians to maintain the Sudan air force C-130s, and Iranian

---

[51] "Sudan", *The Economist Intelligence Unit Limited*, 4th Quarter, 1993, page 21; "Al
Turabi Hails Political Development," *New Horizon*, Khartoum, 6 January 1995".

[52] Samuel M. Katz, *Israel Versus Jibril*, New York: Paragon House, 1993, p. 234.

[53] U.S. Information Agency cable, 20 August 1993, "Evidence of Sudan's Support
for Terrorism." Washington D.C.; *Arabies*, "'Khartoum n'est pas une base ter-
roriste'", February 1992, p. 14; *Newsweek* reports, 25 January 1993, 15 May 1995.

advisers to assist the Sudanese army. In 1992 forty-six Iranian delegations arrived in Khartoum, and Iranian intelligence continued its close cooperation with the Sudanese as did the Iranian *Mostazafan* (Foundation for the Oppressed), the billion dollar Iran relief agency ironically directed by the former bodyguard of Khomeini, Mohsen Rafiqdost. Western intelligence agencies had long considered the *Mostazafan* "a financial and logistical clearinghouse for international terrorism."[54]

The most important delegation from Iran to visit Sudan was led by the Ayatollah Ardabili, the personal representative of Iran's spiritual leader Imam Ali Hussayn Khameini. Ardabili arrived in Khartoum in December 1991 with an entourage including Al Shaykh Gholan Rida, commander in chief of the Pasdaran, and Majid Kamal, who in the early 1980s had played an important role in creating the Lebanese Shiite terrorist group Hizbollah. Kamal was responsible to Deputy Foreign Minister Hossein Sheikoleslam, a onetime student at the University of California, who had helped seize the United States Embassy in Tehran in 1979 and ran terrorist operations out of a secret cell within Iran's foreign ministry. The arrival of Ardabili, Rida, and Kamal reeked of a conspiracy to organize terrorist training in the Sudan. That seemed confirmed when Kamal was named chargé d'affaires in Khartoum in January 1992 and later the Iranian ambassador to the Sudan. In Washington where the Iran-Sudan alliance was viewed with alarm Congressman William Broomfield in the United States House of Representatives issued a stern warning that the Sudan had become "a new haven for terrorists and extremists in Africa" and urged the administration "to step up its efforts to dissuade the Sudanese Government from pursuing this unwise and dangerous policy. Should the Sudan ignore our warnings, it may be time to formally label that country as a terrorist state."[55]

---

[54] *Middle East International*, 20 December 1991, p. 11; "Le Menace," *Africa International*, May 1992, p. 58; "Sudan's Strife Promises to Outlive Rebellion," *The New York Times*, 19 July 1992, Section 4, p. 3; R. Grimmett, *Conventional Arms Transfers to the Third World, 1985–1992* U.S. Library of Congress, Congressional Research Service Report 93–656F, Washington D.C., 19 July 1993, p. 56. On Rafiqdost and the Mostazafan see: R.D. Kaplan, "A Bazaari's World," *The Atlantic Monthly*, March 1996; Peter C. Lyon, "Patronage and Politics in Islamic Banking", *LBJ Journal of Public Affairs*, Austin, Texas, 1998.

[55] *Time*, "Is Sudan Terrorism's New Best Friend," 30 September, 1993; "U.S.

In an interview published in France in February 1992, Sudanese Foreign Minister Ali Sahloul denied, with some passion, a spate of international reports that Khartoum had become a home for Muslim terrorists. By the end of the year, however, the phrase the "Khartoum-Teheran axis" had become common in the media and official pronouncements to describe the relations between the Sudan and Iran. The Research Center of Contemporaneous Criminal Menace reported in May 1992 "the main new threat in the domain of terrorism and islamic activism, as far as Europe is concerned, is Sudan." With the end of the civil war in Lebanon the Sudan had become "the new haven for the Sunni radical muslim groups close to the Muslim brotherhood tradition," and Hasan al-Turabi himself had assisted the movements to "overcome the crisis they had faced during the Gulf war and to reorganize." The alliance between Hamas and the Popular Front for the Liberation of Palestine of Georges Habash had been "forged in Khartoum." Hasan al-Turabi was "orchestrating the spread of radical and violent islam to the muslim part of Africa."[56] The RCC in Khartoum was playing a dangerous game.

Iran, a radical Islamic state, appeared to be using the Sudan in a similar way that it had implanted the Islamic Hizbollah movement in the Bekaa Valley of the Lebanon in 1982. Like the revolutionaries in the Bekaa Valley, the Iranians who appeared in the Sudan were members of the Revolutionary Guards, the Pasdaran. During the Iran-Iraq war they had trained Muslims from many nations in terrorism and revolutionary warfare at camps inside Iran and its notorious school for terrorists at Qom, the holy city of Iran, the site of its most revered theological seminary, and the residence of the Ayatollah Khomeini. As Khomeini grew older and less accessible, the Guards served as an indigenous force of religious zealots whose political mentor, Hojatoleslam Ali Akbar Hashemi Rafsanjani, would

---

Fears Sudan Becoming Terrorists' 'New Lebanon,'" *The Washington Post*, 31 January 1992, p. 13; "Is Sudan Terrorism's New Best Friend?" *Time*, 30 August 1993; note also "Bad Company in Khartoum," *US News & World Report*, 6 September 1993; on Deputy Foreign Minister Hossein Sheikoleslam see: Robin Wright, *Sacred Rage*, New York: Touchstone Books, 1986, pp. 86–90; "The Hon. Wm.S. Broomfield in the House of Representatives, Wednesday, February 5, 1992," see: David Ignatius, "The Sudan: A New Haven for Terrorists and Extremists in Africa?" *The Washington Post*, 5 February 1992.

[56] "Sudan denies 'Khartoum-Tehran Axis,'" *The Washington Post*, 12 March 1992, p. 21; Xavier Raufer, "Ideology of Radical-Islamic Groups: European Implications," *Centre de recherche des Menaces Criminelles Contemporaines*, Paris, May 1992.

assume the secular direction of Iran while the religious mantle would pass to Khameini upon the death of the supreme leader. Thus Rafsanjani was "charged with exporting Islamic Revolution." The Pasdaran revolutionary message found a receptive audience among the 1.5 million Lebanese Shiites, the poorest of the Lebanese poor, many of whom had supported Khomeini, the Iranian revolution, and were attracted to Shiite fundamentalism as the spearhead of a world-wide Islamic revolution. Although the Bakaa Valley itself had been occupied by the Syrians, the Pasdaran soon created an Iranian enclave. By 1986 two Pasdaran divisions (the Hamza and Ansar) had trained some 1,000 Lebanese Hizbollah governed by a twelve-man consultative council that controlled the Islamic Jihad (al-Jihad al-Islami), its military and terrorist arm. The growing influence of Iran in the Muslim world precipitated Congressional hearings on the global reach of a resurgent Islam. In 1986 the United States State Department reported that the Lebanese Hizbollah had become the world's leading supporter of terrorism, and soon afterward representatives of Hizbollah arrived in Khartoum. The Khartoum-Teheran connection seemed the beginning of a historical thrust to move Islam, and particularly Shiite Islam, beyond its frontiers into Africa. Iran had secured a bastion on the Nile with the blessing of that ecumenical Muslim, Hasan al-Turabi that could create in Khartoum a new Mecca for Islamists.[57]

The PLO had opened an office during the dictatorship of Jaafar Numayri, and its members were welcome during the transitional government of General Suwar al-Dahab and the parliamentary government of Sadiq al-Mahdi. Terrorists of Abu Nidal and the Popular Front for the Liberation of Palestine were conspicuous in the capital. The exception was Hamas. Since the publication of its "Covenant" in 1988, it had shown little inclination to support Yassir Arafat and his ambivalent negotiations with Israel and a Hamas office was opened in Tehran in 1991. Hasan al-Turabi was critical of the hostility between the PLO and Hamas. At home and during his many trips to the West, he vehemently denied that the Sudan was training Muslim extremists. He argued, rhetorically and sententiously, that Sudan was too poor to "subsidize world Islamic movements."

---

[57] *Sudan Update*, "the New Mecca?," 30 March 1992, p. 2; Habib Ayeb, "L'Egypte et le Soudan au lendemain de la guerre du Golfe." *Herodote*, No. 65/66, 1992.

Nevertheless, situated on the periphery of the Arab world, Khartoum would be "neutral ground" where competing revolutionary Islamic organizations could quietly meet to work out their differences for the common cause. Just how powerful a personage Turabi had become was demonstrated by the willingness of Hamas and the Fatah faction of Arafat's PLO to use Turabi as a conciliator following a murderous confrontation before a mosque in Gaza.[58] Arafat personally contacted Turabi, and in late 1992 Khartoum was chosen as the place for peace talks between Hamas and the PLO.

In February 1993 they reached a "strategic understanding." Three days later the PLO entered into secret negotiations with Israel at Oslo, Norway, a move that initiated a new stage in the Israel-Palestine peace process, but one that ended the Hamas-PLO negotiations in Khartoum.[59] Unknown to Turabi, Arafat's declining fortunes had been revived by the President of the United States, William Jefferson Clinton, and his personal intervention to bring peace to the Middle East. The Declaration of Principles (the Oslo Accords) signed by the PLO and Israel in September 1993 provided a framework by which the Palestinian-Israeli conflict could have been resolved, but it would have also greatly reduced the influence of the Islamist movement in the Middle East. Since the goals of Fatah and Hamas were significantly different if not hostile, Turabi received praise "for sponsoring the meeting," and "boosting the *intifadah* in the Israeli-occupied territories."[60] Sudan would continue to be a safe-haven for the Palestinians where they could enter freely with visas automatically granted to any Arab.

---

[58] Reported by *Al-Hamishmar*, Israel, 15 June 1992, and appears as footnote 14 in "Hamas, Islamic Jihad and The Muslim Brotherhood: Islamic Extremists and the Terrorist Threat to America," Anti-Defamation League, New York, 1993.

[59] Elie Rekhess, "The Terrorist Connection . . .," Tel Aviv University, 3 April 1995.

[60] *Sudan Update*, London, 16 January 1993, p. 3.

CHAPTER FOUR

THE NIF TAKES CHARGE

In the revolutionary Sudan the change of government was dramatic. The charisma of Turabi, the appeal of the PAIC General Assembly, and the mobilization of the PDF formed the core of a movement that transformed a secular state into an Islamic theocracy by a military coup d'état. In August 1989 Bashir told the U.S. Assistant Secretary of State Herman Cohen that the RCC hoped to emulate the secular government of Turkey's Kemal Ataturk. Two years later, the Sudan government sought to enforce an Islamic cultural identity upon an African country with four hundred different languages and many cultures where Islam and Christians were tolerated but not always embraced with enthusiasm. In 1991 the African Center for Islamic Studies became the African International University under its director, Dr. Abd al-Rahim Ali Ibrahim of NIF, to be the nexus of Islamic and "muslim fundamentalist" outreach throughout the Sudan. Although NIF would vehemently deny it, they were the ghosts of the long history of Islamic xenophobia in the northern and central Sudan.

Curiously and perhaps by chance, the PAIC General Assembly coincided with the first major rift in the RCC. The Minister of the Interior Faisal Abu Salih resigned in April 1991, the same month the PAIC convened. The reasons for his departure from the government were never explained, but it was well known that he was disgusted by interference and infiltration from members of NIF into the ministry of interior. He was particularly upset that Sudanese passports, diplomatic and regular, were being issued to non-Sudanese without his knowledge. Although a devout Muslim, he had clashed with Turabi over his growing involvement with Muslim revolutionaries and specious Muslim relief organizations that had arrived from abroad. Bashir boasted that Faisal Abu Salih and the Chairman of the Political Committee of the RCC Brigadier Osman Ahmad Hassan had been "kicked out." It was a startling turn of events, for Faisal Abu Salih had been promoted from colonel to major general and given the government's most important ministry. Brigadier Osman had served as chairman of the political committee and had been one of those who had planned the coup d'état of 30 June 1989. Like Salih he was a devout Muslim and had worked to ensure the loyalty of the fractious Islamic Association for Student Organizations and responsible for the organization of the shadowy Advisory Council of Forty that gave its counsel to the Political Committee of the RCC. He was the chairmen of popular committees and served as the supervisor for the Northern Region. He had the reputation as an honest broker and was always courteous to Westerners and members of their embassies in Khartoum. Trained in Egypt, some radical Islamists thought that Hassan may have been bought by the Mukhabarat or the CIA. His expulsion from the command council marked the beginning of the ascendancy of NIF in the government.

There was no question in the minds of the Sudanese that Hasan al-Turabi was the philosopher if not the architect of the 30 June revolution.[1] After his release from detention he met regularly with the press to assure them that Bashir would continue to rule the Sudan by an Islamic constitution and the Shari'a law, and after the conclusion of the PAIC General Assembly in April 1991, he made a tour of Arab and Islamic countries to coordinate the fundamentalist organizations and the Islamic relief agencies that provided sanctuaries for the mujahideen. The Islamic African Relief Agency (IARA), *Al-Da'awa al-Islamiyya* (Islamic Call Society), and the Muwafaq (Benevolence) Foundation all served as an outreach arm of the Islamist movement. The IARA and the Egyptian Islamic Jihad used the Kuwait Red Crescent medical operation in Pashawar for cover. The Iranian *Resalat* ("Mission of the Prophet" founded by Ali Akbar Hashemi Rafsanjani), the Pakistani Muslim Relief Agency operating in Kashmir, and the El Hilal and Third World Relief Agency (in the Balkans) provided safe-havens for Sudan based revolutionaries and weapons. Arab and Muslim aid agencies consistently denied they harbored Muslim terrorists, and Muhammad al-Hadi, a Sudanese who ran the Islamic Coordination Committee in Peshawar and Afghanistan, protested that "Foreign Muslims who work with us are here for strict humanitarian reasons."[2]

---

[1] Abdelwahab El Afendi, *Turabi's Revolution: Islam and Power in Sudan*, London: Grey Seal, 1991.
[2] Bruno Philip, Pashawar dateline, *Le Monde*, Paris, 15 May 1993.

After the 30 June Revolution El Bir International and the Muwafaq Foundation established themselves in the Sudan. El Bir had worked in Peshawar and "gained experience providing relief to Afghan refugees in Pakistan and to the Muslim freedom fighters of the Afghan conflict." The Nida al-Jihad, yet another Islamic aid agency, provided funds for training camps in the Sudan for the PDF and supported "the costs of military expeditions." In 1992 the Islamic NGOs were "well along in carrying out a highly politicized and highly directed relief operation that dovetails with the [government] programs to gradually exclude non-Islamic NGOs from working in Sudan."[3] They were all actively engaged in the southern Sudan with government funds from the Islamic charity tax (zakat). After June 30th Islamic NGOs were registered in the ministry of social welfare, and their directors vetted by the Sudan intelligence agencies. The chairman of The Islamic Relief Agency Board of Trustees was the conservative Dr. Al-Juzuli Dafalla, the former prime minister during the Transitional Military Government in 1985–1986. Its director general was the conservative Dr. Said Abdallah and its members were mostly Islamists from NIF as were those in IARA and the Al-Da'awa al-Islamiyya. By 1993 former members of IARA were well placed in the ministry of health and the government's Peace and Development Foundation. Members of Al-Da'awa al-Islamiyya were involved in the PDF, proselytizing in prisons, and administering "Peace Villages" where southern Sudanese were relocated. All government agencies were expected to undertake a comprehensive outreach (da'awa) program for "the renewal" of society's "spiritual life" through a "framework of comprehensive social harmony."[4] The independent Sudanese Red Crescent was dissolved by presidential decree in 1990 and reorganized with a new Islamist board of directors. It continued to work with the United Nations but remained distant from the Western aid agencies.

---

[3] Sue Lautze, "International and National Islamic NGOs in Sudan," Khartoum, November 1992.

[4] "Comprehensive Da'awa Programme Targets Social Renewal," Khartoum, 4 August 1994, p. 2, and "Salih Lashes Out at Population Conference," 7 September 1994, p. 4 in *New Horizon*.

The Price for the Islamist World

After 30 June 1989 life in the multicultural Sudan became more regimented, more intolerant, and more opposed to the traditional open-
ness of Sudanese society. The Islamists became more intransigent.
In September 1992 the command council proscribed the Khatmiyya
Brotherhood (*tariqa*) and tortured Sid Ahmad al-Hussein, the most
senior member of the DUP, the political arm of the Khatmiyya. It
arrested other DUP politicians, and in an attempt to destroy the
Mirghani family, who were the spiritual patrons of the Khatmiyya
and the political leaders of the DUP, the RCC denounced them as
"un-Islamic." The Mirghanis had opposed Turabi for decades, and
now Turabi had his revenge on old political and religious rivals.
Observers felt that Turabi would "go to the last meter and even
beyond it. . . . As far as political power is concerned, he is as hard
as steel."[5] The tolerant Sudanese watched helplessly as the government militia invaded the headquarters of the Khatmiyya and DUP
in Khartoum North, occupied the Khalifa Mosque of the Ansar in
Omdurman and arrested the Khatmiyya leader, Shaykh Muhammad
al-Haddiya.

Turabi regularly dismissed reports of torture in the infamous Ghost
Houses of Khartoum that "resulted primarily from those periods of
one to five days of detention following arrest when the police had
resorted to third-degree methods. . . . This behavior is typical of police around the world. The Sudanese are very sensitive to their dig-
nity and they would call harsh words, a strong light, or an interview
in the middle of the night, 'torture'. . . . The regime intends to retain the preventive detention system until the political system is
fully established."[6] Despite repeated denials there was no doubt that
the RCC approved and ignored indiscriminate torture of suspected
opponents. One journalist reported. "There is, I believe, a deep
psychological process at work in Sudan, in which the state-directed
terror is not acknowledged philosophically by many of the Islamist

---

[5] "Under Islamic Siege," Julie Flint, *Africa Report*, September–October 1993,
p. 26.
[6] "Islam, Democracy, the State and the West; Roundtable with Dr. Hassan
Turabi," *Middle East Policy*, Vol. 1, No. 3, December 1992, pp. 49–61; see also:
"Saudi Denounces Fundamentalists," *The New York Times*, 22 December 1992,
p. 10.

intellectuals—not to the outside world, and perhaps not in any fundamental sense to themselves. . . . There hangs about Turabi himself an atmosphere of reflexive denial. Rather than overtly plotting the political terror, the Islamists turn their backs on it, and let it happen as a matter of distasteful necessity in revolutionary times."[7] His denial was founded on the unity of Islam. "Islam has no problem in dealing with Muslims who may hold views different from the prevailing majority. It is these differences that have brought about the various *madhhabs* [schools of law]." He argued that Islam could "bring all the society together—the Salafis, the sufis, the Ansar, the Khatmiyya, the communists, the trade unionists, the small sects, religious sects, the professions, the artisans." In a united Sudan debate would be free of rancor or personal ambition. The RCC was "not the final model, but the final model will have more of the same." Having confused both friends and enemies, his cryptic prophecy was not reassuring of a benevolent future. "The Sudan does not consider that it has achieved the Islamic model it is working toward, but it has drawn the model."[8]

By 1992 the United States Department of State had become increasingly aware of the Islamic revolutionary activity in the Sudan and that Khartoum had become a center for militant Islamists. There was disagreement within the department and among outside academic experts, however, as to the extent of Islamic militancy in the capital and if revolutionary Sudan was indeed a threat to its neighbors and the Arab countries of the Middle East. The Arabists in the Foreign Service at state argued that the United States should avoid declaring all Islamists and their movements enemies of the United States. The more political advisers to the Secretary of State James Baker were influenced by those political analysts in the department of the Middle East who argued that there was emerging an Islamist movement devoted to the destruction of the secular states throughout the Islamic world often referred to as Muslim fundamentalism or Islamism as preferred by the Islamists themselves.

Two southern ministers in the Bashir government, "Father" George Logokwa Kinga and Aldo Ajo Deng, both of whom fled the Sudan in 1992, disclosed that there were indeed training camps in the

---

[7] William Langewiesche, "Turabi's Law." *The Atlantic Monthly*, August 1994, pp. 26–33.

[8] *Middle East Policy*, Vol. 1, No. 3, December 1992, pp. 49–61.

Sudan where mujahideen received "tough training in all types of combat, violence, and assassination." Turabi vehemently denied these and similar allegations from others; there was "absolutely no basis in fact" that Sudan was involved with terrorism or terrorists or with training camps for "Palestinians, Tunisians or others." The "reports about Sudan's relationship with Iran" were false. There was not a "single Iranian military technician in the Sudan, and Sudan buys no Iranian arms." The only military equipment purchased from Iran were "dual-use Mercedes vehicles." Sudan did "not have much to learn" from Iran and that "no protocols have been signed." Turabi did admit, however, that mutual exchanges were taking place "about how to Islamize public institutions" and ingenuously concluded that "the relationship with Iran doesn't amount to a great deal." The only Iranians were in their embassy in Khartoum.[9] As for Egypt its differences with Sudan were created by Mubarak's fear of indigenous Egyptian Islamist and the alienation "between the state and Islam." Egypt was a very stable and regimented state where the Islamist movement could only develop slowly and that is why the Egyptian government feared "the Sudanese model because Islam could prove its undoing." In Egypt the Islamists where divided that enabled the Egyptian government to exploit their differences with its "very efficient instruments of suppression. . . . after he [Mubarak] goes perhaps the Egyptians may feel it would be wiser to allow Islam to express itself."[10]

Turabi's relations with Ethiopia and Eritrea were equally ambiguous. He would argue that Sudan had an "open frontier" with the Ethiopian people, but his relations with Ethiopia were never cordial after his interview on the BBC in 1992 during which he declared that "an attack on rebel bases in the south had been launched from Ethiopian territory." This revelation "triggered the first diplomatic crisis with Ethiopia, which had secretly agreed to allow its territory to be used for the assault, but was deeply embarrassed when Turabi

[9] Yossef Bodansky, *Bin Ladin: The Man Who Declared War on America*, Prima Publishing, Roseville, California, 1999, p. 65.

[10] *Sudan Update*, 12 December 1992, from Voice of Islamic Republic of Iran, 3 December 1992 and reported in the *Indian Ocean Newsletter*, 5 December 1992; see also: The Reuter Transcript Report, House Foreign Affairs Subcommittee Hearing, Washington, D.C., 20 May 1992; *Middle East Policy*, Vol. 1, No. 3, December 1992, pp. 49–61.

made it public."[11] After the Mengistu government was overthrown relations between President Meles Zenawi and the Sudan had at first been friendly, for he had ended the Ethiopian sanctuary for the SPLA. Three joint ministerial conferences were convened and agreements of cooperation and brotherhood signed in 1992 and 1993. The Ethiopian connection soon turned sour, however, when Ethiopia began to consider major dam building projects on the Blue Nile and Atbara rivers. It joined with Uganda to demand the revision of the historic Nile Waters Agreement of 1959 by which Egypt and the Sudan had divided the Nile waters between them. Relations continued to deteriorate even more rapidly in 1994 when Khartoum began to provide assistance to the Ethiopian rebels of the "Islamic Front for the Liberation of Oromia [OLF]."[12]

Relations with Eritrea were no better. For many years the Muslim Eritrean Liberation Front (ELF) had been supported by Khartoum, but in 1980–81, during an internecine struggle, it lost control of the insurgency movement to the more secular Christian-Muslim Eritrean People's Liberation Front (EPLF). In 1991 it was the EPLF that defeated the Ethiopians and declared the independence of the Eritrean Trust Territory while Muslim Eritreans languished in the Sudan. The NIF sought to drive a division between Christians and Muslims in the EPLF, and after the 30 June 1989 coup d'état the RCC provided clandestine support to the Eritrean Islamic Jihad recruited in refugee camps in Sudan. They were soon to cross the frontier as a Muslim insurgency against the new, independent government of Eritrea.[13] The Sudan government had been incensed when Eritrea recognized Israel, and the Eritrean government of President Isayas Afewerki was infuriated when Bashir supported the Yemen Arab Republic's claims to the Dahlak Archipelago off the coast of Eritrea in the Red Sea.

---

[11] "Sudan's Turabi, 'One of the world's best Islamist thinkers, and worst politicians,'" *Mideast Mirror*, 20 December 1999.

[12] FBIS, "East Africa," 1 March 1993, p. 5.

[13] FBIS, East Africa, 26 April 1994, p. 6 from Radio VBME in Tigrinya, Asmara, 23 April 1994.

Turabi the Traveler

By 1992 Turabi had become the peripatetic spokesperson for the Islamic revival. He enjoyed his debates and interviews with American and European academics and journalists that earned him a good press. The *Christian Science Monitor* could write with equanimity that "Sudan's image as a harsh Islamic dictatorship, imposed by fanatical mullahs in consort with Iran, does not exactly fit." He was no Ayatollah Khomeini but was a spiritual and political counselor to Afghan, Yemeni, and other mujahideen. He was urbane, charming, and well read. The kinder, gentler, avuncular face of "Islamic Fundamentalism" he called the "Islamic Renaissance."[14] In late April Turabi, confident and suave, arrived in London to deliver a speech before the Royal Society for the Encouragement of Arts, Manufactures and Commerce where he defined his Muslim world view. "The most far-reaching prejudice to Muslim unity [was] the introduction of the nation state" with its nationalist ideology, state boundaries, sovereign authority, and "paramount national interests." Decolonization and independence had only solidified the power of nationalism at the expense of the Muslim community, the *Dar al-Islam*. Although the OIC had derived from a spirit of pan-Islamism, it had "turned out to be politically impotent and totally unrepresentative of the true spirit of community that animates the Muslim people." It was the "Gulf War [that] did more than anything else to arouse the Muslim masses and give impetus to the international manifestation of pan-Islam. . . . Charitable, missionary, scholarly, and mystic orders of international dimensions are proliferating among Muslims." Islamic banks, insurance organizations, and business enterprises were "operating multi-nationally." The ease of travel made possible the diffusion of information to revive Islam throughout the Muslim world, for "people in general are associating more and more, indirectly through the media or directly through travel and reunions." And from this web of Islamist interests there was emerging a "popular khilafat drive," the faith by which the Muslim world's "ultimate ideal" could be achieved.[15]

---

[14] *Chrisitan Science Monitor*, 25 March 1993.
[15] Hassan Al-Turabi, "Islam as a Pan National Movement and Nation-States: An Islamic Doctrine of Human Association," Royal Society for the Encouragement of Arts, Manufactures and Commerce, London, 27 April 1992. Published by The Sudan Foundation, London, 1997.

In May he arrived in the United States to attend a roundtable of American scholars of Islam sponsored by the World and Islam Studies Enterprise and the Middle East Committee of the University of South Florida. He lectured at length on "Islam, Democracy, the State and the West," answered questions, and vigorously participated in the discussion. He raised more questions than he answered. The modern Islamic revival, he argued, sought to "reinterpret Islam in terms of the contemporary world," and was more an Islamic renaissance than a "reformation." However, the probity of his arguments and the rationalizations employed for the renaissance of Islam could not justify the brutal repression of Muslims in the northern Sudan and the slaughter of non-Muslims in the South. Rejecting the *dimuqratiyya* neologism and the amorality of Western politics, Turabi argued that the world-wide Islamic movement was "essentially a grass-roots and populist phenomenon and [thus] highly democratic. . . . Islam shuns absolute government, absolute authority, dynastic authority and individual authority" when in fact the RCC and NIF in the Sudan were most certainly not "grass-roots" movements and were most certainly totally absolute. The "Sudan has an experimental system that approximates" true Islam, but Turabi never mentioned the RCC, its elitist civilian cadre from NIF, or its docile TNA. He ignored the torture and arbitrary imprisonment of the civilian opposition, the subjugation of the traditionalist *ulama* with impeccable Muslim credentials, or the suppression of the traditional guardians of Islam in the Sudan, the Khatmiyya and Ansar Brotherhoods. The role of women in the Sudan was not a subject for debate, and he boasted that Sudanese women were "in the movement and in the leadership as well and in the political process." His wife was one of the most progressive women in the Sudan, but in education and government Sudanese women had been forced into a procrustean straightjacket under the RCC.

During the conference Turabi could not avoid discussing the Sudan civil war and the conversion of non-Muslims in the South. He made the astonishing assertion that in "Sudanese society ethnic minorities tend to disappear, as perhaps they were by the government's slaughter of ethnic Nuba in Kordofan and the subjugation of ethnic Fur in the West and ethnic Beja in the East. He added tendentiously even the "army could be a centralizing institution as a professional force which tends to be secularized, but it could also be Islamized. Perhaps a way of achieving this would be to have a small standing army and a large popular defense force drawn from society and

therefore Islamized." Turabi was well aware that the leadership of
the PDF were committed Islamists transforming that force into a
NIF militia. He promised that the southern Sudanese were "to have
autonomy, immunities and freedom as in the model state of the
Prophet, as did the Jews at the time of Muhammad." This was,
however, the confirmation of their second class status. Nor could the
southern Sudanese accept his argument that "in general, people are
more interested in the religious law, not laws as they pertain to constitutional arrangements, e.g. parliament, executive, etc. . . . [in the
Sudan] for example, there is no common consensus or sense of
unity." Yet, despite the different worlds of the non-Arabs in the
North, the Nilotes in the South, the Fur of Darfur in the West, and
the Beja in the East, Turabi blandly proclaimed that "in fact the
Sudanese are Arab in culture. Some are probably Arab in descent
as well, but all are colored people unlike the Arabs. There is no
Arab-African divide anywhere in the Sudan."[16]

From Florida Turabi continued on to Washington to confront the
press and the African Subcommittee of the U.S. House of Representatives Committee on Foreign Affairs. In an interview with Jim
Hoagland of *The Washington Post* he was emphatic that the "new
social order . . . about to be realized" in the Muslim world would
become a reality despite the efforts of the reactionary "old order"
to stop it. The "movement he represented" would never accept the
existence of Israel "or of U.S. support of any kind for Israel" nor
the presence of the U.S. military in the Persian Gulf.[17] In his interview with the *Middle East Times* he argued that the Sudan should
"develop relations with all Islamist movements in the world. . . . [and
that the Sudan government was] "now becoming one of the leading models because it is a complete movement with political, economic, social, cultural dimensions, very well-organized."[18] In Florida
he had described the Gulf War a "blessing in disguise," for in
Morocco, Saudi Arabia, "and other states the mullahs, the ulama
and the Salafi [reformist] establishment have called their regimes
irreligious." Islamist movements were "turned into mass movements"

---

[16] On this meeting see: *Middle East Policy*, Vol. 1, No. 3, December 1992, pp.
49–61.
[17] Jim Hoagland, "The Politics of Playback," *The Washington Post*, 19 May 1992,
p. A19.
[18] "Beguiling Zealot," *Middle East Times*, 19–25 May 1982, p. 15.

and were "radicalized." Turabi warned Washington's foreign policy elite that "the Islamic masses have taken control and many governments and movements are being undermined. They must go popular or perish. There is a 'course of history' that makes the establishment of Islamic states almost inevitable, for as more states go Islamic, pressure on the Sudan and Iran will be reduced and many in the West will realize that Islam cannot be stopped, and they will cease interfering."[19]

Before the Africa Subcommittee of the House of Representatives its members were not amused when he lectured them "about Islamic fundamentalism" telling them that "many Islamics resent" the term. Intellectually acute as ever, he entered into a give-and-take debate with the congressmen who were very disturbed by events in Sudan since the revolution of 30 June 1989. Turabi admitted that the Gulf War had changed regional alliances and allowed Iran to emerge as a major player and that Tehran had "created an alternative to nationalist and socialist revolutions." The Sudan in general and the PAIC General Assembly in particular worked "for reconciliation between Iraq and Iran, between Iraq and Syria, and others," and consequently the Sudan has "turned east to Pakistan, Malaysia, Indonesia and China, and to a lesser extent Iran." The congressmen listened in disbelief when Turabi asserted that "the Sudanese are Arabic speaking and there are thousands of Sudanese who know Islam better than the more learned ulama in Iran ... King Fahd [of Saudi Arabia was] "in quite a mess, and he doesn't know how to save himself." He concluded his testimony with the firm conviction that the "course of history" will make the establishment of Islamic states "almost inevitable."[20]

In a final interview later published in *New Perspectives Quarterly*, an American political journal, Turabi denied he was "the 'new Khomeini,' the new bearer of the flame of Islamic fundamentalism," for he represented "a new, mature wave of the Islamic awakening taking place today from Algeria and Jordan to Khartoum and Kuala Lumpur." The Sudan was "an Islamic state-in-process" that was not "exporting

---

[19] "Islam, Democracy, the State and the West; Roundtable with Dr. Hassan Turabi," *Middle East Policy*, Vol. 1, No. 3, 1992, pp. 49–61.

[20] The Reuter Transcript Report, House Foreign Affairs Subcommittee Hearing, Washington D.C., 20 May 1992; see also: *Middle East Policy*, Vol. 1, No. 3, December 1992, pp. 49–61.

Islamic revolution in consort with Iran" or "the new haven for terrorists." The Iran relationship "has been present for the last three
years" and should be of no particular concern to anyone. "Since we
are a professed Islamic state, what is so surprising about Sudan's
relationship with Iran?. . . . Iran has absolutely no military presence
in Sudan. . . . We have no interest in terrorism. . . . As far as I am
concerned, Islam can have nothing to do with terrorism."[21] Nonetheless, in April 1992 the United States Department of State had
published in *Patterns of Global Terrorism, 1991* that the "apparent presence in Sudan of many different international terrorist organizations,
with the tacit support of the NIF-dominated government. . . . [and]
under the leadership of Hassan al-Turabi, has intensified its domination of the government of Sudanese President General Bashir and
has been the main advocate of closer relations with radical groups
and their sponsors." Five months later the U.S. House of Representatives Republican Research Committee Task Force on Terrorism
and Unconventional Warfare identified the Sudan as a willing ally
at the time when Iran had begun "active preparations for long-term
terrorist operations in Western Europe." Terrorist training and psychological and religious instruction had started in the Sudan in May
1991 after Turabi's first PAIC General Assembly under Brigadier
General Bakri Hassan Salih, Director of the RCC Committee of
Security, who organized those "responsible for training and preparing Islamist terrorists for long-term operations in Western Europe."[22]

Turabi: Assault and Recovery

From Washington Hasan al-Turabi traveled to Ottawa. His purpose
to visit Canada was never made clear. There was a substantial émi-
gré Sudanese community in Canada who had fled the Sudan after
the 30 June Revolution and, not surprisingly, was hostile to him. He
was traveling on a passport with no "Official's Visa" attached so
that the Canadian intelligence service only learned of his impend-

[21] Hassan Al-Turabi, "The Islamic Awakening's Second Wave," *New Perspectives
Quarterly*, Vol. 9, No. 3, Summer 1992.
[22] "Sudan denies 'Khartoum-Tehran Axis,'" *The Washington Post*, 12 March 1992,
p. 21.

ing visit shortly before his arrival when local law enforcement agencies were informed. He was to meet with government officials, members of parliament, and major business interests, particularly for discussions with Arakis, a Canadian oil company that had acquired the concession of Chevron in the Sudan. Upon his arrival at the Ottawa airport he was attacked in the receiving area by a disaffected Sudanese expatriate and karate expert who beat him about the head and left him near-dead. *The Middle East* called it "a bungled attempt" on his life; Turabi himself later called it a Western-inspired assassination. The Security Intelligence Review Committee of the Canadian government prepared a report on the assault that has never been made public.[23] He recovered in a Canadian hospital and was then moved to a clinic in Switzerland to recuperate. He had lost mobility in his right arm and needed a cane to walk. Occasionally, his speech was slurred, his public statements erratic, and for six months he was rarely seen in public. Interviews were few, and the PAIC General Assembly scheduled for the autumn of 1992 was canceled, but by the early months of 1993 he had sufficiently recovered to lead the PAIC meeting scheduled later that year.

In less than two years the PAIC General Assembly had made Khartoum the "the new headquarters of the Islamist International."[24] After the fall of Kabul in April 1992 the expatriate Afghan-Arabs and mujahideen from the Sudan, the Mahgrib, Bosnia, China, the Philippines, and the United States did not belong to that struggle and left Afghanistan for home or to congregate at Pashawar and wait for someone like Turabi to provide inspiration and guidance. The PAIC General Assembly had become the instrument for that guidance, whose resolutions supported "Muslim movements in such places as the Philippines, Burma, Tadjikistan and Kosovo, as well as proclaiming support for the Palestinian people and the Muslims

---

[23] *Sudan Update*, London, 29 July 1992, p. 2; "Sudan: To the Bitter End," *The Middle East*, July 1992, p. 22. "3. Case Studies: (a) Turabi-Attack at the Ottawa Airport," *Annual Report 1992–1993*, Ottawa: Security Intelligence Review Committee, Government of Canada, *1993*, pp. 14–17. The Canadian Government's Security Intelligence Review Committee through the Canadian Association of Security and Intelligence Studies, British Columbia, prepared a secret document, *The Assault on Dr. Hassan Al-Turabi (92/93–07)*, November 1992, which has never been released to the public. There are rumors that Turabi's attacker is an SPLA officer

[24] François Burgat and William Dowell, *The Islamic Movement in North Africa*, Austin: University of Texas Press, 1993, p. 151.

of Bosnia"[25] Uzbekistan, a secular state under attack by Islamist
Afghan-Arabs in the Ferghana Valley, was the first of the former
Soviet Republics in Central Asia to express concern about Turabi
and his PAIC General Assembly and promptly banned the Uzbek
Islamic Renaissance Party from attending. The Egyptians were equally
alarmed.

The Egyptian Connection

By 1992 the Islamist opposition in Egypt to the government of Hosni
Mubarak, led by the *Jama'at al-Islamiyah*, was daily more active and
more outspoken. It attacked Mubarak's political allies, Christian communities, and even personnel in the ministry of interior.[26] Although
the Egyptians had closed the Iranian diplomatic mission to Egypt,
its brand of Muslim fundamentalism was "creating a new challenge"
especially since "Iran supports this movement and gives fundamentalists hope."[27] When the revolutionary government in Khartoum
restored amicable relations with Iran and received economic, intelligence, and military support, Mubarak complained bitterly that the
Sudan had become a threat to Egypt. His accusations, were strongly
supported in December 1992 by the Sudanese opposition exiled in
Cairo. They denounced the Khartoum government for training
Egyptian, Algerian, Tunisian, and Palestinian terrorists at al-'Arusah
in the eastern Sudan on the Red Sea coast "under the supervision
of Iranian experts" where they were incorporated in the training
camps of the PDF to disguise the "sheltering [of] Arab extremists."[28]

In Egypt the more radical of the Muslim Brothers and their allies,
the "street preachers,"—many of whom were influenced by the
Ayatollah Khomeini and his theocratic revolution in Iran—demanded

---

[25] "Africa and Islamic Revival: Historical and Contemporary Perspectives," unpublished lecture by Professor John Hunwick, Northwestern University, at James Madison
University, Virginia, 25 March 1996.
[26] See: "The Battle Against the Leagues," *The Economist*, 4 June 1992, p. 38. On
the *Jama'at al-Islamiyah* see John L. Esposito and John O. Voll, *Islam and Democracy*,
New York: Oxford University Press, 1996, pp. 173–191.
[27] "Threat of Fundamentalism," *The Times of India*, 12 April 1988.
[28] *Al Sharq Al-Awsat*, London, 28 December 1992; FBIS, *Near East & South Asia*,
7 January 1993, p. 17.

an end to tourism, the sale of alcohol, the abolition of interest on loans, and the veiling of women. They rejected Egypt's peace with Israel and any alliance with the United States. They demonstrated their rage by murdering foreign tourists in Egypt that sent the tourist industry, upon which the economy of Egypt depended, into depression when half the expected number of foreign visitors decided to stay home. Despite doubts expressed by the U.S. Embassy in Khartoum and the Department of State in Washington, the Egyptian government was convinced that the terrorist campaign in March 1992 had been initiated by Islamists financed by Iran and trained and supported by the revolutionary government in Khartoum. They were, after all, Egyptians who had disappeared fighting for Iraq, received Islamic "reeducation" in Iranian camps, and returned home, many through the Sudan.

The Mukhabarat was aware that Dr. Ayman al-Zawahiri, an Egyptian physician and prominent member of Al-Jihad in Peshawar had followed Osama bin Laden to the Sudan after which in July 1992 he arranged for financial support from the foreign ministry in Tehran. Having secured the approval of Hasan al-Turabi he opened "camps in Shendi, Khartoum North, and Omdurman to al-Jihad elements." Ostensibly the camps would serve as a transfer point for some 800 mujadiheen, "mostly Egyptian," then located at a camp near Mashad, Iran. The Sudanese camps would be manned by "Lebanese" Hizbollah, supported by Iran to train the men who would form "Arab Liberation Battalions" where needed. The Sudan sites, modeled "after the Iranian camps," had received some 2,000 mujadiheen by the autumn of 1992, including 500 Egyptians from Teheran and Yemen.[29] In addition a military compound at the Khartoum international airport was placed at the disposal of revolutionaries arriving from Afghanistan and Peshawar.[30] The former southern Sudanese minister, George Logokwa Kinga, claimed that in the last six months of 1992 alone the Pasdaran had provided Turabi and his aides with more than $30 million from Teheran to be used in the struggle against the enemies of Islam and particularly Egypt.[31] Sudanese expatriates had also

---

[29] Cairo, *Rose al-Yusuf*, 23 November 92; FBIS, *Near East & South Asia*, 14 December 1992, p. 25.

[30] *Al-Ahram* Radio, Cairo, 1903 GMT, 17 December 1992; FBIS, *Near East and South Asia*, 21 December 1992, p. 28.

[31] *Al Ahram Al-Masai*, Cairo, 3 December 1992, reported by MENA Radio, Cairo,

circulated a report to the U.S. Congress in which they "confirmed" that the NIF government, in "pursuit of the grandiose agenda of an 'Islamic Empire'" had used the Sudan Embassy in Cairo to deliver $5 million to the Egyptian Al-Jihad. An additional million dollars was delivered to Adil Hussein, a member of the Egyptian Muslim Brotherhood and the editor-in-chief of *Al-Shaab* newspaper, "to enable the paper to go on daily circulation." Hasan al-Turabi, "the de facto leader of Sudan" had provided the funds.[32]

The irrepressible Turabi, dressed in his brilliant white *jallabia* (robe) and turban in his white Mercedes, sought to cultivate the Muslim leaders of the Arab world who had become increasingly wary of Sudan's support for Islamic fundamentalists, the Islamists. Opposition gradually surfaced within the OIC whose principal rival was the PAIC General Assembly of Hasan al-Turabi. In October 1992, the influence of Saudi Arabia convinced a majority of the OIC membership to transfer its annual meeting from Khartoum to Pakistan. "It was the second Arab-Islamic blow to Khartoum," for a meeting of Arab information ministers had just accused Sudan of "harboring terrorists—a reference mainly to Islamic fundamentalists but also to members of the Abu Nidal group." The Palestinian organization had moved its center of operations from Libya to Sudan where Hasan al-Turabi and the Iranian ambassador and a professional intelligence officer, Majid Kamal, were strong supporters of their cause.[33] The Egyptian embassy in Khartoum feared that the Sudan, despite its Sunni heritage, was about to become Black Africa's first Islamic Republic based on the Shiite, Iranian model. Cairo was most alarmed by comments from the Iranian Ayatollah Muhammad Yazdi in Teheran that "coordination with Sudan" was to "defend our militant brothers in Egypt" and "to spread the message of Khomeini in Sudan."[34] Saudi Arabia shared Egypt's concern over the Islamists

---

1455 GMT, 3 December 1992; FBIS *Near East & South Asia*, 14 December 1992, p. 17.

[32] The Sudanese Modern Forces for Democratic Action, letter to "The Honorable Harry Johnston and honorable members of the U.S. House of representatives, Subcommittee on Africa," Alexandria, Virginia, March 1993.

[33] *Sudan Update* 19 October 1992, p. 4; at a meeting with US Congressmen on 22 April 1993, CIA Director James Woolsey noted that Majid Kamal was more an intelligence professional than political activist.

[34] *Sudan Update*, 12 December 1992, and the Voice of Islamic Republic of December 1992 and reported in the *Indian Ocean Newsletter*, 5 December 1992.

challenge, and the usually mild-mannered King Fahd, in a "scantly disguised reference to Iran and Sudan," issued his "harshest and most explicit denunciation yet of Saudi Muslim fundamentalism."[35]

Much of the world considered Islamism a religious ideology to be accepted, but the flagrant violation of human rights by the RCC and its brutality of Sudanese citizens was unacceptable.[36] Japan terminated all assistance to Sudan other than humanitarian aid. The European Community issued numerous protests on human rights, and the British House of Lords and the United States Congress condemned "the imprisonment, torture and execution" of Sudanese dissidents. Even the Vatican protested human rights abuse against Sudanese Catholics by the symbolic beatification of Josephine Bakhita, a former Sudanese slave, and protested the persecution of Catholic leaders and Christians in the Sudan by the Islamic Security Bureau. The memory of Fathers Ignaz Knoblecker and Daniel Camboni, who first brought Catholic Christianity to the Upper Nile in the mid-ninteenth century, could not be forgotten. The UN General Assembly expressed "with deep concern reports of grave human rights violations in the Sudan, particularly summary executions, detentions without trial, forced displacement of persons and torture."[37]

The Halayib Imbroglio

In 1991 the RCC granted the International Petroleum Company of Canada rights to drill for oil in the Red Sea. The concession, located east of the Halayib Triangle, an 8,000 square mile wedge of desert that ended on the shores of the Red Sea, was occupied by 20,000 sheep and goats and 20,000 nomad Bisharin of the Beja peoples of the Eastern Sudan. The international boundary between Egypt and

---

[35] *Middle East Policy*, Vol. 1, No. 3, December 1992, pages 49–61; "Saudi Denounces Fundamentalists," *The New York Times*, 22 December 1992, p.10.

[36] For United Nations General Assembly resolutions on human rights in the Sudan see: A/RES/47/142 18 December 1992,/147 20 December 1993,/198 23 December 1994,/197 22 December 1995,/182 29 February 2000; For Commission on Human Rights Reports see: 1 February 1994 E/CN.4/1994/48, 30 January 1995 E/CN.4/1995/58, 20 February 1996 E/CN.4/1996/62, 3 February 1997 E/CN.4/1997/58, 30 January 1998 E/CN.4/1998/66, 18 April 2000 E/CN.4/RES/2000/27, 19 April 2000 E/CN.4/2000/36.

[37] United Nations, "The Situation in the Sudan," UN General Assembly 92nd Plenary Meeting, A/RES/47/142, New York, 18 December 1992.

the Anglo-Egyptian Sudan had been delimited in 1899 at the 22nd Parallel. However, by mutual agreement in 1907, the nomads and their three villages of Shalateen, Abu Ramad, and Halayib situated north of the international boundary were to be administered by the Sudan. Over time the sovereignty to the Halayib Triangle, an administrative convenience, confused both governments and cartographers. Egypt consistently insisted that the international boundary remained fixed at the 22nd Parallel while the Sudan continued to administer its nomads who wandered across it. For a century this arrangement had been to the advantage of the nomads, the Sudan, and Egypt in an arid waste-land of no importance to Egypt or the Sudan. The sands of the Halayib soon became the symbol of the estrangement between the two nations. When the long dormant boundary dispute was revived with a vengeance in 1991, diplomatic protocol was cast on the winds blowing across its sands.

The Halayib Triangle also bordered on the Red Sea coast where European, American, and Canadian oil companies had occasionally expressed an interest, but the Egyptians had been the most aggressive in Red Sea oil exploration passing south and down the coast toward the 22nd Parallel in search of new wells. Mubarak and the Egyptian General Petroleum Corporation, considered Sudanese administration of the triangle an infringement on Egyptian sovereignty designed to deprive Cairo of its historic rights to Halayib. In March 1992 Mubarak used the dispute to sharply criticize the Bashir government in general and Hasan al-Turabi in particular. The Egyptian General Petroleum Corporation immediately authorized exploration of offshore parcels in the Red Sea north of the 22nd parallel but east of the triangle in waters that indisputably belonged to Egypt. The Sudan strongly protested, and Cairo and Khartoum agreed to form a joint committee to study the matter and meet in Cairo in September. Unfortunately, before the Cairo meeting the Egyptian army opened fire on a Sudanese police post in the triangle killing two policemen. The Egyptians followed this attack by increasing the number of their border posts, and Egyptian police began to dispense Egyptian identity cards to the Bisharin residents. In September Egypt "annexed the disputed border area," and when the joint committee finally met late in October the Khartoum government was presented with a fait accompli. There was little to negotiate.[38] Egypt claimed

---

[38] "Scrapping and scrabbling for oil," *The Middle East*, Vol. 4, 1992, p. 41.

Halayib by right of occupation and rejected the Sudanese argument that the Bisharin were Sudanese. In response the Khartoum press called for war against the Egyptian "invasion." Despite the fiery rhetoric the RCC was wise enough to discern that Egypt was looking for an excuse to pick a fight and had found it in Halayib. Unlike the press the RCC was not prepared to declare war, but it reaffirmed the Sudanese claim to the Halayib Triangle. The Egyptian response was to move road-building equipment into the triangle to be followed in December by 600 Egyptian troops who escorted Sudanese officials to the 22nd Parallel.

Outgunned in Halayib and humiliated in Cairo, Khartoum appealed to the United Nations Security Council on 27 December 1992 protesting the Egyptian provocation. Egypt responded that the Sudanese demands contravened the understanding reached at the joint committee meeting held in October. It claimed its sovereignty was predicated on the activity of the Nasr Phosphate Company, which had been mining in Halayib since 1961, and the reopening of the Sinai Manganese Company in Sinai that would require the construction of a Red Sea port at Abu Ramad.[39] The Halayib mines, closed in the 1970s, would be reopened, and the Sinai Manganese Company would use its Sinai ferro-manganese plant (which had recently been upgraded with new equipment by a $50 million investment) to export manganese to Japan and Germany. These plans for development in the Halayib wasteland were more rhetoric than economics, for the triangle lacked "a port and paved roads" and the mineral deposits seemed less than promising.[40] Having succeeded in securing the triangle, Mubarak sought to have the angry Sudanese agree to the Egyptian occupation at a third meeting of the Egypt-Sudan Halayib committee in Cairo on 22–26 February 1993. The Sudanese refused. Egypt then formally annexed (or reincorporated) Halayib. Khartoum supinely declared that Egypt had illegally "annexed the disputed border area."[41]

Faced with a fait accompli and frustrated diplomatically, the NIF government retaliated against Egyptian interests in the Sudan. Egyptian sponsored schools were taken over by the government and Egyptian

---

[39] *Sudan Democratic Gazette*, April 1993, p. 5.
[40] *Sudan Update*, London, 31 January 1993, p. 3; "Bitter Words Between Neighbours," *The Middle East*, May 1993, p. 16.
[41] *Sudan Democratic Gazette*, April 1993, p. 5.

teachers were expelled. The Cairo University Khartoum Branch, operating under Egyptian auspices since 1955, was closed in March 1993 and 125 faculty members returned to Egypt. It was then reopened with Sudanese instructors and renamed the University of the Two Niles. The NIF government would never forget its humiliation in the Halayib. Ten years later, on 17 August 2002, President Bashir announced that Halayib still belonged to the Sudan despite Egyptian occupation of the triangle.

The Saudi Reaction

In December 1992 King Fahd bin Abd al-Aziz of Saudi Arabia denounced in uncharacteristically direct language the Islamists and their foreign allies who opposed his rule, "a scantily disguised reference to Iran and Sudan," whose "foreign currents" were a campaign to destabilize Saudi Arabia.[42] Saudi relations with the Sudan were curiously schizophrenic. Officially, they were cool but correct in diplomatic discourse with the RCC. Privately, insecure Saudi bankers and capitalists ashamed of their private excesses absolved their guilt by supporting the Islamist movement in Sudan. They found satisfaction—theological and psychological—in providing funds for a host of charitable organizations and institutions, including those sponsored by the Saudi royal family. They also financed organizations whose interests and motivations were hardly charitable but like the Sudan Islamic-African Center could spread the message of Islam.

When King Fahd assumed power in 1982 following the death of his brother, he had no more love for the Iranian revolution than he had for Saddam Hussein. He blamed and refused to forgive, the Ayatollah Khomeini and Iran's chief prosecutor, Mussavi Khoinina, for the uprising in Mecca during the 1983 *hajj*. Khomeini had challenged the historic custody of Islam's holy sites by the family of Ibn Saud, and he had employed Iranian Revolutionary Guards and specially trained agitators from other nations to spark riots during the annual pilgrimage to Mecca. The Iranians had exhorted Muslim clerics from Asia and Africa to testify to the meaning of "true Islam"

---

[42] "Saudi Denounces Fundamentalists," *The New York Times*, 22 December 1992, p. A10.

and overthrow the "Godless" Saudi regime.[43] In December 1987 Saudi Arabia publicly accused Iran of ignoring every Arab League and Muslim offer to mediate the devastating war with Iraq and complained that Iran was disseminating an Islamist message, an alien ideology, whose only consequence was to divert attention from the campaign against Israel. The war of words continued through 1990 and Iraq's invasion of Kuwait, and the subsequent Operation Desert Storm. In 1992 the Saudi leadership was still haunted by the Iranian menace and was particularly concerned with the emerging relationship between the RCC and Iran. In the same year they had forced the OIC to move its annual summit meeting from Khartoum to Pakistan, and its leaders were particularly unhappy that the NIF government had allowed Osama bin Laden to use his construction company as a cover for the training of mujahideen in the Sudan.

The Uneasy Sudan-Uganda Relationship

As relations deteriorated between the NIF government, Egypt, Saudi Arabia, and fellow Arabs, those with their African brothers to the south fared no better. In northern Uganda the SPLA had roamed freely for years. The President of Uganda, Yoweri Museveni, had gone to school with John Garang and had since maintained close personal relations with him that helped to confirm his deep distrust of the RCC who were providing arms to Uganda rebels, the Lord's Resistance Army and the West Nile Front insurgents of the former Uganda dictator, Idi Amin, operating in Acholiland in northern Uganda.[44] In 1986 the Sudan began to train, equip, and provide sanctuaries across the border in their own territory for the Lord's Resistance Army and the 2,000 Ugandan Muslims of the West Nile Front who, with "Khartoum's support," had launched raids "into northern Uganda with the intention of eventually capturing the border towns."[45]

After the 30 June Revolution a Sudan-Uganda non-aggression pact seemed to have ended Museveni's problems until he discovered that

---

[43] *The Washington Post*, 8 January 1996; see also: report in *The New York Times*, 28 December 1987.

[44] "Pressures on Garang," *Middle East International*, 11 June 1993, p. 14.

[45] *Sudan Democratic Gazette*, London, Sept. 1993, p. 2.

the Sudanese embassy in Kampala continued to support the insurgents in the north and West Nile. The Iran-Sudan entente and the Sudan army counter-attack in Equatoria in 1992 ended his détente with Sudan when more sophisticated arms supplied by Iran began to appear in the hands of the Lord's Resistance Army and the West Nile Front enabling them to expand their insurgency throughout northern Uganda.[46] Museveni was convinced that the intercession of Hasan al-Turabi had been critical in the decision by the Sudan government to supply these arms to the Lord's Resistance Army, the West Nile Front, and the Allied Democratic Forces in the Democratic Republic of the Congo.[47]

The Lord's Resistance Army soon began to loot and pillage villages in the Sudan-Uganda borderland and threatened the sanctuaries of the SPLA. There were anecdotal accounts that Museveni facilitated the transit of weapons for Garang. In February 1993 a major arms shipment arrived in Kitgum, Uganda, for transit to the SPLA at Ikotos in the southern Sudan. In return the SPLA assisted the Uganda army in its futile attempts to suppress the Lord's Resistance Army and the West Nile Front. It was in this tense atmosphere along the Sudan-Uganda frontier that Pope John II visited Kampala and Khartoum in February 1993. The NIF government was particularly upset that the Vatican appeared to have abandoned its policy of quiet diplomacy with the Sudan government when it had publicly cited numerous "examples of harassment of Christians" in both the northern and southern Sudan.[48] The recent beatification of Josephine Bakhita could be ignored, but the daily direct criticism of the Sudan government by the Holy See for its increasing persecution of Catholics and their leaders by the security services could not. In a calculated insult Hasan al-Turabi, *le Pape Noir de l'islam*, was too busy to meet the Pontiff. Bashir could hardly avoid his presence that was reduced to an exchange of pleasantries.

---

[46] "Iran-armed Islamic forces target Sudan rebels," *The Washington Times*, 3 February 1993.

[47] "Bin Laden First Terrorised Kampala, Says Museveni," *The Monitor*, Kampala, 23 October 2001.

[48] "Sudan: Harsh condemnations," *Middle East International*, 23 October 1992, pp. 13–14.

CHAPTER FIVE

THE UNITED STATES AND THE NIF

In 1992 the Department of State began to evaluate the threat to the United States from Muslim fundamentalism, Islamism, in the Sudan. In the long, hot, humid summer in Washington D.C. the Bureau of Intelligence and Research of the State Department convened a seminar of academic experts to give guidance about the Sudan. The scholars were not very helpful, for they were unable to reach a consensus as to whether the government of the Sudan was a threat or not to its neighbors in Africa or the Arabs in the Middle East. Some academic experts urged that U.S. policy and actions should not further radicalize the Khartoum government at the end of the Cold War by overreacting to a more revolutionary Islam. The United States should distinguish between those Islamists who are extremists and those who are seeking to restructure and direct their societies. There were also those Arabists in the Foreign Service who argued that not all Islamic militants and Islamist movements were enemies of the United States. Some were sincere reformers who should be involved in open discussions to promote democracy. The United States should be ready to work with and assist such leaders once they gained political prominence including Hasan al-Turabi despite his conviction that Western "imperialists will intervene and falsify your [Islamist] will." Advisers to Secretary of State James Baker were not convinced that academics or foreign service officers with close ties to the Middle East could so easily distinguish between those extremists prepared to use revolutionary violence to achieve their ends and those moderates who sought to use the system to achieve power. They were often too ready to accept the views of Egyptian, Tunisian, and Israeli officials that there existed a "worldwide" Islamist conspiracy "directed against secular states in the Islamic world." "There appeared for a time the possibility that the green flag of Islam might be seen by some influential people in Washington as an appropriate replacement for the red banner of communism."[1]

---

[1] Personal correspondence between Foreign Service Officers and the authors; For

In August 1992 Donald Petterson, the new United States Ambassador to the Sudan, presented his credentials to President Bashir at a
time when relationships between Khartoum and Washington had
reached their nadir since the RCC coup d'état of 30 June 1989.
During the next weeks relations continued to deteriorate. In September
the State Department condemned the Sudan government and General
Fatih Urwah for the murder of three Sudanese USAID employees
who had helped to maintain the USAID-Sudan compound in Juba
and had been falsely charged with the misuse of its radio and spy-
ing for the SPLA. All three men were well known in Juba as trusted
and respected professionals, and their summary execution was greeted
with anger by the southern Sudanese residents of the city. This
provocative action immediately created a breach between the United
States and the Sudan. When Assistant Secretary of State for Africa
Herman Cohen testified before the U.S. Senate Subcommittee on
African Affairs in the same month, September 1992, he was very
pessimistic that relations with Sudan would improve and consequently
the Bush administration would not become involved in the Sudan
peace process. The very same month Jan Eliasson, the new Director
of the United Nations Department of Humanitarian Affairs (UN/DHA),
arrived in Khartoum only to be received with ill-disguised hostility.
On 5 October 1992 the United States Senate passed, without any
objection from the State Department, its joint resolution condemning
the Khartoum government for its flagrant disregard of human rights.
The Senate also requested the Department of State to convene a
special meeting of the UN Security Council to review the violation
of human rights in the Sudan. In November the United Nations
General Assembly Committee on Social and Humanitarian Issues
released a report (Second Committee, Item 87, 1992) that censured
the Sudan for its disregard for the human rights of its citizens. The
United Nations General Assembly resolution, supported by 102 nations, expressed "grave concern at the serious human rights violations in the Sudan, including summary executions, detentions without

---

Turabi's views see speech to the PAIC in Nicosia, May–June 1991, Martin Kramer,
"The Mismeasure of Political Islam," in *The Islamism Debate*, ed. Martin Kramer,
Tel Aviv: The Moshe Dayan Center for Middle Eastern and African Studies, 1977,
p. 162.

due process, forced displacement of persons and torture."[2] The UN Human Rights Commission intensified its study of human rights abuse in the Sudan, and Gaspar Biro, a Hungarian lawyer and specialist in minority rights, was appointed its special rapporteur in 1994. He made three investigative journeys to the Sudan, and his report accusing the Sudan government of human rights abuse were consistently dismissed by the Sudanese ambassador to the United Nations as a vicious attack on the religion of Islam. After five years of frustration Biro resigned in 1998 to be replaced by Leonardo Franco, an Argentinian who had led the UN Human Rights Mission to Guatemala.

In Washington when Secretary of State Warren Christopher had announced that Africa would get greater attention from State than in the past, congressional leaders drafted a resolution urging President-elect Bill Clinton to "take immediate action" to deal with the humanitarian crisis in Sudan.[3] In December 1992 Assistant Secretary of State Herman Cohen arrived in Khartoum and explained very clearly that the United States was closely monitoring the support by the government for those Islamic fundamentalists who had found a home in Sudan, but there were those in the State Department who continued to argue that Bashir and the RCC would become more moderate when confronted by their disagreements with the hierarchy of NIF. They were encouraged by the open disputes between them in Khartoum. In an interview earlier in 1992 Turabi had arbitrarily announced that the RCC and NIF had agreed to dissolve the military government. When Turabi declared in a Reuters interview early in 1993 that a revolution in government would occur, the RCC was not prepared to surrender to Hasan al-Turabi and disintegrate

---

[2] "U.N. Panel Rebukes Burmese Military Rulers," *New York Times*, 6 December 1992, p. 10.

[3] "Sudan: Harsh condemnations," *Middle East International*, 23 October 1992, pp. 13–14; in 1993 Human Rights Watch, New York, had published sixteen studies that examined Sudan Government violations; see "Sudan is Described," *The New York Times*, 26 March 1993, p. A3 and the *Congressional Record*, 30 March 1993, p. H1721; on the Clinton foreign policy see Charles William Maynes, "A Workable Clinton Doctrine," *Foreign Policy*, No. 93, Winter 1993/94, pp. 3–21.

as he predicted.[4] The senior officers were determined to retain their paramount role in government and the state.

Somalia

Although disturbed about internal affairs in Sudan, the immediate concern of the Bush administration and Department of State was Sudanese support for radical Islamist groups in Somalia, particularly the Somali Islamic Unity Party (*Al-Ittihad al-Islami al-Somalia*) and General Muhammad Farah Aidid, warlord and leader of the United Somali Congress. In 1992 the PAIC General Assembly had shipped "some 1,000 tons of food and medicine to Somalia" for the Islamic Unity Party when the Sudanese themselves did not have enough food to eat or pharmaceuticals for disease. Such a large shipment could only be explained by ideology "for one reason or another, the Sudanese government has decided to export rather than to feed its own people."[5] The critics argued that the PAIC General Assembly had also convinced the RCC to send arms to Islamist forces in Mogadishu for General Aidid and to Islamists in the Ogaden region on the southern frontier with Kenya. During his visit to Washington in October 1992 the foreign minister of Kenya discussed its deteriorating relations with the Sudan and Somalia. He accused Khartoum of supporting the Islamic Party of Kenya (IPK) "and warned that a religious war" would engulf eastern Africa "if the international community does not recognize the dangers of such actions."[6] President Daniel Arap Moi was especially alarmed at the growing religious tensions in Kenya, and in April 1992 he had objected after Turabi had publicly expressed his support for the IPK. Founded at Mombasa on 15 January 1992, by mid-year the IPK was agitating for political recognition. Led by Omar Mwiny, Secretary-General Abulrahman Wandata, and charismatic street preachers like Shaykh Khalid Balala, it was a small but growing movement whose members were residents of Mombasa but were active all along the coast of East Africa. Even before the 30 June 1989 Revolution, NIF was active in Kenya,

---

[4] "Sudan: Turabi raises political tension," *Middle East Economic Development*, 22 January 1993.

[5] "Issues in the News: Starving Sudan Sends Supplies to Somalia," *Washington Report on Middle East Affairs*, December/January 1992/93.

[6] *Sudan Update*, London, 19 October 1992, p. 3.

sponsoring the education of young students at Muslim institutions in the Sudan, especially the African Center for Islamic Studies at Khartoum. Provided with funds from NIF, members of the IPK began to disseminate propaganda and initiate a terrorist campaign along the Somalia frontier and coastal Kenya.[7]

In Somalia the Sudanese were increasingly active. General Fatih Urwah, later the Sudanese ambassador to the UN, was the official liaison officer of the RCC to Farah Aidid. Mahdi Ibrahim, later the Sudan ambassador to the United States, was the Sudan link with the Somali Islamist civilian community. Ali Osman Muhammad Taha, later the powerful vice-president of Sudan, acted as the intermediary between Saudi and Somali bankers, most notably Osman Otto. A well-known Sudanese intelligence agent and Islamist named Al-Tayib Zein al-Abdin apparently was the principal representative of the RCC in Somalia during 1992–1993 to an equally shadowy Iran-Sudan task force on Somalia.[8] Despite a 1993 United Nations resolution that banned arms shipments to Somalia, Sudanese C-130s were being used to transport Iranian arms from Port Sudan to small airfields in Somalia. Hasan al-Turabi himself had ties to the *Al-Ittihad al-Islami al-Somalia*, the most radical of the Somali Islamist movements, and when its leadership visited Khartoum in 1992, Turabi arranged to have them meet with Osama bin Laden.

Osama bin Laden himself was determined to support the Islamists in Somalia. In 1992 he sent his trusted lieutenant Muhammad Atef (Abu Hafs) to southern Somalia. He was followed by Abu Ubaidah al-Banshiri, who, with four other Al Qaeda members, would later drown in a ferry accident on Lake Victoria in 1996. Abu Ubaidah returned to Khartoum in October 1992 to provide Al Qaeda with an assessment of the Islamists and conditions in Somalia. He warned that the Americans were becoming actively involved in Somalia because of the prospect of widespread famine in the south. At an important meeting in November 1992, held on the usual Thursday at the Al Qaeda guesthouse in Riyadh, Khartoum, a *fatwa* was written by Abu Hajer al-Iraqi (Mamdouh Mahmud Salim) and Saad

---

[7] Karl Vick, "FBI Trails Embassy Bombing Suspect," *The Washington Post*, 17 September 1998, p. A01; see also, "Soudan: la guerre est-elle finie?" *Jeune Afrique*, 30 April–13 May 1992, p. 61.

[8] Al-Tayib was last seen in Bosnia in 1995 attached to the Muwafaqah Brigade of 900 Islamic mujahideen being supplied by Iran and supported by Sudan.

al-Sharif and approved by Osama bin Laden to confront United States intervention in Somalia. The *fatwa*, an opinion on legal or religious matters, was issued by the two *mujtahid* who were acceptable to Bin Laden of deriving law from textual sources. The Khartoum *fatwa* was based on the historical works of Ibn al-Taymiyah, a 7th century cleric (*mufti*) and the legal case he constructed to justify Muslim warfare against the invading Tartars. Osama bin Laden had previously used Taymayah's arguments to give legitimacy to his opposition to the presence of United States military forces in Saudi Arabia. Equipped with the *fatwa* Muhammad Odeh and Abu Siad, the latter an important member of the military committee of Al Qaeda, were sent to Somalia to organize and train Muslims whose beliefs were sympathetic to those of Al Qaeda. Teams of Al-Qaeda soon followed. Three were sent to the Afars in the arid lands north of Hargaysa near the Djibouti frontier, two to the Ogaden, and others to join forces with the *Al-Ittihad al-Islami al-Somalia* that operated in Mogadishu. Two other teams went further south to the Gedo region and the Kenya frontier.

Only much later would Osama bin Laden admit that he and the Arab mujahideen of Al Qaeda were involved in Somalia, but at the time he was eager to help with arms and spiritual guidance to the warlords fighting amongst themselves for control of Mogadishu and southern Somalia.[9] Al Qaeda did not respect Aidid, but even with the support of Muhammad Ali Mahdi, who controlled the Abgal quarter of the city, Aidid could not be dislodged. After the death of the "perpetual dictator," Mohammed Siad Barre in January 1991, expatriates of the United Somali Congress had proclaimed Muhammad Ali Mahdi president of the Republic of Somalia. Few Somalis inside the country accepted this decision imposed by those in the Somali diaspora, and his authority was tenuous at best. In June 1991 Muhammad Farah Aidid, who Siad Barre had jailed for plotting a coup and then exiled as ambassador to India, was elected chairman of the United Somali Congress (USC). Ali Mahdi, however, refused to step down as president of Somalia, and in October he formed a

---

[9] "Mujahideen Spokesman on Their Repulsion of Ethiopian Aggression: Nidaʿul Islam Interviews the spokesman for the Islamic Union of the Mujahideen of Ogadin," *Al-Nidaʿul Islam*, Report 19, date unknown, appeared on http://www.islam.org.au./articles/19/.

government, which Aidid refused to recognize, claiming that his USC was the only legitimate government of Somalia. Ali Mahdi declared war only to suffer a quick and overwhelming defeat. Aidid then attacked the remnants of Siad Barre's army in southern Somalia.

Anarchy now ruled in Somalia—in Mogadishu, in southern cities, towns, and villages and in the countryside. Tragically, the struggle for power among the Somali warlords coincided with a major drought. Tens of thousands of Somalis had fled from war and famine across international borders to settle in ramshackle refugee camps in Kenya, Ethiopia, and Eritrea. In Somalia desperately poor Somalis, who could not flee, were trapped in a whirlwind of violence as a score of warlords sought to carve out satrapies within the once Republic of Somalia. By 1992 Somalia was "a state without a government," and there was no one able to respond to the drought that threatened famine for a half-million Somalis. By April 1992 starvation crisscrossed throughout the country, but the international humanitarian aid organizations found it nearly impossible to deliver food to the starving across the fiercely defended turf of the warlords. It was this widespread famine and endemic banditry that led the United Nations to attempt to restore some semblance of political order. To halt the death and destruction the UN Security Council Resolution 794 authorized the delivery of food, medicine, and other aid in "Operation Provide Relief" backed by military force. The international food aid agencies and NGOs had hired their own bodyguards and had for months begged the United Nations for protection from the warlord's militias who commandeered food intended for the starving Somali. Many of the NGOs had participated in the UN's massive Operation Lifeline Sudan program and their personnel had worked in the southern Sudan, but they had never experienced the danger confronting them in 1992 in Somalia from automatic weapons, mortars, grenades, and landmines of the warring Somali clans "armed, financed, and equipped, apparently with Iranian and Sudanese money." In April 1993 William Millward, a Canadian government anti-terrorist expert, reported "there are now signs of expanding joint Iranian/Sudanese contacts with Islamic militants in Somalia."[10]

---

[10] "Relapse to clan warfare," *The Middle East*, January 1992, page 25; UN General Assembly, A/RES/47/162, "Emergency Assistance to Sudan," New York, 18 December 1992; William Millward, "The Rising tide of Islamic Fundamentalism (11)," *Canadian Security Intelligence Service, Commentary*, No. 31, April 1993.

Given the "rapid deterioration of [the] situation, heavy loss of
human life and material damage," UN Resolution 733 of the General
Assembly in1992 ordered the "complete embargo on weapons and
military equipment to Somalia." When that resolution was ignored,
a second resolution by the UN Security Council (S/RES/751 of 24
April 1992) reinforced the arms embargo of the General Assembly.
Both resolutions had no effect on violence and famine in Somalia.
Finally the UN Security Council Resolution 794, adopted on 3
December 1992 and supported by both the OAU and the OIC,
ordered that action be taken "to establish a secure environment" in
Somalia so that humanitarian relief operations could deliver food
and medical supplies to more than a half-million famine-stricken
people. A Security Council Sanctions Committee had been created
to oversee the imposition of sanctions but its lack of success led the
newly-elected UN Secretary-General, Boutros Boutros Ghali, to urge
the United States to use American military forces to protect the various agencies of the UN's humanitarian mission in Somalia. He was
convinced that the UN operation would fail without military support and was able to persuade the Bush administration in November
1992 to deploy U.S. military units in Somalia. The UN's "Operation
Provide Relief" was replaced by the UN's "Operation Restore Hope,"
an entirely new and unexpected use of United States military power
in the post-Cold War era that would involve 25,000 Americans. The
irony of this decision to send American military units to Somalia to
escort, defend, and protect humanitarian agencies providing relief to
starving Somali when the U.S. had never considered sending its
military forces to do the same in the southern Sudan was not lost
on the southern Sudanese or their supporters in Congress. "How
does one justify intervention in Somalia but not a few hundred miles
away in Sudan where a seemingly interminable civil war has claimed
the lives of tens of thousands of innocent civilians?" If the decision
of President Bush stressed both the humanitarian purpose and the
limited nature of the U.S. military involvement in Somalia, could
not the same decision be applied to the Sudan where drought and
civil war threatened the lives of many thousands of southern Sudanese?[11]

---

[11] Ted Galen Carpenter, "Setting a Dangerous Precedent in Somalia," Cato
Foreign Policy Briefing, No. 20, December 18, 1992, The Cato Institute, Washington
D.C.

In the glare of television lights a unit of U.S. Marines that formed part of a twenty-four nation coalition waded ashore at Mogadishu on 9 December 1992. Given the overwhelming firepower of the Marines the forces of Muhammad Farah Aidid and the Somali Islamic Unity Party prudently held their fire as the race began to get food to the starving. The Somali warrior chiefs representing fourteen warring clans were subsequently cajoled into attending yet another Somalis Reconciliation Conference at Addis Ababa where the Sudanese ambassador to Ethiopia, Uthman al-Sayyid Fadl, mediated a cease-fire agreement signed on 15 January 1993. Uthman Fadl was appointed only after he received the approval of Hasan al-Turabi and was known to have been involved in providing assistance to the Ogaden Islamic Union seeking to secede from Ethiopia. Once the cease-fire had been established, the Marines were able to provide effective security for relief agencies, but the fragile Somali cease-fire could not survive the deep rivalries of the warlords and their clans.

Herman Cohen and the Sudan

When William Jefferson Clinton was elected president in November 1992, Assistant Secretary of State for Africa Herman J. Cohen was about to conclude a long and distinguished diplomatic career. After more than three years as assistant secretary he could offer little hope that the Sudanese civil war would be peacefully resolved. His proposal to demilitarize Juba, the beleaguered capital of the southern Sudan, and to institute a cease-fire under the supervision of international monitors had been rejected by Khartoum. When he arrived at the capital of the Sudan in December, the principal concerns of the Department of State were human rights violations and the presence of terrorists, while the Agency for International Development (AID) was preoccupied with the famine produced by annual drought and endless war that threatened hundreds of thousands of southern Sudanese. The UN General Assembly had "noted with satisfaction" that Sudan cereal production had increased in the 1992–1993 harvest and any surplus should be "used to meet the needs of the people," but the NIF government in Khartoum did nothing to relieve starvation in the South. By January 1993 an estimated 800,000 people needed immediate supplies of food and another 1.5 million were

living on less than subsistence to stay alive.[12] The United States
pledged $53 million in humanitarian assistance. The Senate had
reluctantly approved, but its members were less interested in foreign
aid now that the Cold War had come to an end. In the House of
Representatives, where for over a decade, many members had regularly supported humanitarian assistance for the Sudan, there was a
growing unwillingness to provide yet more food to help the NIF government. Some members were determined to provide disaster relief
only to the southern Sudanese because they were sure that Khartoum
would make no honest effort to relieve the southern famine, end its
massive human rights violations in the Upper Nile, or take seriously
peace talks with the SPLA. During his last visit to the Sudan Cohen
had warned Bashir that the United States was deeply concerned
about their support for Islamic fundamentalists who had found a
home in the Sudan and their failure to respond to the growing
famine in the South. He captured the attention of the RCC, however, when he warned that the prospect of famine in the Sudan was
as grave as that which had just led the United Nations to intervene
in Somalia. This was an implicit warning that if the Sudan did not
permit UN relief agencies unrestricted access to the southern Sudan,
the United States would review other options to ensure the delivery
of relief supplies as it had done in Somalia. His admonitions were
publicly scorned by Ali al-Haj and politely ignored by other members of the RCC once the lame duck at State had departed.

Herman Cohen was a singularly decent and solicitous diplomat
whose life as the Assistant Secretary for Africa had not been made
easy by the revolutionary government in Sudan. Unfortunately, Cohen
had his critics in the United States. They argued that by providing
food to starving Sudanese through a totalitarian regime, the United
States undermined the regional self-reliance of the SPLA and thus
prolonged the civil war. Like most senior diplomats about to leave
the State Department, he had hoped for an easy transition between
the end of one administration and the arrival of Secretary of State
Warren Christopher and his Africa team. The Clinton administration, however, was excruciatingly dilatory in filling crucial African
policy positions in the State Department and the Pentagon so that

---

[12] Ioan Lewis, "In the Land of the Living Dead," *The Sunday Times*, London, 30
August 1992; *Sudan Update*, London, 12 December 1992, p. 1.

Cohen stayed on as Assistant Secretary for Africa until March 1993. His departure coincided with the hectic days following the Trade Tower bombing at a time when the Sudan was suddenly becoming a topic not only for the Department of State but the national media.

In his official capacity as assistant secretary, Herman Cohen gave his last testimony to the House Foreign Affairs Subcommittee on Africa in March that the Sudan and the United States were on a collision course. He strongly condemned the "coercive Islamization of non-Muslim Sudanese," the presence of Muslim terrorist organizations in the Sudan, and an increase in Iranian activity in Sudan after the visit of President Rafsanjani to Khartoum in December 1991. Sudan could shortly join Libya, Iran, Syria, Iraq, North Korea, and Cuba on the State Department's list of nations sanctioned for state-sponsored terrorist activity. "We are monitoring the situation closely and have made it clear to the Sudanese that under U.S. law, they are extremely close to being designated a state sponsor of terrorism." His testimony was not totally pessimistic. He recommended a positive alternative proposed by Roger Winter of the U.S. Committee for Refugees and Frank Wolf, the influential Republican Congressman, to "establish demilitarized zones in Southern Sudan to protect hundreds of thousands of vulnerable Sudanese civilians," not unlike those established by the United Nations for the Kurds in northern Iraq.[13] In the same month, March 1993, thirty-five nations signed the U.S. Committee for Refugees first public condemnation of the human rights record of the Sudan government. Meanwhile at Geneva in January 1993 the 49th Session of the United Nations Human Rights Commission had previously reported numerous instances of torture employed by the Sudanese government including the execution of over 300 civilians of Juba after the government garrison had repulsed an attempt by the SPLA to capture the provincial capital. Further human rights abuse had accompanied the continuing forced resettlement of hundreds of thousands of internally displaced people throughout the Sudan.

The new Clinton administration soon learned of the problem of the Sudan that had been a conundrum for Herman Cohen. The

---

[13] "News from the U.S. Committee for Refugees," Washington D.C., 9 March 1993; Cohen, H., "The Situation in Sudan," Testimony of Asst. Secretary of State Herman J. Cohen," House Subcommittee on Africa, 10 March 1993, U.S. Department of State, March 1993.

Paris journal, *Al-Watan Al-Arabi*, published an extensive report on the "comprehensive terrorist plan" being prepared in Tehran and Khartoum. Yemeni Afghan-Arabs would be trained in Iran and Sudan to overthrow the secular government in Yemen. Other Afghan-Arabs were to assist Islamist movements in North Africa. The Sudan was needed as a sanctuary and the country from which the Islamist revolution could be carried into the heart of Africa south of the Sahara. The Islamist insurgency against the Yemen was one action in a larger design for the spread of the Islamic revolution by Hasan al-Turabi.[14] In America *Newsweek* reported "now aided by Iran, the first Sunni Muslim Islamic republic—Sudan—has become the linchpin of an aggressive, Pan-Arab Islamic front."[15]

The New York World Trade Center Bombing

On 26 February 1993 a bomb exploded in the World Trade Center in New York. The attack, which caused extensive damage to one tower of America's largest business complex, was a terrorist act of unprecedented magnitude in the United States. Investigations by the FBI immediately established a Muslim connection, and agents began to review information previously gathered from mosques in Brooklyn, New Jersey, and Virginia that were well-known for the affiliation of their members with revolutionaries and terrorist organizations in Europe and Asia. Within days the investigations led to the activities of Sudanese diplomats in New York particularly the Sudanese Mission to the United Nations and those Sudanese at the Washington embassy who seemed to enjoy more independence and authority than the ambassador. The normal interest in the activities of the Muslim Brotherhood in the United States became more rigorous when young student Brothers had first entered the United States in significant numbers during the nineteen fifties. They had established community organizations, Islamic schools, and in 1963 founded the Muslim Students' Association of the United States and Canada. Financial support from the Middle East for these organizations was often transmitted through diplomatic channels including the Sudan embassy.

---

[14] *Al-Watan Al-Arabi*, (translation from the Arabic), Paris, 22 January 1993, pp. 18–21.
[15] "Building an Enemy," *Newsweek*, 15 February 1993, p. 28.

On 24 June 1993 a Sudanese with the Sudan UN mission, Siddig Ibrahim Siddig Ali who was preparing to carry out yet another bombing, was arrested. He and two Sudanese friends, who were presumed to be intelligence agents, used their diplomatic immunity to leave the United States. Two months later the Sudan was added to the list of state-sponsored terrorist nations, for the investigation of the Trade Center bombing had discovered that the blind Shaykh Omar Abd al-Rahman and his *Jama'at al-Islamiyah* had approved or assisted in the bombing. The Shaykh was arrested and Sudanese diplomats were clearly implicated as accessories, but President Bashir persistently denied that any Sudanese had been involved in the terrorist attack. Shaykh Omar Abd al-Rahman, who had entered the United States from Sudan in 1990 and had successfully fought all efforts by Egypt to extradite him, was indicted for the murder of the six Americans who died in the Trade Center bombing. The Shaykh had been on the State Department "look-out" list since 1987, yet had received his visa. President Mubarak and the Egyptian authorities were understandably perplexed how he was able to obtain a visa to enter the United States at its embassy in Khartoum, or why, after arrival in the United States, he was allowed to leave New York for London and return in October 1990 and several times in 1991.[16]

Eventually, the FBI were able to arrest most of the those responsible for both the Trade Center bombing and for plotting other terrorist attacks in New York. Mahmoud Abouhalima, an Egyptian, the Shaykh's driver, and former Afghan-Arab had planned the bombing. Siddiq Ali had been with Abouhalima in Afghanistan in 1988–1990 and was Shaykh Omar's interpreter in the United States. After the bombing Ali had assisted Abouhalima to leave the United States for the Sudan where he planned an attempt to assassinate President Mubarak during his visit to New York in March 1993. The FBI also "intercepted a telephone call" from the Sudanese representative at the UN to Hasan al-Turabi, the contents of which were never disclosed but involved references to an Osama bin Laden.[17] In June Siddiq Ali "and his mostly Sudanese recruits were arrested in flagrante delicto manufacturing bombs to be deployed at New York

---

[16] US v. Omar Ahmad Ali Abdel Rahman, et al., (S5) 93 Cr. 181 (MBM). New York; "Luqsor Massacre: Shedding Light on Western Support for Terrorism", (translated from the Arabic), *Al-Sha'ab al-Arabi*, Cairo, 1 January 1998.

[17] James Kitfield, *National Journal*, 12 October 2001.

landmarks."[18] In London Mohamed Osman al Mirghani, the exiled leader of the Khatmiyya, confirmed, that despite denials by President Bashir that any Sudanese in the United States were terrorists, it was Ali who had arranged a meeting with the Sudanese community during his visit to the United Nations in 1991. When Turabi had visited the United States in 1992, Ali had been one of his bodyguards.[19] Five Sudanese were arrested in the conspiracy, as was Muhammad Saleh, an important Hamas operative, who had been responsible to arrange for its military training in the Sudan. Osama bin Laden was named as one of the many co-conspirators.

The investigation into the Trade Towers bombing led FBI agents from New York to Pakistan in May 1993. Coincidentally with their arrival, among the recent pilgrims to Peshawar had been Shaykh Omar Abd al-Rahman, Rashid al-Ghannushi, Yemeni fundamentalist Abd al-Majid al-Zandani, Hasan al-Turabi, and members of the Egyptian Islamic Jihad masquerading as employees of the Kuwait Red Crescent. A visiting team of Egyptian intelligence agents met with the FBI. Pakistan police had rounded up the "Arabs of Peshawar" including 600 foreign Muslims who had once worked in Pashawar with middle-eastern charities. Another 154 of some 2,624 "non-Pakistani" Muslims, including Sudanese, Mahgrebians, Bosnians, Filipinos, and even African-Americans who had been registered between 1987 and 1992, were arrested, mostly for unauthorized possession of firearms or fake passports. The Pakistani police had only scratched the surface of their "Islamic mercenaries" Afghan-Arab problem, for their 800 mile border with Afghanistan was virtually "ungovernable."[20] In the end, the government of Pakistan would force hundreds of Afghan-Arabs to find a new home and among the Egyptian expatriates" all but two went to the Sudan."[21]

The Trade Center bombing set off an international chain reaction against Muslim extremists. The government of Algeria terminated diplomatic relations with Iran and recalled its ambassador from

[18] Andrew C. McCarthy, "Prosecuting the New York Sheikh," *Middle East Quarterly*, March 1997.

[19] *Al-Sharq al-Awsat*, London, 3 July 1993, page 1; Bruno Philip, *Le Monde*, Paris, 15 May 1993.

[20] Bruno Philip, *Le Monde*, Paris, 15 May 1993.

[21] In his popular *Join The Caravan (Ilhaq bil-q filah)*, Pakistan, 1987, Shaykh Abdullah Azzam acknowledged he would instill two virtues in all Muslims, the duty of *jihad* (fighting), and the duty of arousing all believers.

Khartoum claiming Iran assisted Muslim mujadiheen fighting with the Islamists in the Algerian civil war. The Sudanese ambassador in Teheran denied the Algerian accusations "blaming problems at home [in Algeria] on the Sudan and Iran." In Khartoum the government labeled the accusations a "mere lie. . . . raised by certain countries, the U.S. in particular, that Islamic activists are being trained in Sudan with financial support of Iran."[22] The Egyptian response to Muslim radicalism was more decisive and thorough. When President Hosni Mubarak paid an official visit to Europe and the United States in April 1993, he had declared all-out war on Egypt's Muslim extremists. He would not have Islamist radicals from the Sudan, the Maghrib, Palestine, Lebanon, and Jordan operating in Egypt or attempting to isolate Egypt from the Arab world. In June Egypt arrested dozen of students at Al-Mina University in Upper Egypt as spies for the Sudan and Iran that precipitated a threatening response from Khartoum that the Sudan might reconsider its support for Egyptian interests in the Nile waters.[23] The Islamism preached by Hasan al-Turabi and his allies was a danger to Egypt and the West. In Washington Mubarak's message was confirmed by the sophisticated Mansour Khalid, the foreign minister of the Sudan under Numayri and now spokesman for the SPLA, and Mubarak al-Fadl al-Mahdi, Sadiq al-Mahdi's cousin and confidant. Both were aware that there were dangerous Islamists in the mosques in the United States from Alexandria, Virginia, to St. Louis, Missouri.

It took some time, but Western newspapers began to respect the State Department's claim that Sudan facilitated the activity and movement of terrorists and that Khartoum had become a meeting place for Afghan-Arabs and radicals from the Islamic Jihad, Hamas, Lebanese Hizbollah, and Abu Nidal. The Sudan and its involvement in the terrorist "conspiracy" had come to the attention of the media and the American public after the arrest of the five Sudanese living in the United States scheming to plant bombs in the United Nations and the FBI building in New York. All five had close ties to NIF and moved in Islamic fundamentalist circles on the east coast of the United States. A few had links with Sudanese diplomats accredited to the United Nations, and all were companions or admirers of

---

[22] "Algeria breaks Iran ties, recalls envoy to Sudan," *The Washington Times*, 28 March 1993, p. A14; IRNA Report, Teheran, 29 March 1993.

[23] AFP, 10 June 1993; Ghazi Salah al-Din Atabani in *Al-Safir*, 11 June 1993.

Shaykh Omar Abd al-Rahman, who had settled in Jersey City, New Jersey, and were members of his large following.[24]

At the time no effort was made to arrest Shaykh Omar. Inexplicably, he was allowed his freedom even though the Egyptian Higher State Security Court had issued an order for his arrest on charges dealing with terrorist acts in Egypt and sought his extradition from the United States. He remained active in and out of the mosque warning Mubarak not to proceed with the execution of twenty-two Egyptians convicted of terrorism and cautioning the United States government that it would have to pay a heavy price for its continued support of Egypt. Finally in April 1993 the U.S. immigration service ordered his deportation. The Board of Immigration had discovered he lied on his immigration papers and declared him to be a danger to the security of the United States. Before immigration took action, however, Shaykh Omar was arrested in New York on charges of associating with terrorists and an accomplice in terrorist acts carried out in the United States. He and nine others were tried and convicted for their participation in the World Trade Center bombing and for planning the destruction of other targets in the United States. Abu Abdallah, the Islamic Jihad envoy to Sudan, predicted the United States "could expect more" attacks similar to the Trade Center bombing "because the Islamic World is very angry."[25]

The United States, Sudan, and Somalia

In April the new Assistant Secretary of State for African Affairs George E. Moose, who was a senior at Grinnell College when John Garang de Mabior was a freshman, arrived in Lokichokkio in northern Kenya. He told skeptical relief workers that the Sudan was a priority because "it is a major humanitarian crisis," but he was "not terribly optimistic" that it was possible for the United States to broker a peace agreement. "With trouble mounting in Somalia and the West still reluctant to use force in the Balkans, the prospect of forceful intervention in Sudan seems remote." Relief organizations would have "to operate with little more than grain bags and moral

---

[24] "Specter of Terror," *The New York Times*, 27 June 1993, p. 28.
[25] "Sudan Suspected," *The Washington Times*, 17 August 93, p. A3.

suasion."[26] Having returned from Africa Moose testified in May before the Senate Foreign Relations Subcommittee on Africa where he urged all nations to suspend arms shipments to the Sudan and end all economic aid other than humanitarian assistance. The Senate agreed and responded with Senate Resolution 94 that was confirmed by the House of Representatives Concurrent Resolution 131 to express "the sense of the Congress with respect to the situation in the Sudan."[27] In the House there was anger at the massive human rights violations perpetrated by the Sudan government. Congressman Harry Johnston argued. "An entire generation of southern Sudanese is being wiped out in one of the world's most neglected civil wars."[28] It was apparent, however, that the Clinton administration was narrowly preoccupied with nation-building in Somalia, and that the Sudan would receive little attention.

In Somalia, Operation Restore Hope and the Marines had imposed an uneasy truce, but military action "demonstrated how slippery the distinction between the political and the humanitarian goals is becoming." It would soon become even more slippery when the Islamists who dominated the governments of Sudan and Iran responded to the Western presence in Somalia. During a visit to Khartoum the Iranian Deputy Foreign Minister Ali Janati made the astonishing statement that "the presence in Somalia of the United States under the umbrella of the United Nations troops is a threat against Sudan."[29] Long before U.S. Marines patrolled the streets of Mogadishu the NIF government had sent Mahdi Ibrahim from the foreign ministry to forge closer ties with the more radical Muslim elements in Somalia.[30] In December another Iranian delegation arrived in Khartoum, the eighth to visit the Sudan in 1992, but this time led by the Ayatollah Ardabili and Revolutionary Guards Commander Gholan Rida. The Sudanese delegation, in which President Bashir "was simply a

[26] "U.N. Makes Aid Appeal," *The Washington Times*, 8 April 1993, p. A10: "Fighting in Sudan Halts Food Relief," *The New York Times*, 18 April 1993, p. 7.
[27] Reuters, Washington D.C., 4 May 1993.
[28] "House Panel Approves Measure Against Sudan," Reuters, Washington, 4 August 1993; "International Democracy Report: Focus on Sudan," Ross & Green [Lobbyists], Washington D.C.,1 September 1993.
[29] "Iran, Sudan Interested in Broadening Religions," IRNA, Khartoum, 14 July 1993; "Iran, Sudan Discuss Cultural Cooperation," IRNA, Khartoum, 17 July 1993; "Pressures on Garang," *Middle East International*, 11 June 1993, p. 14.
[30] *Middle East Confidential*, 18 December 1992.

member," was led by Hasan al-Turabi to seek and support a policy to defy the Western presence in Somalia.[31]

Iran was soon to support three training camps for mujahideen in Mogadishu, Bosaso, and Marka. Western NGOs would be replaced by Islamic relief agencies from the Sudan and the *Al-Da'awa al-Islamiyya* while the Khartoum government disingenuously announced scholarships for 10,000 Somali students.[32] In March Abd al-Bagi Muhammad Hassan was named Sudanese ambassador to Somalia, and thereafter the Sudanese embassy in Mogadishu became the center for operations opposed to the United Nations in Somalia. The Iran-Sudan policy had an immediate impact, and even Aidid's rival, Muhammad Ali Mahdi of the Somali Unified Congress, expressed his appreciation for food and scholarships from the Sudan and the close ties between the two peoples.[33] Iran was now moving arms through Port Sudan for the Sudan to transfer them by air to Somalia. Hajatoleslam Ali Fallahian, director of the Iranian intelligence services, and Nafi Ali Nafi, a senior member of NIF and Head of Sudan State Security, met at an undisclosed location to discuss the means by which to confront American and French forces in Somalia.[34] Nafi had previously worked with Ali Menshawi, director of the Pasdaran.[35] Another secret protocol was signed in January 1993 by which Sudanese pilots would be trained by the Iranian air force, and Iran would purchase twenty Chinese ground attack aircraft for the Sudan that never arrived. In addition Khartoum would receive $300 million in military assistance including 120 tanks Iran had captured in its war with Iraq, along with "enough uniforms, small arms and ammunition to equip 10 battalions."[36]

---

[31] "Chief Justice Holds Meetings With Senior Iranian Officials," *New Horizon*, 9 June 1994, p. 4; "Further notes on Aideed's Khartoum connection," *Somali News Update*, 10 November 1993, and quoted in Gabriel Warburg, "Hot Spot: Egypt and Sudan Wrangle over Halayib," *Middle East Forum*, March 1994; "Sudanese-Iranian Relations Shift Up a Gear," *Sudan Democratic Gazette*, London, February 1993, p. 4.

[32] *Indian Ocean Newsletter*, 11 September 1993; reported in *Sudan Update* 8 October 1993, p. 3.

[33] SUNA Radio, Khartoum, 1637 GMT, 12 January 1993; FBIS, *Near East and South Asia*, 15 January 1993, p. 1.

[34] SUNA Radio, Khartoum, 1637 GMT, 12 January 1993; FBIS, *Near East and South Asia*, 15 January 1993, p. 1.

[35] *Middle East Confidential*, 18 December 1992; *Indian Ocean Newsletter*, 11 September 1993; *Sudan Update*, 8 October 1993, p. 3.

[36] U.S. Department of State, *Patterns of Global Terrorism*, 1993.

General Muhammad Farah Aidid later denied that Sudan was involved in the training of his troops, but in March 1993 he was flown to Khartoum in a Sudan C-130 and met with Hasan al-Turabi during which the latter, "offered General Aidid help in training his loyalists and General Aidid accepted."[37] On 8 April Radio Omdurman announced that Dr. Ghazi Salah al-Din Atabani, minister of state at the presidency, expressed support for Somalia after Aidid had a long private meeting with President Bashir.[38] In June Aidid returned to Khartoum to participate "in special consultations conducted under the cover of a special session" of the PAIC General Assembly "chaired by Turabi" accompanied by Bin Laden, Zawahiri, and Iranian intelligence officers.[39]

Humanitarian Missions

In Khartoum the United States Ambassador to Sudan Donald Petterson, on his own initiative and to the surprise of the Sudan Government, visited the southern Sudan in May 1993 hoping to mediate a cease-fire in order to reactivate the distribution of food to those Nilotic Sudanese dying from famine caused by the civil war and the hostilities among the rival factions of the SPLA. He stopped at Ayod, Kongor, Bor, and Nzara, and met with Riak Machar, who led the Nuer faction of the SPLA against John Garang and his Dinka. Although Riak seemed disinterested in famine relief, Petterson continued to use his influence as the ambassador of the United States to provide food aid. In April the United Nations declared some 2.8 million people were at risk in the southern Sudan and urged the international donor community to honor its commitments to Operation Lifeline Sudan. The UN had received only $15 million of the $130 million required to fund Operation Lifeline Sudan in 1993 because the usual donor nations had been loathe to provide assistance that would support a government which restricted access to areas in need.

---

[37] "Iran-armed Islamic Forces Target Sudan Rebels," *The Washington Times*, 3 February 1993, p. A9.

[38] "Foreign Help Seen in Aidid Tactics," *The Washington Times*, 8 October 1993; FBIS, *Arab Africa*," 9 April 1993, p. 12.

[39] Yossef Bodansky, *Bin Ladin: The Man Who Declared War on America*, Roseville, California: Prima Publishing, 2001, pp. 76–79.

In Washington Senate Resolution 94 (which served as a follow-up to Senate Resolution 140 of October 1992) requested the administration to provide greater humanitarian assistance to the Sudanese. Senator Paul Simon, who had taken the lead in moving the resolution, acknowledged that "the suffering of the Sudanese people has not been alleviated," that the government was "abusing its citizens," and that there seemed no end to the civil war. He argued that the regime ill-treated southern Sudanese, used the PDF to terrorize its minorities, and employed the quasi-paramilitary Popular Police Force to intimidate the urban populace. In the end the Senate supported Operation Lifeline Sudan and, in order to sustain the UN efforts to monitor human rights violations in Sudan recommended that the president should appoint a special representative to work with the UN, the OAU, and other interested parties to create internationally monitored demilitarized zones and resettlement routes that could be used until a permanent cease fire was achieved.[40]

In late May 1993 Ambassador Petterson returned to the South to Ulang and Nasir in Upper Nile where he again met Riak Machar and succeeded in obtaining his verbal agreement to demilitarize the area within the so-called Waat-Yuai-Ayod "triangle of death." Petterson then continued on to Nairobi to visit Garang and received his approval for the creation of a safe-haven that would have permitted Operation Lifeline Sudan to distribute food only to be confronted by an abrupt withdrawal by Riak of his previous promise. On 1 June he "absolutely rejected" Petterson's proposal.[41] A few days later the ambassador returned to the United States. He was outspoken that Khartoum had done nothing to improve its human rights record. The Sudan government had made access to southern Sudan extremely difficult for humanitarian agencies, and in a very frank report to his government he was emphatic that United States "relations with Sudan are poor and that's exactly what I told Mr. Bashir."[42] Khartoum was not pleased. Dr. Ali al-Haj scornfully rejected the Petterson plan for a demilitarized zone.

In May 1993 Assistant Secretary of State for Africa George Moose testified before the Senate Foreign Relations Committee where he

---

[40] *The Congressional Record*, S4509, 3 April 1993.
[41] *The Washington Times*, 29 May 1993, p. A2; FBIS, *Arab-Africa*, 1 June 1993, p. 21; Johnson, *The Root Causes of Sudan's Civil War*, p. 120.
[42] Private correspondence in the authors' possession, 25 June 1993.

expressed the Department's growing distress about the well-known presence of terrorists in the Sudan. When questioned closely Moose would only promise to give the senators a confidential briefing in private. Other nations were equally troubled. In February King Fahd of Saudi Arabia had sought to use his personal diplomacy to end the civil war in Afghanistan. The king hoped that if his efforts succeeded the arms trade and support for Afghan-Arab terrorists, who were making their appearance throughout the Muslim world, could be diminished. Unfortuately, the splintering of Afghan mujahideen into a half-dozen disparate commands, each with its own demands, led them to reject the Saudi peace plan. Shortly thereafter, The Arab Monetary Fund, which was dominated by the Saudis, halted all loans to Sudan, explaining that Khartoum was already $220 million in arrears.

Although the evidence of terrorist training in the Sudan appeared to some self-evident, there were those critics, including former President Jimmy Carter, who thought that the United States government was overreacting to the supposed presence of Sudan sponsored terrorist training camps. Ironically, that view was shared by Ambassador Donald Petterson who was well aware of the presence in the Sudan of Hamas, Hizbollah, *Jama'at al-Islamiyah*, Islamic Jihad (Palestine), and the Abu Nidal. However, he "did not think the evidence was sufficiently conclusive" to put Sudan on the list of state-sponsors of terrorism until he was personally told by Assistant Secretary of State George Moose in Washington in August 1993 that there was in fact good reason to do so. Petterson, whose years in the Foreign Service had been spent mostly in Africa south of the Sahara, was not particularly knowledgeable of the Middle East or Muslim terrorist groups, for the Department of State normally regarded the Sudan as more in Africa than the Middle East. In later years he was convinced that during his three year tenure in the Sudan the information Egypt provided on terrorism was part of a "disinformation campaign." Bin Laden "did not figure" and "we in Khartoum were not really concerned about him," even though there were many in Washington who thought otherwise.[43]

---

[43] Donald Petterson, *Inside Sudan: Political Islam, Conflict and Catastrophe*, Boulder Colorado: Westview Press, 1999, pp. 42–43, 69. Petterson quotes appeared in the *Vanity Fair* article by David Rose, "Clinton staff rejected bin Laden info," *Vanity Fair*, Los Angeles, 30 November 2001.

CHAPTER SIX

STATE SPONSORED TERRORISM

It took Hasan al-Turabi six months to recover from the severe beating in Canada. Although often lacking in physical stamina, he seemed to be his old self by mid-1993. There was nothing wrong with his mind, and he reemerged as statesman and apologist for the Islamist state stronger than ever and reassumed the leadership of the PAIC General Assembly while still projecting an aura of mystery. An American journalist who interviewed Turabi wrote that "despite his obvious authority, he remains in what might be called the foreground of the background" that created ambiguity as to who was in charge in Khartoum, "the military strongmen, who are increasingly reviled for their bloody ways, or their brainier friends outside the army, the Islamist intellectuals led by Turabi. . . . As factions shift within factions" Turabi moves adroitly "to duck responsibility and claim credit as needed."[1] Another American who met with Turabi could not decide whether he was talking to the snake charmer or the cobra.

During its first four years the revolutionary military government had purged numerous dissidents, crushed attempted coups, and pursued with vigor the war against the SPLA. The alliance between NIF and the RCC seemed secure, and although the ministry of defense and the presidency remained in military hands by the fourth anniversary of the 30 June coup d'état, there was "an identity of views between Bashir and Turabi on issues internal, international, and ideological."[2] It thus came as a shock to many Sudanese when Turabi was quoted in January 1993 that the RCC would be dissolved "in months rather than days. . . . [there was] "no place, actually, for [them] any more." Bashir had agreed in 1992 to dissolve the command council at some future date, but in the spring of 1993 the military leadership was reluctant to accept early retirement or

---

[1] William Langwiesche, "Turabi's Law," *The Atlantic Monthly*, August 1994, pp. 26–33.
[2] "The French and American policies on Algeria: Vive la différence," *Mideast Mirror*, Vol. 8, No. 196, London, 11 October 1994.

permit the decentralization of government. Turabi's statements generated "confusion and anger and contradictory responses from different government offices" until their disgreements were reconciled, and the military agreed to the incremental decentralization of government that had always been part of its rhetoric for a new Sudan since August 1989.[3] In October 1993 three constitutional decrees officially abolished the National Salvation Revolutionary Command Council, but Bashir was named president and the RCC executive and administrative functions were devolved to him. All significant political decisions would still require the approval of Bashir and the small military circle that surrounded him, but administrative decisions and economic policies would continue to be made by the civilians most of whom were beholden to Hasan al-Turabi. As president, Bashir would enjoy the same prerogatives as he had as leader of the RCC, but there would be a civilian cabinet and the Transitional National Assembly (TNA) would ensure the evolution of an Islamist federal form of government by 1997. The TNA was dominated by NIF and Hasan al-Turabi.

By 1994 the Sudanese military dictatorship shared power, if not openly at least tacitly, with the party hierarchy of NIF. Turabi regarded the Sudan as "a model state advancing towards the ideals of Islam," a nation that would "definitely be a sense of inspiration in the new world order."[4] Washington was skeptical. It had long argued that the RCC had only "nominally ruled Sudan," for NIF and Hasan al-Turabi "effectively controlled the Government." Now that the RCC had agreed to dissolve, NIF had "further tightened its grip on the state" and its members occupied "most key positions in the Government, security forces, judiciary, academia, and media."[5] Washington, however, seemed unaware or did not appreciate the importance and influence of Hasan-al-Turabi's organization for the Islamist revolution, the PAIC General Assembly. The PAIC was an instrument to combine and promote his omnificent view of a modern, evolutionary Islam with that of the narrower revolutionary vision that had recently emerged in Shiite Iran. He not only created an

---

[3] "Sudan: Turabi raises political tension," *Middle East Economic Development*, 22 January 1993.
[4] "Sudan spreads Islamic Extremism," *Foreign Report*, Jane's Information Group, Ltd., United Kingdom, 15 June 1995.
[5] "Sudan Human Rights Practices, 1993," U.S. Department of State, Washington D.C., 31 January 1994.

institute, but a movement. The congress was to bring together a millennium of Islamic factionalism. By the strength of his personality
and his learning, Turabi sought to use the PAIC General Assembly
to forge a single, cohesive, and unified Islamic organization uniting
the *umma* (the Muslim community) from West Africa to the Philippines.
Iran and Iraq and even Yemen, Qatar, and Malaysia provided funds
for the next meeting of the congress in 1993 that brought Islamists
to Khartoum from more than fifty nations and many Muslim organizations. It became the nexus in the expansion of the Islamist revolution and a platform to denounce the West.

Turabi was much too sophisticated and subtle to use the congress
for publicity that would attract unwanted attention to his movement.
It did not issue blood curdling manifestoes, but it bonded together
Islamists from far and wide with a common purpose. As the organization gained prominence, however, Turabi was forced to devote
substantial energy to defend its aims and objectives. During the second PAIC General Assembly in Khartoum in December 1993 he
projected his image as a benign Islamic revivalist, but in special sessions he and Dr. Ayman al-Zawahiri devised an Iraq-Iran-Sudan
"contingency plan" to confront United States military forces in
Somalia.[6] After the PAIC adjourned Turabi proposed to organize
and host the annual conference of the Islamic Organization in Africa
(IOA) that usually met at its headquarters in Nigeria. His reputation and support from the Nigerian Muslim Brothers enabled him
to transfer the venue for that year to Friendship Hall in Khartoum.
The Sudan media was given freedom to publicize the meetings of
the conference, a privilege it did not have in reporting on the meetings of the PAIC General Assembly. The IOA conference was
described as the first fruit of a "New Islamic Order" whose members stood ready "to confront the New World Order which was tar-
geting Islam and Muslims throughout the world." Muslim scholars
from Tanzania, Nigeria, Senegal, Uganda, Mauritania, and other
African states attended. They talked, listened, and exchanged ideas.
Hasan al-Turabi dominated the meetings. In his closing remarks he
declared that despite the "Western and Colonial blockade" Africa
was witnessing the birth of a "modern Islamic movement," one in

---

[6] Yossef Bodansky, *Bin Laden: the Man Who declared War on Americans*, Roseville,
California: Prima Publishing, 1999, p. 76.

which the Sudan would "continue to serve as an axis for the unity of the Muslim nation." He reminded his Islamist colleagues that "Africa had been known as a point of radiation of Islam," and a "refuge for Muslims at the beginning of Islam." It was, therefore, the duty, the responsibility of the African delegates to carry forward "the message of Islam in order to reform the unjust international order."[7] The meeting ended, the participants returned home, and during the following weeks there were reports of Islamist activity in Tanzania, Uganda, and Nigeria with support from Turabi's PAIC and the NIF government.

The United States and Sudan Sponsored Terrorism

The spread of Turabi's reputation and influence coincided with the continued support of the Sudan government for what the State Department called "state-sponsored terrorism."[8] There was an explosion of reports within the United States intelligence community about the activities of radical Islamist groups operating in and from the Sudan. Hasan al-Turabi had met in Teheran with members of the Lebanese Hizbollah and the Palestinian Hamas in order to open a Sudanese embassy in Muslim-held West Beirut where Sudanese security agents with diplomatic passports could supply "weapons and related equipment and information" to terrorists.[9] After a "systematic 180-day review" the State Department on 18 August 1993 added the Sudan to its list of countries that supported international terrorism for using "its territory as sanctuary for terrorists . . . [providing] safe houses and other facilities used to support radical groups." Operating from Khartoum there was the Popular Front for the Liberation of Palestine, the Democratic Front for the Liberation of

---

[7] "Islam, Democracy, the State and the West; Roundtable with Dr. Hassan Turabi," *Middle East Policy*, Volume 1, No. 3, 1992, pages 49–61. The quotes were attributed to Turabi during a private visit to the United States in May 1992; also see FBIS-NES-93-092, 14 May 93, page 6; Radio Omdurman in Arabic, 0430 GMT, 11 May 93, FBIS-NES-93-092, 14 May 1993.

[8] The International Security Assistance and Arms Export Control Act of 1976 and the Export Administration Act of 1979 prohibited foreign aid to countries that assisted international terrorism. In 1979 the U.S. Department of State created a "terrorism list" of countries participating in terrorism.

[9] "Egypt and Sudan Make Up," *Middle East International*, 9 July 1993, p. 12; "Mubarak and Bashir Meet," *The Washington Times*, 1 July 1993, p. A2.

Palestine, Hamas, Islamic Jihad, Hizbollah, the Algerian FIS, Tunisia's *Al-Nada, Al-Islah* from the Yemen, and Egypt's *Jama'at al-Islamiyah.* There were credible "reports of training in Sudan of militant extremists that commit acts of terrorism in neighboring countries." The Sudan was added to the State Department's list because it "failed to respond to repeated requests for information on suspected training sites, safe houses, and other terrorist activity." Such support was "directly related to the extension of the National Islamic Front (NIF) influence over the Government of Sudan." Neither Bashir nor Turabi could claim they had not been warned. In the State Department report, *Patterns of Global Terrorism,* 1991, published in April 1992, it noted that Turabi and NIF had intensified their domination of the Bashir government and had been the main advocate of closer relations with radical groups and their sponsors."[10]

In Khartoum the government made no effort to disguise its support for the revolutionary organizations on the United States terrorist list. In June 1993 Munir Said, who had opened the Hamas office in Khartoum, led a public march protesting the peace negotiations between the PLO and Israel. There was no end to human rights violations by the Bashir government and no tolerance of dissent, and since copies of the security services reports were sent directly to the NIF leadership, the marginalized ethnic minorities—the Nubians of the north, the Nuba of Kordofan, the Zaghawa of Darfur, and the Beja of the Red Sea Hills—had much to fear. Sudanese diplomats would not be expelled from the United States, but there would no longer be economic or military aid for Khartoum and no wheat deals as in the past. The United States used its considerable influence to block international bank loans for the Sudan, but it still supported humanitarian aid for the southern Sudanese. It provided funds for the United Nations Operation Lifeline Sudan that involved the Department of State in a "tricky double-track Sudan policy." On the one hand, the United States was attempting to discourage the regime's support for terrorism. On the other, the United States was trying "to reach the Sudanese people with a $70 million humanitarian

---

[10] "In Sudan's Beirut Embassy," Foreign Report, *The Economist,* London, 1 July 1993, p. 5. "Terrorists Helped by Sudan, U.S. Says," *The New York Times,* 19 August 1993; Yehudit Ronen, "Sudan and the United States: Is a Decade of Tension Winding Down?" *Middle East Policy,* Vol. 9, No. 1, March 2002, p. 96.

aid program" that required the good will of the NIF government, the sponsor of state terrorism.[11]

The Sudanese government vehemently denied the report on state sponsored terrorism by the Department of State and launched a barrage of venomous verbal assaults and orchestrated violent anti-American street demonstrations. The regime and its media repeatedly accused the United States of a conspiracy against Islam by placing Sudan on the list of state sponsored terrorism. Bashir denounced the charges of supporting terrorism as "baseless accusations," but the government did admit that members of Iran's Revolutionary Guards were training recruits in the five camps of the PDF. In Teheran, Muhammad al-Amin Khalifa, the speaker of the National Assembly, denounced the United States for accusing "independence-seeking nations of terrorism and fundamentalism."[12] Others reported that the Iranians were "well advanced in the process of transforming Sudan into their main operation base to export the Islamic Revolution northward to Egypt and other Arab countries of Africa."[13] Even World Bank officials knew that Iran was buying weapons from North Korea and China for the Sudan. By 1993 Iran was providing $850 million in arms, "$500 million as an outright gift, the rest as a loan."[14] In September 1993 there were more round table discussions between academics and diplomats at the State Department about the Sudan that resulted in mutual frustration produced more from a failure to communicate intelligence information than ideological differences. The following month, October, 1993, President Clinton personally admonished the new Sudanese ambassador, Ahmad Suleiman, when presenting his credentials that the United States was deeply concerned about Sudan's human rights violations and its support of terrorist organizations. The Sudan was forced to close its consular section at the United Nations in New York "which had been operating without proper sanction in the USA."[15]

---

[11] "Evidence of Sudan's Support for Terrorism," U.S. Information Agency Cable 41279, 20 August 1993; "Terrorists Sudan," *The Washington Post*, 20 august 1993.

[12] "Islam Main Factor Behind Iran-Sudan Friendship-President," IRAN, Tehran; "Sudanese Speaker on U.S. Animosity Towards His Country"; "Qods Belongs to Islamic Ummah Says Sudanese Speaker," IRNA, Tehran, 14 November 1993.

[13] "Elite Iran Unit Said To Control Sudan's Security," *The Washington Times*, 28 August 1993, p. A7.

[14] *Africa Report*, September/October 1993, p. 25; *Jane's Defence Weekly*, 3 July 1996.

[15] *Sudan Democratic Gazette*, November 1993, p. 10; *The Washington Times*, 12 October 1993, p. A12.

In its annual review on human rights published in 1994 the State Department was more convinced than ever that NIF and Hasan al-Turabi "effectively controlled the Government . . . [and had] further tightened its grip on the state . . . [by placing its supporters in the most] key positions in the Government, security forces, judiciary, academia, and media."[16] Turabi had never denied his close ties with Iran and radical Arab groups to promote Pan-Islam and his condemnation of the morals and mores of the West. He became increasingly contemptuous of those Arab rulers whose secular ideas and actions were "judged too close to the West and too far from God." When Siraj Yussif and Ahmad Muhammad, the two officials from the Sudanese mission at the United Nations implicated in planning bomb attacks in New York, Turabi had "personally informed Sudan's U.N. ambassador that even though the two had diplomatic cover, they were in fact intelligence operatives."[17] In August federal agents believed that "Sudan's Islamic government was involved in the thwarted plot to bomb the UN and FBI buildings."[18] Turabi later dismissed these allegations of state sponsored terrorism. Americans were "very ignorant [and] know little about the world" to equate Islamic fundamentalism with terrorism.[19] Even former President Jimmy Carter was skeptical about the charges against the Sudan, accusations that inspired him to launch a one-man effort to achieve peace in the Sudan from his Carter Center in Atlanta. Knowing the Carter initiative would come to nothing, the Sudanese embassy in Washington welcomed his initiative for the purpose of its own propaganda value.[20]

---

[16] *Sudan Human Rights Practices, 1993*, Washington D.C., Department of State, 31 January 1994.

[17] "Iran, Abu Nidal, and Hamas," *Foreign Report, Economist Newspaper Ltd.*, 10 June 1993; *San Francisco Chronicle*, 19 July 1993, p. A11; *Sudan Update*, 8 October 1993, p. 3.

[18] Todd Shields and R.Z. Chesnoff, "Maestros of mayhem: Sudan's colonels and clerics wage war on their own people and the West," *U.S. News & World Report*, 30 August 1993; "Sudan Suspected," *The Washington Times*, 17 August 1993, p. A3. The State Department and FBI refused to comment on these disclosures.

[19] "Sudan Denies Backing Terrorists," *The Washington Times* and "Terrorists Helped by Sudan, U.S. Says," *The New York Times*, 19 August 1993; The Turabi quotes are from an interview published in *Haberler* (Turkish Press Review), 15 August 1995.

[20] *Sudanews*, Washington D.C.: Embassy of the Republic of the Sudan, 16 and 30 September 1993, p. 1. Many Sudanese who had attended a conference in communications held at Howard University, Washington D.C. in May 1989 were supporters of NIF, including Ali al-Haj Muhammad. After the Gulf War the Sudan retained a Washington D.C. public relations firm to give the country a new image

Hasan al-Turabi and the Second Popular Arab and Islamic Congress

The second PAIC General Assembly was held 2–4 December 1993 in Khartoum that Hasan al-Turabi now envisaged as the center if not the headquarters of the new Islamic world. Five hundred delegates swarmed into the capital, and Turabi had personally invited an all-star cast of Islamists that included Ayatollah Mahdi Karrubi, head of the Society of Combatant Clergy, from Teheran and Husayn Fadlallah of the Lebanese branch of Hezbollah. Gulbaddin Hekmatyar represented the Afghan Islamists. Rashid al-Ghannushi, the Tunisian Islamist leader, and from Algeria Abdallah Jaballah and Rabih Kabir of the FIS were in attendance. Omar Abd al-Rahman came from Egypt amidst a swarm of lesser-known Islamists including Yasser al-Masri and Abu Qatadah who later were to face terrorism charges in Great Britain. Under his skillful management Turabi was enthusiastically elected secretary-general of the congress and using his office promptly organ-ized the election of an international council of shaykhs that included one of the most active members of the PAIC General Assembly, Osama bin Laden.

The issues discussed and debated at the congress were numerous: the "New World Order" precipitated by the demise of the Soviet Union; the role that the congress could play in promoting Islamic hegemony in the Muslim world; the challenge from the repression of Muslim minorities in Europe and the United States; the Western challenge to Islam. As during the first PAIC General Assembly in 1991 the media was strictly regulated, and the only television coverage to reach the West was provided by the Canadian Broadcasting Company that included rather staged chants of "down with the USA" in English and "death to the Jews" in Arabic.[21]

During the congress the prominent Russian Islamist, Geidar Jemal, took the opportunity to discuss with Hasan al-Turabi the problems of Muslims in Russia. Turabi was sympathetic, and he denounced the "traitorous policies" of the Russian Foreign Minister Andrei Kozyrei that had produced a "huge tragedy for the Islamic world"

---

by the embassy publishing *Sudanews*, a weekly newsletter to confront the enemies of the revolutionary government in America.

[21] Mira L. Boland, "Sheikh Gilani's American Disciples," *The Weekly Standard*, Washington D.C., Vol. 7, Issuse 26, 10 March 2002.

and had helped to deprive Russia of its superpower status. Turabi proposed an Islamic committee for Russia with Jemal as chairman that would serve as "an organ representing the religio-political will" of Russian Muslims.[22] Another influential Islamist to attend the second PAIC General Assembly was the former Pakistan commander-in-chief (1988–1991), General Mirza Aslam Beg, who read a paper on the "Dynamics of Global Conflict and the Ummah's Response." He was accompanied by Lieutenant General Hamid Gul, the former director of the ISI. Gul had strongly opposed American intervention in the Gulf War and had ignored the profitable Pakistan narcotics trade that financed covert operations for the emerging Taliban in Afghanistan and Islamists against India in Kashmir. General Beg was an honored guest in Khartoum, for he had a long relationship with Osama bin Laden and had political ambitions of his own.[23] His appearance at the congress confirmed the support by the ISI for the Islamist Taliban in Afghanistan, the mujahideen in Kashmir, and the *Markaz-Dawat-al-Arshad*, a Pakistani charitable front organization that boasted of its connections with international Islamic terrorism. Not surprisingly, the "conference discussed Pakistan's role in the Armed Islamic Movement and international terrorism,"[24]

At its conclusion Turabi would confidently declare that "objectively, the future is ours."[25] After all, the RCC had been effectively dissolved in October, and its executive authority was now dominated by civilian cabinet members who were all Turabi supporters. Legislative powers had been given to the TNA that Turabi controlled. By 1994 the influence of the PAIC General Assembly permeated every political and social development in the Sudan and as far distant as Burma, the Philippines, and Tajikistan.[26] In Burma it supported the Rohingya, indigenous Muslims, and their Arakan Liberation Front. In the

---

[22] "The Taliban is our Ally," (translated from the Russian), *Novy Peterburg*, No. 55, 13 December 2001.

[23] Paul W. Rasche, "The Politics of Three: Pakistant, Saudi Arabia, Israel," *Sudien von Zeitfragen* on-line service, August 2001.

[24] Subhash Kapita, "International Terrorism: The Pakistan Connection," Institute of Peace and Conflict, New Delhi, No. 602, October 2001.

[25] "Dudaev Calls for Islamic Alliance Against West," Radio Free Europe/Radio Liberty Research Institute Daily Report, Washington D.C., No. 226, 26 November 1993.

[26] John Hunwick, "Africa and Islamic Revival: Historical and Contemporary Perspectives," unpublished lecture (private distribution) at James Madison University, Virginia, 25 March 1996.

southern Philippine islands it promoted the radical Abu Sayyaf led by Muhammad Jamal Khalifa, a member of Al Qaeda and a brother-in-law to Osama bin Laden. He was the link to Malaysia and southern Thailand to reactivate the Pattani United Liberation Organization after a decade of its inactivity. The Abu Sayyaf also supported the nascent Islamic Defenders Front in Indonesia and financed the Yemeni Shaykh Muqbil Bin Hadi in the Molluccas of Indonesia. Al Qaeda maintained a guesthouse and had investments in Tadjikistan, and after the outbreak of civil war in May 1992, it operated along the Afghanistan-Tajikistan frontier. By 1994 the PAIC General Assembly was directly participating in most of the evolving Islamist movements from the Atlantic to the Pacific.

Embolden by this international support at the PAIC General Assembly Turabi and the Islamists were prepared to challenge the older and more formal OIC and other traditional Muslim institutions for the soul of Islam. At the sixth Student Union Conference at the University of Khartoum Turabi urged Muslim youths throughout the world "to take up the challenge of uniting the Islamic countries [that] could never be achieved without *jihad*. . . . the Islamic era will prevail, where truth defeats falsehood and all Moslems live in a united Islamic Nation."[27]

Sudanese Islamists Beyond the Sudan

When Muhammad al-Amin Khalifa, the speaker of the newly constituted TNA, met in November 1993 with Hojatoleslam Ali Akbar Natiq Nouri, the former reactionary minister of interior, leading member of the Iran Islamic Republic, and perhaps a successor to Prime Minister Rafsanjani, the "Balkans Problem" was discussed. Khalifa was angry about the "massacre of Muslims in Bosnia," Western hostility to Islamists, and that international "forums are killing time in order to destroy Islam in Europe and the whole world." He particularly criticized the Balkan policy of the United States that should accept "the presence of Iranian forces in Bosnia."[28]

---

[27] Nhial Bol, "Sudan Religion: Drawing the Line Between Islam and Ethnicity," IPS, Khartoum, 3 April 1995; *New Horizon*, Khartoum, 9 June 1994, p. 1.

[28] "Nateq-Nour Confers With Sudanese Counterpart," IRNA, Tehran, 13 November 1993; "Iran Sticking to Islamic Cause—Speaker Ali Akbar Nateq-Nouri," IRNA,

During that same autumn of 1993 the NIF government received arms from Iran and Afghanistan. On 22 August 1993, four days after the Department of State added Sudan to its list of state sponsored terrorism, a Boeing 707 cargo plane arrived with arms from Afghanistan followed by four other flights in September.[29] The NIF government was desperate to acquire arms from anyone, for it was "left with no choice but to opt for a military solution for the problem of the southern Sudan."[30] The weapons were flown from Kabul, and it was ironic that the pilot's name was Osama, an uncommon surname, that reminded those in Khartoum of Osama bin Laden who had been supporting the Afghan-Arab mujadiheen since the Soviet invasion in December 1979.

The arms shipments from Kabul were approved by Dr. Mustafa Osman Ismail, a strong supporter of NIF, a disciple of Hasan al-Turabi, and the secretary-general of the Council for International People's Friendship (CIPF). Ismail was ambitious but diplomatic rather than a clandestine conspirator. He had been appointed secretary-general through his close friendship with the chairman of the political committee of the RCC, Brigadier Osman Ahmad Hassan Osman. Osman had previously supported Ismail's nomination as secretary-general of the Islamic Association of Student Organizations where he proved to be a ruthless administrator that brought control over that fractious student society. He had a background in manipulating the media which he used to defend the 30 June 1989 revolution with inspired enthusiasm. The CIPF had been created in 1980 by President Jaafar Numayri to promote friendship with other nations by fostering political and cultural ties with the Muslim world. It was a benevolent and innocuous agency of no importance in the Sudan or among the Islamic nations. After the revolution, however, the CIPF became a place where Islamists could discuss their future, conspire, and plot while conducting dialogues in an ecumenical meeting house about the Quran, Shar'ia, and the philosophy of revolution. The council soon evolved as a friendly face to the Islamic world and

---

Tehran, 14 November 1993; see also "Lifting of Arms Embargo on Bosnian Muslims Called For," IRNA, Tehran, 19 March 1994.

[29] "Kabul is Khartoum's latest Arms Supplier," *Sudan Democratic Gazette*, London, October 1993, p. 6; the information was apparently supplied by Osman al-Mirghani and first published in *Al-Sharq al-Awsat*, London.

[30] *Sudan Update*, 8 October 1993, p. 1.

the Siamese twin of the PAIC General Assembly, both dedicated to the Islamist movement led by Hasan al-Turabi. The CIPF was the host for numerous bi-national organizations such as the Sudan-Iraq, Sudan-Qatar, and Sudan-Libya friendship societies and the first Conference on Inter-Faith Religious Dialogue in April 1993. Unlike the more aloof Turabi, Dr. Mustafa Osman Ismail was the government's greeter and stage director for the flood of Islamic visitors to Khartoum.

The CIFP was, of course, overshadowed by the PAIC General Assembly with its theological and political issues, while Dr. Mustafa devoted his time to meeting the many delegations arriving in Khartoum and holding "lengthy discussions" to "potential investors from various parts of the world" what "the Sudan offers to them for secure, viable, and profitable investment conditions."[31] He was young, affable, and a rising star in NIF. After the attack on Turabi in Canada in 1992, Mustafa managed the affairs of PAIC until Turabi regained his health. In 1991 the CIPF had sponsored the Multaqa Sudan Global Peace Conference which the Khartoum media proudly declared was the first major interfaith conference held in Africa. It provided a forum for meeting and discussion by Islamists from Chad, Ethiopia, Lebanon, Iran, Jordan, Syria, Zaire, and Bosnia. Unlike the PAIC General Assembly, the CIPF seemed harmless and open in its activities and consequently became a more transparent front for Islamists to extend "brotherly financial aid to the Mujahideen of Afghanistan, the Bosnia Muslims, Somalia [and others] facing difficulties."[32] Increasingly, the friendship council became politically involved and through its international contacts supported Islamists in Eritrea, Kenya, and Shaykh Abd al-Majid al-Zandani's efforts to open the Al-Imam Islamic University in Sanaa, Yemen, in 1995, a location from which the "Gulf Battalion" of Osama bin Laden operated.[33]

---

[31] Adil Bayoumi, "Strengthening Sudan's Foreign Relations," *New Horizon*, Khartoum, 6 July 1994, p. 4.
[32] "CIPF Investment Contacts," *New Horizon*, Khartoum, 29 November 1994.
[33] FBIS-NES-95–092, Washington D.C., 29 November 1994.

The Bosnia Connection

Mustafa Osman Ismail was also used as an intermediary in the
Afghanistan arms shipments to avoid any connection with Hasan al-
Turabi and his PAIC, for these arms were not destined for the Sudan
army but to the Muslims in Bosnia. Upon the dissolution of Yugoslavia
in 1991 the ancient animosities between Muslims and Christians in
the Balkans revived with all the implacable hostility of religious war.
When the Clinton administration refused to lift its embargo on arms
to Muslims in Bosnia and ignored the peace proposals of former
Secretary of State Cyrus Vance and David Owen of Britain, the
Muslims of Bosnia frantically searched for weapons to protect themselves between the Serbian hammer and the Croatian anvil. They
were not disappointed. Support for the Bosnian Muslims appears to
have begun at Tehran in February 1993 after Russia announced it
would provide $360 million in weapons to "Serbia and Serbia-con-
trolled areas of Bosnia and Croatia."[34] Russian weapons for the Serbs
were far superior to those being shipped through Croatia to Bosnia.

In April 1993 Muslim volunteers including Afghan-Arabs began
to appear in Bosnia. Iran began to coordinate support for Bosnian
Muslims, and in May the first ambassador from the Muslim government of Bosnia-Herzegovina presented his credentials in Tehran
to the dismay of the OIC led by Saudi Arabia that did not want
to see Shiite Iran dominate Sunni Muslims in Bosnia.[35] In July 1993
sixteen representatives from Muslim states met at the OIC conclave
held at Islamabad. It urged the United Nations to lift the arms
embargo to Bosnia and offered an Islamic peacekeeping force that
included 10,000 soldiers from Iran, a proposal that was politely
declined by the UN. Frustrated members of the conference, notably
from Brunei and Saudi Arabi, began to provide funds to support
Muslim aid agencies in former Yugoslavia, and although the Sudan
did not attend the conference, Sudanese airports became the principal transit port to Bosnia for mujahideen and arms from Iran,

---

[34] "Tough Choices Face U.S.," *The Christian Science Monitor*, 3 February 1993,
p. 1; "Bosnia Peace Plan," *Newsday*, New York, 11 February 1993; "Clinton Wary
of Peace Plan," *The Dallas Morning News*, 6 February 1993; "1st U.S. Airdrop," *The
Chicago Tribune*, 1 March 1993, p. 3.
[35] "Velayati: OIC Plan," IRNA, Zagreb, 14 July 1993.

Pakistan, and Afghanistan. In June 1993 "a large quantity of arms" for Bosnian Muslims disguised as humanitarian aid was shipped from the Sudan through Maribor, the airport in Slovenia, after Igor Umek, the Slovenian minister for transportation and communication, had signed three agreements in Tehran for sea and air links between the two republics.[36]

The Austrians had also been prepared to support the Bosnia Muslims and in an unexpected, if not bizarre, maneuver invited President Museveni of Uganda and from the Sudan President Bashir and Mahdi Ibrahim, NIF leader and head of the political department of the foreign ministry, to Vienna ostensibly to revive the moribund IGAD initiative. In Austria Bashir had the opportunity to meet with members of its substantial Sudanese community among whom was Al-Fatih Ali Hassanein who had been a student in Yugoslavia in the 1970s.[37] Al-Fatih had maintained contact with Turabi, Bin Laden, and Shaykh Omar Abd al-Rahman, and in 1987 he had founded The Third World Relief Agency (TWRA). Organized as an humanitarian organization in Austria, it transferred weapons through the Sudan to Croatia and the Balkans. The TWRA had prospered from the arms trade to become a powerful financial institution. Al-Fatih opened offices in Bosnia, Turkey, and Russia and became the principal financier of the Sarajevo government. He opened accounts in Liechtenstein and Monaco to launder $80 million dollars remitted in 1992 to the First Austrian Bank and another $231 million in 1993 from Saudi Arabia, Iran, Sudan, Pakistan, Brunei, Malaysia, and Turkey.[38] The funds were used to purchase weapons for Bosnian Muslims and make payments to those who moved them to the Bosnian mujahideen. "With the knowledge of the Austrian government" Al-Fatih had employed Viennese banks to "cover the expenses of the international tours of the Bosnian Moslem politicians and their propaganda campaigns."[39] When the activities of Al-Fatih became well-known to the intelligence community in Europe, his office was searched by the Austrian police. He was forced to surrender his

---

[36] Goran Bradic, "Muslim Humanitarian Organization Delivered Arms to Bosnia-Herzegovina," TANJUG, Belgrade, Zagreb, 14 June 1993.

[37] "New Peace Bid," *New Horizon*, Khartoum, 2 June 1994.

[38] Alexandre del Valle, "La Bosnie: un Etat islamiste pro-american en plein coeur du monde orthodoxe," www. geo-islam.org, Paris, 4 May 2000.

[39] *Wirtschafts Woche*, 1995; *Serbia Today*, Part IV, Belgrade, 2 April 1996.

Sudanese diplomatic passport in 1993 and soon left Vienna for Istanbul.[40]

Given the secrecy that surrounded the support for the Bosnian Muslims, it is difficult to know the extent of the commitment by the PAIC and CIPF. Nevertheless, Turabi and other Islamist leaders approved of the Bosnian operation in a *fatwa* issued at a PAIC-sponsored conference at El Obeid in Kordofan province in April 1993. The *fatwa* was a "precedent-setting text for legislating relations between Muslims and non-Muslims in areas where the infidels" would not accept subjugation "by the Muslim forces."[41] Although its formula justified the jihad against the SPLA in the southern Sudan, it was subsequently cited to give legitimacy to Sudanese support for the Muslims in Bosnia and other Islamist revolutionary movements from Algeria to the Philippines.

By 1993 veterans of the Afghan wars and volunteers from the Sudan and other Muslim states had been absorbed into the Bosnian army. They had entered Bosnian as humanitarian relief workers under the auspices of the United Nations and were often financed by Osama bin Laden. He admitted to the journalist Robert Fisk, however, that the number of mujahideen who had reached Bosnia were few because "the situation there does not provide the same opportunities as Afghanistan." The Croats had made it difficult for the Muslim mujahideen to reach Bosnia, but those who did were being "armed and equipped by friendly nations such as Iran, Sudan, and Malaysia."[42] By spring 1993 a significant body of Afghan-Arabs had congregated near Travnik where they formed a "Mujahideen Battalion" that operated throughout the Zenica district of Bosnia and reportedly had close ties to the Saudi Muwafaq Foundation in the Sudan.

---

[40] "On the Terrorist Centres in Bosnia," *Serbia Bulletin* (Tanjug, Tel Aviv) October 1996; www. Yugoslavia.com.

[41] Yossef Bodansky, *Offensive in the Balkans*, Alexandria, VA.: International Strategic Studies Association, 1995.

[42] Robert Fisk, "Anti-Soviet warrior puts his army on the road to peace," *The Independent*, London, 3 and 6 May 1993; "The Prosecution's Evidentiary Proffer Submitted in Advance of the Trial of Defendant Accused of Using A Religious Charity to Raise Funds for Usama bin Laden and al-Qaeda," United States District Court, Northern District of Illinois, Eastern Division ("United States of America v. Enaam Arnout"), February 2003, p. 24; see also Christopher Long, "Balkans Reporting," http://www.christopherlong.co.uk/rad.musrea.html.

During these years, 1993 and 1994, it is difficult to ascertain the interest of Osama bin Laden in the Sudan or if his activities in support of Islamic movements were compatible with those of Turabi and NIF. For most Sudanese who knew of him Bin Laden was as much an enigma as his inaccessibility. The Khartoum press reports concerning the assault by an outlawed Muslim sect on his home in the Khartoum suburb of Riyadh in February 1994 were perfunctory and without explanation. His rare public appearances were occasions expected by the chairman of the board of his Al-Hijra Company. When he signed a contract to begin the second phase of the $29 million "Challenge Road" between Shendi and Atbara, the simple ceremony featured only the Sudanese minister of transport and Brigadier Abd al-Rahim Muhammad Hussein who preferred anonymity. The former director of military intelligence in IS-SOR, Abd al-Rahim was now in 1993 minister of the interior, confidant of Bashir, and the most dependable ally of NIF in the military.[43] Reportedly, Al Qaeda worked directly with Hussein to obtain communications equipment of sophisticated radios and satellite cell phones sought by Bin Laden to enhance the Al Qaeda communications network. Another Afghan-Arab, former Saudi businessman, and close associate of Bin Laden, Khalid al-Fawwaz, moved from London to Khartoum in 1994 where he founded the Advice and Reform Committee. The committee was to coordinate communications and provide documentation and facilities for Al Qaeda members moving through Europe. Tuarabi, who from his youth had been absorbed with the dissemination of propaganda, must have been apprised of this expanding web for Islamist communications.

If the Sudanese were secretly involved in Bosnia, they were transparently enmeshed in their convoluted relationships with Eritrea. In October 1993 President Isayas Afewerki denounced the NIF government for "exploiting Eritrean refugees in Sudan by forcibly recruiting and militarily training them in an attempt to destabilize Eritrea."[44] Despite the usual appeals of friendship a succession of governments in Khartoum had supported the Eritrean Muslims, in and out of Eritrea, with money and weapons for thirty years. In April 1965 the

---

[43] "The Challenge Road's Second Phase Starts," *New Horizon*, Khartoum, 13 July 1994.

[44] *Sudan Democratic Gazette*, November 1993, p. 10.

ICF under the leadership of Hasan al-Turabi had been "accused of being involved in the smuggling of arms" to the Eritrean Liberation Front (ELF).[45] A quarter of a century later Isayas Afewerki had to confront his successors in the RCC because his arch rivals, the ELF were seeking to divide Eritrea in two, the Arab Muslim dominated lowlands bordering on the Sudan "and the [Christian] highlands bordering the Ethiopian province of Tigre."[46] The NIF government was incensed when Eritrea recognized Israel, and President Afewerki was flown to Sheba Hospital in Israel for treatment of malaria.[47] In May 1993 the Sudan retaliated. The RCC provided generous funds for the Eritrean Islamic Jihad (EIJ), a new revolutionary movement very active among Eritrean refugee camps in the Sudan whose leadership worked assiduously to overthrow Afewerki.[48] Khartoum continued to support the political aims of the Eritrean Liberation Front-Revolutionary Council (ELF-RC), but its exploits were so egregious that even Eritreans opposed to Afewerki protested that NIF should cease to interfere in the internal affairs of Eritrea. This was not to be.

In December 1993 the EIJ initiated well-planned assaults "from base camps in the Sudan" shortly after the close of the second PAIC General Assembly in Khartoum at which Muslims from Eritrea had a substantial delegation.[49] The Sudan was forcibly recruiting Eritrean refugees and training them in the camps of the PDF and planting antipersonnel mines along the heavily traveled roads that crossed the frontier into Eritrea. Eritrea lodged a formal complaint with the United Nations Security Council after its security forces had killed twenty assailants of the EIJ that included some Afghan-Arab "mercenaries."[50] Hasan al-Turabi at a conference in Madrid exclaimed. "There is not a single non-Sudanese training anywhere in the Sudan."

---

[45] M.O. Beshir, *The Southern Sudan: From Conflict to Peace*, Khartoum: the Khartoum Bookshop, 1975, p. 29.

[46] "Sudan's Eritrean Diplomacy," *Foreign Report*, 1975, p. 29.

[47] "Eritrea's New Friend-Israel," *Israel Foreign Affairs*, 5 February 1993, p. 5.

[48] "Eritrea, Example of Judeo-Christian Plot Against Muslims; Eritrean Islamic Jihad Movement Confronts Plot to Eradicate Arab Islamic Identity in Eritrea," *Al-Ribat*, Jordan, FBIS-AFR-93–147, "East Africa," 3 August 1993, pp. 3–5.

[49] *Eritrean Human Rights Practices, 1994*, Washington D.C.: U.S. Department of State, 1994.

[50] "Radicals Gain Strength in Horn of Africa," *The Washington Post*, 5 January 1994, p. A26.

Isayas Afewerki remained unconvinced.[51] The Eritrean foreign ministry denounced the NIF government which, "from its political bases in Sudan," created the EIJ in 1989 and then "continued to support this group until and after the independence of Eritrea."[52] In April, however, Eritrea sent a delegation to Khartoum. There were four months of negotiations, rhetoric, and an agreement for mutual non-interference in the internal affairs of their countries that was more paper than substance. On the first anniversary of the founding of Eritrea President Afewerki announced that all young men must give eighteen months of military service to defend the nation from the incursions and attacks by Sudan on the Eritrean border.

The Sudan, Yemen, and Egypt

In May 1994 a simmering dispute erupted into civil war between the Yemen Socialist Party (YSP) of Aden and the government of Yemen dominated by northern Yemenis in Sanaa. Led by Ali Salim al-Baidh in southern Yemen, the YSP rejected the unequal distribution of political power that favored Sanaa in the north over Aden in the south. The governments of the Arab world soon took sides in the conflict. The YSP charged that Islah Party Islamist functionaries from the north had traveled to Iraq in search of arms. When the southern Yemeni rebels declared their secession, Hasan al-Turabi and Osama bin Laden supported the government in Sanaa and their fellow Islamists in the Yemen Islah Party. In April 1994 Turabi made a "secret visit" to Sanaa where he offered his assistance to Abdallah al-Ahmar, speaker of the Yemen Parliament and head of the Islamist Islah Party. Afterward, when hundreds of "volunteers" departed from Port Sudan for camps in Yemen, the YSP claimed that Turabi had given his personal approval for the northern offensive against their forces.[53] Although the Sudan foreign ministry denied that any Sudanese troops were in the Yemen, the southern

---

[51] "Islamic Fundamentalism in the Sunni and Shia Worlds by Dr. Hassan al-Turabi," Occasional Paper, The Sudan Foundation, London, 1998.
[52] "Foreign Ministry Reviews Talks with Sudan," FBIS, Africa, 26 April 1994, p. 6.
[53] "Yemeni rivals lobby for Arab backing," Mideast Mirror, Vol. 8, No. 89, 11 May 1994.

rebels charged that the Sudan had armed "fundamentalist volunteers" and placed its airfields at the disposal of Sanaa.[54]

Shortly after the outbreak of hostilities in May 1994 Osama bin Laden was seen in Sanaa. This was no surprise, for he had family ties in Yemen and had personally been involved in Yemen affairs since the early 1980s when he provided money and arms to support the destruction of the Communist leadership of South Yemen. Despite his enduring relationship with Prince Turki bin Faisal and Prince Salman bin Abdel Aziz, the powerful governor of Riyadh, the intervention of Bin Laden in the Yemen civil war could not be tolerated by Saudi Arabia. He was declared *persona non grata*, an enemy of the state, and his passport publicly revoked. As hostilities intensified, President Ali Abdallah Saleh in Sanaa complained that Egypt, Syria, and Saudi Arabia were providing material assistance to South Yemen. As an immediate neighbor Saudi Arabia preferred a divided and consequently weakened Yemen to a strong central government on its southern flank. Its government feared the presence of an Islamist and revolutionary government at Sanaa. In Saudi Arabia itself the government had expressed concern about the Committee for the Defense of Legitimate Rights (CDLR), an Islamist movement founded in Riyadh on 3 May 1993 and officially banned a week later. Led by prominent Saudi intellectuals who were critical of the legitimacy of Saudi rule, its leader, Muhammad al-Massari, was soon in prison. Six months later Massari made his escape through Yemen, a CDLR safe-haven, and traveled to London where he opened a CDLR office in April 1994. In London Massari worked closely with Khalid al-Fawwaz who had returned from Khartoum to London where he opened an office for the Advice and Reform Movement. Massari's CDLR and Bin Laden's Advice and Reform Movement would henceforth remain critics and a considerable annoyance to the Saudi government by sending polemics to thousands of Islamist allies through their intricate communications networks.

In the Sudan most of the Afghan-Arab leadership had found a home from which to travel individually or in small groups to Bosnia, the Philippines, or to return quietly to Egypt to infiltrate the legiti-

---

[54] Radio Omdurman, in Arabic, 10 May 1994; Reuters, "Sanaa Says Egypt, Syria, Sudan Support Yemen Unity," 3 June 1994; "The Arab/Islamic World," *Mideast Mirror*, Vol. 08, No. 89, 11 May 1994 from *Al-Sharq Al Awsat*.

mate political parties and the porous student and faculty organizations in the universities. Mubarak sought to check the spread of the
Egyptian Afghan-Arabs by urging them to abandon terrorism and
join or form a legal political party, but parties based "on religious
grounds" would not be tolerated "since all religions will then demand
that they have their own parties."[55] His overtures were studiously
ignored, but in the Sudan Hasan al-Turabi with the encouragement
of the RCC publicly urged the Egyptian government to "send an
official delegation to visit every part of the country [Sudan], inspect
every inch of it, and talk to anyone it wants to talk to."[56] Egypt and
the Sudan were "the heart of the Arab world in terms of size and
position." The NIF had never supported terrorism against neighboring states, and the alliance between Egypt and the Sudan was a
"necessary foundation for the achievement of Arab unity and the
establishment of the Islamic edifice on it." He would be willing to
meet with Mubarak so long as "it did not cause any sensitivity or
embarrassment to the official quarters."[57] President Hosni Mubarak
remained aloof from Turabi's invitation, but no matter how much
he distrusted him and despised Omar Hassan Ahmad al-Bashir, he
could not ignore the Sudan at the confluence of the Blue and White
Niles. The NIF government in Khartoum was despicable to Cairo,
perhaps a momentary irritant, but the long term interests of Egypt
were its strategic concerns over the Nile waters in Ethiopia and
Uganda.

---

[55] *Al-Bilad*, Amman, 22 June 1994.
[56] "Sudan-Al-Turabi Willing To Open Dialogue With Egypt," *Al-Quds al-Arabi*,
in Arabic, London, 20 July 1994.
[57] "Dialogue With Egypt," *Al-Quds al-Arabi* in Arabic, London. 20 July 1994.

CHAPTER SEVEN

THE FRENCH CONNECTION

While most of the Western world began to ostracize the NIF government in Khartoum for its flagrant violations of human rights and growing involvement with international terrorism, France was the exception. After the 30 June Revolution the French had been very solicitous of the RCC in a spirit of accommodation. During the domination of Britain in the Anglo-Egyptian Sudan in the first half of the twentieth century the French government, its intellectuals, and commercial community had little presence in the Sudan. After their humiliation at Fashoda in 1898 by the Anglo-Egyptian army of General Horatio Herbert Kitchener, they could hardly expect the British to welcome them back to Khartoum. Their relationship with the Sudanese from a somnolent embassy in Khartoum was confined to the western frontier province of Darfur whose inhabitants, Fur, Zaghawa, Baggara, had close ties to kinsmen in Chad and French Equatorial Africa.[1] When Sudan achieved independence in 1956, France was preoccupied with the rebellion in Algeria, and it was not until the 1970s and the relatively tranquil era after Algerian independence that France began to cultivate cultural and commercial exchanges with Khartoum.

The French Total Oil Company received a concession for oil exploration in the southern Sudan, and the French construction conglomerate, Compagnie de Constructions Internationales (CCI), began the excavation of the Jonglei Canal in 1978. The Jonglei Canal was to be the longest navigable canal in the world, 224 miles (360 kilometers) to bring down the fresh waters of the great equatorial lakes to the Sudan and Egypt without the massive losses in the Sudd, the great swamps of the Upper Nile. There had been much opposition to the construction of the canal by the Nilotes of the southern Sudan.

---

[1] See J. Millard Burr and Robert O. Collins, *Africa's Thirty Years' War: Chad, Libya, and the Sudan, 1963–1993*, Boulder: Westview Press, 1999.

Dr. John Garang de Mabior, the leader of the SPLA, had written his doctoral dissertation at Iowa State University condemning the Jonglei Canal, and on Friday, 10 February 1984, the SPLA destroyed the French base camp at the Sobat ending the excavation at mile 166 (267 kilometers). Total immediately suspended its oil explorations in the southern Sudan. The attack on Sobat Camp earned the bitter enmity of the French for the SPLA and a decade later French antagonism for the SPLA had turned to mutual hostility. The SPLA simply did not trust the French or their commercial and diplomatic representatives. Garang was especially suspicious of Turabi's intellectual and personal relationships in France, and his agents often visited London, Berlin, and Washington but not Paris. Offices of the SPLA were opened in England, Italy, Germany, Canada, Sweden, the United States, and in various African nations, but the SPLA would not send emissaries to France or open an office.

After the withdrawal of the French from the Jonglei Canal and prospective oil fields France displayed little interest in the Sudan even after the restoration of civilian government under Sadiq al-Mahdi in 1986. The European Community (EC) and a consortium of European nations continued to provide millions of dollars and thousands of tons of food to alleviate famine produced by drought and war in the Sudan, but the embassy of France performed only a very minor role in the relief efforts. The famine of 1988 was particularly devastating. Tens of thousands of southern Sudanese starved to death, and during the crisis the French embassy remained silent when its fellow members of the EC office in Khartoum openly criticized Sadiq al-Mahdi's unconscionable indifference to the famine rapidly spreading throughout the southern Sudan.[2] The British Foreign Minister Geoffrey Howe arrived in Khartoum to express his government's concern about famine conditions in the Sudan, and the EC implored Sadiq al-Mahdi to permit food flights to the South. In the meantime, the French were holding "secret" talks in Addis Ababa with representatives of the SPLA to inform them that France would use the United Nations to denounce the rebel movement if Garang

---

[2] Ironically, while the French Embassy was quiescent, heroic efforts were undertaken by the French non-governmental humanitarian organizations, Médicins Sans Frontières (MSF) and Action International Contre la Faim.

did not begin to work for peace.[3] During these discussions the SPLA regarded the French "lectures" as paternalistic and demeaning, but they agreed not to interfere with French commercial activity which at the time was confined to a monopoly of Iranex dominated by NIF capitalists that purchased and marketed gum Arabic from Kordofan and Darfur where the SPLA had no presence.[4]

Shortly before the coup d'état in 1989 a delegation from the French Geological and Mineral Research Bureau arrived in Khartoum to negotiate with Beshir Omer, minister of sudan energy and mines, for a joint venture to mine gold and other minerals in the Ariab region of the Eastern Sudan. Preliminary studies had indicated that there was a recoverable potential of perhaps as much as 24 tons of gold.[5] The French ambassador and chargé d'affaires continued to work quietly in support of this proposal after the change of government, meeting with the senior members of the RCC.[6] They were successful. By 1991 the Ariab Mining Company Limited had been granted a concession whose ownership was divided 60–40 between the government and French investors and had already extracted a half-ton of gold, exceeding all expectations. The following year the Ariab mine increased its production to 1.3 tons, 3 tons in 1994, 4 tons in 1995, and 5.7 tons in 1998.

When the Islamists in the RCC began to remake the Sudan's educational system, they focused their efforts for reform on the University of Khartoum by eliminating English as a language of instruction. Throughout Arab Africa France had consistently promoted the French language in local secondary schools and realized that the reduction of English language instruction in the Sudan provided a unique opportunity to introduce courses in French language and culture in Sudanese secondary schools. The French Cultural Center in Khartoum, a dilapidated outpost of their cultural empire in Africa, was remodeled, and in December 1989 a French representative for Technical and Educational Cooperation from the foreign ministry discussed with Mahgoub al-Badawi, minister for education, efforts to promote

---

[3] "Sudan: Prospects for Peace," *Africa Confidential*, 16 December 1988, p. 3.
[4] Statement to Millard Burr by SPLA official, 1990, and later confirmed by NDA and SPLA representatives at a meeting held at a private home in Washington, D.C. in 1991.
[5] SUNA, *Daily Report*, Khartoum, 7 June 1989.
[6] SUNA, *Daily Report*, Khartoum, 7 November 1989.

the teaching of French and the establishment of a French technical school in Khartoum. Michel Trichet, director of the Agence France Press office in Sudan, began to work closely with SUNA, the official Sudan government news agency and provided generous stipends for Sudanese journalists to visit France.

Franco-Sudanese relations remained very cordial even after the SPAF in the Bahr al-Ghazal shot down an airplane of the French humanitarian agency, Médicins Sans Frontières-France (MSF) taking off from Aweil on 21 December killing three Frenchmen and one Sudanese employee. MSF-France was a respected and renowned NGO that had its largest program in Sudan. Forty doctors and technicians worked at nine sites in the southern Sudan in some of its most troubled villages and towns where they frequently encountered the hostility of local traditional authorities and rival conservative Muslim relief agencies. The French embassy in Khartoum tactfully did not request an official investigation into this unprovoked incident that shocked the humanitarian community in Sudan. Subsequently, the French ambassador personally asked Bashir when the report of the incident would be concluded. The president replied with some surprise. "Why should you worry about it? After all, they were not French government employees." The French ambassador brushed off the insult and went on to another topic.[7] When the RCC finally delivered its official report in February 1990, the plane was reported to have been destroyed by a "Sam 6 missile fired from the Rebel Movement camp at Bariak."[8] The French embassy quietly accepted this mendacious response to the murder of French citizens, but French officials in Khartoum were personally troubled that all French foreign aid was now being allocated only to projects in the northern Sudan.

Despite their somnolent impression, the French embassy was most certainly not inactive. President Mitterand extended an invitation to Foreign Minister Ali Ahmad Sahlul and other Sudanese officials to attend the exclusive Summit Conference of Francophone Nations in

---

[7] Ambassade de France au Soudan, Khartoum, Report No. 22/MAE, 14 January 1990. The Embassy report and information on the subsequent meeting with Bashir was given to Millard Burr by a Sudanese government official and confirmed by a European official.

[8] Government of Sudan-Ministry of Foreign Affairs, Khartoum, Memorandum MFA/EO/1/1/31/A., 2 February 1990.

Casablanca, Morocco, on 23–24 November 1989, and to the subsequent Euro-Arab dialogue held in Paris on 22 December 1989. As relations continued to deteriorate between the RCC, Britain, and the United States, France perceived an opportunity to extend its economic influence. The French-Sudan Ariab Mining Company had been granted an extensive concession in the Red Sea region, and the Total Oil Company had revived its interest in Sudan. Total had suspended its operation after the SPLA attack on the CCI Sobat Camp in 1984, but it had never abandoned its concession in the Upper Nile and now expressed interest in obtaining the Chevron concession, offshore oil exploration in the Red Sea, and return to work in the Upper Nile. French financial firms were especially interested in Islamic banking in the Sudan mostly controlled by the Muslim Brothers and loyal supporters of NIF. In March 1990 Sudan was a welcome participant at the 38th executive session of the Union of Arab and French Banks.

After the Sudan government supported the Iraq invasion of Kuwait, most of the Western embassies recalled their personnel in protest. French diplomats, however, remained as did the French military intelligence agents from the *Direction Générale de la Sécurité Extérieure* (DGSE) including Colonel Jean-Claude Mantion and Paul Fontbonne, each with many years experience in Africa, especially in the Central African Republic and Chad. Both served as intermediaries in the negotiations that led to the restoration of diplomatic relations between the Central African Republic and Sudan in February 1990. They were also directly involved in arming and funding the Chadian rebels led by Idriss Deby, an ethnic Zaghawa, that enabled the insurgents to launch their assaults across the Sudan-Chad border from the Sudan province of Darfur. Well-armed and protected in their Sudan sanctuary Deby's men attacked and routed the Chad army thinly stretched on the long Chad-Sudan frontier. By December 1990 Idriss Deby had entered Ndjamena, the capital, and driven President Hissene Habre into exile.

The renewed French interest in the Sudan became increasingly complicated by competition within the French government as to which ministry would take charge of relations between Khartoum and Paris, the foreign ministry at the Quai d'Orsay, the ministry of interior, or the ministry of defense. In June 1991 President Bashir boasted of his close personal relationship with Jean-Cristophe, the son of President François Mitterand. The younger Mitterand was an influential member of the "Africa Cell" at the Quai d'Orsay that included Paul Dijoud, a close friend of the French president and Director of African Affairs at the ministry. In January 1992 Dijoud met with Turabi and Bashir in Khartoum ostensibly to assist the Sudan in its balance of payments problem in return for economic concessions and the support of the Sudan government to assist in a settlement to the vicious civil war in Algeria. In April 1993 Hasan al-Turabi, the Sorbonne graduate, expressed his "warming" toward France, which, he argued, was understandable given the mature worldview of the French. This worldview was most evident in the French press coverage of the Islamist Revolution in the Sudan. In 1990 Jean Gueyras in *Le Monde* was one of the few Western journalists to appreciate the influence of Hasan al-Turabi, particularly in the RCC, and the importance of Shari'a as the law of the Sudan. In November 1993 *Le Monde* was the first to report the arrival of Turabi in Afghanistan for the second time in the last eighteen months to mediate conflicts among Afghan warlords. Upon his return to take charge of the second PAIC General Assembly *Le Monde* had reported that among the 450 Muslim delegates from 60 countries Hasan al-Turabi was the "powerful presence," a leading figure in the Islamic world.[9] By 1994 the ministerial spheres of influence had been clarified, and Charles Marchiani, the dominant figure in the "Africa Network" of Charles Pascua in the ministry of interior, was now working closely with Colonel Mantion who had been given the Sudan desk in 1993. He used his close relationship with General Fatih Urwa, Bashir's adviser on security, to gain the friendship of the Sudanese president that had given him a considerable advantage over his rivals in Paris.

Washington did not share the blissful belief of Hasan al-Turabi in the worldview of the French. By 1993 the documented violations of human rights by the Sudan government had become of great concern to the United States Congress and to the EC. In February the United States Senate Committee on Foreign Relations supported efforts to sponsor a UN resolution to condemn human rights violations in the Sudan, and the US with the European Community,

---

[9] Jean Gueyras, "Soudan," *Le Monde*, 12 April, 3 July 1990; On Turabi in Afghanistan see "Afghanistan," *Le Monde*, 23 November 1993 and "Reunis á Khartoum les mouvements islamistes," *Le Monde*, 7 December 1993.

except for France, requested the United Nations to appoint a "special rapporteur" for the Sudan.[10]

At the meeting of the UN Human Rights Commission the following month in Geneva, the U.S. delegate accused the Sudan government of terrorizing the residents of Juba and executing hundreds. The justice minister of the RCC, Abd al Aziz Shiddo, denied the charges but received a special hearing in France where his counterarguments were fully and favorably reported. France was now importing Sudanese sorghum even though the Sudan government claimed it could not deliver the 150,000 tons it had promised to UN Operation Lifeline Sudan.[11] Revenue from the grain sales may have helped to buy four A-320 Airbuses obtained through a hire-purchase plan financed by the French bank, Credit Agricole. The Sudan had a serious balance of payments deficit with France, $20 million in exports against $86 million in imports, but that appears not to have deterred French commercial interests willing to invest in agriculture and mining.

Carlos the Jackal

On 13 August 1994 the Sudan government issued the surprising announcement that the notorious international terrorist Ilich Ramirez Sanchez, "Carlos the Jackal," had been captured in Khartoum and extradited to France. It was riveting theater. French security agencies had spent years in their hunt for "the Jackal" after his terrorist bombing of the Saint-Germaine Drugstore in Paris in 1974 and the subsequent murder of two French intelligence officers in 1975. The United States Central Intelligence Agency had been tracking the perambulations of Carlos since 1992. Previously protected by the Popular Front for the Liberation of Palestine-General Command, the Ahmad Jabril terrorist organization that operated in the eastern Mediterranean, Carlos had left Syria in 1993. He was traced to the

---

[10] "Claiborne Pell, et al., to George F. Ward, Acting Asst. Secretary of State for International Organizations," U.S. Senate Committee on Foreign Relations, Washington D.C., 25 February 1993; also see, *The Washington Post*, 24 February 1993; "Back to Abuja?" *Middle East International*, 5 March 1993.

[11] The Agricultural Bank of the Sudan planned to export 230,000 tons of grain to France, Turkey, Italy, and Holland. *Africa Economic Digest*, 17 May 1993, p. 10.

Sudan by a CIA counterintelligence officer, and once in Khartoum
he was placed under surveillance by American and British intelligence agents. There he lived "with the full knowledge and protection of senior levels of the NIF and Sudanese government," and
"bragged about his ties to senior government officials."[12] With the
assistance of Hasan al-Turabi and Nafi Ali Nafi Carlos had found
a home in the quiet Amarat quarter of the capital.

In Khartoum Carlos offered his services to train NIF officials in
subversion and regularly lectured to recruits in the PDF on the fine
art of exporting terrorism. It seems, however, that his relationship
with the puritanical members of NIF was compromised from the
day he arrived at the Khartoum airport. He was a Venezuelan
Marxist, not a Muslim or an Islamist. He drank heavily and forni-
cated with abandon that scandalized many Sudanese who were not
members of NIF. Despite his personal behavior he was at first protected by a small circle of government officials, and apparently he
took some part in the short-lived civil war in Yemen in which Osama
bin Laden, Turabi, and the PAIC General Assembly had taken a
personal interest.

When the United States informed the French government that
Carlos was in the Sudan, General Philippe Rondot was sent to
Khartoum. A counterintelligence expert known as "the Arabist" and
special adviser to Charles Pascua, Rondot had been following Carlos
for years. The Sudanese government officially denied he was in the
Sudan, but Rondot identified Carlos at the meeting of the second
PAIC General Assembly held in Khartoum 2–4 December 1993.[13]
Rondot initiated "intense negotiations" with the Sudanese Minister
of the Interior "Sikha" Khair to give up Carlos rather than the international terrorist, Abu Nidal, who was also enjoying the sanctuary
of Khartoum.[14] It was rather curious that neither President Mitterand
nor the DGSE alerted their ambassador that Carlos was living in
Khartoum until it became common knowledge in diplomatic circles,
and then, not to flush Carlos prematurely, the ambassador was

---

[12] *Patterns of Global Terrorism*, Washington, D.C.: U.S. Department of State, April
1995, p. 23. Carlos reportedly arrived from Damascus using a Yemeni passport;
See, "Journey's End," *The Middle East*, October 1994, p. 12.
[13] "Sudan's Offer to France—Carlos or Nidal," *The Sunday Times*, London, 25
September 1994.
[14] "Journey's End," *The Middle East*, October 1994, p. 12; "Sudan: Inside the
Jackal's Lair, *Africa Confidential*, 26 August 1994.

informed of French plans to capture him and told to remain silent. It soon became apparent that the NIF government was not prepared to extradite anyone, and that the return of Carlos to France would have to be by stealth and force. Numerous military delegations passed back and forth between Khartoum and the south of France. The agreement that was finally reached to permit French agents to kidnap Carlos was more to advance the foreign policy objectives of the Sudan than any altruistic desire to turn over a wanted terrorist to European authorities.

Ostensibly the French had warned Bashir in private that if France could not obtain Carlos, it would publicly announce that Carlos was in Khartoum at the service and protected by the Sudan government. In effect, Bashir, the RCC, and NIF had to decide to sacrifice a non-Muslim, Marxist terrorist in order to avoid international embarrassment and receive French good will. The "Ghost" had to go, and France would confirm "to the world" that Sudan was "a peace loving country" that "would not entertain the presence of terrorism in the country."[15] In return Khartoum would specifically receive French military equipment, intelligence, training for Sudanese police, financial assistance for Sudan Airways, and a desalinization plant for Port Sudan. Carlos the Jackal did not come cheap. Although many assumed that the RCC was desperate to escape its isolation from Europe by a symbolic gesture, it was probably Hasan al-Turabi, not Bashir and his colleagues in the RCC, who decided that Carlos was expendable to secure for himself a personal "strategic alliance" with France.[16] After a meeting with French intelligence in 1993, Turabi had been told that in return for his cooperation in the affair of the Jackal, France would acknowledge his preeminent role among Islamist intellectuals and a role in French mediation with the Algerian Islamic movements. In July 1994 Turabi flew to Paris where he met with Charles Pasqua, minister of the interior. There is no record of the discussions, but a few weeks later and only three days after Carlos had been abducted to France, Pascua announced on 16 August that the Khartoum regime had broken with terrorism. The French media had their own view of the Carlos affair that portrayed Turabi as an "intermediary" between his friend, the jailed Algerian leader

---

[15] "The 'Ghost' Must Go," *New Horizon*, Khartoum, 18 August 1994, p. 4.

[16] Bernard Violet, *Carlos: les reseaux secrets du terrorisme international*, Paris: Seuil, 1996.

Abbasi Madani of the FIS, and the government of France. France would acknowledge Turabi's "asserted ambition to be the instigator of a 'third path' for Islamic militants" between the "outdated" Gulf monarchies and the violent and inflexible Iran. Working together, Paris and Khartoum would influence the rebel FIS and Algerian President Liamine Zeroual to accept a cease-fire and the institution of a government along the Sudanese model, a military leadership blessed by Islamic militants.[17]

The "sale" of Carlos exacerbated dissension within the ranks of NIF. In December 1993 Turabi and the "traditional" NIF leadership had strongly disapproved of "commando tactics much favored by hawks" when an Eritrean Jihad operation in the Sudan had resulted in open hostility between presidents Afewerki and Bashir.[18] In the debate over the Carlos kidnapping Nafi Ali Nafi, Ghazi Salah al-Din Atabani, and Ali Osman Muhammad Taha vigorously condemned the abduction of Carlos.[19] Taha's disapproval, however, did not last long, for he was already distancing himself from Turabi and his small circle of friends. Often referred to as a leader of the "radical wing" of NIF, Taha had been a favorite among its younger members, but by 1992 he had became more closely associated with Bashir and his military colleagues in the RCC. Perhaps to remain in a position of power as minister of social planning he had no other choice. It was rumored that Asim Hasan al-Turabi, son of Hasan al-Turabi and a notorious currency dealer, had twice fired a pistol at Taha. True or false the relationship between Taha and Turabi had become perceptively cool.

Whether Turabi realized it or not, the betrayal of Carlos and the method of his abduction planted a worm of mistrust among some Islamists that the Sudan might no longer be a safe-haven for terrorists or a trustworthy ally in the struggle against the West and Zionism. No one was about to question Turabi's commitment to the Islamist movement, but the manner by which President Bashir had

---

[17] "France-Sudan: Well Understood Intentions," *The European Press Survey*, September 7–20, 1994, derived from *Liberacion*, Paris.

[18] "Sudan: Plunging Headlong into Islamic Activities," *The Indian Ocean Newsletter*, 8 January 1994, p. 1.

[19] "A Palestinian View of Carlos," *Israel and Palestine Political Report*, Paris, No. 189, September/October 1994, p. 20; See also, "The Carlos Affair," and "Muddy Waters in Khartoum," *Middle East International*, 26 August 1994, p. 10.

agreed to the kidnapping indicated to some that he was delighted to use l'affaire Carlos to tranquilize his government's reputation for terrorism. His subsequent decisions certainly indicated a determination to demonstrate his independence. The direction, communication, and responsibility within the Sudanese intelligence community was often confused and muddled by the counselor for national security of the RCC who was to coordinate for the council the activities and analysis of the Sudan intelligence agencies. The first counselor was the incompetent Brigadier Ibrahim Nial Adam, a Nuba. He was soon replaced in December 1989 by Bakri Hassan Salih who immediately purged the remaining members of the former Sudan security bureau of President Numayri. He then rooted out corruption in the service and exposed enemies of the RCC. A fanatical fundamentalist he had, by 1991, consolidated the daily control of Sudanese security within the ministry of interior. Despite his association with a Libyan fundamentalist, who was responsible for the bombing of an Omdurman mosque in February 1994, he established a feared position in the government that even Nafi Ali Nafi was reluctant to challenge. In July 1994 when Muhammad Hussein was replaced by Lt. Colonel Al-Tayib Ibrahim Muhammad "Sikha" Khair, a former dentist, Islamic fundamentalist, and NIF activist as the minister of cabinet affairs, "Sikha" immediately formed a partnership with Bakri Hassan Salih who officially controlled the internal and external security agenies. He and Nafi Ali Nafi, who in August 1994 had been promoted minister of state at the presidency, designed the High Court for Peace, often called the Supreme Peace Council that would spread Islam throughout the southern Sudan with the assistance of the PDF.

The promulgation of the General Security Act of January 1995 and the appointment of Nafi Ali Nafi as director of internal security and Major General Hassan Muhammad Dhahawi the director of external security insured that the Islamists had gained control of Sudanese intelligence. Dhahawi was forty-five and a Baggara Arab of the Missiriya from Muglad in southern Kordofan. In 1986 he was made the press adviser to the army commander-in-chief and after the 30 June Revolution to President Bashir and later a "Moral Orientation Officer" in the PDF. Like Nafi and Interior Minister "Sikha" Khair, he was ruthless. As a colonel he was a member of the first delegation sent by the RCC to meet with the SPLA in August 1989 and to the Nairobi peace talks that opened in November.

These changes in the intelligence leadership firmly established the legacy of a two-track intelligence organization with internal security under the control of Nafi Ali Nafi suppressing all civilian opposition and Dhahawi ensuring the purity of the military that included his authority over military attaches and Sudanese government intelligence abroad. Both men were now firmly beholden to President Bashir not Hasan al-Turabi.

The Aftermath of L'Affaire Carlos

There were as many interpretations of the Carlos affair as there were observers, most of which were stimulated and then embellished by the exotic past of Carlos himself. The truth will probably never be known. Among the more prescient but petty explanations was that the NIF government and France had used each other as revenge against Yoweri Museveni who supported the SPLA to the fury of Khartoum and the Rwanda Patriotic Front that "deliberately appealed to French resentment" and French aspirations in Rwanda.[20] Others argued that it was Hasan al-Turabi who had worked out a deal to hand over Carlos to the French in return for a few million dollars transferred through a French bank to provide a down payment on the Sudan's debt to the International Monetary Fund. The Egyptians, of course, had their own theories. Carlos had become an obsolete commodity who had outlived his usefulness, and France had employed Turabi to strike a deal whereby his exchange would result in French political, economic, and financial assistance. In Morocco the L'Affaire Carlos was "Sudangate" that only elicited contempt from the Moroccans. It brought no credit to the Sudan, Turabi, or Islam and certainly none to France.[21]

In Khartoum the Islamists were divided over the betrayal of Carlos, but the Sudanese military leaders in the RCC were more anxious to have France as an ally than Carlos as a resident liability. Once Carlos was snatched, drugged, hooded, and flown from Khartoum,

---

[20] *The French Connection: Report on the Political, Economic and Military Collaboration between Khartoum and Paris*, Brussels: Pax Christi, International, October 1994, p. 6.

[21] Arab Republic of Egypt Radio Network in Arabic, Cairo, 19 August 1994; "Sudangate," *L'Opinion*, Rabat, Morocco, 26 August 1994.

France began to provide arms and essential intelligence to the Sudan military. Aerial photography from the European SPOT satellite in Noordwijk, the Netherlands, covering southern Sudan and the Sudan frontier along the Congo-Nile watershed with Zaire and the Central African Republic where the SPLA was in control of the countryside was of great tactical value to the SPAF. In January 1995 the French were influential in arranging permission for a Sudan military expedition to move across the border into the Central African Republic and Zaire during its campaign that enabled the SPAF to inflict a devastating defeat on the SPLA forces in western Equatoria under Commander Samuel Abu John.[22] In France Charles Pasqua vehemently denied there was any quid pro quo in return for Carlos and tendentiously argued it was the imagination of "twisted minds." French journalists were unimpressed, and Claude Wauthier reported that *L'Affaire Carlos* was "une aide militaire multiforme."[23] Four years later in 1998 Michel Porta, chairman of Aeronautique et Sytemes of France, was alleged to have been involved six weeks after the kidnapping of Carlos in a secret $3 million "unlawful export of war material" consisting of five drone aircraft to the Sudan identical to the military Marula model developed by Sagem industries of France. Porta claimed the aircraft were only for civilian use.[24]

The real role Turabi played in the Carlos affair remains a mystery, precisely because he wished it so. For years he denied any special relations with the French "Exterior Minister." He made the absurd assertion that the "American administration" had made possible the entry of Carlos into the Sudan in order to provide proof that the country harbored terrorists. It appears, nevertheless, that Turabi was very much involved in the Carlos affair and willing to trade the terrorist for the support of Charles Pasqua "to approach the World Bank and the International Monetary Fund" in order "to secure loans to eventually erase Sudan's foreign debt."[25] Nothing

---

[22] On the alliance see: "French Plan Meeting With Junta," *The Indian Ocean Newsletter*, 21 December 1991, p. 2; "Pot-pourri franco-soudanais," *Le Nouvelle Afrique Asie*, No. 67, April 1995, p. 19; Gerard Prunier, "Luttes armees au cour de l'Afrique", *Monde Diplomatique*, February 1997, pp. 8–9.

[23] Claude Wauthier, "Appetits americains et compromissions francaises," *Le Monde Diplomatique*, October 1994, p. 10.

[24] Wauthier, "Appetits americains et compromissions francaises."

[25] SUNA, *Daily Report*, Khartoum, 12 August 1994.

came of these discussions leaving Turabi to imply that Sudan had been unfairly regarded as a terrorist state.

In the United States Washington considered the Carlos affair a Machiavellian maneuver for internal Sudanese reasons concerning the relationship between France and the Sudan. It would not cause a rift in the Khartoum and Teheran axis nor with other radical states.[26] It would, however, encourage France to make more dramatic moves to cement close relations with Turabi and the NIF government in Khartoum. In September 1994 the French chargé d'affaires in Khartoum met with the deputy speaker of the Transitional National Assembly, Professor Muhammad al-Amin al-Bashir. He extolled the "religious tolerance prevailing" in Sudan and praised the close relations between Paris and Khartoum, a relationship "based on frankness, consultation and seriousness." The "Sudan's handing over of the terrorist Carlos to France refutes the terrorism charge against the Sudan."[27] Ironically, a few days later the Department of State "gave Khartoum solid, incontrovertible information about the location of a military facility north of Khartoum at which training, including small arms familiarization, had been provided to non-Sudanese extremists."[28] A week later the Ariab Mining Company reported that gold production had reached three tons.

---

[26] "Lucrative Spin-off in Carlos Affair," *Indian Ocean Newsletter*, 10 September 1994, p. 2.

[27] "Deputy Speaker Receives Iranian, French Charge d'Affaires, *New Horizon*, Khartoum 13 September 1994.

[28] "Deputy Speaker Receives Iranian, French Charge d'Affaires.

CHAPTER EIGHT

THE PAIC GENERAL ASSEMBLY, THE MIDDLE EAST, EUROPE, AND AFRICA

In October 1994 Hasan al-Turabi opened and chaired the second Conference on Inter-Religious Dialogue in Khartoum organized by Dr. Mustafa Osman Ismail and his CIPF. The purpose of this conference, like the first in April 1993, was "to define common ground between Islam and Christianity." All the well-known Islamists were present, many of whom had participated in the PAIC General Assembly in December 1993. The formidable Nigerian Cardinal Francis Arinze represented the Vatican. Cloaked in the lambskin of religious ecumenism, Turabi explained that the conference was to introduce a dialogue (*hiwar*) to close "the gap" between Western and Arab-Islamic civilizations. He denied there were "secular and national" differences in Sudan, and suggested that the conferees should distinguish between the "Islamic evolution" in Sudan and the "Islamic revolution" in Iran, a country with which the Sudan had no economic or cultural relations! Ignoring the devastating civil war in the South that had killed two million non-Muslims, he rejected the use of violence in welcoming the religious leaders who had made their way to Khartoum. His speech received loud applause, but it did not open any serious religious dialogue in the Sudan or the world beyond.[1] The Christian and Muslim delegates were not about to be reconciled, but at this conference Hasan al-Turabi cemented his image as one of the major leaders in the Islamic world. The conference endorsed his demand that women should participate in elections, employment in the professions, and that the *umma* (Islamic Community) must be the source of all authority.[2] In the Sudanese tradition Turabi was the perfect host, greeting each delegation. There were Christian

---

[1] Adrian Kreye, "Unter Moslembrudern," Munich, Germany, privately printed, 1994; "Khartoum conference seeks solutions in moral realm," *Executive Intelligence Review*, 11 November 1994, pp. 48–51.

[2] Hashem Kassem, "Muslim Brotherhood," *EastWest Record* internet site: www.eastwestrecord.com, file copy, Beirut, 19 April 2002.

clergymen, Sudanese clerics, mullahs, Islamic radicals, and other dignitaries, including Dr. Ayman al-Zawahiri, who listened and applauded when the "Lenin of Islam" castigated the "unbelievers" who thought they controlled the world. Turabi's platitudinous essay, "Inter-Religious Dialogue: Challenges and Horizons" was widely distributed.[3] He specifically praised Osama bin Laden for his faith to invest in the Sudan. Delegates were flown to Juba to see for themselves the war on the frontier of Islam.

After this personal triumph, the following month he sent his representative, Yassin Omar al-Imam, to offer his services as a mediator for peace among the warring Afghan factions. In Khartoum he argued disingenuously that the problem of the Sudan was not the Sudanese but the United States for "leading a world campaign against Islam" and spreading anti-Sudanese propaganda.[4] He continued to deny rumors of Iranian military experts in Sudan. There were, of course, personnel from the Iranian embassy, but "not one Iranian businessman or even tourist."[5] No one in Khartoum believed him, for by February 1995 the Construction Jihad of Iran, under the direction of Minister Gholamreza Foruzesh, had been busy building roads and mechanized agriculture on a 10,000 hectare farm at Wadi Ramli. Iran agreed to train annually 250 agricultural technicians, distribute medicines to villages, build a new hospital at Umm Zouban, south of Khartoum, and the Imam Ali secondary school in a Khartoum suburb. In 1994 Iran provided funds for the Fatimah Zahra Training Center to instruct Sudanese women in a multitude of activities from sewing to computer programming.

In March 1995 a delegation from the Iran foreign ministry arrived in Khartoum led by Hussein Sheikholeslam, deputy foreign minister for Arab-African Affairs, to inform the Sudanese "on the position of Iran in relation to the current regional situation and international developments."[6] A few weeks later a larger delegation arrived led by the chairman of the Islamic Consultative Assembly (*Majlis-e-Shura-e-Islami*), Natiq-Nouri, that included numerous military officers. Although

---

[3] "Al-Turabi Calls for Multi-Religious Front," *New Horizon*, 11 October 1994.

[4] "Sudan to Maintain Relations with All States-Al-Bashir;" "Progress of Bilateral Agreements Implementation," *New Horizon*, Khartoum, 28 November 1994.

[5] IRNA Report, Athens, 3 December 1994.

[6] "Sudanese Ambassador Calls For Expansion of Ties with Iran," IRNA, Tehran, 22 February 1995; "Iranian Dy FM Discusses Regional, Int'l Situation With Sudan Officials, IRNA, Tehran, 17 March 1995.

Turabi held no government post, he took charge of the negotiations. Iran received unrestricted access to Port Sudan and Suakin on the Red Sea Coast to provide "yet another springboard" for subversion in the Red Sea region and the Horn of Africa.[7] The Sudanese opposition, The National Democratic Alliance (NDA), and particularly Eritrea opposed Iranian warships in the Red Sea that would threaten regional security and would be an insult to "Sudanese national honor and pride."[8] The Beja Congress were the peoples of the eastern Sudan led by Imam Taha Ahmad Taha who had joined the NDA against Khartoum. The Hadendowa Beja, the formidable "Fuzzy-Wuzzies" of Kipling, had lost land in the Gash River delta to Osama bin Laden where the NIF government gave him considerable land grants in return for his financial support and the construction of a paved road from Kassala to Port Sudan. The Imam Taha, a respected Muslim cleric, was accused of holding opinions contrary to the Quran, imprisoned, and his schools and mosques closed. The Hadendowa and their cousins, the Amara and Bisharyin Beja, crossed the border into Eritrea to join the NDA.

In August 1994 Ibrahim al-Sanoussi of the PAIC General Assembly and the chairman of CIPF, Mustafa Osman Ismail, arrived in Yemen to congratulate the northerners on their "victory over the [Marxist] separatists in the south of Yemen."[9] The short, sharp civil war had lasted only two months but at a cost of more than 25,000 casualties. It ended with the capture of Mukalla, the port and capital of the Hadramawt from where Salim al-Baidh, the leader of the Democratic Republic of Yemen, fled to Jiddah and exile in Saudi Arabia. Iran had supported the Sudan in its assistance for Yemen during the conflict that led the foreign minister of Eritrea, Petros Salomon, to accuse the Sudan of trying to destabilize the region, and that Hasan al-Turabi was the strategist assisting the Eritrean Jihad, the Ittihad in Somalia, and the Oromo insurgents in Ethiopia. It was another example of the ever-increasing estrangement between Asmara and Khartoum.

---

[7] Guy Roux, "Hassan Turabi—Tehran's Sudanese Puppet," *International Review*, Vol. 16, No. 40, Autumn 1995.

[8] *New Horizon*, Khartoum, 13 August 1994.

[9] Yossef Bodansky, "Peres and The New Middle East," *The Maccabean Online*, Houston: The Freeman Institute, December 1995.

As the PAIC General Assembly grew in age, it grew in numbers. When the general assembly convened at Khartoum from 30 March to 2 April 1995, two members of the *Usbat al-Ansar* (Gathering of Followers), a small, well-armed, secretive Lebanese-based group comprised of Sunni mujahideen, were present. Its leader, Abd al-Karim al-Saadi, also known as Abu Mahjin, had fled from Lebanon in 1995 after being involved in the assassination of the Mufti of Tripoli. Often at odds with Yasser Arafat and other Palestinians, members of the *Usbat al-Ansar* had received training in the Sudan, and later "Sudanese officers arrived in Beirut to coordinate with [*Usbat*] Al Ansar leaders, and assist in an assassination of a rival faction leader."[10] Turabi and the PAIC General Assembly also welcomed mujahideen from Iran and the director of military intelligence for Hizbollah, Imad Mughniya, and one of 18 persons designated by the United States government as terrorists "that threaten to disrupt the Middle East peace process." Mughniya was wanted by the United States for the murder and kidnapping of U.S. citizens in Lebanon between 1982 and 1983 and for the bomb attacks against the U.S. marine barracks in Beirut. The meeting of Mughniya and Bin Laden in the Sudan was a sinister moment in the history of Middle East terrorism, for it brought together four of the world's most influential and effective terrorist organizations: Hizbollah, Hamas, Islamic Jihad, and Al Qaeda. Now collaborators working in concert, Mughniya and Bin Laden with Turabi and his PAIC General Assembly could provide both direct and indirect support for mujahideen dedicated to the establishment of Islamist states and the extirpation of Israel. After the congress Mughniya stopped over in Saudi Arabia on his way to Teheran, and although apprised of his itinerary the Saudi authorities failed to arrest him, perhaps, Washington intelligence authorities speculated, out of fear of the growing power of the terrorist axis.[11]

The gatherings of professional terrorists among the 300 delegates from 80 countries at the PAIC General Assembly in April 1995 were "not isolated or discrete incidents," but the "components of a major Islamist offensive" directed against moderate Middle East regimes.

---

[10] "Syria and Iran vie for Control of Militant Fundamentalists," *EastWest Record*, www.eastwestrecord.com, 15 October 2001.

[11] "Saudi-U.S. relations clouded by Terrorist," *The Washington Times*, 24 April 1995.

In addressing the opening session Turabi "accused the West of trying to wipe out Muslim independence." Many conferees used the meeting to launch inflammatory diatribes against tyranny, imperialism, the West, and the "Great Satan." Members of the Abu Sayyaf organization were present. Secretary-General of NATO, Willy Claes, warned that the "Islamic fundamentalists" who attended the PAIC General Assembly had openly "appealed to fellow Muslims to break free from a military, economic and cultural stranglehold" the West had imposed upon them.[12]

Unlike the past this PAIC General Assembly received international publicity in the media of East and West. Hasan al-Turabi was now the "strong man" of the Sudan. With charm and reason he argued that the PAIC General Assembly did not represent the Islamic world. It was a "non-governmental alternative" to the more conservative Organization of the Islamic Conference (OIC). He envisaged the creation of an international Islamic human rights organization and a new ecumenism that "suggested reformulating an Islamic human rights charter according to our view, which is close to the real Christian view," not that of the condemnation of human rights in the Sudan by Amnesty International who were in the pay of British intelligence.[13] There were those in the conference who disagreed. Shaykh Muhammad Bashir Osmani from Benin wanted to delete "Arab" from the name Popular Arab and Islamic Congress General Assembly. His motion threatened to divide the conference between Arabs and Africans along racial lines. Backed by African delegates from Eritrea, Kenya, Nigeria, Senegal, South Africa, and even by the Afro-American Muslim organization of Louis Farrakan from the United States, Shaykh Osmani "made it clear to Dr. Hassan Abdalla al Turabi, the secretary-general of the organization, that the word Arab must be removed because it will create racism and discrimination among the Muslim people." Osmani argued that "Arab" had to be eliminated "because as 'an African and a Muslim,'" he and

---

[12] Yossef Bodansky, "Like the Wings of a Bird: The Myths and Reality in PLO-HAMAS Relationship," *The Maccabean Online*, Houston: The Freeman Institute, April 1996; also see Andrew Bilski, "Islamic Fundamentalism," *Maclean's*, Canada, 17 April 1995.

[13] "Issues in the News: Turabi Raps Rights Groups," *Washington Report on Middle East Affairs*, p. 23, June 1995.

the 2.5 million Muslims in Benin would otherwise "not fit into the organization." The motion was opposed by the representatives from the Mahgrib who objected to the change "at a time when the Islamic world is facing a serious challenge" from the West. The debate was raucous, uncontrolled, and led some Arab delegates to leave when a vote favored a name change, but in the end Turabi prevailed "to the chagrin of the non-Arab delegates." He postponed any action on the vote until the next year "under tremendous pressure from the Arab lobby to make no change."[14]

Although seemingly dysfunctional, the conference did acquiesce or quietly accepted plans by the "Islamists" to begin in the summer of 1995 "very professional preparations" to destabilize moderate Arab regimes and to train "larger and more professional terrorist cadres . . . in Pakistan, Sudan, and Iran pending deployment to Egypt and the inevitable escalation of the Islamist armed struggle."[15] Although he had crushed the Islamist opposition in Syria, Hafez Assad was "fully aware" of the threat presented by the Islamist revival in the Islamic world and the presence of Syrian Islamists at the PAIC General Assembly in Khartoum. By the summer of 1995 there had been a "marked improvement of the already intimate strategic cooperation" between Damascus and Teheran to contain the Islamists in Khartoum.[16] The Egyptian government was, not surprisingly, even more concerned than Assad at the gathering of Islamists in Khartoum. A delegation of Egyptian Muslim Brothers and the Egyptian Labor Party were in attendance when Turabi was able to broker a secret truce between Egypt's radical Islamic Jihad and the Islamic Group (*Jama'at al-Islamiyah*) of the jailed Shaykh Omar Abd al-Rahman. It was the first time since 1983 that the two revolutionary movements had agreed to "unite their activity."

The Algerian Islamist insurgents, including many former Afghan-Arabs, were also at the PAIC General Assembly during which the leaders of the Armed Islamic Group (GIA) rejected the "moderation" of the umbrella Algerian FIS. Long before the PAIC was

---

[14] Nhial Bol, "Sudan-Religion: Drawing The Line Between Islam and Ethnicity," IPS, Khartoum, 3 April 1995.

[15] Yossef Bodansky, "Peres and The New Middle East," *The Maccabean Online*, Houston: The Freeman Institute, December 1995.

[16] Yossef Bodansky, *Like the Wings of a Bird: The Myths and Reality in PLO-HAMAS Relationship* (privately published), April 1996.

convened it had become common knowledge that the Sudan was used as a base for arms shipments to Algerian rebels operating from Chad and Niger where Bin Laden and his Al Qaeda were directly involved in support of the Islamist revolution in Algeria. At the time of the PAIC General Assembly, however, the Algerian Islamists had suffered a series of defeats with heavy losses by Algerian government forces. Anwar Haddam, the FIS rebel, and its representative in the United States, spoke to a gathering of Muslim leaders at the general assembly during which he promised the FIS would "not accept any compromise on our religion," and "the jihad" to establish an Algerian Islamic State "would continue."[17] The fears that they were exporting their revolution appear to have been confirmed when terrorists from the Armed Islamic Group were seized by French officials in their abortive attempt to hijack an Air France passenger jet to crash in Paris, reportedly at the Eiffel Tower.[18]

There were others who were neither Islamists nor Muslims that followed the proceedings and discussions at this PAIC General Assembly. Edward P. Djerejian, the director of the James A. Baker III Institute for Public Policy at Rice University and former U.S. Ambassador to Syria and Israel and Assistant Secretary of State for Near Eastern Affairs, warned that "the current revival of Islam as a political force has caused the West, the United States specifically, to treat Muslims as enemies in a new cold war." He argued that despite the activities occurring in Iran and Sudan, "the United States Government does not view Islam as the next 'ism' confronting the West or threatening world peace." Unlike Samuel Huntington, whose provocative essay argued that the West and Islam were entrapped in a "clash of civilizations," Djerejian regarded a war of worlds as a simplistic response to a complex reality and "a perception [that] plays into the hands of the extremists." On the sixteenth anniversary of the Islamic Revolution in Iran, President Hashemi Rafsanjani had stressed that "the West and particularly the United States wants to confront Islamic fundamentalism the same way they challenged

---

[17] Chris Hedges, "Sudan Linked to Rebellion in Algeria," *The New York Times*, 24 December 1994, p. A5; James Phillips, "The Rising Threat of Revolutionary Islam in Algeria," *Backgrounder*, No. 1060, Washington D.C.: The Heritage Foundation, 9 November 1995; Youssef Ibrahim, "As Islamic Violence Accelerates, Fears of a Showdown in Algeria," *The New York Times*, 22 February 1995, p. A5.

[18] "Algeria claims spectacular success in sweep of militants' stronghold," *The Washington Times*, 2 April 1995.

Communism. . . . [but this was] a mistaken comparison and a policy that will only strengthen the movement."[19]

Khalid Duran, a Spanish-born Moroccan Muslim intellectual warned his Western counterparts to reflect on Hasan al-Turabi, his congress, and the Sudan. "He tells the Western media what they want to hear, but in practice he implements a program for society that is one of the most obscurantist and one of the cruelest in regard to human rights." He denounced the NIF government of Sudan for its violence, and Turabi's tacit acceptance of terrorism. The Muslim Brotherhood had set in motion an Islamic fascism that would substitute religion for race and institute renewal (*tajdid*) without reform (*islah*). The Islamist movement was a dangerous phenomenon sowing the seeds of hate, violence, and the psychological disruption of Muslim society. What, indeed, have the Islamists "brought to Iran, Sudan, Afghanistan, Kashmir, Palestine, and Algeria if not hate?"[20]

The Iran-Iraq-Sudan Axis and Bosnia

During 1994 and 1995 the Sudan had became the home for wandering and refugee Islamists, Afghan-Arabs, and others drawn to the rhetoric, resources, and charm of Hasan al-Turabi. The Inter-Faith Religious Dialogue conference of October 1994 had provided the opportunity for Islamists to confer, and shortly afterwards for Turabi to declare "that Islamic radicalism will win by force in countries where the government refuses to grant freedom to the Islamists, such as Egypt and Algeria."[21] During the next six months before the PAIC General Assembly in the spring of 1995 Islamists had met in Teheran, Khartoum, and Larnaca, Cyprus, to define the strategy to achieve the objectives of their movement. In Teheran in January 1995 Al Qaeda decided to operate in the West, including the United States, and by April Al Qaeda cells were being established throughout the

---

[19] Edward P. Djerejian, "United States Policy Toward Islam and the Arc of Crisis," Baker Institute Study No. 1, Houston, 1995. Also see, Samuel J. Huntington, *The Clash of Civilizations*, Simon and Schuster, New York, 1996.

[20] Aicha Lemsine, "Muslim Scholars Face Down Fanaticism," *Washington Report on Middle East Affairs*, June 1995, pp. 17, 92.

[21] AFP and BBC, *Summary of World Broadcasting: The Middle East and Africa*, 21 October 1994.

Muslim world. They were financed by Bin Laden whose accounts in Italian and Cyprus banks transferred remittances from wealthy supporters in Saudi Arabia.[22] By the summer of 1995 an Iraq-Iran-Sudan axis had been forged by secret agreements involving the Iraqi Social Affairs Minister Latif Nusayyif Jasim and members of NIF close to President Bashir. In order to implement this entente, "about 20 intelligence officers were added to the Iraqi Embassy in Khartoum," to assist the Sudan military to respond to "the mounting crisis with Egypt . . . [by reorganizing] the Sudan Army "along the same lines as the Iraqi Republican Guard."[23] Hasan al-Turabi warmly encouraged the Islamic relationship between the Sudan and Iraq. He condemned the insistence that Iraqi oil be sold through United Nations channels and found solace in the belief that "France was the only European country" that did not take orders from the United States.[24]

While Hasan al-Turabi was beguiling his guests at the Inter-Faith Religious Dialogue Conference in October 1994, the German Federal Intelligence Service, the *Bundesnachrichtendienst*, usually known as the BND, published its report on the presence of Weapons of Mass Destruction (WMD) in Iraq. The RCC and NIF had supported the Iraq invasion of Kuwait in 1990, and in August "Iraq established a major expeditionary force in Sudan in order to strike Egypt and western Saudi Arabia. . . . deployment included several South African made G-5 155mm guns equipped with both high-explosive and chemical shells, as well as 14 SCUD-B launchers with several missiles each that were originally deployed along the Red Sea coast across from Yanbu and Jidda. . . . [and in the northern Sudan that could reach] southern Egypt and the Aswan High Dam." After the defeat of Iraq and the end of the Gulf War, President Bashir agreed to the request of Deputy Prime Minister Tariq Aziz of Iraq "to move Iraqi chemical weapons and additional SCUD missiles to Sudan in order to circumvent their destruction by the UN." In the summer

---

[22] Yossef Bodansky, *Bin Laden: The Man Who Declared War on America*, pp. 102–110.

[23] "The Iraqi WMD Challenge: Myth and Reality," Task Force on Terrorism & Unconventional Warfare, House of Representatives, Washington, D.C., *Task Froce Report, 10 February 1998*; see also: *Global Trade, Local Impact: Arms Transfers to All Sides in the Civil War in the Sudan*, New York: Human Rights Watch, August 1998.

[24] *New Horizon*, Khartoum, 20 January 1995; Turabi's comment was reported in "Sudan's Islamic Leader Hassan Abdullah al-Turabi," IRNA, Athens, 12 March 1995.

of 1991 Iraq relocated an estimated 400 SCUD missiles to Yemen and Sudan and transferred "some nuclear material to Sudan for temporary storage. . . . via Jordan utilizing Sudanese diplomatic mail privileges."[25] Very little was known about the Iraq Weapons of Mass Destruction program whose elimination the UN Security Council had approved. The first major independent study of the magnitude of the WMD program in Iraq had been in 1994. By that time it was apparent to everyone that the UN inspectors would be in Iraq for some time to come. In 1993 Iraq had sent more chemical weapons to the Sudan, and in the fall of 1993 Iraqi forces established camps in the Red Sea Hills near Port Sudan and at Dalawat near the Halayib Triangle equipped with "computers, missiles, defense systems, anti-aircraft, and radar systems. In the waning cool months of 1993, the regions surrounding these installations were experiencing strict security measures and 24-hour armed patrols."[26] The Beja nomads were removed from their grazing grounds for reasons of security.

The message and meaning of Hasan al-Turabi at congresses of the PAIC General Assembly was pan-Islam, the unifying of Muslims, their coming together as the *umma*, the community of the Faithful. He welcomed "as many disenfranchised Muslims and Islamic groups as possible as a means of bolstering his pan-Islamist credentials."[27] Bosnia received particular attention. By early 1995 an Islamic battalion comprised almost entirely of foreign mujahideen was operating in Bosnia. The unit was "closely associated with the Armed Islamist Movement (AIM)," an Iran-funded umbrella organization that provided assistance to many Muslim terrorist groups including the little-known Islamic International Brigade and the Legion of Islam operating in Europe. The AIM traced its roots to the revolutionary movement in Iran spawned by the Ayatollah Khomeini and supported by the revolutionary guards. In Lebanon it had created the Hizbollah and in the Sudan was closely associated with the "Sudan-based National Islamic Front," Its activities "were conducted under

---

[25] "The Iraqi WMD Challenge: Myths and Reality," Task Force on Terrorism & Unconventional Warfare, House of Representatives, Washington, D.C., *Task Force Report*, 10 February 1998.

[26] "The Iraqi WMD Challenge: Myths and Reality."

[27] Andrew Hammond, "Sudan overseeing militant merger: Alfi," *Middle East Times*, Cairo, 3–9 September 1995.

the guidance of the new Islamist headquarters in Teheran and Karachi." The AIM in Teheran was responsible for training, arming, and provisioning the force in Bosnia. Its Islamists in Karachi were responsible for its activities in the Serbian province of Kosovo. This division of labor had been agreed to at the PAIC General Assembly "convened in Khartoum in the first days of April 1995."[28]

In May 1995 a "mujahideen battalion" of non-Bosnian volunteers and unknown "ansar" that had been operating in the Travnik and Zenica districts of Bosnia was incorporated into the Bosnian army's III Corps as the Armija Republike BiH, 3 Korpus, Odred el-Mujahedin, soon to become known as the Al-Muwafaqa Brigade. Commanded by an Egyptian "Afghan" with the title and nom de guerre of Ameer Kateebat al-Mujahedin Abu al-Ma'ali, the Al-Muwafaqa Brigade was supported by the TWRA in Vienna who had been smuggling "large quantities of arms" to Muslim mujahideen in Bosnia.[29] Ironically, the Al-Muwafaqa Brigade soon became a dangerous threat to the Bosnians themselves in Travnik and the UN peacekeepers. After the cease-fire brought about by the Dayton Accords in the United States, the Al-Muwafaqa Brigade was no longer a combat unit, but the 700 men of the brigade did not disappear. Although its base and headquarters were closed, the men remained at Travnik under their Iranian advisers. Some held Bosnian passports. Some had married Bosnian women. In 1996 there were still an estimated 300 mujahideen in Bosnia, some of whom had made their way to Muslim villages in Kosovo where another war between Christians and Muslims was brewing.[30]

The Sudanese Opposition Begins to Revive

During the years that Hasan al-Turabi was holding his PAIC General Assembly congresses and consolidating his leadership in the Islamic

[28] Yossef Bodansky, *Offensive in the Balkans*, Alexandria, Va.: International Strategic Studies Association, 1995, Chapt. 8, "The Bosnian Jihad," pp. 71–78.

[29] Goran Bradic, "Muslim Humanitarian Organization Delivered Arms to Bosnia-Herzegovina," TANJUG Agency, Belgrade, 5 October 1995.

[30] Jan Urban and Yvonne Badal, "Muslim Fighters Switch to Training," Sarajevo dateline, OMRI, Czechoslovakia, 19 February 1996; Michael Mihalka, "Iranians and Foreign Fighters Continue to Plague Bosnian Operation", OMRI, Czechoslovakia, 24 February 1996.

world, the hitherto moribund Sudanese opposition, the NDA, began to demonstrate that it was still alive. At a meeting in London in March 1992 the leaders of the NDA had agreed that "religion, race and culture would not become a special qualification for Sudanese in any field of endeavor" and that "the basic qualification for Sudanese citizenship would be through birth and not religion," but these pedantic principles found little support in the Sudan for an opposition movement that was long on rhetoric and short on results.[31] The continuing and repressive human rights violations of Sudanese, arrests, torture in Ghost Houses of even mild critics of the regime by the agents of the NIF government, and the polemical campaign against former respected Sudanese political leaders in exile led to the impassioned denunciation of the Sudan Government by the European Community led by the Baroness Cox in the British House of Lords. The leaders of the Umma and DUP, historic and bitter rivals, began to put aside their differences. Despite serious disagreement between the "secularists" and "sectarians," by 1993 the fragile unity of the Alliance appeared the only viable opposition to the Khartoum government given the deep divisions among the southerners and their defections to the government.[32]

In March 1993 General Fathi Ali Ahmad the president of the NDA, a senior, respected general with little dynamism or political vision, visited Algeria seeking funds for the alliance since Algeria was confronted with its own insurgency and should be sympathetic. He received no money but the polite promise of some logistic support. He continued on to the United Arab Emirates who agreed to provide both military and financial assistance on condition that the NDA organize its limited armed forces to be equal to those of the African SPLA. In Saudi Arabia he was encouraged by the determination of the Saudis to restrict the movements of its Islamists and then traveled on to Nairobi for a meeting with the SPLA on 17 April 1993. Here a "Nairobi Declaration" was signed to separate religion from politics in a new constitution for the Sudan in an effort to unify the opposition in the North and South against the NIF government in

---

[31] On the problems within the National Democratic Alliance see "NDA Affirms Commitment to Non-Religious Democracy," *Sudan Democratic Gazette*, December 1992, p. 4.

[32] "Sudan: Wheeling and dealing," *Middle East International*, 18 December 1992, pp. 13–14.

Khartoum. General Fathi continued on his peregrinations seeking moral and material support for the NDA/SPLA. The Egyptians were not impressed with the general or the NDA. They refused to permit the alliance to operate from the Halayib Triangle and restricted their activities in Cairo to rhetorical statements in the Egyptian press.

In June 1993 General Fathi arrived in Washington. He confessed that the NDA had no armed force of any consequence and was dependent on the SPLA of John Garang to do its fighting. Like the Egyptians the Pentagon was not prepared to provide military assistance to the NDA-SPLA. The State Department was equally unwilling to give any diplomatic assistance. On Capitol Hill John Garang, the Dinka commander of the SPLA, would remain the favorite rather than Riak Machar, the Nuer, or Lam Akol, the Shilluk, both of whom had now defected to the government in Khartoum and whose militia were more interested in shedding southern blood than seeking peace with the northerners. Fathi, a sincere but ineffectual advocate of democracy, warned that the "NIF Government would one day soon threaten United States interests in the Middle East."[33] In 1988 the war in the Sudan was estimated by the NDA to cost $1 million a day. By 1993 the cost had risen to an estimated $2 million.

Upon returning to Egypt General Fathi found a more favorable climate toward the NDA. President Mubarak permitted him and other leading members greater freedom of movement and speech. He had reacted with equanimity, if not satisfaction, upon the arrest in May 1994 of Sadiq al-Mahdi and his three confidants, Dr. Hammad Umar Baqadi, a member of the Umma Political Bureau, retired Brigadier General Abd-al-Rahman Farah, who had been responsible for security, and Sayf al-Din Said, a member of the Umma Security Committee. They were charged with conspiracy to overthrow the Sudan Government. The arrest of Sadiq finally convinced the fractious opposition within the NDA that only unity could overcome the RCC and the NIF government. Muhammed Uthman al-Mirghani, the leader of the powerful Khatmiyya Brotherhood and its DUP, declared in June 1994 that there would be no negotiations or reconciliation with the Bashir regime. Farouq Abu Isa, the secretary general of the Arab Lawyers' Federation and chairman of the

---

[33] On Egyptian reporting see "Opposition Group Denounces 'Repression,'" FBIS, Arab Africa, 7 June 93, p. 23.

Coordination Committee of the Sudanese National Democratic Grouping (NDG), announced that President Mubarak had given his permission for the NDA to install a transmitter to broadcast anti-Bashir and anti-NIF government propaganda from Cairo.[34]

The Inter-Governmental Authority on Drought and Development

After the abortive peace conferences in Abuja Nigeria in 1992 and 1993 failed to bring peace to the Sudan, the Inter-Governmental Authority on Drought and Development (IGADD) sought to revive negotiations between the NIF government and the SPLA. IGADD consisted of representatives from Kenya, Uganda, Ethiopia, and Eritrea who had originally come together over the severe drought in eastern Africa and the Horn. They were soon confronted with the political issues of war and peace in the Sudan. In April 1994 their efforts to restart peace talks were frustrated when representatives of the NIF government met with the Nuer faction of Riak Machar that had broken with the SPLA.[35] When President Museveni of Uganda met with President Bashir of the Sudan in Austria in May, the discussions were an exercise in futility. Museveni was convinced that Bashir and his NIF government were neither interested in peace nor the IGADD mediation.[36] Thereafter the Khartoum government media repeatedly denounced Museveni for his support of the SPLA, and Kampala responded by condemning the arms that Khartoum supplied to the Lord's Resistance Army rebels in the Acholi territory of the southern Sudan and northern Uganda. Trying to be helpful in a humanitarian cause, President Clinton appointed Ambassador Melissa Wells as his special representative on Sudan in May 1994 to "promote the regional peace effort ... and to help smooth delivery of humanitarian assistance" to the South and assist the IGADD partners to bring about a peaceful settlement of the civil war.[37] Wells visited Khartoum and held consultations with the

---

[34] *Al-Wasat*, London, 30 May 1994; *Al-Hayah* in Arabic, London, 19 June 1994; Cairo MENA in Arabic, 18 June 1994.

[35] "Cardinal Danneels, President of Pax Christi International, Visits Sudan," *Pax Christi International*, Nairobi, 1 March 1994.

[36] "Al Bashir Returns from Austria," *New Horizon*, Khartoum, 2 June 1994.

[37] Radio Omdurman, 11 June 1994, interview with Melissa Wells.

members of IGADD. Bashir had hoped to use this opportunity to
revive relations with Washington, but it soon became apparent that
her negotiations where doomed to fail when "Khartoum stalemated the
talks in September by refusing to cooperate in substantive discussions."[38]

The failure of the IGADD mediation in 1994 coincided with the
deterioration in relations between Eritrea and the Sudan. The president of Eritrea, Isayas Afewerki, daily expressed his dismay that the
Sudanese government was providing substantial assistance to Shaykh
Muhammad Arafah and his EIJ that operated from bases in the
eastern Sudan. The EIJ had begun a campaign to assassinate Eritrean
government officials as a means to create an Islamist government in
Eritrea then dominated by Christians. Although the population of
Eritrea was only one-eighth that of the Sudan, President Afewerki
commanded an army tempered by three decades of war with Ethiopia,
and he was confident of victory in any border war with Shaykh
Arafah and his Sudanese patrons. Eritrea was a poor but proud
nation, and despite the shortage of funds the government managed
to provide assistance to Sudanese refugees who had fled to Eritrea
and Sudanese political leaders who were given asylum in its capital,
Asmara, while accomodating other Eritreans returning home from
the Sudan. Despite the incredible complications resettling the returning Eritreans, the government repatriated more than 100,000 refugees
from the Sudan. Another 50,000 Eritreans returned on their own as
tensions within the Sudan encouraged their return.[39]

The Sudan and Ethiopia had signed agreements of cooperation
in 1992 and 1993. A joint committee was created to assess and pro-
pose a settlement of the long-standing border dispute between them,
and both nations agreed to deny their territory as a sanctuary for
insurgents seeking to overthrow neighboring governments. Ethiopian
territory would not be used "to destabilize Sudan," and the Sudan
would not permit Ethiopian rebels to use its territory as a safe-
haven.[40] Soon after the signing of these paper accords, relations began

---

[38] "U.S. Policy Toward Sudan," Testimony of Edward Brynn, Acting Assistant
Secretary of State, House Committee on International Relations Subcommittee on
Africa, 22 March 1995.
[39] By 1996 Eritrea had repatriated more than 150,000 people; See "Eritrea,"
World Refugee Survey, Washington D.C.: U.S. Committee for Refugees, 1993, 1994, 1995.
[40] FBIS-AFR-93–198, 15 October 1993, p. 1; FBIS-AFR-93–242, 20 December
1993, p. 4.

to deteriorate. Khartoum declared that any attempt to solve border incursion by use of force would complicate matters between the two neighbors. Former President Jimmy Carter was unhelpful. In his usual unsolicited remarks, he said that President Zenawi was "the most remarkable leader I have met anywhere in the third world," and that he would attempt to "persuade Washington to give Meles Zenawi a role in negotiating an end to the Sudanese conflict [with Ethiopia]."[41] The NIF government in Khartoum was not amused.

In 1994 drought, ethnic, and religious conflict along the border between the Sudan and Ethiopia precipitated a new wave of Ethiopian refugees into the Sudan creating additional tensions between Addis Ababa and Khartoum. The NIF government used the confusion to revive that long-dormant disagreement over the delimitation of their 1,500 mile boundary. The focus of contention was the Ashiga Triangle and Gallabat on the frontier of the Red Sea Province. Like the Halayib Triangle it was an old dispute over worthless territory but which had nearly led to war between Ethiopia and the Sudan in the 1970s.[42] Squabbles over ownership of the land extending from Metema to Humera, settlements that straddled the ill-defined border, was not new, but they became very visible when large numbers of Sudanese crossed into Ethiopia searching for firewood. Firewood had become a scare commodity in the borderlands, and "nine Sudanese citizens" chopping trees and collecting wood at Fashiga were killed by the Ethiopian inhabitants. This border incident soon blossomed into a frontier war between the Ethiopian army and the Sudanese PDF who were sent to protect Sudanese farmers. Although both the Sudanese and Ethiopians regarded this incident as "manageable," when President Bashir paid a surprise visit to Ethiopia shortly thereafter, his conversations with Ethiopian government officials about the affair were considered inflammatory.[43]

---

[41] *Sudan Democratic Gazette*, London, November 1993, p. 10.

[42] *New Horizon*, Khartoum, 8 July 1994; On the history of this issue see: Faisal Abdel Rahman Ali Taha, *The Sudan-Ethiopia Boundary Dispute*, Khartoum: University of Khartoum Press, 1983; Ian Brownlie, *African Boundaries: A Legal and Diplomatic Encyclopedia*, Berkeley: University of California Press, 1979, pp. 852–887.

[43] "Ethiopia-Sudan: Border Dispute Mars Relations," IPS, Addis Ababa, 29 July 1994.

This historic bickering over border disputes was a reflection on
the internal administrative reorganization of the Sudan. Throughout
the twentieth century the Sudan had been divided into nine large
provinces that were a heritage from the *Turkiyya*, Turko-Egyptian
rule in the nineteenth century. In order to advance the cause of
Islam on its frontiers the NIF government arbitrarily divided the
Sudan into twenty-six provinces in February 1994, including seven
additional provinces in the southern Sudan that sub-divided the
traditional administrative districts of the Upper Nile, the Bahr al-
Ghazal, and Equatoria. The creation of a plethora of petty provinces
enabled the NIF government to provide administrative employment
for their followers in the marginal regions—west, east, and south—
on the periphery surrounding the heartland of the Sudan where the
awlad al-bilad, the riverine villagers from which NIF recruited its
followers, were scattered along the banks of the Nile. The NIF officials
sent to administer the hinterland were most certainly not welcome
in their new satrapies and complicated the demoralized efforts of
IGADD to negotiate a peace. In April the SPLA responded to this
arbitrary gerrymandering of the South at its National Convention
held in Eastern Equatoria that attracted nearly 500 supporters who
bravely hailed "the birth of a New Sudan" in the traditional provinces
of the Bahr al-Ghazal, Equatoria, Upper Nile, and in Southern
Kordofan, and Southern Blue Nile, two enclaves in the northern
Sudan inhabited by African Sudanese. The rhetoric declaring a "New
Sudan" could not disguise the fact that the SPLA was desperate. It
had been unable to stop the renewed offensive of the Sudan army
or to achieve a reconciliation with Riak Machar and his South Sudan
Independence Movement (SSIM) who had joined the government
forces as a militia.

Relations were no better between the representatives of IGADD
and those of the Sudan Government. IGADD held monthly meetings but nothing was ever accomplished. The NIF government
appeared only to be going through the motions in order to derive
some propaganda from its relationship with the states in the Horn
of Africa. Efforts to revive the IGADD negotiations were left to
President Daniel Arap Moi of Kenya. He was not enthusiastic
for the NIF government of the Sudan was "training terrorists to
infiltrate" into Kenya, Uganda, Zaire, and the Central African
Republic, and Hasan al-Turabi and his PAIC General Assembly

were providing cash and comfort to the illegal Islamic Party of Kenya.[44]

Other African leaders were also aware that the PAIC General Assembly was actively promoting Islamic outreach (da'awa) south of the Sahara. The "Islamic Civilization Project" of Hasan al-Turabi devoted to the spread of Islamist ideology to Africa accompanied by seminars and conferences for the "Islamisation of Africa south of the Sahara" caused widespread consternation.[45] The government of Senegal deported an official from a Sudanese NGO and closed the offices of five foreign Muslim charitable organizations it accused of attempting to destabilize its government. In Mauritania its indigenous Islamic Movement had ties with Islamic organizations in Sudan that were regarded as seditious. In East Africa Swahili Muslims, who considered themselves the guardians of an Islamic heritage, responded enthusiastically when Sudanese Islamists proclaimed that they represented "a return to 'Afro-Islamic authenticity.'"[46] In the United States there were those who revived the fear of a Muslim incursion into Africa accompanied by "Islamic fundamentalist inspired terrorism" and "an emerging Muslim insurgency in Central and Southern Africa."[47]

The infiltration of Islamists into Kenya was a powerful motivation for President Moi himself to make a major effort to resolve the conflict in the Sudan that threatened to destabilize his own government. On 18 June 1994 as chairman of a revived IGADD peace initiative he opened the conference by thanking the European community for the financial assistance to IGADD and the United States ambassador to the Sudan Donald Petterson for his efforts to provide food to 1.5 million southerner Sudanese in need of emergency assistance. President Moi, like his predecessors, had failed in the past to reconcile the two hostile factions of the SPLA or, for that matter, the factions within the government in Khartoum. He now hoped

---

[44] *Sudan Democratic Gazette*, London, February 1994, p. 5.

[45] "Past over Present," Issue No. 462, *Al-Ahram Weekly On-line*, http://www.ahram.org., Cairo, 30 December 1999–5 January 2000.

[46] Heather Deegan, "Contemporary Islamic influences in sub-Saharan Africa: An alternative development agenda," *The Middle Eastern Environment*, ed. Eric Watkins, St Malo Press, 1995.

[47] Clark Staten, "Muslim Incursion Into Africa," Emergency Response & Research Institute, Chicago, 6 May 1996.

to "break new ground and give the people of Sudan the peace and development they so much deserve" but was frustrated from the moment the talks began.[48] Salva Kiir, the SPLA delegate, had arrived in Nairobi in a sour mood, asserting that Khartoum had "intensified its military offensive" against the SPLA "signifying its faith in a military victory and the determination to impose an Islamic state on the whole country." The NIF government was led by the speaker of the National Transitional Assembly, Muhammad al-Amin Khalifa, and included Dr. Ali al-Haj Muhammed, minister for regional government, and Nafi al Nafi, minister for state. Ironically, before the talks began Hasan al-Turabi's youngest brother, a recent engineering graduate from the University of Khartoum and volunteer in the PDF, had been killed fighting in the southern Sudan. The civil war was taking its toll as the bodies were brought back to the northern Sudan. Bashir soon lost a brother, another volunteer in the PDF. Muhammad al-Amin argued that the SPLA was dwelling in the past and should consider "the new realities" (a Federal Islamic Sudan). After an appeal from President Moi the SPLA responded by declaring a unilateral cease-fire on 23 July, but the talks soon sank into an impasse when President Bashir announced in Khartoum that the Shari'a and the secession of the southern Sudan were "not negotiable". The conference was adjourned on 28 July.[49] When Turabi later met with President Moi, he made it quite clear that the Sudan was determined to "pierce this blister [SPLA] once and for all." Moi understood that the struggle in the Sudan was between Islam and "paganism" and quietly lost interest as a mediator between two irreconcilable religions.[50]

During the Nairobi conference the fact that the Khartoum delegation seemed to spend more time trying to suborn several former SPLA leaders than it had in substantive talks led the SPLA delegation to depart in frustration and anger. The SPLA had been under considerable internal criticism by its dissident members against the

---

[48] "Sudan-Politics: Talk of Peace but the Guns of War Roar On," IPS, Nairobi, 19 July 1994.
[49] "War Lords Seek Peaceful Settlement," *New Horizon*, Khartoum, 8 June 1994, p. 6; "Sudan talks in Nairobi are adjourned until September," DPA, Nairobi, 29 July 1994.
[50] "New Phase To Begin in Sudan's War Against Rebels in the South," *The Washington Times*, 3 November 1994, p. A14.

firm and autocratic rule of John Garang. Southern Sudanese Nilotic societies were known for the individual independence of their people who would recognize the power of religious diviners but not that of chiefs. In the Upper Nile there were no historic kingdoms except for the Shilluk, the Nilotes looking after their cattle and themselves. This cultural past and present followed them to Nairobi where numerous southerners, mostly Nilotes, were determined to defy Garang's attempt, no matter how ruthless, to impose his authority on the southern Sudanese. The result was "a number of rebels" who "confirmed their desire to return to the country and contribute to achieving a just and comprehensive peace."[51] Responding to accusations that the SPLA was a dictatorial movement beholden only to John Garang, the SPLA expanded its National Liberation Council to 183 members from every district in the southern Sudan and an Executive Council of twenty-seven members to impose civilian authority in the "New Sudan" under SPLA control. John Garang remained the military leader and Chairman of the Executive Council. Commander Salva Kiir, his deputy, was named foreign and interior director. Deng Alor was made head of state affairs, Dr. Justin Yak became the minister of health, and Commander Yusuf Kuwa the SPLA agent for affairs in Kordofan.[52]

Garang and the SPLA became more aggressive in their search for external support. Its leaders met in Cairo with those of the DUP during which Yusuf Kawa of the SPLA Executive Council declared that the SPLA had abandoned its "quest for self-determination in order to achieve the highest degree of coordination with other opposition forces in the coming phase. . . . [in order to] "achieve a democratic and secular Sudan, a society that respects ethnic, cultural, and religious diversity." In September the fifth round by IGADD seeking a peace agreement "collapsed" in Nairobi after one day of acrimonious discussion over the usual principal issues, "self-determination for the South and a secular constitution." President Museveni once again accused Bashir of providing support to the Lord's Resistance Army of Joseph Kony in northern Uganda. President Bashir accused Museveni of supporting the SPLA. A meeting of foreign ministers on 6 September ended with the Sudanese Minister of State Ghazi

---

[51] Radio Omdurman in Arabic, 20 July 1994.
[52] *Al-Hayah*, in Arabic, London, 16 June 1994.

Salah al-Din Atabani declaring that the Sudan would continue its "divine mission of Islamizing Africa." President Bashir announced over Khartoum television that IGADD "had outlived its usefulness."[53] Thereafter, the chairman of the IGADD mediation committee, Dr. Zakaria Onyonka of Kenya, was given the impossible task of keeping the discussion alive while Jimmy Carter unsuccessfully continued to urge Khartoum and the SPLA to enter into direct negotiations.

Frustrated, the IGADD mediation committee (Kenya, Uganda, Eritrea and Ethiopia) requested the United Nations in January 1995 to become directly involved in order to resolve the Sudanese civil war, and U.N. Secretary General Boutros Boutros Ghali agreed to send an observer to future peace talks. The NIF government in Khartoum was resolutely opposed to any United Nations or international intervention in what it considered an internal affair. A month later the Netherlands, United States, Norway, Canada, and Italy formed the "Friends of IGADD" under Dutch leadership in an attempt to generate international support for the peace process. When Khartoum refused to acknowledge the "Friends," this initiative collapsed, and the IGADD mediation committee ceased to function.[54]

Discouraged by the failure of IGADD and angry at the infiltration of Sudanese Islamists into Eritrea, President Isayas Afewerki broke diplomatic relations with Sudan in December 1994. He ordered the Sudanese embassy in Asmara closed and invited the NDA to make its headquarters in the building. After taking over the embassy and issuing a "Declaration of Political Agreement" signed by all the members of the Sudanese opposition in December 1994, Afewerki openly supported the Sudanese NDA, Arab and African, and permitted them to use Eritrean bases. Here in the former Sudanese embassy in Asmara the leaders of the NDA and the SPLA met from 15–23 June 1995 to conclude an agreement of their mutual relationship that would perhaps at some time in the future serve as a constitution for the Sudan. The critical article of The Asmara Declaration

---

[53] "Sudan Abandons Peace and Resumes War," *New African*, November 1994, p. 34; Salah al-Din's comment was quoted by SPLA Representative Steven Wondu in: "Unrealistic Portrait of Life in Sudan?" *The Washington Times*, 25 August 1996.

[54] "Dr. Ghazi Meets French Ambassador," *New Horizon*, Khartoum, 12 January 1995, p. 4.

recognized that the peoples of the southern Sudan should have the right to self-determination. The SPLA and the NDA leadership had pursued a long and difficult path since the 30 June 1989 Revolution.

CHAPTER NINE

THE PLOT TO ASSASSINATE PRESIDENT MUBARAK AND THE SUDAN

By the middle of the 1990s the influence of Hasan al-Turabi had precipitated a soul-searching debate in the Muslim world undergoing an Islamist renaissance. At the seventh summit of the OIC in Casablanca in December 1994 Algeria and Egypt led a group of moderate Muslims who expressed their deep concern that the Islamist revival would lead to the spread of terrorism throughout the Islamic world. Egypt had identified "17 secret training camps" for "Islamic militants" in the Sudan.[1] A code of conduct designed to confront and combat militant Islamic groups was drafted and signed by all fifty-two members of the conference to deny a safe-haven in their countries or support for extremists involved in terrorist acts against brother Islamic countries. Much of this was conventional conference rhetoric, for there were no provisions for enforcement. Iran and the Sudan grudgingly agreed to sign but only after arguing that the code equated Islam with violence. If Iran were to carry out the terms required by the OIC, it would betray its Islamic revolutionary message. For the Sudan to implement its provisions would hopelessly compromise the NIF government in the eyes of the more radical defenders of the faith.

Hosni Mubarak and the Egyptian establishment possessed a very different perspective. After a decade of internecine political warfare and terrorist attacks against his government, President Mubarak was determined to prevent the Muslim Brotherhood and its allies coming to power in Egypt by the ballot box or by terror, for it would mean the end of democracy and the historic secular parties. Mubarak employed the Egyptian interior ministry to contain the Islamists. Whether they were Egyptians, like the Islamic Jihad, or Al-Qaeda, the Palestinian Islamic Resistance Movement, Hamas, the Arab-Afghans,

---

[1] Georgia Anne Geyer, "Seeking to change society by force?," *The Washington Times*, 22 February 1995.

or the Iranian-sponsored Lebanese Hizbollah, none of these revolutionaries were welcomed or tolerated in Egypt. In January 1995 thirty Muslim Brothers were arrested and charged with holding illegal meetings and inciting terrorist activity. The government then initiated an intensive investigation of Egyptian relief agencies, particularly the Humanitarian Relief Committee that operated in Bosnia, Burundi, Somalia, and Yemen. They were charged with using humanitarian aid as cover for paramilitary training and for terrorists in the Sudan and Iran. The U.S. Department of State, however, reported that it had no evidence of specific acts of terrorism by the Sudan in 1994, but the U.S. Ambassador in Khartoum, Donald Petterson, had specifically cabled Washington in September that terrorists were being trained at the Merkhiyat PDF camp northwest of Khartoum.

In February 1995 there were significant changes in the cabinet of the NIF government. The ambitious Ali Osman Muhammad Taha was named foreign minister, and another staunch member of NIF, Dr. Ghazi Salah al-Din Atabani, was made state minister, number two, in the ministry of foreign affairs that guaranteed Islamist control of the Sudan's foreign affairs. Another NIF stalwart, Dr. Mustafa Osman Ismail who was the secretary-general of the PAIC General Assembly, became chairman of the Sudanese People's Committee for the Defense of Sudanese that had been charged with the Trade Towers bombing and on trial in New York. In Khartoum the question of who was first among equals, Bashir or Turabi, had become the subject of endless debate. They were opposite sides of the same coin and used each other as the coin changed hands. Turabi dominated politics. Bashir dominated the military that has always been the decisive factor in the independent Sudan. The appointment of Muhammad Taha and Ghazi Salah al-Din Atabani to the foreign ministry produced speculation that Turabi was now confronted by a schism within NIF. Either the two "pragmatic" Islamists had joined Bashir and the "military wing" of the NIF government or "Turabi and his followers [had] entrenched themselves so skillfully—far more than any previous regime—that it may be impossible to get them out."[2]

After the bombing of a bus in Tel Aviv in October 1994 by a Hamas militant that killed twenty-two Israeli civilians, Turabi had

---

[2] As reported in "Sudan's Islamic Leader Hassan Abdullah al-Turabi," IRNA, Athens Dateline, 12 March 1995.

declared it "an honorable act."[3] Munier Said, director of the Hamas "Aqsa Information Center" in Khartoum, admitted there were 400 or 500 Palestinians living in Sudan but disingenuously claimed that Hamas activists received training *only* in Palestine.[4] Not surprisingly, Turabi was one of 497 Islamists, *ulama* (religious scholars), intellectuals, politicians, pan-Arab nationalists, cultural, professional, and trade union leaders who signed a "Statement of Support and Solidarity" for Hamas published in the Saudi-owned Arab London daily *Al-Hayat*. The signatories included the Tunisian Islamist Rashid al-Ghannushi, leaders of the Egyptian, Jordanian, and Syrian branches of the Muslim Brotherhood, Husayn Fadlallah the secretary-general of Lebanon's pro-Iranian Hizbollah, and Anwar Haddam of Algeria's FIS. Non-Arabs from Pakistan, Kashmir, Bangladesh, and Turkey with ties to radical Islamic movements gave their support. The statement declared Muslim solidarity with the Palestinian people and Hamas, for Palestine was "the central cause of the Arab and Moslem nation." Under no circumstances would Islam forsake "any part of its blessed land." Jerusalem and the Al-Aqsa Mosque were not "open to bargaining and any settlement which consecrates the (Israeli) occupation of any part of the city or precludes Moslem rights in it is rejected by the (Arab and Muslim) nation, which will not be bound by it. . . . [Islam was] duty-bound to assist the Palestinian people with all available means and support their legitimate right to liberation, repatriation and self-determination until the [Israeli] occupation is ended. . . . The option of jihad to liberate Palestine is the nation's legitimate option. Any other option that consecrates the presence of the occupation on any part of the blessed land has no legitimacy."[5]

The Attempt to Assassinate Hosni Mubarak

During his presidency Hosni Mubarak and his Mukhabarat had vigorously circumscribed the Islamists in Egypt whether they were

---

    [3] "Firefight on Border Worsens Egypt-Sudan Political Feud," *The New York Times*, 29 June 1995.
    [4] "Nearly 500 Islamist and nationalist figures from Arab and Moslem world voice their support for the militant group in al-Hayat ad," *Mideast Mirror*, London, Vol. 09, No. 86, 5 May 1995.
    [5] Milton Viorst, "The Islamic Cauldron?," *Foreign Affairs*, May/June 1995.

Muslim Brothers or Islamic Jihad. Mubarak had been a strong supporter of the Gulf War against Saddam Hussein, and he had sent 40,000 men to take part in Operation Desert Storm. In the fall of 1994 Khartoum became the place where Islamists could safely devise a plan to assassinate Hosni Mubarak. Prior to opening the PAIC General Assembly Turabi had met early in March 1995 with the Egyptian revolutionaries, Mustafa Hamza and Rifai Ahmad Taha, the Khartoum and Peshawar commanders respectively of *Al-Jama'at al-Islamiyah*, and Dr. Ayman al-Zawahiri of the Egyptian Islamic Jihad to plot the assassination of Mubarak. After the PAIC General Assembly had adjourned, Turabi met again with Zawahiri in Geneva where he undoubtedly received details of the plot which he appears to have made no effort to obstruct.

In June 1995 President Mubarak arrived in Addis Ababa to attend the annual summit meeting of the OAU. On the 26 June his limousine was fired upon by two gunmen from the Egyptian *Jama'at al-Islamiyah* based in Khartoum. The two assassins were killed in the exchange of gun fire with Mubarak's bodyguards. Three others were shot dead in their Addis Ababa hideout five days later. Three others were arrested, but three more escaped Ethiopian security agents including one gunman and two others whom the Ethiopian government claimed had planned the assassination in Khartoum. Mubarak immediately blamed the Islamists and their revolutionary organizations for the outrage, but the Ethiopian government soon confirmed that the NIF government in Khartoum had provided the assassins with Sudanese and Yemeni passports. Their weapons had been delivered to Addis Ababa by Sudan Airways.

Radio Cairo immediately denounced the Khartoum government and specifically Hasan al-Turabi for "masterminding" the plot. On that same evening of 26 June Hasan al-Turabi issued a bland statement over Radio Omdurman denying any connection with the attempted assassination but managed to express his "deep regret."[6] He subsequently did little to conciliate Mubarak's fury, calling the assassins "messengers of the Islamic faith." He accused Mubarak of having no personal faith, and that "Egypt is today experiencing a

---

[6] Radio Cairo, 28 June 1995; Statements by Hasan al-Turabi, Radio Omdurman, 26, 27 June 1995 and *Al-Sharq al-Awsat*, 27 June 1995.

drought in faith and religion, but Allah wants Islam to be revived from Sudan and flow along with the waters of the Nile to purge Egypt from obscenity."[7] He lectured foreign journalists at his home in Omdurman that their use of the term "fundamentalism" to describe militant Islam was associated with terrorism: It was "a misleading word . . . started by the Americans," who were "very ignorant" and knew "very little about the world." He denied that the Sudan had supported terrorist groups like Egypt's Islamic Jihad (*Jama'at al-Islamiyah*) that, with Hamas, had claimed responsibility for the attack on Hosni Mubarak. "What's happening today is that Sudan is asserting Islamic values in public life. There is an Islamic renaissance going on in the world and it's going to express itself. I don't think history can be stopped." He "saluted" the mujahideen who "grew from Egyptian soil and hunted down the Egyptian pharaoh."[8]

An angry Mubarak denounced the NIF government for providing asylum to the leader of the assassins who was wanted by Egyptian police for his involvement in the assassination of Anwar al-Sadat in 1981. The house the killers used in Addis Ababa had been rented by a Sudanese, Mohammad Seraj, in the pay of the NIF intelligence chief, Nafi Ali Nafi.[9] Ethiopian President Meles Zenawi, whose Ethiopia People's Revolutionary Democratic Front (EPRDF) had just won an overwhelming victory in Ethiopia's first multi-party election, was enraged and lashed out at Sudan for its apparent involvement in the affair. The NIF government arrogantly ignored the Ethiopia assertions of its complicity and with little sensibility claimed that anger was clouding Mubarak's good sense. Mubarak's charges, however, were believed in Washington, by Jaafar Numayri the former Sudanese military dictator now in exile in Egypt, and by Yitzhak Rabin of Israel. Radio Cairo unleashed a stream of vitriolic accusations

---

[7] *Al-Sharq al-Aswat*, 6 July 1995.

[8] Mary Anne Weaver, "Blowback," *The Atlantic Monthly* (digital edition), May 1996; See also, Counsel of Record, Re: US v Omar Ahmad Ali Abedl Rahman, et al., (S5) 93 Cr. 181 (MBM); Yossef Bodansky, *Bin Laden: The Man Who Declared War on America*, Roseville, CA, Prima Publishing, 2001, pp. 122–125; Tim Niblock, "Sanctions and Pariahhood: The Case of Sudan," Fifth International Conference on the Sudan Studies, University of Durham, 30 August–1 September 2000.

[9] Salah Nasrawi, Associated Press, Khartoum, 3 July 1995, reported that former Sudanese intelligence official Col. Abdel-Aziz Gaafer told Egypt's *Al-Akhbar* newspaper that Mohammed Seraj, the key suspect, had been working for Nafi Ali Nafi. The charge was repeated in IWR Daily Update, Vol. 2, No. 169, 4 July 1995.

that exceeded its accustomed vehemence for NIF, the RCC, and Sudanese Islamists. "When this pygmy despot [President Bashir], who wishes to conceal his domestic problems, and his master, Turabi, get so bold as to raise weapons against the Egyptian people and their national symbol, President Mubarak . . . things become unforgiveable."[10] Once Islamic Jihad had claimed responsibility for the attack the government organized massive street demonstrations condemning the Sudan as a "fountain of terrorism" and a "hub of murderers and assassins." Upon leaving Addis Ababa after the OAU summit meeting, President Bashir strongly declared that his country was being falsely accused. He denied the charges by the Egyptian media that Sudanese were involved with the curious question. "Would this be the responsibility of the state?"[11] Osama al-Baz, "a senior political advisor to the President" announced that the government was awaiting the result of investigations. Other spokesmen protested that Khartoum had no culpability in the crime and complained that Mubarak should await the outcome of the Ethiopian investigation before seeking to incriminate the Sudan.

Mubarak dismissed the Sudanese protests, for "unfortunately, all suspicions are that the operation came out of Sudan." He was convinced that Hasan al-Turabi was personally involved, and that the assassins had been "planning this operation since March." President Omar Hasan Ahmad al-Bashir "was just Turabi's secretary." For the first time Mubarak publicly met with the leaders of the Sudanese opposition residing in Egypt. Ahmad Seif Hamad and Mabrouk Mubarak of the DUP suddenly received widespread press coverage in which they announced that the DUP was actively purchasing arms "from friendly countries" to wage war against the Khartoum government. The Egyptian official media began to repeat the accusations by the Sudanese NDA spokesman, Farouq Abu Isa, who had claimed that two senior Sudanese officials, Major General Fatih Urwa, Bashir's security advisor, and Muhammad Ahmad Dabi, Sudan's chief of military intelligence, had participated in planning the assassination. In contrast Egyptian Foreign Minister Amr Musa urged caution. Egypt was "loathe to interfere in Sudan's internal affairs or take military action against it that would lead to loss of

---

[10] Radio Cairo, 28 June 1995.

[11] "Egypt, Sudan," *Mideast Mirror*, London, Vol. 9, No. 123, 29 June 1995.

life. He argued: "The Sudanese people are able to deal with their leaders, they can take the decisions they deem fit and carry them out ... We are not required to intervene with forces or anything like that."[12] The doyen of Egyptian journalism, Muhammad Hassanein Haykal, also urged restraint. The Egyptian government should evict the leadership of the Sudanese opposition, the NDA, residing in Egypt and refrain from a policy of confrontation that could only lead to an African conflict that would be Egypt's Vietnam. Haykal, who over his long career had often seemed paralyzed by unexpected phenomena, did not offer a course of action for Mubarak and his government against Islamists who were using the Sudan to destabilize Egypt.[13] Despite these words of moderation the Cairo media generally remained unforgiving. *Al-Ahram* urged the government to attack "terrorist training camps" in Sudan with air strikes and speculated that the discovery of an arms cache in Upper Egypt was part of the plot to assassinate Mubarak and overthrow the Egyptian government.

Mubarak remained implacable and ominously warned that the Egyptian armed forces could eliminate the Bashir regime in less than two weeks, and he hinted that air strikes might be launched against camps in the Sudan suspected of training Egyptian militant Islamists. Egyptian air power was, however, insufficient to intimidate the Sudanese. History had demonstrated that to march successfully along the Nile for 1,500 miles through harsh desert required a line of communication easily disrupted by guerrilla warfare that made the prospect of an Egyptian invasion more rhetorical than real. Egypt had "indirectly involved itself in Somalia and Ethiopia" and was "subjecting its vital interests to danger by its engagement in the internal affairs of Sudan." Although the Egyptian foreign minister denied the implications in the Egyptian media of any Iranian involvement in the assassination attempt, Iran strongly supported the Sudan. The Iranian Minister of Interior Muhammad Ali Besharati deplored Mubarak's effort to push the Sudan into "a corner that would never benefit

---

[12] Ronald Bleier, "Will Nile Water Go to Israel?," *Middle East Policy*, Vol. V, No. 3, 1997, pp. 113–24.

[13] "Haykal Calls for the Expulsion of the Sudanese Opposition and Warns of a Vietnam Style War," *Al-Quds* (based on a *Rose al-Yousif*, Cairo, interview), Cairo, 24 June 1995.

the Muslims of the region."[14] In Teheran and Khartoum a wide range of cooperation was discussed including the formation of a joint political commission and even "presidential meetings."[15] Iran was particularly interested in the development of Sudan petroleum. In Khartoum Turabi gave his usual suave analysis that the assassination of President Sadat had made Mubarak obsessed with Islamism that he considering a menace to his government and to him.[16]

Early in 1996 the Egyptians used the attempt at assassination as an excuse to eliminate the last vestiges of the Sudanese presence in the Halayib Triangle. In a press conference Mubarak announced that he had personally ordered the expulsion of seventy Sudanese policemen located at four guard posts in the triangle because of numerous Sudanese provocations. He had no interest in spilling Sudanese blood, but he would take "measure after measure" against Khartoum unless the Sudan government ended its policy of confrontation. The Sudanese government claimed that the Egyptian "aggressive escalation" was Mubarak's revenge against Sudan and its "peaceful and responsible Islamic and patriotic orientation."[17] Egyptian troops then launched an attack on the Abu Ramad police post in the Halayib, killing one and wounding many. Skirmishes then erupted between Egyptian and Sudanese forces throughout the enclave. The Halayib dispute was, in fact, only a symbol of the deep, historic hostility between Egypt and the Sudan that had now surfaced in the guise of the Islamist state inimical to Mubarak and secular Egyptians. Turabi understood this all too well when he remarked in an interview with *Al-Sharq al-Awsat* that Halayib was merely "a small piece of land which would add nothing to either Egypt or Sudan. It is only being used as a pretext to create tension in the relations because Egypt wants to display superiority over Sudan."[18]

In the furor that followed the Addis Ababa assassination affair no one seemed to have appreciated the fact that on 6 August 1995 the

---

[14] "Iran's 1st Deputy FM Hopes Khartoum-Cairo Will Resolve Differences," IRNA, Tehran, 5 July 1995; "Sudan's Ambassador Deplores Mubarak's Incrimination of Sudan," IRNA, Tehran, 6 July 1995.

[15] IRNA reporting, Tehran dateline, 24 July 1995, 10 September 1995, 22 October 1995, 24 October 1995.

[16] R. Gauffin, "Ce que m'a dit Tourabi," *Jeune Afrique*, 6–12 July 1995, p. 33.

[17] R. Gauffin, "Ce que m'a dit Tourabi;" *Al-Sudan al-Hadith*, 3 March 1996; *Sudanow* (Khartoum), April 1996.

[18] An interview with *Al-Sharq al-Awsat*, 19 May 1996.

Sudan had quietly abandoned its policy that permitted any Arab or Muslim to enter the Sudan without a visa. In the future they would be subject to the same regulations as other foreign nationals.[19] Mubarak was not impressed. He remained convinced that Egyptian Islamists would continue to use the Sudan to plot against his government, and he was determined to circumscribe if not crush their activities in Egypt. In July more Muslim Brothers were arrested. They were charged with terrorism, participating in revolutionary activity in Upper Egypt and Sudan, and plotting to assassinate Mubarak. In September forty-five of them were put on trial in military courts, and more were arbitrarily detained after a sweeping roundup of the Brothers. Mamoun al-Hudaybi, a well-known Muslim Brother, denounced the arrest of "popular candidates" as a transparent attempt to keep the Brotherhood and its allies in the Labor Party from winning seats in the forthcoming Egyptian elections in November. He denied any association between the Brotherhood and Hasan al-Turabi, but Mubarak did not believe. The president's conviction that he and his government were under attack was confirmed in November just before the Egyptian elections when a powerful truck bomb exploded outside the Egypt embassy in Islamabad. The offices of the ambassador, security, and the visa section, whose records may have been the immediate target, were totally destroyed by the suicide bomber assembling a composition of ammonium nitrate and fuel oil, the same mixture used in the World Trade Center bombing and later at the Khobar Towers in Saudi Arabia. Eighteen people, including five Egyptian diplomats, were killed in the explosion that left a crater twelve feet deep and fourteen feet wide. The Egyptian government immediately accused Egyptian Afghan-Arabs and the *Jama'at al-Islamiyah* of Dr. Ayman al-Zawahiri who was then believed to be living in Peshawar. Al Qaeda was also suspected to be involved in the bombing as was Osama bin Laden. Mubarak described Bin Laden as a "megalomaniac" determined to "take over the world." His name had already been well-known among the 173 conspirators listed by the United States government in the trial of Shaykh Omar Abd al-Rahman and eleven others being tried in New York.[20]

---

[19] "Tehran-Khartoum Parliamentary Relations Discussed," IRNA, Tehran, 18 July 1995.
[20] Mary Anne Weaver, "Blowback," *The Atlantic Monthly* (digital edition), May

Sudan Intelligence Agencies and the Sudan Alliance Forces

Despite statements by Hasan al-Turabi and President Bashir that they had complete confidence in the information they received, there was obviously something very wrong within the Sudanese intelligence apparatus. After the Carlos affair rumors had spread that a serious split had developed between those in the intelligence community who favored and those who opposed the extradition of terrorists. After the attempted assassination of President Mubarak, this division became more acute and these differences soon emerged in the leadership of the government. Was the NIF government seeking a scapegoat in the intelligence agencies for the Mubarak affair or was it concerned that its agents had actually supported and failed to kill Mubarak? In September 1995 at a meeting of Arab League foreign ministers in Cairo Ali Osman Muhammad Taha denied the rumors of a widening rift between Bashir and Turabi or that a "collision between the military and the NIF" was imminent. Despite his protestations, all was not well in Khartoum.[21] The American Ambassador Donald Petterson had frequently complained of the difficulty to conduct proper diplomatic relations when the State Department sought information on the many terrorist organizations that maintain offices in Khartoum whose personnel could move freely in and out of the Sudan. Two officials of the U.S. Embassy, both members of the CIA, had been harassed resulting in a strong protest by Ambassador Petterson. Khartoum reacted quickly to his strong protests. Ghazi Salah al-Din Atabani warned Bin Laden that further actions against diplomats in the Sudan could not be tolerated, and there were questions in the Bashir regime of the cost of doing business with Bin Laden and his Al Qaeda. Increasingly, after the Mubarak affair Bashir and his military officers in the RCC began to discuss, assess, and evaluate the cost to Khartoum of doing business with him and his Al Qaeda.

Both the Sudan intelligence agencies, internal and external, were under the authority of the Sudanese ministry of interior. Since the coup d'état of 30 June 1989, there had been numerous changes that

---

1996; see: All Counsel of Record, Re: US v. Omar Ahmad Ali Abdel Rahman, et al., (S5) 93 Cr. 181 (MBM).

[21] "Sudan Minister Denies Split in Leadership," Reuters, Cairo, 19 September 1995.

had a direct impact on the gathering and analysis of intelligence for
the government. The first Minister of Interior Major General Faisal
Ali Abu Salih was expelled from the RCC in April 1991. Military
control over the intelligence apparatus continued, however, when
Major General Al-Zubeir Muhammad Salih, the deputy vice chairman of the RCC, was appointed minister of the interior. His tenure
was brief to be followed in January 1993 by the air force general,
Abd al-Rahim Muhammad Hussein. His appointment was a significant
change from the military to the political and growing influence of
NIF in the decisions of government. Hussein had been secretary-
general of the RCC since 1989 and was regarded as a protégé of
Bashir and known as an Islamist and "hardliner" in the deliberations of the council. Hussein left the supervision of military counterintelligence to General Hashim Abu Said, an intelligence officer
during the Numayri regime who concentrated on internal affairs and
a favorite in the officers corps of the Sudan army. Counterintelligence,
however, was peripheral. Internal intelligence was crucial to the
regime. By February 1994 Hussein had consolidated his authority
over all intelligence branches, but he left the investigative organization of internal security to Nafi Ali Nafi who administered internal
security as a quasi-independent agency.

In the aftermath of the Mubarak affair there were massive demonstrations against the government in September during which students
led 15,000 protestors marching through the streets of Khartoum. For
the first time the security forces and NIF militia were called out to
suppress the determined demonstrators twenty of whom were killed
in the violence that spread from the capital to El Obeid, Wad
Medani, and Port Sudan. Bashir was very disturbed that his internal intelligence agencies had not anticipated the September riots and
used savage reprisals to force the students from the streets. The RCC
ordered a sweeping reorganization of the intelligence apparatus.
Interior minister "Sikha" Khair, Nafi Ali Nafi, Hassan Dhahawi, and
Police Chief Lt. General Hassan Ahmad al-Siddiq, who was considered remiss for his handling of the student riots, were demoted
or transferred. Khair was replaced by Bakri Hassan Salih and shunted
into the ministry of labor and administrative reform, Nafi Ali Nafi
by Brigadier Muhammad Ahmad Mustafa al-Dabi, a confidant of
President Bashir, and General Dhahawi by Brigadier Al-Hadi Abdallah
Hassan who was appointed state minister at the presidency. In effect,
intelligence operations were returned from the Islamists to the military.

Although the Islamists in NIF dismissed the change in the security agencies as a "cosmetic exercise," it was most certainly not an ornamental reorganization. The military had regained control of its intelligence services.

In August the Government of Eritrea had announced the formation of the Sudanese Allied Forces (SAF), another rebel army led by former Sudanese Brigadier Abd al-Aziz Khalid. The SAF was conceived as a multi-ethnic force operating into the Sudan from Eritrea and the Ethiopia borderlands. Although small in numbers in 1996, it would open a new front in the East and divert forces of the SPAF and the PDF from operations against the SPLA in the southern Sudan. Abd al-Aziz Khalid had joined General Fathi and the NDA in Cairo but frustrated by the incompetence of his military leadership, he broke with him in 1993 and moved to Eritrea. Here he began the difficult task of melding a secular political organization of dissident professionals and politicians while organizing a multi-ethnic army from those who had fled the Sudan. He also began to build a "Fifth Column" of the Sudanese in the three towns at the confluence of the Niles and in the Red Sea province from the embittered Beja and Hadendowa. Khalid was a contemporary of President Bashir and the valedictorian of their graduating class at the military academy. In 1989 he had been one of the officers instrumental in forcing Sadiq al-Mahdi to consider peace with the South. As commander of SAF he was accepted by the Eritreans as a committed warrior, unlike general Fathi, and he could be counted on to attack the Eritrean Jihad operating from Sudan.

While Khalid was organizing the SAF in Asmara, dissent in Khartoum had been suppressed, but it did not disappear. There was a dramatic rise in the price of bread. Petrol was scarce, and the PDF was arbitrarily conscripting Sudanese youth to fill the unpopular demands for jihad. For the first time there were chants in the street demonstrations of Khartoum. "Prison for Turabi," "the people are hungry," and referring to the civilian revolution that had toppled the Abboud military dictatorship "bring back October [1964]."[22] Bashir had hoped to use the reorganization of his cabinet and security services to impress the 104th ministerial meeting of the Arab League that opened in Cairo in mid-September, but the

---

[22] "Sudan," *The Economist Intelligence Unit*, London, 4th Quarter, 1995, p. 7.

Khartoum riots were regarded as a sign of weakness in the regime. The Arab League, meeting under the eye of Hosni Mubarak, refused a Sudanese request to include Halayib on its agenda, for it would "only cause more divisions" within the membership.[23]

The student protests of September 1995 were followed by the usual spate of arrests. The PDF patrolled the streets of the capital. Nafi Ali Nafi was now a personal aide to Hasan al-Turabi who was unhappy that Bashir had fired a man he had handpicked to run internal Sudanese intelligence. Arab-Afghans, Pakistanis, and Iranians were now conspicuous in the offices of Sudanese security, frequently replacing Sudanese, and the appearance of foreigners in the government's intelligence apparatus was of grave concern to the Sudanese abroad, the NDA, and Sadiq al-Mahdi of the powerful Umma Party. After the demonstrations in September the NIF government had approached the Umma leadership in Khartoum and in exile seeking a rapprochement. The Umma, however, was offered no share in the cabinet, and patronage would remain a prerogative of NIF. Sadiq's acerbic response was published in *Al-Hayat* in December 1995. He denied the legitimacy of the NIF government, and strongly supported the Asmara Declaration of the NDA and SPLA in June 1995 as the basis for a new Sudanese constitution. As for the civil war in the Sudan he observed that "the NIF is now the only party in the country that still believes in a military solution to the conflict."[24]

The Isolation of the Sudan

With unfriendly nations to the south and east and an angry Mubarak to the north, the RCC in the summer of 1994 sought to break out of its international isolation. By September 1994 Muammar Qaddafi had completed the reorganization of his Libyan intelligence apparatus whose Islamists were replaced by members of his family clan. When Bashir attended the 25th anniversary of Libya's revolution,

---

[23] "Government of Sudan and Rebel Forces Both Guilty of Abuses Against Children," *Human Rights Watch*, New York, September 1995; "Darkest Days Yet for Sudanese Regime," *Middle East Times*, 17–23 September 1995, p. 1; "Egypt Snubs Sudanese Reconciliation Overtures," *Middle East Times*, 24–30 September 1995.

[24] "Regime Puts Foreign Fundamentalists in Control of National Security," *Sudan Democratic Gazette*, London, January 1996, p. 7.

Qaddafi was the friendly mediator between Bashir and Algerian President Liamine Zeroual to resolve the latter's accusations that Algerian Islamists were openly operating against him from Sudan. In November 1994 Hasan al-Turabi met with Qaddafi in Tobruk to discuss "problems of Islamic movements in Libya and North Africa," the means by which the sanctions imposed on both nations could be "eased," and how the implementation of the "apparatus for integration" of the Sudan and Libya could begin. Turabi, Vice President Zubeir, Chairman Ismail of CIPF and secretary-general of the Sudan-Libya ministerial committee, and Major General Muhammad Osman, met with Qaddafi in an effort to revive the moribund Sudanese-Libyan ministerial committee, "the apparatus for integration." Turabi announced that the talks had "strengthened my relations with Gaddafi after a long break."[25]

This was an illusion. Qaddafi was confronted by an economy in recession, the flight of domestic capital through expatriate worker remittances, and the rise of Muslim fundamentalism in his own country. Thus, despite an initial outburst of enthusiasm for his perennial Pan-Arab message, he could not forget that his Pan-Arab quest had been consistently rejected in the past by Turabi and NIF. They were more Pan-Islamists than Pan-Arabs. He was not about to embark on another plan for integration with the Sudan when relations with Egypt, after years of hostility, had changed after Qaddafi strongly supported Mubarak in the wake of the Addis Ababa affair. When Libya failed to obtain a UN Security Council seat in 1995, it supported Egypt as its replacement. Qaddafi effusively responded when the Egyptian Foreign Minister Amr Musa proposed to remove the international sanctions on Libya as a result of the complicity of Libyans in the Lockerbie disaster in April 1982. Relations between Cairo and Tripoli became even more cordial when the national oil companies of both countries agreed to fund a joint $300 million 600 kilometer-long pipeline which would move 150,000 barrels a day of Libyan oil from Tobruk to Alexandria.[26] The pipeline agreement

---

[25] "Sudan, Libya aim to revive merger pact," Reuters, Cairo, 20 November 1994.

[26] James Bruce, "As Khadafy Celebrates 27 Years, His Fundamentalist Challenge Grows," *DefenseWeb*, www.pollux.com/defenseweb: 1996; also note Reuters, "Sudanese Deported from Libya Arrive Home," 13 September 1995; "Plot to Kill Qaddafi," *Foreign Report*, Jane's Information Group Ltd., 28 September 1995, pp. 2–3.

dramatically improved relations between Tripoli and Cairo at a time when those between Tripoli and Khartoum were deteriorating.

In order to strengthen his economy and assuage the growing animosity of his Libyan subjects, Qaddafi began the expulsion of foreigners who comprised about one-third of Libya's workforce many of whom were Sudanese. The long economic recession, the revived activity of Libyan Islamists, and the fear that foreigners were becoming involved in Libyan politics led him to send home hundreds of thousands of expatriates. The pace of expulsions accelerated after an attempt to assassinate him failed in Sirte in September 1995 to be followed by a series of clashes in Benghazi between the security forces and 3,500 "Islamic activists," many of whom were armed.[27] The Libyan demonstrators were led by Islamists of the so-called "Martyr's Movement" but were supported by liberals opposed to Qaddafi and members of the Sannusiya brotherhood whom Qaddafi had singularly suppressed. There were 400 Islamists who had broken out of Benghazi's notorious Al-Kuwairfiya prison in March 1996. Senior Libyan security officials were assassinated, most notably the "commander of Libya's *Mukafaha Zandaka*, or 'anti-heresy force,' formed by Khadafy to counter the mounting fundamentalist opposition."[28]

These Islamist demonstrations and assassinations were the first real challenge to Qaddafi's Jamahiriya in a quarter century. He was furious, declaring that the attempt to assassinate him showed a "remarkable similarity" to the attack on Mubarak in Addis Ababa. He responded by expelling 70,000 Sudanese from Libya. When he was informed that Sudanese were involved in the clashes in Benghazi, he denounced the NIF government for training the "Muslim militants opposing him."[29] Thousands of Sudanese, many without identification papers, arrived in Darfur, Northern Kordofan, and at Dongola in the Northern State. Qaddafi had closed the door on his relationships with the NIF government. Although Libyan security agents also expelled Egyptian merchants from Tripoli, Benghazi, and Tobruk, the Egyptian-Libyan rapprochement had been solidified by the oil pipeline and Mubarak's sympathy with Qaddafi's concern and suppression of the Islamists, particularly after more clashes erupted in

---

[27] "Libya puts clamps on Muslim activists," *The Washington Times*, 11 September 1993.
[28] *Al-Sharq al-Awsat*, London, 9 July 1996.
[29] *Al-Sharq al-Awsat*.

Benghazi between police and "fundamentalist groups."[30] When in July Qaddafi ordered the Libyan air force to use jets and helicopter gunships to attack the base camps of Islamist-led rebels operating from the Jabal Akhdar region on the Egyptian border, Mubarak did not object.

Thunder on the Nile

Throughout 1995 and 1996 Presidents Bashir and Mubarak continued their war of words. The Sudan should not be a scapegoat for Egyptian Islamist militants when Mubarak had been unable to resolve his differences with his own dissidents. Bashir appeared convinced Egyptian efforts to implicate the Sudan in the Mubarak assassination was part of a wider conspiracy to overthrow his government that began when the Eritrean government severed diplomatic relations and invited the NDA opposition to make its headquarters in Asmara. Three days after the attack on Mubarak in June 1995 at Addis Ababa the SPLM, DUP, Umma, Union of Sudan African Parties, the Sudan Communist Party, Trade Unions, the LMC, the SAF, and the Beja Congress had signed a Declaration of Political Agreement to continue the war until the NIF government in Khartoum was overthrown.[31] Known as the "Asmara Accords" the declaration affirmed the right of self-determination as a "basic, original and democratic right of all peoples . . . with the support and blessing of neighboring states" who were actively plotting to overthrow the NIF government of President Bashir. The NDA formally established the Sudanese Allied Forces commanded by Brigadier Abd al-Aziz Khalid which was the first northern military force committed to bring down the NIF government.[32] The SAF was not a formidable army, but its "mobile forces" included 500 Beja who in May 1996 dominated the eastern Sudan and the Eritrea frontier.

Bashir thundered that his government would confront the NDA participants at Asmara in a manner that "astounds the world." The presence of the ambassador of the United States and Western

---

[30] *Al-Hayat*, London, 10 July 1996.

[31] "The Final Communique," The National Democratic Alliance Conference on the Issues of Destiny," Asmara, Eritrea, 23 June 1995.

[32] *Al-Watan Al-Arabi*, interview with Brigadier General Abd al-Aziz Khalid, Sudanese Allied Forces chief, Paris, 7 June 1996.

diplomats at Asmara gave a boost to morale and perhaps covert funds to the NDA. The members of IGADD were unimpressed by Bashir's bashing. It had been Bashir and his government who had frustrated IGADD efforts to end the civil war in the Sudan in 1994, and in 1995 Khartoum's disinterest had led IGADD to postpone its heads of state summit meeting. The European Community expressed its dismay at the disabling of IGADD by Bashir "as a result of the non-cooperative posturing of the Government of Sudan."[33] A week later in Washington the Sudan Minister for Foreign Affairs Dr. Ghazi Salah al-Din Atabani pronounced the IGADD process spent, "only the Sudanese can bring a peace process—the role of IGADD should be a catalytic one only."[34] Having no interest in the peace process, Khartoum launched a military offensive from Juba against the SPLA in Equatoria, and the Transitional National Assembly prepared for elections controlled by the government to be held in March 1996 for a permanent National Assembly (*Majlis al-Watani*) that would officially confirm a NIF dominated government.

From Libya in the northwest to Eritrea in the southeast, there emerged in Khartoum a feeling that it was surrounded by weak friends and determined enemies who formed a "circle of animosity." After the Asmara Accords the SPAF appeared to be confronted by "an alliance of exiled opponents that [was] putting on muscle." African statesmen publicly agreed that the NIF government of Omar Hasan Ahmad al-Bashir and Hasan al-Turabi was racist, bigoted, and totalitarian. Egypt, Eritrea, Ethiopia, Kenya, and Uganda were all hostile. On the Congo-Nile watershed, the southwestern border of the Sudan, eastern Zaire was plunging into anarchy, the Central African Republic and Chad were impoverished and unstable. In the past Sudanese governments could count on allies in the Gulf and in the West to overcome internal political problems and international tensions on its borders. No other country in the great Nile basin and the Horn of Africa "has ever been encircled like Sudan is today, apart from South Africa."[35] The main perceived threat was from Uganda on the Sudan's southern border.

---

[33] ACP-EU Joint Assembly Report ACP-EU/AP1607/95/COMP, 27 September 1995, p. 2.

[34] Dr. Ghazi Salah al-Din Atabani at the Center for Strategic and International Studies, Washington D.C., 4 October 1995.

[35] "Sudan almost ringed by foreign and exiled foes," Reuters dispatch, 18 February 1996 for a report published in *The Kenya Times*, Nairobi, 18 February 1996.

President Museveni of Uganda had sought to bring peace to the southern Sudan, for the fighting spilled over into northern Uganda where he had little political support from the Acholi. Bashir consequently began to arm the rebels in northern Uganda and its West Nile District from the headquarters of the Sudan army in Juba in order to contain the hostility from Kampala. During the decade of the nineties Khartoum had provided funds for the Tabliq Youth organized by radical Islamist elements within the Muslim population of Uganda. Moreover, Alice Lakwena's Holy Spirit Movement, which was certainly not Muslim but committed many murders of innocent civilians, had only been crushed by the Ugandan army in 1987, but no sooner was her movement brought to an end, than Khartoum began to supply arms and sanctuary to a new Christian fundamentalist movement led by the "prophet" Joseph Kony.

Kony, a former Catholic altar boy and "herbalist," proclaimed the coming of a new millennium. He attracted thousands of Acholi from the Sudan-Uganda borderlands to his Lord's Resistance Army (LRA) promising them that Uganda would be ruled by the Ten Commandments. "Thousands of young men were abducted into his army; hundreds of young women were torn from their families for general use among the military." They were trained in the "fine arts of murder, torture, and learned that either death or a good beating awaited those who tried to escape."[36] As the children matured they were utterly merciless in the treatment of the helpless civilian population of southern Sudan and northern Uganda and cowardly when opposed by military elements. Despite operation "Iron Fist" of the Uganda Defense Force the LRA continued to raid and pillage refugee camps and protected villages during the summer of 2002. Besides supporting the LRA the SPAF also trained and armed a Muslim force of 2,000, smaller than the LRA, but which raided throughout northern Uganda "with the intention of eventually capturing the border towns with Khartoum's support."[37] In 1994 the Uganda People's Defense Force in the West Nile District defeated the radical Muslim Tabliq Youth who fled into Zaire to become "the core of the West

---

[36] Robin Denslow, "Terror fo the 'Lord's Army,'" *South Africa Weekly Mail & Guardian*, 23 August 1996.
[37] *Sudan Democratic Gazette*, London, September 1993, p. 2.

Nile Bank Front," the loyal, former soldiers of Idi Amin from his homeland west of the Nile.

In 1995 the Sudan launched a dry-season offensive to take the SPLA stronghold at Kaya that required encroachment into Uganda territory, and the antiquated Russian Antonov bombers, which began high altitude bombing in February, could not discriminate between Sudan and Uganda territory. The SPAF frequently crossed the border unopposed into the West Nile District. and continued to support Joseph Kony's Lord's Resistance Army that was killing hundreds of civilians and destroying scores of villages east of the Albert Nile in Acholi land in northern Uganda. Exasperated, Museveni broke off diplomatic relations in April and closed the large Sudanese embassy, a "nest of spies," in Kampala. Only Jimmy Carter seemed interested in reviving peace talks. He arrived again in Khartoum in July, and as a former president of the United States, he was able to embarrass the Khartoum government to respect a cease-fire in order for him to launch his well-organized humanitarian campaign to eradicate river blindness in the southern Sudan. Even the Islamists, who had few friends, could not resist his appeal and agreed to a cease-fire, but Minister of State Ghazi Salah al-Din Atabani grumbled that a cease-fire only benefited the SPLA.[38] The hope that Carter, by his position and personal diplomacy, could restart the peace process was naïve. He and his staff knew little of the Sudan and less of the Sudanese. When a proposed reconciliation conference that included all major and minor southern Sudanese military and political organizations to begin in Nairobi on 15 August was postponed indefinitely, the Carter mission returned to Georgia.

In that same August the Sudan army and the West Bank Nile Front (WBNF) led by Colonel Juma Oris overran the SPLA at Kaya on the Uganda border, and the men of the WBNF pursued the remnants of the SPLA into Zaire and Uganda. "Whatever the diplomatic cover is put over the situation, the reality is that Uganda and Sudan are effectively at war."[39] In August Tehran announced to a visiting Sudanese delegation that it would offer its mediation in the

---

[38] "Sudanese Reconciliation Postponed," *The Middle East Times*, 20–26 August 1995.
[39] Private correspondence in possession of the authors.

Uganda and Sudan dispute that became irrelevant after the SPLA won its first decisive victory in three years during its 1995 offensive in October. President Bashir blamed the unexpected defeat of his army on Uganda that drove relations with Uganda from bad to worse.

Eritrea, Uganda, Ethiopia, and the Sudan

In 1995 the most determined enemy of the NIF government in Khartoum was President Isayas Afewerki of Eritrea. He had proudly hosted the crucial meetings of the NDA in 1994 and 1995 and had given them the former Sudanese embassy in Asmara from which to overthrow the Islamist regime in the Sudan. "Our conflict with Sudan comes from Khartoum's dream of spreading its brand of Islam across Africa."[40] No sooner had the Asmara Accords been signed by the members of the NDA in 1995 than the Beja, armed by Eritrea, began their raids throughout the eastern Sudan. The Beja were yet another ethnic minority known for their martial prowess. For centuries they have been committed Muslims, but their practice of Islam was mixed with ancient non-Muslim rituals that the Islamists in Khartoum considered heterodox at best and heretical at worse. More important the Beja leaders had bitterly complained that the government had done nothing to help hundreds of thousands of their nomadic herders to recover from a series of disastrous droughts during 1983–1985.[41]

Despite negotiations held in June in Blantyre, Malawi, between Presidents Museveni and Bashir the Sudan government continued to bomb villages and towns in the southern Sudan of no military importance, killing only cows and civilians. With the coming of the spring and summer rains, however, the SPLA took the offensive for the first time since 1989. In Uganda they attacked the LRA whose units retreated to Juba and the protection of the SPAF that launched its own offensive into Equatoria driving another 300,000 southerners

---

[40] "Sudan almost ringed by foreign and exiled foes," Reuters dispatch, 18 February 1996, from a report published in *The Kenya Times*, Nairobi, 18 February 1996.
[41] Radio SPLA (clandestine), 1300 hours, 22 June 1985.

into Zaire and Uganda. In February 1996, the LRA, supplied with arms and their safe-havens in the Sudan, launched a campaign of terror in northern Uganda raiding refugee camps, burning villages, looting shops, and abducting children to fill the depleted cadres of its movement.[42] In Kampala Museveni was quick to appreciate that the LRA rebels, who had been around for years but were only a nuisance, had now been rearmed by the Sudan army. The Sudanese Islamist infiltration into Uganda was not confined to arming the LRA. Shaykh Saad Ibrahim Luwemba, the Mufti of Uganda and a close friend of President Museveni, warned that the militant Tabliq Youth were still being trained by the Sudan to devise a "new plan by Islamic fundamentalists to wage war on the government."[43]

After the attempted assassination of Hosni Mubarak the Ethiopian President Meles Zenawi joined Museveni and Afewerki in outright opposition to the Sudanese government. He had offered to mediate in the Sudan civil war. "In our entire region we have probably gone the farthest in trying to convince Khartoum that its course runs great risks."[44] There had long been Islamist proselytizing among Somali refugees in Ethiopia, and Somali irredentists were active in the Ogaden financed by the Wahhabi of Saudi Arabia. President Zenawi was appalled that Somali Muslims would use Ethiopia to attack a member of the OAU and the Inter-Governmental Authority on Drought (now IGAD), for he had succeeded in melding the Oromo, Issa, Afar, and Amhara into a parliamentary alliance, and his EPRDF had begun the decentralization of government that promised greater regional autonomy. He had also expended considerable effort conferring with Somali leaders to institute a stable government in the Ogaden and Somalia. Meanwhile, Sudanese assistance continued to pass through the *Al-Da'awa al-Islamiyya* and the Islamic Relief Agency (ISRA) supported by the Somali Islamic Union Party, *Al-Ittihad*, from its center at Burao in northern Somalia.

---

[42] "Uganda says 500 rebels cross from south Sudan," Reuters, Kampala, 13 February 1996; "Ugandan rebels kill 12 in raid on northern town," Reuters, Kampala, 16 February 1996; "Report on the Mission to Sudan, Eritrea and Ethiopia, 26 August–2 September 1995" (Lord Plumb, Mr. Boulle, Mrs Kinnock and Mrs. Robinson), ACP-EU Joint Assembly, AP/1586, 25 September 1995.
[43] *South Africa Weekly Mail & Guardian*, All Africa Press Service, Kampala dateline, August 29, 1996.
[44] "Radicals Gain Strength in Horn of Africa," *The Washington Post*, 5 January 1994, p. A26.

In December the UN Security Council demanded that the Sudan extradite to Ethiopia the three missing gunmen in the attempted assassination of President Mubarak The Sudan government responded it had no proof that the suspects had entered its territory. In January 1996 the UN Security Council unanimously passed Resolution No. 1044 that imposed sanctions on the Sudan for refusing to cooperate in the assassination investigation. The United States accused the Sudan of "complicity in supporting and sheltering" the terrorists. When the Sudanese public prosecutor pleaded ignorance of the whereabouts of the assassins and issued a public request they turn themselves into the government, the Ethiopian ministry of foreign affairs responded in disbelief. "Since Sudan knows full well where the three gunmen are being sheltered and protected by its own security personnel, the notice issued by its prosecutor is the latest confirmation that Sudan is not about to comply with the request of the Security Council. . . . Above and beyond [Sudan's] lack of sincerity, this call by Sudan to the three suspects to report to police, six months after the Ethiopian request for their extradition, confirms without a shadow of doubt that Sudan will never, ever co-operate with the Security Council."[45] Some thought that Ali Osman Muhammad Taha was "behind the assassination" and provided passports and transportation to the three terrorists to leave the Sudan that "enabled them to move on to Afghanistan."[46]

Relations between Addis Ababa and Khartoum continued to deteriorate after the SPLA overran units of SPAF and captured the border town of Kurmuk on the Ethiopian frontier in January 1996. The NIF government denounced Ethiopia for its support in this "two-week offensive." Ethiopia denied the accusation, arguing that Sudan was only trying to undermine Ethiopian efforts in the UN Security Council designed to hand over the three terrorists accused in the attempted Mubarak assassination. President Bashir responded in turn by accusing Egypt and the United States of involving Eritrea, Ethiopia, Kenya, and Uganda in a plan to overthrow his government. The rhetoric, not surprisingly, was accompanied by military activity. In March 1996 Ethiopian mechanized units shelled border villages along

---

[45] United Nations, New York, Press Release, 31 January 1966, 26 April 1996.
[46] Correspondence between Millard Burr and Dr. Eric Reeves, Smith College, Northampton, Massachusetts, 15 October 2001.

the frontier in support of the SPLA offensive that captured the small
towns of Yabus and Pochalla on the Ethiopian-Sudan border.[47]

On 26 April 1996 the UN Security Council, on which Egypt was
the only Arab member, passed Resolution 1054 that authorized further sanctions against the Sudan for its refusal to cooperate in the
assassination investigation. It required the Sudan government to turn
over the suspects within two weeks or suffer penalties that included
the reduction of Sudanese diplomatic representation in the United
Nations and restricted travel in the United States for its diplomats.
Ethiopia had waited more than half a year for the Sudan to respond
to its request to extradite the three gunmen by which time the United
States now recognized the complicity of Khartoum in sheltering the
terrorists. In Addis Ababa the United States Secretary of Defense
Assistance Secretary for International Security Affairs Vincent Kern
told the Ethiopian parliamentary defense committee that "The United
States was ready to share with Ethiopia its rich democratic military
experience gained over the past 200 years."[48] Kern's strong statement was followed by the announcement that the United States
would assist the reorganization and equipment for the Ethiopian air
force. The Egyptians, who had experienced two thousand years of
hostile relations with the Ethiopians, were not as cooperative as the
Americans. After the attempted assassination the Egyptian government sought to "usurp the official investigations in Ethiopia, believ-
ing that the Ethiopians would perhaps not do a thorough job."
Egyptian officiousness angered the Ethiopian government, that was
as determined as Cairo to fix, find, and try the culprits. The Ethiopian
investigation was very thorough and gave Egypt no cause for complaint particularly if it implicated the NIF regime in Khartoum. In
March 1996 the Egyptian terrorists went on trial in Addis Ababa.

One of the indicted, Safwat Hassan Abd al-Ghani, admitted he
had received military training in Afghanistan and in the 1980s had
fought with mujahideen guerrillas. When the war ended, he joined
the Egyptian *Jama'at al-Islamiyah* (Islamic Jihad) and went to Kenya
and the Sudan where he "stayed for a number of years" with brother
revolutionaries "on a farm that was used for our gathering." The

---

[47] Reuters datelines, Addis Ababa, Ethiopia, 26, 27 March 1996.
[48] Reuters datelines Addis Ababa, 8 February 1996, 12 February 1996; *Jane's Defence Weekly*, 3 July 1996.

farm was Osama bin Laden's favorite retreat on the Blue Nile. Al-Ghani then moved to Addis Ababa where he opened an auto spare parts shop financed by the Islamic Jihad, but the Sudanese government "is our only solace. It upholds the flag of truth for the glory of Islam and Moslems."[49]

---

[49] Reuters datelines, Addis Ababa, Ethiopia, 26, 27 March 1996.

CHAPTER TEN

SEARCHING FOR FRIENDS, SURROUNDED BY ENEMIES

The attempted assassination of Hosni Mubarak and the gatherings of Islamists at the PAIC General Assembly finally isolated Khartoum from nearly all Arab and African governments. From Morocco through Libya, from Mali through Chad, and in Africa south of the Sahara, the Sudan could not rely on a single ally. Its friends were in the Yemen, Qatar, Syria, Iran, Iraq, Afghanistan, Malaysia, and China. It was not a union of nations that inspired much trust. Although the RCC in 1989 had never attracted popular support at home, its isolation in international affairs began in 1991, coinciding with the PAIC General Assembly and the arrival in Khartoum of Osama bin Laden. The PAIC attracted the leading Muslim fundamentalists, and a parade of theorists and terrorists many of whom settled in the Sudan. By 1994 Turabi's PAIC General Assembly had become the political arm of a world-wide Islamist movement that accepted terrorism as a just instrument to be wielded in an evil world dominated by the West.

In less than three years the Sudan, a Nilotic backwater, had achieved a new image in the twentieth century that had its heritage in the Sudanese Islamic revolution of Muhmmad Ahmad al-Mahdi in the nineteenth. Hasan al-Turabi emerged as the Islamist spokesman for a new age. Despite his charm and discourse, he could be both discreet and secretive. There would be no handouts to the press at the meetings of PAIC General Assembly, and the conferees would come and go quietly without any publicity. The congress would have carried on their deliberations in relative obscurity were it not for a major miscalculation. In 1991 both Al Qaeda and the Egyptian Islamic Jihad leadership, financed by Osama bin Laden, and hundreds of Afghan-Arabs arrived from Afghanistan and Pakistan in the Sudan with the approval of President Bashir and Hasan al-Turabi. It is apparent that they both misjudged the impact in the Sudan and on the international community of these militant visitors. There were scores of Egyptian jihad revolutionaries. Turabi knew the Afghan-Arabs very well. President Bashir knew much less than he should, but it probably would not have mattered for both would have welcomed anyone to ensure the survival of their Islamist state.

Although Sudan intelligence issued passports, provided false documents, and organized travel arrangements, the Afghan-Arabs, Bin
Laden, Dr. Ayman al-Zawahiri, and the Egyptian Islamic Jihad group
became an increasing liability for President Omar Hasan Ahmad al-
Bashir. The U.S. Department of State added the Sudan to its list
of state-sponsored terrorism in 1993, and the United States had
become so antagonistic that it used its powerful presence in the international community to condemn the policies and practices of the
Sudan government. After the PAIC General Assembly opened in
Khartoum at the end of March 1995, there was increasing interest
from the international community in the moral support given by
Turabi and the funds funneled through Bin Laden and his Al Qaeda
front organization for mujahideen in Bosnia, Albania, Kashmir,
Somalia, Ethiopia, Chechnya, and Tadjikistan. Bin Laden was known
as the mujahideen financier, and in Sudan he had invested $50 million in the Islamic Al-Shamal Bank in Khartoum and in mechanized agricultural schemes that provided work for some 4,000 people.[1]
He found employment for his Afghan-Arabs and Muslims who were
trained in arms and explosives including Egyptians associated with
Islamic Jihad and its "Vanguards of Conquest" leadership.

The attempted assassination of Hosni Mubarak and rumors that
Al Qaeda would assassinate Sadiq al-Mahdi had antagonized his
large following, the Ansar and Umma, who were a constant threat
to the survival of an unpopular NIF government.[2] Disillusioned by
the Gulf War and the Saudi royal family Bin Laden had begun to
reorganize Al Qaeda. No longer welcome in Saudi Arabia he was
able from the sanctuary of Khartoum to finance much of the anti-
royalist propaganda disseminated in Saudi Arabia. His presence and
activities certainly contributed to the growing rift between the Sudan
and Saudi Arabia. In November 1995 a bomb destroyed a training
facility of the Saudi Arabian National Guard in Riyadh, killing seven
people, including five Americans, and revived Saudi interest in Osama

---

[1] "Suspected terrorist in Ontario court says he's been falsely accused," Canadian
Press Newswire, 27 February 2001.
[2] "Terror group weighed poisoning, bombing," UPI, New York, 13 February
2001.

bin Laden. He had become the "main bankroller of Islamic fundamentalist organizations throughout the Arab world and Europe" and
was devoted to the destruction of the Saudi royal family for its corruption, the Westernizing of Saudi Arabia, and for allowing an
American military presence in the country.[3] A few days after the
incident in Riyadh the Egyptian embassy in Islamabad, Pakistan,
was destroyed by a large car bomb planted by militant Islamists associated with Osama bin Laden and Hasan al-Turabi. Prince Turki,
the director of Saudi Arabian intelligence services, flew to Cairo for
meetings with his Egyptian counterparts during which a "pan-Islamic
link" was established. Pakistan was pressured by Egypt and Saudi
Arabia to expel "the Peshawar-based, non-Afghan mujahideen fighters"
who were exporting *jihad* "back home to their respective countries. . . .
Pakistan expelled about 230 Egyptians," a number of whom after
leaving Iran arrived in the Sudan accompanied by "shipments of
arms and documents from Pakistan to Egyptian terrorist groups in
Sudan."[4] In Khartoum Bin Laden denied any association with the
four Saudi Afghan mujahideen who were arrested and accused of
the Riyadh bombing, apostasy, and plotting against the Saudi Arabian
government. The terrorists appeared on Saudi television in April
1996. "They confessed to being influenced by extremist groups" and
by "views circulated by Muhammad al-Massari and Osama Bin
Ladin."[5] The four Saudi terrorists were beheaded in the public square
of Riyadh.[6]

Hasan al-Turabi and the National Council

In 1995 President Bashir approved the Thirteenth Constitutional
Decree of the RCC. "Decree 13" was the result of "the popular
movements" that began in 1992 when 16,000 local conferences were
convened and elections held for constituent councils. Elections to

---

[3] "Saudi Millionaire Denies Role in Riyadh Bombing," COMPASS News Service,
Washington D.C., 29 April 1996.
[4] Tarun Basu, "Pakistan Called an 'Incubator' of Terrorism," *India Abroad Publications
Inc.*, 1 December 1995.
[5] "Riyadh Bombing Culprits Arrested," Embassy of Saudi Arabia press release,
Washington D.C., 22 April 1996.
[6] "Saudi Arabia sends warning to dissidents-analysts," Reuters, Dubai, 23 April
1996.

provincial councils followed shortly, and from them delegates were elected to a national conference in Khartoum. Here the national conference, in its extended deliberations, constructed the "Charter of the Sudanese People" that authorized direct elections, defined the functions of the president and parliament for an elected government to succeed the military dictatorship of the RCC. The president would be elected for five years by a majority vote that was a rare phenomena in the plethora of Sudanese political parties. "Decree 13" ended the rule by the command council and introduced a form of federalism by a 400 member National Council, a national parliament, the *shura* envisaged by Hasan al-Turabi, to govern the Sudan. After the Inter-Religious Dialogue Conference in Khartoum in October 1994 he was emphatic that "the Sudanese model is not a military government supported by an Islamic movement." His political model for the new Sudan would become a reality only when an Islamist military would become subservient to an Islamists *shura* chosen by the Sudanese people. The years between the coup d'état of 30 June 1989 and the elections of 1996 were just "a transition" during which NIF had remade the military, the police, the universities, and privatized the economy by "the democratization of government" that would lead to the creation of an "Islamic model of government."[7]

Of the 400 seats in the National Council a 125 were appointed in January 1996 and another fifty seats went to candidates, including loyal NIF supporters, ministers, academics, and the professions nominated by the NIF government. The other half of the National Council were to be chosen by elections launched on 22 February 1996. With typical Sudanese exuberance and the frustration of the past when elections had been prohibited, over 1,000 citizens campaigned for the remaining 275 seats in the council from March 6 to 17. The candidates were "favored," however, by "popular committees" of NIF supporters in the voting districts. Indeed, electoral registers were missing and thousands complained they were unable to vote especially where unpopular politicians and non-NIF members were running for office. Brigadier Youssef Abd al-Fatah, Brigadier Al-Taib Ibrahim Muhammad Khair, Ali Osman Muhammad Taha, Muhammad Al-Amin Khalifa, Mohamed Khogali Saliheen,

---

[7] "Interview with Sudanese Leaders Al-Turabi and Al-Attabani," *Contemporary Islamic Political Views*, November 1994 and April 1996.

ran unopposed as did some forty-seven parliamentary candidates. In Khartoum there was considerable competition, 184 candidates standing for its thirty-eight constituencies.

During the election Turabi remained the master dissembler denying he had any interest in political office. He was an Islamic theologian, lawyer, and leader of the PAIC General Asembly, not a politician. Nevertheless, he stood for election in the Al-Sahafa District south of Khartoum where he had lost an embarrassing election in 1986 that had brought Sadiq al-Mahdi to power. His two Islamists opponents, Abd al-Rahman al-Sallawi, a businessman, and Dr. Abass Awadallah Abass, Dean of the Shari'a Faculty at the Al-Imam Al-Mahdi University in Omdurman, withdrew claiming election fraud. Turabi returned triumphant to public life and was immediately elected speaker of parliament. He was now the most powerful personality in the Sudan who controlled a parliament of his NIF supporters to build the "new Sudan."

After the elections the RCC kept its word given in 1989 to return the government to civilian control. Omar Hasan Ahmad al-Bashir was elected president with over 75 percent of the vote, but historically when the Sudan was ruled by parliamentary governments, the president had been more a figurehead than the dominate political figure. Bashir, however, still controlled the military, a check on ambitious new civilian politicians. There were few changes in the cabinet except for the Minister of Economics Abdallah Hassah Ahmed who was retired to be governor of the Bank of Sudan. It was Islamist politics as usual with a government dominated by NIF, its supporters now led by Hasan al-Turabi as speaker of parliament, but this new NIF government sought to improve its international image by a disingenuous display of democracy. Democracy Sudanese style was more coercion at the voting booth than open debate in city and countryside that resulted in the landslide election of NIF supporters to all but one of the seats in the new national parliament.

Sadiq al-Mahdi described the elections as a farce. Khartoum had become the capital of a rogue government that issued passports to terrorists "and to individuals who have actually declared war against their governments and have used violence" to achieve their ends.[8]

---

[8] Associated Press, Khartoum, 31 March 1996.

Moreover, there had been serious disagreements between the Muslim Brotherhood and Turabi. Mustapha Mansoor, the General Guide of the Muslim Brotherhood, admitted there were "some disagreements between Turabi and the Brotherhood" that had led to their going separate ways. He did not regard Turabi's new *Majlis al-Shura* as "the ideal Islamic model for "Islam does not approve of the principle of [achieving] power through military revolution." Sadiq al-Mahdi regarded the new parliament as absurd; Mansoor dismissed it as an appointed body, not the elective council envisaged by Hasan al-Turabi.[9] Others thought that radical Islam in the Sudan was not the product of Hasan al-Turabi, but "more a product of student activism at Leeds Polytechnic and London University in the sixties than of the Mahdi Mohammedans," and his movement represented only "an elite of educated young men who have secured the most important civil service and military jobs, but are struggling to take the rest of society with them."[10]

The ambiguity about Hasan al-Turabi, the Islamists, and the NIF government was not confined among the Sudanese. In 1995 the Department of State Coordinator for Counter-Terrorism Ambassador Philip C. Wilcox, Jr. did not believe that the Sudan government was involved in the bombing of the World Trade Center. He did not appreciate the spread and determination of both Al Qaeda and the PAIC General Assembly or the direct support mujahideen had received from numerous states including the Sudan. Wilcox described Ramzi Ahmad Yousif of Al Qaeda "and his gang" as a "group of freelance terrorists, many of whom were trained in Afghanistan who came from various nations but who did not rely on support from any state."[11] The Director of the United States Central Intelligence Agency John Deutch did not agree. He testified before Congress in February 1996 that the Sudan had emerged "as a clear threat to the stability of nearby African and Middle Eastern states because of its support for subversive activities of regional opposition groups' and this threat would remain as long as the "NIF is the dominant political force" in Sudan. "In its effort to spread its version of Islamic

---

[9] "MSA News: Muslim Brotherhood Interview with Mustapha Mansoor," msamews.mynet.net/MSANEWS/ 20 June 1996.
[10] Philip Van Niekerk, "Sudan's own apartheid ghettoes," *Mail & Guardian*, South Africa, 4 April 1997.
[11] "Amb. Wilcox on Patterns of Global Terrorism," Daily Press Briefing, U.S. Department of State, Washington D.C., 30 April 1996.

fundamentalism beyond Sudan and destabilize moderate Muslim governments friendly to the United States, the NIF supports insurgent
and terrorist groups opposed to the governments of Egypt, Eritrea,
Ethiopia, and Uganda." The Sudan continued to provide a safe
haven for "radical groups" including Hizbollah, Hamas, the Abu
Nidal Organization, and Algerian extremists while Khartoum continued its "repressive internal policies against the Sudanese people,
particularly non-Muslim southerners."[12] There was little chance of
constructive relations between the United States and Sudan with
Turabi and his Islamists in power until Osama bin Laden had become
a liability. Perhaps ebullient at the prospect of an Islamist *shura* to
replace a military dictatorship or the confirmation of his arrogance
as its speaker, "in August [1996], Turabi sent an 'olive branch' letter to President Clinton" through a trusted intermediary proposing
that he use his influence and dominate position in Khartoum to
improve relations between the Sudan and the United States. "There
was no reply."[13]

Osama bin Laden for Sale

By January 1996 Hasan al-Turabi had become aware that Osama
bin Laden, the guest he had graciously greeted in 1991, was no
longer welcome in the Sudan. It is unknown if he was aware that
President Bashir was determined to rid his government of Osama
bin Laden. He first offered to extradite Bin Laden to Saudi Arabia,
but the proposal was refused by the leaders within the Saudi royal
family. They were rightly apprehensive that his return and trial would
create unwanted if not drastic domestic repercussions. If the Saudi
government refused to take Bin Laden, Bashir then requested them
to act as intermediaries to facilitate his delivery to the United States.
He used his confidant, Al-Fatih Urwah, who met with representatives of the CIA in a hotel room in Rosslyn, Virginia. Here he vol-
unteered the services of Sudanese security to seize Bin Laden and

---

[12] John M. Deutch, Director, Central Intelligence Agency, "Worldwide Threat
Assessment Brief," Senate Select Committee on Intelligence, Washington D.C., 22
February 1996.
[13] Mansoor Ijaz and Timothy Carney, "Intelligence Failure? Let's Go Back to
Sudan," *The Washington Post*, 30 June 2002.

legally extradite him to Saudi Arabia where he would be turned over to American authorities.

In Washington officials at the Department of State were apparently baffled by the offer. Their deep distrust of the Sudan government, RCC or NIF, gave them no confidence to accept this unique opportunity forgetting that the French displayed no such squeamishness over snatching Carlos the Jackal. Steve Simon, Director of Counter-Terrorism at the National Security Council during the Clinton administration, would later claim that there was not sufficient "evidence that could have led to his indictment on U.S. soil," even though Bin Laden had already been named as an a co-conspirator but not indicted during the process that brought Shaykh Omar Abd al-Rahman to trial in New York. Simon sententiously made clear that extra-judicial kidnapping was not possible, for "that's not the kind of country we live in." Even Susan Rice, director of the African Bureau at the National Security Agency, who regarded the NIF government as "one of the most slippery, dishonest governments in the world," displayed no public interest in Bin Laden or his activities.[14] As he and some fifty American diplomatic staff were preparing to close the United States embassy in Khartoum, Ambassador Tim Carney was informed by senior Sudanese officials that Osama bin Laden was no longer welcome in the Sudan. He argued this was not the time to close the embassy. Carney was overruled, for by 1996 the Sudan had "become a nest of Islamic radicalism" where 4,000 mujahideen received training in twenty Sudanese camps. The Sudanese Foreign Minister Ali Osman Muhammad Taha continued to deny these allegations, for the Sudan was "not a base for any military or political operations" and the extremist groups were but "a refuge for some of these individuals."[15]

While Bashir pursued one course of action to be rid of Osama bin Laden, Turabi decided on another. To forestall a scandal that could damage his image, political career, the PAIC General Assembly, and his position as secretary-general to the NIF parliament, Turabi contacted the Sudanese ambassador to Afghanistan, Atiya Badawi, and urged him to facilitate Bin Laden's return. A former Afghan-Arab who spoke Pushtu, Badawi received approval from three former

---

[14] S. Kalita, "Missed Chance," *Newsday*, New York, 2 December 2001.
[15] "A Diplomatic Retreat." *Time International*, Vol. 147, No. 8, 19 February 1996.

mujahideen commanders who operated from Jalalabad.[16] It was just
in time, for presidents Mubarak and Clinton had convened the
"Summit of the Peacemakers" at Sharm al-Shaykh to coordinate
anti-terrorism. Although the conference was primarily concerned with
suicide bombings in Israel by Palestinian terrorists, the growing hostility toward Khartoum in both the Arab and Western worlds convinced President Bashir to improve his image. The following month,
April 1996, he warned expatriate residents living in the Sudan to
either cease their hostile activities against other governments or be
expelled. Rumors circulated that the Hamas office in Khartoum
would be closed. On 18 May Osama bin Laden quietly disappeared
from the Sudan on a chartered plane for Peshawar and Afghanistan
with his family, a few friends, and twenty bodyguards. There are
conflicting accounts about his hasty departure, but Isam al-Turabi,
the son of Hasan al-Turabi and a business partner with Bin Laden
in buying Arabian horses, warned him that he was to be the next
Carlos in a deal between the intelligence agencies of Saudi Arabia
and the Sudan.[17] Bin Laden was next seen in Peshawar during the
last months of the internecine struggle that would bring the Taliban
movement to power in Afghanistan. He eventually made peace with
the Taliban, received the support of the Iranian Pasdaran, and
through the mediation of Dr. Ayam al-Zawahiri established the headquarters of Al Qaeda in Kandahar surrounded by many Afghan-
Arabs of his former 055 Brigade.

There is no doubt that President Bashir was delighted to be rid
of the Bin Laden liability. The Sudanese ambassador to the United
Nations, Ali Osman Yassin, sent an official letter to the Security
Council confirming that Bin Laden had departed and had only been
in the Sudan for purposes of financial investment. The Sudanese foreign ministry reported that he had left the country for his road building contract had come to an end, and he was seeking new areas of
investment. The secretary to the ministry of information, Muhammad
al-Hadi, claimed that Bin Laden "and other Arab brothers" had left

---

[16] "The Making of the World's Most Wanted Man: Part 2," *The Observer*, 28
October 2001.
[17] "Anyone seen Ussama Bin Laden?" *The Indian Ocean Newsletter*, Paris 14 September
1996.

of their own volition because of those "enemies of Islam" determined to damage the image of the Sudan.[18] Perhaps the reactionary Sharaf al-Din Banaga, minister of engineering and housing for Khartoum State, was the most candid when he gave the "main reason" for the departure of Osama bin Laden was "to improve relations between Saudi Arabi and our country."[19] The ambitious Dr. Mustafa Osman, who through the influence of Turabi had become the minister of state for foreign affairs from his previous position as director of CIPF, announced that "all Arab Afghans in Sudan are less than 1,000 people" and that the "policy to expel them is continuing and will be completed."[20]

Expel the Afghan-Arabs they might, but before his departure Bin Laden had been able "to terminate all his business" later claiming that "he had invested badly" in the Sudan and had never been fully paid for the Khartoum-Port Sudan road project.[21] He complained that his ventures in the Sudan lost "more than $160 million" and described the NIF government as a "mixture of religion and organized crime."[22] Shaykh Tunisi was placed in charge of the remaining Bin Laden enterprises in the Sudan selling them off at bargain basement prices. As members of Al Qaeda left the Sudan Bin Laden's trusted lieutenant, Madani al-Tayib, also known as Abu Fadl al-Makki and married to Bin Laden's niece, returned to Saudi Arabi to inform Saudi intelligence about Al Qaeda and its operations. In Peshawar Bin Laden and his entourage appeared at the *Bayt Ashuhada*, the House of Martyrs, which he had established in the 1980s. From Peshawar he moved to Jalalabad, Afghanistan, where he was protected by Yunus Khalis, a former mujahideen commander.

---

[18] "An Interview With the Secretary of the Sudanese Information Ministry, br. Muhammad Al-Bahir Muhammad Al-Hady," *Nida'ul Islam*, Issue 17, February–March 1997.

[19] Reuters, Dubai dateline, 18 June 1996.

[20] "Sudanese Minister: We have asked 1,000 'Arab Afghans To Leave the Country," *Al-Wasat*, London, 15 July 1996.

[21] "Bin Laden no longer has investments in Sudan: foreign minister," *AFP*, Khartoum, 28 April 2000.

[22] "In War on Terroism, Sudan Struck a Blow by Fleecing bin Laden," *The Wall Street Journal*, 3 December 2001.

Egyptian Sudanese Rapprochement

In 1996 President Hosni Mubarak sought to restore relations with
Khartoum. At the Arab Summit Conference in June in Cairo, the
first since the invasion of Kuwait in 1990, Mubarak personally welcomed Bashir to Cairo and met with him for an hour to discuss
matters of mutual concern. He discussed the support of the Sudan
for Islamists and their "Afghani" janissaries. Egypt was desperate to
reduce Islamist violence that had a deleterious affect on the tourist
trade so crucial to the Egyptian economy. Some 280 revolutionaries had been killed by Egyptian security in 1995, and despite the
departure of Bin Laden and Dr. Ayman al-Zawahiri from the Sudan,
Mubarak still held Khartoum responsible for sheltering the Egyptian
Afghan-Arabs.[23] He enigmatically described his talks with Bashir as
"somewhat positive." The Egyptian Foreign Minister Amr Mousa
described them as "frank, friendly, and positive." The Sudanese
Foreign Minister Ali Osman Mohamad Taha announced that personnel from each ministry of interior would establish a committee
to review matters of mutual concern, terrorism, sequestration of property, and the activities of expatriates to change an "era of tension
and conflict" to one of "cooperation and coordination."[24]

These were all fine words, but there was little evidence that
Khartoum was prepared to reduce the activities of the Islamist militants in the Sudan that was essential if relations with Egypt were
to improve. President Bashir was regarded more as a figurehead
where the real political power was in the hands of Hasan al-Turabi
who was the dominant figure in the NIF government.[25] The prospect
for a reconciliation between Egypt and the Sudan was left to the
Sudanese ambassador to the United Nations, Ali Osman Yassin, and
Egypt's former ambassador in the Sudan, Hassan Gad Al-Haqq. Al-
Haqq had been recalled from Khartoum when Egypt in protest
reduced its diplomatic representation in September 1995. Between
them they reviewed outstanding issues that had produced tension

---

[23] "Violence Victims Increase at 25% in Egypt," Arab Organization for Human
Rights quoted in *Al-Sharq Al-Awast*, London, 10 October 1996.
[24] Reuters reporting, Cairo dateline 23, 25 June and 9 July 1996.
[25] G.G. LaBelle, "Sudan'scharges of terrorism, claims of Democracy," Associated
Press, Khartoum, 31 March 1996

between Egypt and the Sudan.[26] These discussions were accompanied by favorable commentary in the Khartoum and Cairo press but produced no "clearing of the atmosphere."[27] Egyptian security officials who visited the Sudan seeking information about the Egyptian *Al-Jama'at Islamiyah* and Islamic Jihad received little. President Bashir continued to deny that the three assassins who sought to kill Mubarak were in the Sudan and the offices of the known revolutionary movements remained open. Having made a facile effort to reduce tensions with Egypt, President Bashir sought a similar effort to cultivate relations with Saudi Arabia now that Osama bin Laden had fled to Afghanistan.

Hasan al-Turabi appears to have had no objection to Bashir's rapprochement with Saudi Arabia. The Sudanese Minister of Culture and Information Al-Tayib Ibrahim Muhammad Khair revoked the law against the importation of Saudi newspapers and journals into the Sudan and encouraged the state controlled media to emphasize the close relations between the Sudan and Saudi Arabia. King Fahd and the Saudis reciprocated. The offices of the Sudanese opposition, the NDA, were closed in Riyadh and told to cease political activity in Saudi Arabia.[28] President Bashir, on his part, declared that his government would combat "terrorism and drug trafficking." The reference to "drug trafficking" was unusual and may have been the result of a report soon to be published by the UN International Narcotics Control Board (INCB) that the eastern Sudan, particularly Port Sudan and the adjacent area of Gedaref, had become a center of cannabis in the traditional lands of the Beja that had "already been expropriated and is now controlled by Usma [sic] Ben Laden (a businessman working under government protection who bankrolls international fundamentalist movements)."[29] Upon the departure of Osama bin Laden the concern of drug trafficking soon disappeared in the criticism of the NIF government. Terrorism was another matter.

[26] "Sudanese Extraordinary Ambassador to Cairo," *Al-Sharq Al-Awsat*, 8 July 1996.
[27] "Sudan did not Respond to Security Requests, Mubarak Says," *Al-Sharq Al-Awsat*, 10 July 1996.
[28] *Al-Nasr*, Cairo, 27 July 1996.
[29] *The World Geopolitics of Drugs, 1995/1996; Annual Report, Obseratoire Geoplitique de Drogues*, Nantes, France, September 1997.

In 1992 the Council of Arab Interior Ministers and the Council
for Arab Justice Ministers began to address terrorism—its morphology, practice, and, most important, its definition—that troubled the
members of the Arab League. Committees of experts had been meeting to review more than one-hundred recommendations on ways to
combat terrorism. In 1996 the interior ministers adopted "a code of
ethics" by which Arab states would commit to combating terrorism
and "abstain from participating or engaging in terrorist actions or
offering asylum to the perpetrators of such acts." In August 1996
the interior ministers defined terrorism that excluded "armed struggles
by peoples under foreign occupation to free their lands and realize
their rights of self-determination."[30] By 1997 the Sudanese representatives were taking an active part in the meetings, and in January
Khartoum agreed to share intelligence and tighten border controls
with other members of the league.

The Khobar Towers Bombing

Although Bin Laden had left the Sudan, he was determined to strike
at the American presence in Saudi Arabia. In June 1996 a truck
carrying the equivalent of a 5,000 pound bomb destroyed the Khobar
Towers in Dhahran killing nineteen United States servicemen and
wounding another 250. Bin Laden declared that the explosion marked
"the beginning of war between Muslims and the United States."[31]
After the bombing there was not one "Western government who
wouldn't like to talk to Osama."[32] Robert Fisk of *The Independent*, one
of the few Western journalists known to have interviewed Bin Laden,
reported that he was in a remote mountain area of Afghanistan. He
was emphatic that all Western crusaders must withdraw from Saudi
Arabia. "Not long ago, I gave advice to the Americans to withdraw
their troops from Saudi Arabia ... Now let us give some advice to
the governments of Britain and France to take their troops out
because [of] what happened in Riyadh and Khobar (Dhahran)

---

[30] Hasan al-Turabi, "Women in Islam and Muslim Society," 1993, translation
from Young Muslims, Canada, www. youngmuslims.ca/online library.
[31] Reuters, London, 10 July 1996.
[32] Kathy Evans, "World-wide hunt is on for terrorist leader," E-Mail Essay, *Weekly
Mail & Guardian*, South Africa, 28 June 1996.

showed that the people who did this have a deep understanding in choosing their targets. . . . They hit their main enemy, which is the Americans." When asked if he was declaring war on the West he replied. "It is not a declaration of war, it's a description of the situation. This doesn't mean declaring war against the West and Western people but against the American regime which is against every Muslim."[33] Mustafa Hamza, a member of the Egyptian *Al-Jama'at al-Islamiyah* charged with the attempted assassination of Mubarak, admitted that those bombing the Khobar Towers were Pakistanis with "the identity papers of Yemeni nationals."[34]

President Bashir strongly condemned the bombing to distance himself from Osama bin Laden whose ghost still resided in the suburb of Riyadh in Khartoum. Hasan al-Turabi, however, praised the *fatwa* issued by Bin Laden from Afghanistan on 23 August. The "message from Usama bin Laden to his Muslim Brothers in the Whole World and Especially in the Arabian Peninsula: Declaration of Jihad against Americans occupying the land of the Two Holy Mosques; Expel the Heretics from the Arabian Peninsula [threatening death to all Americans] occupying the land of the two shrines . . . the presence of the American crusader military forces in the Muslim Gulf states . . . is the greatest danger and the largest harm which threatens the world's biggest oil reserve."[35] Within days after the bombing Bin Laden disappeared from Jalalabad and was reported to have joined the Taliban in the hills ready to destabilize the government in Kabul. A few weeks later rumors circulated that he had attended a conference in Tehran on 21–23 June 1996 with Al-Zawahiri, Muhammad Ali Ahmad, another Al Qaeda member, and some thirty other terrorist organizations. His days of using or being used by the Sudanese were finally over. His absence from Khartoum greatly diminished the importance of the Sudan as a safe-haven and a place to meet for Islamists.

---

[33] Reuters, London, 10 July 1996; G.G. LaBelle, "Alleged sponsers of terror join in condemnation of bombing," Associated Press, Cairo, 27 June 1996.

[34] M.H. Faruqi Report, *Al-Balagh* ("Deliverance"), Vol. 1, No. 5, Electronic Mail Submission, kbaig@delphi.com, London, 24 September 1996.

[35] FAJR News Service, *Muslim World News*, 31 August 1996.

Subtle Changes in the Sudan

When Hasan al-Turabi became the speaker of the national parliament, he confirmed by his official position that he was, indeed, the
dominant figure in Sudanese politics. That task absorbed his ener-
gies previously devoted to the PAIC General Assembly. Moreover,
his Islamic congress was now circumscribed by the international travel
bans and diplomatic sanctions imposed on the Sudan by the UN
Security Council Resolution 1054 of 26 April 1996. When the Sudan
diplomatic representatives in the UN did not respond to Resolution
Number 1054 the UN Security Council imposed even more stringent sanctions on 10 July 1996 that severely limited Sudanese owned
or chartered aircraft to use the airspace of UN member nations and
threatened to impose an embargo on Sudan Airways, all of which
hindered the facility to travel to Khartoum. Nevertheless, during his
visit to Syria Turabi, ever confident, dispensed the impression that
Khartoum was not about to abandon its Islamist friends and particularly the Hamas office in Khartoum whose director, Munir Said,
had unlimited access to the speaker of parliament.

The election of Hasan al-Turabi to speaker of the national parliament changed his image from an Islamist theologian to a stolid
parliamentarian. Although Ali Natiq Nouri, president of the Iranian
Consultative Assembly (*Majlis-e-Shura-e-Islami*), had to assure Turabi
that the two nations had treaty agreements and that Iran had been
generous in arms, equipment, and advisers to the Sudan military,
the departure of Bin Laden to Afghanistan had diminished Iranian
interest in the speaker of parliament. It was unlikely that the NIF
government in Khartoum would soon break out from its isolation
and consequently no longer able to continue its support for Muslim
extremists and the Arab-Afghans sponsored by Iran. Osama bin
Laden appears to have returned briefly to the Sudan in August 1997
where he met with Turabi and the Yemeni Islamist Abd al-Majid
al-Zandani, but there was no longer money or enthusiasm for a new
PAIC General Assembly.

Although Egypt had welcomed elections in the Sudan, Mubarak
was not pleased with the results. In a speech to Egyptian academics
he declared that he would "have nothing more to do with the
Sudanese government because it continues to shelter and support
Egyptian militants. . . . We are still eager that nothing should affect

the Sudanese people, but we will not deal with the current regime or the Turabi front or whatever. . . . [There are] more details and they are bitter. There are terrorists they are sheltering, and they make Sudanese passports for them and they get paid by them."[36] Turabi retaliated with his own interpretation of Egypt's hostility for the Sudan. "In the nineteenth century, Egypt colonized the Sudan. After independence Egypt saw that Sudan was rich and that it is governed by the current Islamic trend, while Egypt lags behind us on that score. It is all about jealousy. The faith is very strong in Egyptian society but is less strong as you rise up through the country's leadership. In Sudan it is the other way around and that is why Egypt is afraid that Sudan could influence Egyptian society with its tendency toward uprising. This is why it supports the opposition and its guerillas."[37] The Sudan had only its Islamist friends for financial, military, and moral support. The Khartoum government was conspicuously absent at the meeting of the Ad Hoc Committee Combating Terrorism of the Arab interior ministers held in Cairo. The Sudan claimed that the Egyptian embassy in Khartoum had refused to issue visas for the Sudan delegation. Without the Sudanese the fifteen Arab ministers adopted a proposal to prohibit the use of their territories to plan, organize, or carry out acts of terrorism, to "tighten the stranglehold on terrorists" by coordination among the Arab security agencies.[38] In the Sudan the former U.N. Human Rights Commissioner Gaspar Biro was invited to return to Khartoum after having been banned from the Sudan for two years because of his critical study released in February 1994 of the government's human rights abuses. The Sudan government media reported that he had been allowed to come back to the Sudan after his "apology" to the government, which this Hungarian lawyer of impeccable integrity never made, but his return, not surprisingly, accomplished little.

---

[36] Reuters, Cairo, 22 August 1996.
[37] SUNA, 21 and BBC, 23 August 1996; *Al-Inqadh al-Watani*, 22 August 1996; *El Mundo* (Madrid), 18 March 1996.
[38] "Adoption of Draft Arab Strategy to Confront Terrorism," *Al-Sharq Al-Awsat*, London, 1 August 1946.

The Flight of Sadiq al-Mahdi

Despite the creation of a national parliament and futile attempts to
end the isolation of the government of NIF, the economy continued
to decline and neither Bashir nor the parliament with Hasan al-
Turabi as speaker inspired any confidence among the Sudanese community. The lethargy of the Islamist state was only enlivened when
Sadiq al-Mahdi made a dramatic escape from Khartoum to Asmara
in December 1996. He disappeared when his brother-in-law, Hasan
al-Turabi, was attending a large wedding ceremony in Sadiq's own
garden that enabled him to elude his close confinement. He was
warmly welcomed in Eritrea by the leaders of the NDA, the SPLA,
and particularly the members of his own Umma Party in exile. There
were Sudanese cynics who remarked that Bashir and Turabi let Sadiq
escape knowing that he would only create disarray within the NDA
opposition which ultimately proved to be the case. At the time, however, his dramatic flight was a great propaganda coup for the political opposition in Ertirea, Egypt, the southern Sudan, and to the
thousands of Sudanese exiles abroad. Sadiq had been jailed once in
Kobar Prison, detained five times, and for seven years had been
held hostage in house arrest during which he had continued to
demand, as the last prime minister, a return to civilian government.
In January Sadiq was in Cairo to meet with his historic political
rival, Muhamed Osman al-Mirghani, the titular leader of the NDA.
They met with the Egyptian political leaders, President Mubarak
and Foreign Minister Amr Musa, during which they discussed their
opposition and plans against the NIF government in Khartoum. In
his interview with *Al-Hayat* Sadiq made it clear that the NDA had
"made several attempts to solve their problems peacefully without
bloodshed" and urged that the government form a transitional national
government that would include the SPLA to call a constitutional
conference to be followed by free elections. Hasan al-Turabi was not
impressed with this unrealistic and ambiguous rhetoric. "The question of an unholy alliance between Sadiq al-Mahdi and John Garang
is insignificant. Sadiq is unlikely to join a political organization headed
by someone other than himself."[39]

---

[39] MENA, London, 26 January 1997; Radio Monte Carlo, 26 January 1997;
"Crisis in Sudan: Interview with Dr. Hassan al-Turabi," *Southern Sudan Bulletin*, Vol.
2, No. 3, London, January 1997.

The arrival of Sadiq in Asmara in December 1996 certainly invigorated the NDA, but his presence cannot account for the January 1997 offensive by the SPLA along a 300 mile front from Eritrea and Ethiopia. The year before, in January 1996, the leadership of the NDA that included Nour al-Deim of the Umma Party, party leaders from the DUP, John Garang from the SPLA, and Fathi Muhammad Ali from the Sudan People's Democratic Movement had met in Asmara "to coordinate their campaign" of popular revolt within the Sudan and military action across the frontier "to overthrow the government in Khartoum" from their bases in Eritrea.[40] Victories by the SPLA and sporadic but successful attacks by the Beja in the winter of 1997 resulted in support for the government from Arab states and particularly Egypt. The Sudanese Foreign Minister Ali Osman Muhammad Taha appealed before the national parliament that "There should be found an effective mechanism and more efforts should be exerted for reducing diplomatic confrontations and eliminating the causes of tension in Sudanese-Egyptian relations." Arab League ministers meeting in Cairo announced "their support for Sudan against 'any foreign threat' and reiterated their backing for Sudan's sovereignty and territorial integrity."[41] The members of the Arab League were not about to have the Africans of the southern Sudan marching down El Nil Boulevard to the Palace in Khartoum on the banks of the Blue Nile. Arab arms were sent to Khartoum and the Islamic Jihad in Eritrea.[42]

After successful victories by the SPLA and the Beja along its eastern frontier with Eritrea and Ethiopia in January 1997, the Sudan requested an emergency session of the United Nations Security Council during which Ali Osman Muhammad Taha urged the council "to take steps to ensure that Ethiopia withdraws from positions inside Sudan and refrains from carrying out further attacks."[43] The leading officials in the Sudan government were sent throughout the Islamic world seeking support for the *jihad* against the African and Arab infidels to receive overwhelming public backing from the Arabs that was more rhetoric than material substance. After seven years the Arab states had become accustomed to frantic calls from Islamists

[40] "Sudanese opposition gathers in Eritrea," Reuters, Cairo, 9 January 1996.
[41] AFP, Khartoum, 2 April 1997.
[42] "Global Muslim News," *Nida'ul Islam*, July–August 1997.
[43] "Sudan regime's plea to UN," Reuters, Cairo, 15 January 1997.

in Khartoum for assistance when their rag-tag army had suffered military defeat in the field. In Beirut, which was then known as the regional center for Sudanese informational and diplomatic activities, the Sudan Ambassador Uthman Al-Dardiri met with Shaykh Husayn Fadlallah of Hizbollah and Ali Al-Shaykh Ammar of *Al-Jama'at al-Islamiyah* who urged resistance to the African opposition. The Fatah of Yasser Arafat denounced the aggression. In the defense of the regime Khartoum was able to "raise $200 million, $20 million of which came from Qatar. With cash in hand the NIF representatives departed for Beijing to purchase Chinese arms.

While the Sudanese were seeking to purchase Chinese weapons, President Bashir arrived in Nairobi for discussions with President Daniel Toroitich arap Moi seeking his mediation in the long standing war in the Sudan. Moi refused, for he did not accept the Sudanese contention that Ethiopia, Eritrea, and Uganda were giving direct support to the SPLA. The East Africans had been intrigued by the proposal in the autumn of 1996 from the Clinton Administration for the creation of an African Crisis Response Force that would number 10,000 African troops to "intervene in that continent's trouble spots," including the southern Sudan.[44] The French were opposed and the proposal was quietly put to rest at a time when the SPLA offensive had been brought to a halt. They had taken Kajo Kaji on the Uganda border but did not have the resources to take the heavily fortified capital of Juba.[45] The result was stalemate. The Sudan army occupied the principal towns in the southern Sudan; the SPLA controlled the countryside. Although there were further discussions between Sudanese and Uganda representatives, the war dragged on.[46] In Khartoum university students and civil servants, "young men between 18 and 32 will be pursued and forced to do their military service."[47] Some 70,000 secondary school graduates were to be given military training, but many failed to appear for service knowing they

---

[44] "Clinton Administration Revamps Plans For Trouble-Shooting All-African Force," *Washington Post*, 9 February 1997, p. A28.

[45] "Sudanese President Optimistic About Ties with Uganda," PANA News Agency, Khartoum, 11 May 1997.

[46] "Sudan secret Talks Between Sudanese Government and Opposition," PANA News Agency, April 17, 1997.

[47] "27 Sudanese students died fighting rebels: minister," AFP, Khartoum, 23 October 1997.

would be sent from their arid lands in the north to the hostile grass and woodlands of the war zone in the southern Sudan.

During his visit to Washington in the autumn of 1997 President Isayas Afewerki of Eritrea accused the Sudan for disrupting the peace process while rearming to launching another military offensive. He still hoped there could be future peace, for "we are destined to live together in the region, and no political group or ideology will ever divide the region and bring about an endless crisis." In time the problem of the Sudan would "pass down the road," and "the peoples of the region will find ways of living together irrespective of the politics and ideologies that prevail today." Few believed Afewerki's optimism for the future. When the Eritrean Ambassador Semere Russom presented his credentials at a White House ceremony, President Bill Clinton remarked that "The government in Sudan continues to wage a fratricidal war against its internal enemies and to seek the destabilization of its neighbors, including Eritrea. Obviously, Sudan's history of aggression toward its neighbors must stop."[48] Two weeks later the Sudan government and the SPLA, both exhausted by war and a declining economy, agreed to reopen discussions in Nairobi ostensibly committed to a "negotiated settlement."

In Washington there was indecision.[49] While welcoming the return to negotiations for peace, the administration refused to reopen the United States embassy in Khartoum and on 4 November 1997 President Clinton issued an Executive Order prohibiting the importation of any goods or services of Sudanese origin. These sanctions were even more strict than those imposed in 1993 because of blatant Sudanese violations of international human rights and religious persecution of southern Sudanese. Since the Islamist Revolution in 1989 the United States had provided more than $650 million in humanitarian assistance to the "victims of Sudan's civil war" and would continue to help. Sanctions were to "deprive the regime in Khartoum of the financial and material benefits of US trade and investment, including investment in Sudan's petroleum sector." These

---

[48] "Eritrean President Chides Sudanese Regime for Stalling Peace Talks," United States Information Agency, Washington D.C., 18 September 1997.

[49] Mark Hubard, "Khartoum seeks to divide its opponents," *Financial Times*, 25 September 1997; "Retreat From Sudan Announcement Reveals Confusion at State," *The Washington Post*, 30 September 1997, p. A18.

were stringent requirements, but they were made cynical when the importation of Sudanese gum Arabic which was an essential ingredient in the manufacture of American soft drinks and adhesives was made an exemption.[50] More important, there was renewed interest in the petroleum resources of the Sudan, and American interests close to the Clinton Administration sought to exclude the activity of American oil companies from economic sanctions.

[50] Madeleine K. Albright, "Remarks on New Economic Sanctions Against Sudan," U.S. Department of State, Washington D.C., 4 November 1997; Jonathan Clarke, "The cost of confusion in our foreign Policy," Cato Institute, Washington D.C., 17 September 1998.

CHAPTER ELEVEN

ARAKIS, OIL, AND CHINA

The elections of 1996 did little to resolve the civil war nor improve the economy which was in disarray. Hasan al-Turabi appealed to the Sudanese to be patient in adversity, for the Sudan was sitting on "lakes of oil." The scramble for oil in the Sudan dates from the early 1960s when a number of foreign oil companies—Union Texas, Total, Sun, and Texas Eastern—began exploration in the coastal waters of the Red Sea with little success. Fifteen years later in February 1980 Chevron Overseas Petroleum Incorporated (COPI) struck oil in the Unity Field in southern Kordofan south east of Muglad and north of the Bahr al-Ghazal, 480 miles south of Khartoum. Two years later Chevron discovered oil in The Heglig Field forty-three miles northwest of the Unity Field and half its size. The wells were located on the northern margin of the historic pastures of Arab and Nilotic peoples between the dry Sahelian zone to the north and the rich grasslands south of the Bahr al-Arab (Kiir) River where Chevron found another promising discovery north of the Kiir near Bentiu, a sleepy Nuer administrative center located eighty-five miles southeast of Muglad.

Suddenly, the Sudan evolved from a passive to an active player in the world of oil. Tentative estimates predicted that the Muglad Rift Basin contained at least 300 million barrels of oil that decided Chevron to spend another $1 billion to develop its concession. Since that time the discovery of "black gold" has aroused the cupidity of a succession of Sudanese governments. The military dictatorship of President Jaafar Numayri (1969–1985), the civilian coalition of Prime Minister Sadiq al-Mahdi (1986–1989), the RCC of Omar Hasan Ahmad al-Bashir, and Hasan al-Turabi all visualized that oil was the key to unlock untold riches for a nation long on human but short on natural resources. Oil could have saved a succession of inept governments from their incompetent management of the nation's economy, but the Chevron discovery proved to be no blessing. In the 1990s an evil jinni bottled for less than a decade was decanted and all the regional and ethnic distrust that characterized the first quarter century of Sudanese independence was let loose in the Sudan. From the moment of its discovery oil would cause political problems. The government needed its revenue to reverse a deteriorating economy, but the discovery could not have occurred in a more unfortunate location. The Al-Muglad Rift Basin in the Sudan lay astride the Arab North and the African South, the large reserves being in the southern Sudan, and the prospect of great wealth opened old wounds that had not healed since the conclusion of the Sudan's first civil war in 1972. The impoverished southerners had never believed that Numayri would distribute the revenues from oil to their benefit. They were, of course, correct.

Approached rationally, the distribution of oil wealth could also have been the lubricant to unite a Sudan whose fissiparous political and cultural tendencies were self-evident from the moment the nation achieved independence in 1956. The Chevron discoveries were in the southern Sudan whose people had been historically dismissed as *abid*, slaves, by the politically dominant riverain Arabs, the *awlad al-bilad* who ruled from Khartoum. President Jaafar Numayri used the prospect of oil to exacerbate divisions between North and South. And it was northern greed and the emerging Islamist policies of Numayri, supported by Hasan al-Turabi, that led the southern military to rebel against the central government in May 1983. It set South against North, African Christians and traditionalists in the South against Muslims in the North, African against Arab cultures. It was the deadly combination of greed and an Islamist government that would revive historic hostilities. It would ruin the South and cause the death of two million southerners and another four million displaced person in that impoverished region. For two decades Islam and oil would result in the tragic conflict of the Republic of Sudan.

Drilling for Black Gold

Sudan oil for the past two decades has attracted both strange corporations and a passel of extraordinary characters as slick as the crude oil they pursued. They were the rich and famous like Adnan Kasshoggi and Rowland "Tiny" Roland, and the not so rich and famous Canadian, J. Terry Alexander. Tiny Rowland had considerable holdings in the *Nairobi Standard*, and his Lonhro Corporation had invested heavily in Sudan which had been nationalized without proper compensation by Jaafar Numayri. Rowland got along well with Garang and served as a silent backer and member of the Sudanese Peoples Liberation Movement (SPLM), the political wing of the SPLA. It was understood that a Rowland investment in a concession in the Upper Nile oil fields and gold mines near Kapoeta in Equatoria would be confirmed once the civil war was concluded. He did not live long enough to realize the profits from such high risk ventures, but there were other players like the Lundins, a rich and secretive Swedish family, and the Canadian-based Lutfur Khan of State Petroleum and Arakis Oil who did. The national oil companies of Iran, China, Malaysia, and Qatar would all use their friendship with Khartoum to have a role in the search for oil. And Russia, Azerbaijan, and India were anxious to become players in the game.

By 1983, ironically the year the civil war in the Sudan broke out once again, the Chevron discoveries in the Muglad Rift Basin were only partly developed, but the Unity Field already had an estimated yield of 35,000 barrels of oil a day (bopd), while another additional 15,000 barrels came from Heglig. Chevron, which sought not to choose sides, was planning to begin the construction of a pipeline from the Unity Field in a direct line northeast to Port Sudan where a marina (Marsa Numayri) would be built south of the port. While the rebels began to organize, Chevron was still studying the engineering problems associated with moving the oil by pipeline to the Red Sea. In February 1984 a rogue element of southern Sudanese insurgents known as Anya-Nya II, who had never accepted the Addis Ababa Agreement of 1972 granting autonomy to the South, attacked the Chevron camp at Rub Kona killing four employees and resulted in the determination of the company to terminate its successful drilling operations and withdraw to Khartoum. During the heated discussions that followed the Rub Kona incident President Numayri sought to "pressure Chevron to resume operations," by signing a joint venture agreement that permitted the Saudi investor Adnan Khashoggi to "acquire any oil assets not then being developed" as required by Chevron's lease agreement with the Government of Sudan (GOS).[1] Nobody's fool, Khashoggi quickly lost interest in oil exploration in the midst of a revived and violent civil war. Chevron limited its

---

[1] Maps that delimit the oil concessions can be found in Peter Verney, "Oil and Conflict in Sudan," *Sudan Update, Special Report*, London, December 1999; on Khashogi see Ronald Kesseler, *The Richest Man in the World*, Warner Books, 1986, p. 251.

activities to seismic work to keep its concession, estimated recoverable oil reserves at 600–800 million barrel range or an oil field containing 4–6 billion barrels, "in place".

The Oil Economics of NIF

After the coup d'état of 30 June the RCC was fortunate that Muammar Qaddafi agreed to deliver oil within days of the revolution and continued to provide sixty percent of Sudan's need until the summer of 1990 when Qaddafi could no longer tolerate the Islamists giving his enemies sanctuary in the Sudan. He promptly terminated his oil shipments creating consternation and concern in Khartoum, and justifiably so, as to their supply of oil. Sudanese exports were only $350 million a year while the government imported $450 million in petroleum products alone. Since most imported oil was consumed in the war, petrol shortages were a daily fact of life in the capital and other Sudanese cities and towns. They were so pervasive that the RCC economic committee chairman and Minister of Energy and Mining Brigadier Salah al-Din Muhammad Ahmad Karrar ("Colonel Dollar") urged companies in the private sector to import petroleum, but when the government announced it would supervise its distribution, private companies lost interest. The petroleum crisis was further aggravated in April 1992 when Qaddafi demanded that Khartoum make some effort to repay its oil debt to Libya of $500–$800 million.[2] When Khartoum did not respond with even token payments, Libya refused to continue shipments on its previous generous terms.

Qaddafi can be excused for his petulance. The NIF government had rejected any close banking ties with Libya and then, despite the many Libyan oil shipments, Khartoum chose the millionaire Sudanese banker and NIF supporter, Osman Khalid Mudawi, and the Saudi Arabian Baraka Bank, "to centralize all future oil negotiations." All international financial transactions would be handled through the Islamist banking system in the Sudan. Khartoum was desperate for a dependable supplier of petroleum, and by January 1993 the government was spending $20 million a month simply to purchase oil on the Rotterdam spot market. Without Libyan largess the NIF gov-

---

[2] "Why So Gloomy?" *The Middle East*, January 1993, p. 37.

ernment next approached Iran. Tehran agreed to provide oil exports, but it preferred to swap Iranian oil for Chinese arms some of which were delivered to the Sudan instead of petroleum.[3] Oil imports remained largely responsible for the growth of Sudan's external debt that exceeded $13.5 billion in 1993 and whose repayment was a practical impossibility.[4] At mid-year Finance Minister Abd al-Rahim Hamdi admitted there was practically no foreign exchange available, and the Sudanese pound fell to 220:1 against the dollar and by October to 300:1. Hamdi had supported most of the draconian demands from the IMF, and although dismissed in December 1993, he would continue to inform his Muslim Brotherhood friends and investors of petroleum developments in the Sudan.

In December 1991 the International Petroleum Sudan Limited (IPSL), a wholly-owned subsidiary of the International Petroleum Corporation (IPC), resumed offshore exploration in the Suakin concession in the Tokar Delta Block. International Petroleum was a curious operation. It was partly owned and totally operated by the Lundin family of Sweden but incorporated in Canada. Its corporate headquarters were located in Dubai, and its shares traded on Swedish, Canadian, and United States stock markets. IPC had operated with infrequent success in Africa and Asia, and its explorations in the Red Sea proved to be unpromising. It did, however, follow events closely in the Sudan. In June 1992 Chevron firmly decided to invest no more in the Sudan and leave as soon as possible. It sold outright its production and exploration rights to Concorp, a Sudanese construction company, at the bargain basement price of $12 million for the concession. Concorp was owned by Muhammad Abdullah Jar al-Nabi and was backed by other Sudanese capitalists—Shaykh Abd al-Basri, Osman Khalid Mudawi, and Al-Tayib al-Nus—who were aligned with the Faisal, Tadamun, and Baraka banks of Sudan who, in turn, were close to Hasan al-Turabi and had helped finance NIF. After the sale Chevron walked away from its Unity and Heglig fields and several other incompletely evaluated discoveries and left behind promising and untouched oil regions in the South. With Chevron gone, the NIF government would eventually sub-divide the

[3] "Chinese arms for Sudan's Army," *The Indian Ocean* Newsletter, 23 December 1995, p. 5.
[4] "Sudan," *Middle East Economic Digest*, 15 October 1993, p. 28.

huge concession into smaller exploration blocks, keeping a small percentage for itself and then inviting international concerns to bid on them.

Once Chevron had departed the unknown State Petroleum Corporation of Canada (SPCC) was first to express an interest in the Chevron concession. In contrast to Chevron, State Petroleum was a small and insignificant oil company. Its chairman of the board and CEO, Lutfur Rahman Khan, was born and educated in Pakistan from where he immigrated to Canada. He had only founded SPCC in November 1991. At the time he was the director of a number of small operations including Constellation Oil and Gas Limited, Pacwest Resources Limited, both private companies engaged in oil and gas exploration and development, and in Larnite Capital Corporation and Trivalence Mining Corporation, the latter a public company primarily engaged in West African diamond mining. Khan and his negotiating team had first contacted the Khartoum government in early 1991, and its spokesman, Arman Aziz, a former Pakistani civil servant and professor at Punjab University who had immigrated to Canada in 1980, apparently succeeded in finding favor with the Sudanese leadership at that time isolated by its support for Iraq. Khan was reportedly close to Qutbi al-Mahdi, the former ambassador to Iran and NIF party leader who had studied in Canada and who was then serving as acting first undersecretary in the minister of foreign affairs. Dr. Asif Ali Syed, M.D., a founding member of State Petroleum and its corporate secretary, also had many friends in the NIF government. These three Pakistanis were able to sell the Sudan Petroleum Affairs Board and the Exploration and Production Authority—both state owned entities responsible for oil industry activity—that the State Petroleum Corporation of Canada, though small, was a serious organization.

In 1992 Khan himself received an invitation to visit the Sudan, and he personally inspected the Chevron facilities and wells in Heglig. After demonstrating his interest in the concession and knowledge of the petroleum industry Khartoum astonishingly allowed State Petroleum to review all of Chevron's crucial and irreplaceable seismic data. The fact that SPCC was not a serious producer of petroleum did not deter the enthusiasm in the ministry of energy and mining or the ministry of finance, for Hasan al-Turabi and his friends in NIF had given State Petroleum their unqualified support. SPCC would receive seventy percent of production revenues (later reduced to sixty per cent) until its initial investment was recovered. Thereafter, revenue would be evenly split between SPCC and the government.[5] The company acquired thirty-four wells but, more important, Chevron's impressive seismic database that would allow SPCC to build on an existing estimated 300 million barrels of recoverable reserves. In return State Petroleum agreed to finance a pipeline from the oil fields to the Red Sea.

To explore and exploit the Muglad Basin, State Petroleum should have approached one of the larger oil companies for collaboration, but in late 1992 it turned instead to the unknown Arakis Energy Corporation of Canada for help in financing the Sudan project. It was a bizarre, extraordinary, or perhaps shrewd maneuver. Arakis, another small Canadian oil company involved in minor natural gas fields in the United States, was working at the time unpromising concessions in the Sultanate of Oman and Papua New Guinea. Although Arakis had been interested in a production sharing agreement with Khartoum, it had little "upstream" exploration and producing experience and no "downstream" marketing or refining capability. Worse, it did not have a productive oil field and thus no serious cash flow from operations.

The relationship between State Petroleum and Arakis remains a mystery. On or about June 26, 1992, approximately the same time that the Sudanese Concorp was granted the Chevron concession, an agreement had been concluded between SPCC and Arakis president J. Terry Alexander. State Petroleum would obtain "certain oil and gas concessions located in the Republic of the Sudan, Arakis would acquire all of the issued and outstanding shares of State." Arakis took over State Petroleum and the concession for the Heglig, Unity, and Kaikang fields. In exchange for giving up control of SPCC, the Pakistanis would receive five million shares of Arakis Energy stock. A group of European financiers were to receive one million shares that undoubtedly included the Lundin family.[6] Named chief executive of State Petroleum, the secretive Lutfur Khan was as smooth as Arakis Energy CEO Terry Alexander was energetic. Together they

---

[5] *Blatt's Oilgram News*, 8 December 1992.

[6] "In the Matter of the Securities Act, R.S.B.C. 1996, C418 and in the Matter of Arakis Energy Corporation," British Columbia Securities Commission, Alberta, 11 May 1998; see David Baines, "Regulators probe Arakis officials' share dealings," *The Vancouver Sun*, 28 July 1997.

made a good team. On 29 August 1993, a year after Khan and
Alexander had begun negotiations, the fast-talking chairman of Arakis
secured a production sharing agreement with the NIF government.
Alexander remained president of Arakis Energy, but Khan and his
Pakistanis gained investor control of the corporation through the distribution of stock, but to begin operations in the Chevron concession Arakis had to raise money in the capital markets.

Overnight a minor and unknown oil company, Arakis Energy,
owned a 12.2 million acre concession and held an option on the
remainder that comprised the former Chevron block. Although Arakis
would have to relinquish forty percent of the concession to the Sudan
government at the end of the third year (August 1996) if it had not
met all its contractual conditions, Arakis had secured an astonishing
opportunity. Relinquishments are both legal and common in oil practice. State Petroleum had proven wells and invaluable seismic material from Chevron. The contract that Khan signed with Khartoum
was, in most particulars, quite fair, but the cost of developing the
oil fields forced Arakis either to seek partners or raise cash. Given
the insecurity in the southern Sudan international banks would not
provide financing. A joint venture would require intricate negotiations, and to issue more Arakis shares to raise money would dilute
shareholder value and depress the price of its stock (AKSEF) that
traded on the Vancouver and NASDAQ stock exchanges. Nevertheless,
Terry Alexander promised to seek some $140 million in commer-
cial financing, a proposition that would attract only the bravest of
speculators.[7]

While Arakis was seeking investors, the Sudanese Concorp began
to pump a small quantity of oil from the Abu Jabra field in May
1993. The oil was trucked to El Obeid where a small refinery with
a capacity of 25,000 bopd had been constructed and operated by
the Sudanese. Elsewhere, Khartoum quietly awarded a generous contract for exploration to Lundin in "Block 5A," a 29,412 square kilometer parcel carved out of the Arakis concession and working secretly
with five foreign oil companies, "in association with the [Sudan]
state-run petroleum company," began exploration adjacent to the
former Chevron concession.[8] Lundin's IPC and Malaysia's state oil

---

[7] *Africa Economic Digest*, 6 September 1993, p. 10.
[8] *Sudan Update*, London, 6 June 1993, p. 2.

company, Petronas, were the first after Arakis to begin work in the former Chevron concession followed by the Chinese in a joint Sino-Sudanese oil exploration company. The French Total Oil Company remained aloof, reluctant to resume operations in its dormant concession until "the circumstances were appropriate."[9] As long as the civil war continued in the Sudan the "circumstances" were not propitious, and the French had memories of the destruction of their Jonglei Canal by an SPLA unit that had passed through the Total concession.

In 1994 the NIF government began a new round of contacts with international oil companies. The "country was in dire need of oil," and the Islamization of the Sudan and its banks discouraged foreign investment.[10] The external debt of $13.5 billion was unmanageable, and as a result of "persistent failure to fulfill its obligations," the IMF declared the Sudan "an uncooperative nation." The development of the oilfields appeared the only hope to revive the economy and restore confidence in the world's international financial community. Arakis appeared to be the solution. Having obtained the former Chevron concession Arakis, as had Chevron, agreed in May 1994 to construct a 950 mile pipeline from Heglig in Kordofan to Port Sudan on the Red Sea coast. In the same month Arakis Energy purchased the remaining shares of SPCC despite the fact that Arakis Energy "had been unsuccessful in obtaining the necessary financing for completion of the Sudan Project."

The history of Chevron in the Sudan and its endless civil war had discouraged the international financial community from investing in the Sudan and big petroleum companies to operate its oil fields, but in December 1994 the Arab Group International for Investment and Acquisitions Co., Ltd. (AIG) chaired by "His Highness Prince Sultan bin Saud bin Abdullah al-Saud" of Saudi Arabia expressed considerable interest. SPCC had used the trucks of AGI to move materiel and drilling rigs from Port Sudan to Heglig but knew little of the company except it was located in Riyadh. During the next six months of negotiations Arakis learned little more about the secretive Prince Sultan who carried a diplomatic passport from Saudi

---

[9] BBC World Broadcast, MEW/0312, 14 December 1993.
[10] "Oil the Hope for Development," 1 August 1994 and "Mutual Oil Benefits," 8 December 1994, *New Horizon*, Khartoum.

Arabia and was accompanied by advisers and security personnel to give the impression of a wealthy and successful businessman knowledgeable about oil and gas and international finance. Arab Group International appeared the solution to Arakis financial problems.

Arakis Takes Charge

At the beginning of 1995 Arakis was bubbling with optimism. It announced that $30 million would be spent on an expanded program of testing and exploratory drilling including fourteen new wells, but the company still had a cash flow problem and the various options to finance the pipeline project estimated at $300 million. Despite these difficulties Arakis Energy stock continued to surge upward during February 1995 to reach $10 on heavy volume. Those who followed petroleum developments in Africa believed that the Arakis field formed the eastern hinge of a huge and promising oil producing area. Geologically similar rift basins had been located along a line that stretched more than 1,000 miles from the Muglad and Melut basins in central Sudan to southern Chad where Exxon, Elf, and Shell had also experienced successful explorations, but it was not until July 1995 that interest in Arakis Energy stock became visible after Arakis had entered into a contract with AGI "for the purpose of financing the Company's Sudan petroleum project, which is owned through the Company's wholly-owned subsidiary State Petroleum Corporation." After extensive negotiations AGI agreed to provide $750 million and to assume the management of the exploration, drilling, and development of oil fields within the 12.2 million acre concession. Arab Group International would also undertake the construction of a twenty-four inch pipeline with a capacity of 150,000 barrels of oil per day to Marsa Numayri marina south of Port Sudan and the construction of its terminal facilities.

Arakis agreed to issue twenty-three million shares at $15 a share ($345 million) to be issued in three separate tranches and purchased by AGI and payable "in cash or other acceptable consideration." Prince Sultan would purchase 10 million shares and Abbas Salih, managing director of AGI, another 10 million. A mysterious Mr. Haroun Hamid Haroun, who became business manager of AGI and a close associate of Prince Sultan, agreed to purchase the final three million shares so that Arab Group International would acquire a forty percent stake in Arakis. Doubts about the financing began to arise when the first issue of private placement shares on 27 July was "held in abeyance pending shareholder and regulatory approval of the Equity Financing." An additional $405 million in the form of loans were to be secured by a letter of credit and could be "drawn upon at the discretion of the Company in respect to pipeline completion costs or development costs of the oilfields." The issue of shares and the company's reorganization required Arakis to file a "Statement of Material Facts" with the Vancouver stock exchange and the British Columbia Securities Commission and a registration statement with the United States Securities and Exchange Commission with respect to the terms of sale pertinent to the shares obtained by AGI.

It all looked perfect on paper, but the promise of $345 million proved ephemeral. Oddly, no one in Arakis seemed to have much information about AGI, but its proposed investment was welcomed by Arakis and there would be no change in the Arakis company management. J. Terry Alexander would remain president and CEO and Lutfur Rahman Khan would remain the president and CEO of State Petroleum. The Arakis board of directors would expand to include His Royal Highness Prince Sultan bin Saud Abdullah al-Saud, chairman of AGI who became chairman of the Arakis board on 25 July 1995.[11] Arakis predicted that its Sudan oil fields would be producing 300,000 barrels a day by 1999.[12] Speculators drove Arakis stock to $27 despite those on Wall Street who had neither confidence in the management of Arakis or AGI. The investors did not know, however, that the embassy of Saudi Arabia in Washington had informed the U.S. State Department that "Prince Sultan" was a very distant relative of the royal family whose creditability and cash was questionable. In two weeks the share price fell forty

[11] "US $30 Million Exploration Program for 1995 Begins," Arakis Energy Corporation, Vancouver, 11 January 1995; Arakis Energy Obtains US $750,000,000 Project Finance," *Canadian Corporate News*, Vancouver, 6 July 1995. "Arakis Energy Corporation—Financing Update," *Canadian Corporate News*, Vancouver, 22 September 1995.

[12] "Arab Group International for Investments and Acquisitions Co., Ltd. New Release," *Canadian Corporate News*, for Arakis Energy Corporation, Riyadh, Saudi Arabia, 2 August 1995.

percent from a high of $25.60 in late July to $16.50 on 7 August as Terry Alexander and other directors were able to manipulate the stocks.[13]

Arakis continued to provide optimistic press releases. On 2 August it announced that Prince Sultan was proceeding with the first tranche of $750 million, but the second tranche of $295 million would be issued only as goods and equipment were delivered to SPCC and when internationally accepted irrevocable letters of credit were delivered to the company. Arakis stock rose to $23 in mid-August amid renewed optimism.[14] That would soon change. On 16 August the British Columbia Securities Commission and the Vancouver stock exchange discovered that the proposed $750 million only included $40 million in cash instead of $345 million so that the offering did not conform to the exchange's requirements "for private placement of shares."[15] Trading in Arakis would remain "temporarily halted pending submission of specific detailed regulatory information regarding prior disclosures made by the Company with respect to the Financing." Angry traders were not satisfied when Arakis President J. Terry Alexander claimed the "company had always expected only $40m in cash." The business manager of AGI, Haroun Hamid Haroun, and Prince Sultan declined to attend a special meeting of the Arakis board of directors on 24 August to consummate the formal signing of the agreement between Arakis and AGI.

Although Prince Sultan "carried a diplomatic passport from Saudi Arabia and was accompanied by several advisers and security personnel," and "Messrs. Salih and Haroun all gave the appearance of being wealthy and successful businessmen and displayed knowledge and experience in oil and gas and financing matters," Arakis had curiously not sought independent information about the financial resources of AGI or its principal officials. Now under close scrutiny from the Canadian regulatory agencies, Arakis suddenly announced it would "voluntarily delist" its shares from trading on the Vancouver stock exchange but not NASDAQ. Investors responded by selling large blocks of Arakis stock which soon declined to $12 by 22 August

---

[13] *Oil and Gas Interests Newsletter*, January 1996.

[14] "Oil Fluctuations," *Sudan Update*, Vol. 6, No. 13, 24 August 1995; "Arakis Energy Reports Further on Approval Process for Sudan Project Financing," *Canadian Corporate News*, 15 August 1995.

[15] *Oil Daily Energy Compass*, 22 August 1995.

1995. By September Arakis stockholders still believed that the Arakis concession contained "over 395 million barrels of recoverable reserves with additional potential of 3.5 billion barrels of recoverable reserves," but on the 18 September AGI abandoned is financing agreement with Arakis.[16] Trading was not resumed on the NASDAQ until 22 September when Arakis stock fell to $5 and by 1996 was selling at $3. Some analysts predicted it would become another speculative "penny stock."[17] Arakis had lost shareholder confidence and was still without financing.

Arakis, Stockholders, and Khartoum

Having failed to mollify petulant stockholders at home and confronted by disgusted officials in the Sudan, Terry Alexander resigned as chairman of Arakis in January 1996 to be replaced as president and CEO by John McCloud, a knowledgeable oil man who moved the company office from the unfriendly atmosphere of staid British Columbia to the entrepreneurial oil capital of Calgary, Alberta. He terminated the Arakis agreement with Walid Al-Omarand and his company, Rosscape A.I.D. for no "evidence of performance."[18] The taciturn Lutfur Khan, who had joined the Arakis board of directors in June 1995, remained president and CEO of SPCC, the Arakis subsidiary, and his colleague, Arman Aziz, joined the Arakis board of directors. In reality control of Arakis had devolved to the Pakistanis. Khan worked from a nondescript office in Vancouver whose walls were covered with photographs of important people—President Omar Hasan Ahmad al-Bashir, Hasan al-Turabi, and the Vice President of the United States, Albert Gore. He refused to give interviews. In May 1996 the future of Arakis appeared perceptibly brighter. Testing had confirmed that Arakis had "made a major new field discovery" forty kilometers southeast of the Greater Heglig oilfield and had "defined a new exploration fairway parallel to the eastern edge of the Muglad Basin."[19] There was no longer doubt that Arakis was

---

[16] "Arakis Energy Reports Further on Approval Process for Sudan Project Financing," *Canadian Corporate News*, 15 August 1995.

[17] "Arakis says interest in joint venture high," Reuters, Calgary, 20 June 1996.

[18] "Arakis Terminates Arrangement with Walid Al-Omar and Rosscape A.I.D.," *Canadian Corporate News*, 23 February 1996.

[19] Arakis Energy Company Press Release, May 23, 1996.

sitting on a substantial pool of oil, but the company would never enjoy the fruits of its Sudanese investment unless it could interest wealthy investors. McCloud had begun a frantic effort to scrape-up funds to keep operations moving, and by midyear he had raised $70 million, and a $143 million in debentures were sold to European speculators at a discount that, however, could not be re-sold in the United States for at least forty days after purchase. Such offerings were usually a warning that a company was in trouble and to save itself was diluting its stock.

Arakis had disclosed in July 1996 that it had $80 million in working capital to cover its Sudan operations and "other financial commitments" for its proposed work program in the Sudan during 1996 and 1997. In late August, however, the company completed another private placement of convertible debentures totaling $37.5 million. The number of outstanding shares was difficult to determine. In December 1994 there were 21 million shares; in March 1995 there were 33 million shares, and on 30 August 1996 there were 67.8 million shares issued and outstanding. Once all debentures were converted, the number of shares would exceed 90 million by 1997. Arakis stock had essentially become worthless in 1996, but who could tell about the future? When asked what might solve the problems of the Sudan, Hasan al-Turabi replied "God and southern oil."[20] Chuck Strain, the Houston oil analyst and Arakis adviser arrived in Khartoum in May 1996 to meet with President Bashir, Turabi, the energy and foreign affairs ministers. Strain Consultants estimated a minimum of two billion barrels of reserves with a potential of ten to twenty billion barrels but projected the cost of the pipeline to be $900 million and the total cost of the project at $1.1 billion. With reserves of two billion barrels he predicted the fair market price per share for Arakis should rise to $24. An expert in oil but politically and culturally ignorant, Strain argued that the government was not "fundamental Muslim."[21]

In April 1996 the Arakis subsidiary in the Sudan, State Petroleum Corporation of Canada, had begun an "Early Production System" which transported some 47,000 barrels of crude oil by truck from

---

[20] Tom Heaton, "Sudan in Turmoil Despite Government Denial," *All Africa News Agency*, Khartoum, 12 October 1998.
[21] "Chuck Strain Goes on a Safari," *Strain Consultants*, 1998.

Heglig to the government refinery being enlarged at El Obeid. In June the site was still under construction but at the time could refine 10,000 bopd. In July President Bashir officially inaugurated the El Obeid oil refinery and jubilantly proclaimed that Sudanese crude, whose reserves were "enormous," had already begun to cover a significant portion of its imports.[22] The Arakis-Government of Sudan production sharing agreement covering the Heglig Unity and Kaikang was both "valid and in force," and the SPCC would continue its exploration and development activities. In return, State Petroleum "with cooperation from the Government of the Sudan," promised within six months to "seek to establish a consortium of companies to participate in and complete Phase I of the $927 million Sudan Petroleum Project." McCloud was told that either Arakis must move quickly or the government would negotiate a new agreement or even end the concession. Arakis development costs in the Sudan already exceeded $100 million and though determined "to move forward with its exploration and development program," it could not do so indefinitely. Arakis shares plunged to a new low on the New York stock exchange.[23]

Despite the civil war in the Sudan the Arakis concession was of substantial interest to many oil companies. At the annual meeting of its stockholders in June 1996, McCloud announced that Arakis had "signed 18 confidentiality and non-competition agreements with various companies and groups" but declined to name the corporations interested in a joint venture agreement in Sudan oil and the pipeline to the Red Sea. A few days after the annual meeting rumors circulated throughout Canada and the United States that the Chinese National Oil Development Corporation (CNODC) was in direct talks with Arakis as was the Malaysia government state petroleum company, Petronas. Both were impressed by the two very successful Arakis wells between the Heglig and Unity fields.

---

[22] "Melham Karam interview with President al-Bashir," *La Revue du Liban*, Internet On-Line, #1908, 7 September 1996.

[23] "Arakis Energy-Valid Status of Sudan Concession Reconfirmed," *Business Wire*, 1 August 1996.

The Chinese and Sudan Oil

China had a long and mutually agreeable relationship with a succession of Khartoum governments before the coup d'état of 30 June 1989. Chinese funds had been used to construct a major textile mill near El Hasaheisa, and Chinese money, architects, and personnel had built the Friendship Hall in Khartoum. That curious structure, whose oriental finish seemed incongruous in Khartoum, became the meeting place of all important functions by the governments of the Sudan, its assemblies, and international gatherings. During the first six months after the coup d'état the Chinese embassy remained aloof from the feverish diplomatic activity that followed the change of government, but in the spring of 1990 the relationship blossomed when the RCC was selling Sudan grain to China in order to earn foreign exchange, the profits of which were believed "to have been spent on weaponry from China to continue the civil war."[24] In the Numayri regime the Sudan armed forces had purchased Chinese small arms and anti-tank and anti-personnel mines that probably account for more than half of the one million mines still scattered about the southern Sudan. The first official Chinese military delegation to the RCC arrived in Khartoum in January 1990.[25] The Sudan army Chief-of-Staff General Ishaq Ibrahim Omar received the Chinese delegation with typical Sudanese hospitality at the Wadi Sayyedna military base. With cash or commodity exchange the Sudan could become a valuable customer for Chinese weapons.

In 1990 the United States still viewed Iran as a threat to vital U.S. security interests in the Persian Gulf and was particularly concerned with Iran's support for a plethora of known terrorist organizations operating in Europe, Asia, and against Israel. When reports began to circulate in Khartoum in 1991 that Iran was to purchase Chinese arms for shipment to the Sudan, Washington was not amused. During the Soviet invasion of Afghanistan in 1979 China and Iran had provided military support to the Afghan insurgents. After the outbreak of the Iran-Iraq war in September 1980 China had fur-

---

[24] "African Dilemma: Food Air May Prolong War and Famine," *The New York Times*, 12 May 1991.
[25] SUNA Radio in English, Khartoum, 0925GMT, 23 February 1990.

nished military support to Iran that established a partnership and Chinese arms. Chinese policy and the Chinese arms industry could profit by a wise choice of friends in the small engagements in the unstable African world. After the Gulf War in 1991 Iran and China became the most dependable trading partners for the Islamist Sudan. The arms it shipped to the Sudan were hardly a trifle, and the United Nations Register of Conventional Arms Report for 1992 confirmed Beijing's growing interest in the Sudan. By 1993 officials from the World Bank were reporting that weapons "from China and North Korea," paid by Iran, were arriving in the Sudan, including "at least twenty attack aircraft from China for delivery to Sudan."[26] In its third year in power the RCC had received substantial modern arms from Libya, Iraq, and China including Chinese fighter aircraft that were copies of Russian MIGs.

Sudanese exports to China in 1993 were only $30 million, but in the following year they nearly tripled to $84 million and accounted for very nearly twenty percent of its exports. In return China had become a significant donor of foreign aid, providing in 1994 $180 million in grants.[27] In July a Chinese Workers Union delegation visited Khartoum, and the Chinese Friendship Society was invited to visit the Sudan "in the context of developing relations between the Sudanese and Chinese peoples." Their arrival in Khartoum the following month began a week of "Sino-Sudanese" celebration in August organized by the Sudan Olympic Committee. Thereafter, there was a continuous flow of delegations and journalists between the two countries.[28] The Chinese built a $12 million 1,500 bed hospital at Umbadda north of Omdurman, and the Chinese ambassador, who had hitherto been inscrutable, became more visible in Khartoum. In October 1994 he attended a well-publicized meeting with Muhammad Al-Amin Khalifa, the speaker of the Transitional National Assembly, during which Khalifa praised "China's stance towards Sudan and Arab issues in international forums."[29]

---

[26] *Jane's Defence Weekly*, 3 July 1996.

[27] Michael Winchester, "Inside Story: China, Beijing vs. Islam," *Asiaweek*, 24 October 1997.

[28] "Sudanese Diplomacy Promotes Joint Relations," 29 June 1994; Expanding Sudanese Chinese Mutual Ties," 18 January 1995, *New Horizon*, Khartoum.

[29] "Chinese Friendship Delegation to Visit Sudan," 26 June 1994 and "Objectives of Chinese Society's Visit," 8 August 1994, *New Horizons*, Khartoum.

The Sudanese reciprocated. In October a delegation from the Sudan Business Owners' Association that included the most influential Sudanese industrial and commercial entrepreneurs visited China. The Sudanese businessmen, most of them members of NIF, were eager to establish ties with those Chinese of similar interests. They sold 4,000 tons of sunflower oil that resulted in a dramatic increase in acreage devoted to sunflower production in the Sudan. Upon the return of the delegation the Sudanese Foreign Minister Dr. Hussein Sulayman Abu Salih left for China on an official visit where he signed "educational, agro-industrial, economic, technological and cultural cooperation agreements" and announced that Sino-Sudanese relations had changed from "traditional" to "strategic."[30] Militarily, China was the Sudan's most dependable source of arms. Politically, it was considered one of the countries upon which Sudan could rely to defend its Islamist issues in international politics. Having been isolated from the West as an ally of Iraq's Saddam Hussein, this support was very important to Khartoum. The Sudan needed a friend in the UN Security Council and China served that purpose. China, however, had no surplus oil to export to the Sudan, and was itself quietly seeking new sources of petroleum. A joint committee for commercial and technological cooperation led by Minister of Industry and Commerce Dr. Taj al-Sir Mustafa visited China to cooperate in the exploration and exploitation of Sudan oil. He was followed by President Bashir on a state visit to China in October 1995 where he was warmly received. Three months later the Sudan air force "received an additional six Chengdu F-7s (MiG-21s) [built in] China" paid for by Iran.

During the regimes of Jaafar Numayri (1969–1985) and Sadiq al-Mahdi (1986–1989) relations between China and Sudan had been correct but not close. The prospect in 1995 of operations to extract Sudan oil changed that relationship when General Manager of China Oil and Gas Corp Wang Tao invited Sudanese Minister of Energy and Mines Major General Salah al-Din Muhammad Ahmad Karrar to China. In June Karrar met with Wang and Chinese Vice-Premier and Foreign Minister Qian Qichen in Beijing. Although the Chinese expressed interest in cooperating with the Sudanese to develop their

---

[30] "Abu Salih on Sino-Sudanese Ties," 23 February 1994; "Foreign Minister to Visit China," 31 October 1994, *New Horizon*, Khartoum.

potential petroleum, there were apparently no agreements to do so.[31] Three weeks after Karrar returned to Khartoum the Sudanese Finance Minister Abdallah Hassan Ahmed announced in the Khartoum newspaper *Al-Sharq al-Awsat* that the agreement between the government and the Arakis Energy Company of Canada had expired and was "awaiting a decision for renewal," and the Sudan foreign ministry announced that China had loaned the Sudan $18 million, $13 million of which would be used "to help Sudan explore its oil deposits and train its engineers."[32]

After President Bashir returned from Beijing there were a spate of press reports that China National Petroleum Corporation (CNPC) would join Qatar's Gulf International Corporation in the latter's ongoing search for oil in a concession negotiated with the RCC. Qatar had been one of the few friendly nations to support the NIF government and had shipped oil to the Sudan when it was desperately needed. Although Shaykh Hamad and his brilliant Foreign Minister Hamad bin Jasim bin Jaber maintained friendly relations with Iraq, Iran, and Sudan and tolerated Islamist radicals and the ubiquitous Hasan al-Turabi, Qatar, ironically, still served as a friendly base for the U.S. Navy. In December CNPC opened an office in Khartoum.[33] Chinese interest in Sudan's oil reserves should have come as no surprise. In 1993 China had become a net oil importer. The Chinese had anticipated a serious "petroleum demand-supply gap" beginning in the early 1990s for a burgeoning Chinese economy that would require 50 million tons of imported oil a year by 2001.

In July 1996 there were rumors in Calgary and New York investment circles that Arakis had approached the CNPC to take a share in the old Chevron concession. It was clear from an Arakis Energy Corporation statement to stockholders that its private negotiations with prospective joint venture partners had been progressing very slowly at the same time it only had six months left to fulfill their contractual conditions with the Government of Sudan or all would be lost. The Arakis concession remained "valid and in force," but

---

[31] "Sudanese Energy Minister Discusses Oil Cooperation with China," Radio Broadcast in English, Xinhua News Agency, Beijing, 5 June 1995.

[32] Nhial Bol, "Foreign Firms Go for Gold," IPS, Khartoum, 29 May 1995.

[33] Bo Xiong, Daluo JIA, *China News Digest-Global*, 11 December 1995.

the company was obligated by agreement to return forty percent of its concession in August 1996 if it had not met the contractual requirements agreed to in August 1993. Arakis requested another year's extension arguing that unexpected delays were often the fault of the ministry of mining and energy. The government pointed out that Arakis had yet to make a thorough evaluation of its 12.2 million acre concession, "one of the largest undeveloped oil properties in the world." By October some thirty oil companies had demonstrated an interest in joining Arakis and twelve had discussed their offers with the minister of mining and energy. Eleven companies had provided the "due diligence" required by the Sudanese government before they could be seriously considered. By early October the list had been reduced to three finalists.

Later in October Arakis President John McCloud flew to Khartoum to review negotiations with the government over the pipeline whereby shares in Arakis Energy rose nearly thirty-five percent on speculation that the company was close to securing financing for the pipeline that would "change the entire economic picture of the country." The following month, November, he proudly announced that Arakis had drilled the first well of its 1997 exploration program at El Saqr 25 miles south of the Heglig base camp.[34] On 2 December with great fanfare a temporary agreement was signed by Lutfur Khan, Chairman of SPCC, and its the new partners in the consortium. CNPC acquired forty percent of the concession and Petronas Carigali, a subsidiary of the National Petroleum Company of Malaysia, another thirty percent while the Sudan Government continued to have a five percent holding to see that its interests were respected. The day before, 1 December, the Sudan ministry of energy and mining had announced that a crude oil pipeline agreement and a lease agreement had been signed with Petronas-Chinese National Petroleum(CNPC) and State-Sudapet (the contractors of Blocks 1, 2 and 4) for the construction and operation of an export pipeline transporting up to 250,000 bopd to an oil export terminal to be constructed on the Red Sea coast south of Port Sudan.

Arakis was now part of a joint operating company, but it would no longer have to invest capital in the Sudan. Strapped for cash,

---

[34] *The Atlanta Journal and Constitution*, Constitution Edition, p. 4F, 9 October 1996; Carol S. Remond, "Arakis Energy: Bentiu Oil Production States in S. Sudan," AP-Dow Jones News Service, New York, 25 November 1996.

SPCC had been forced to reduce its holding which came as no surprise to its long-suffering stockholders. Arakis argued that "CNPC and Petronas and their respective governments have a significant level of commitment to the Sudan and the financial ability to absorb the balance of the Project costs." In exchange for its reduction in working interest and reserves, the consortium partners agreed to fund all of the costs of ongoing exploration and development and a 1,500 kilometer export pipeline until the Arakis investment, $175 million, was matched on a pro rata basis. Arakis might continue to lead the venture, but nearly all future financing—at least $400 million from CNPC and $300 million from Petronas—would come from two nations seemingly immune to Western pressure or world opinion. With this infusion of new capital the partners announced a production of 150,000 barrels a day and that the first commercial oil shipments from the Muglad basin would begin "as soon as 1999."[35]

These agreements had been worked out by Robert Fleming & Co. Ltd, a London corporation with extensive experience in China, and Arakis had been in discussions with Fleming for a year "to accelerate exploration and development" of the Sudan project.[36] Fleming Energy Group would advise Arakis "in seeking an international appraisal to assess additions to the value of the Sudan Petroleum Project between 1993 and the present." It was agreed that the partners would "recognize both the unaudited capital contribution and the appraised value added to the concession" by Arakis, and the partners would assume "State's expenses up to the value of State's recognized capital contribution and value added to the project." Since Arakis had invested $175 million, CNPC and Petronas Carigali would invest $300 million on exploration and development activity and $225 million on the pipeline transportation system before Arakis would be required to invest another cent in the project.

The CNPC had scored a major success in the competitive world of international petroleum. Beijing boasted that after fierce international competition it had emerged victorious to join Arakis in the Sudan, and the signing ceremony in Khartoum was broadcast live on Beijing radio and television in March 1997. The immediate goal

---

[35] Jeffrey Jones, Reuters Ltd., Calgary, 6 December 1996.
[36] "Arakis Appoints Flemings as Advisor," *Canadian Corporate News*, Calgary, 13 December 1996.

was to raise Sudanese crude oil production from 10,000 bopd to 150,000 barrels by mid-1999 and to make the Sudan self-sufficient in oil when CNPC built a new refinery to be completed some time in 1999 with a capacity of 50,000 bopd, the amount consumed daily in the Sudan. The Sudan oil field construction project was the largest undertaken abroad by CNPC. Speaking at the 15th World Petroleum Congress held in Beijing in 1997, Wang Tao, the senior adviser and former head of the CNPC warned that "the growth of oil production in China is no longer matching economic development."[37] In 1996 the volume of oil imported into China was eight percent of domestic consumption. Wang Tao intimated that China would have to import 195 million tons annually by 2000 and 265 million tons by 2010.

China, the world's third largest oil producer, was starving for oil and its rapid economic growth had outstripped the ability of CNPC to find new reserves to replace older fields. "China might have to import four million barrels a day by the year 2015, the equivalent of half of Saudi Arabia's total current output." Wang made it clear that "We will keep on developing ties with some countries for oil imports."[38] On 28 February CNPC took over the largest percentage of the 12.2 million acre Arakis concession in southern Sudan and began to search for contractors to build the thousand-mile pipeline. Arakis was now a minor player, and on 18 August 1998 Lutfur Khan sold the Arakis Energy Corporation to the Talisman Energy Corporation of Canada for $175 million. Dr. Jim Buckee, Talisman president, assured Khartoum that his company would invest at least $780 million in order to complete the Sudan project by 2001. Three days after the Arakis sale was concluded missiles fired from United States frigates in the Red Sea destroyed the Al-Shifa pharmaceutical plant in Khartoum in what Washington called a response to its production of chemical nerve gas. The raid once again raised doubts in international capital markets as to the viability of the Talisman investment in the Sudan.

---

[37] "Arakis Appoints Flemings as Advisor."
[38] "Oil: Sleepy giants are stirring," *Financial Times*, London, 19 August, 1997.

CHAPTER TWELVE

THE END OF AN ISLAMIST EXPERIMENT

After the departure of Osama bin Laden from the Sudan in the spring of 1996 the PAIC General Assembly lost one of its most wealthy financial supporters, and it led Hasan al-Turabi to postpone the next Islamic congress until January 1999. Despite his visionary leadership the Sudan was too poor and too marginal to serve as the base for a universal Islamic revolution, but he was determined to continue his Islamic mission.[1] In an interview in the *La Revue du Liban* he argued with pride that "man is torn between regionalism and internationalism," but it is the Islamist model in the Sudan that will have a "universal impact." The PAIC General Assembly was international attracting Islamic youth from all over the world to visit the Sudan and return to their homes "to establish local chapters." Asked if he approved of suicide bombers, Turabi dodged the issue by arguing that "religious text legalizes and supports every military action against every force of occupation or tyranny," but his vision of a universal Islamic movement did little to end the international isolation of the Sudan.[2]

When the SPLA began its offensive in the Muslim eastern Sudan during the winter of 1996–1997, the government had sent emissaries throughout the Middle East seeking military assistance. Their defeats in the east and the south were attributed not to the PDF or superior tactics by the SPLA, but the conspiracy by external forces, the United States and the Zionists who supported Eritrean-Ethiopian aggression. In Beirut the Hizbollah leader, Shaykh Husayn Fadlallah, fulminated that "all Moslems should confront the conspiracy" in the southern Sudan, a conspiracy with "an African face." Muslims were urged to "come to the help of Arab and Islamic Sudan," but the

---

[1] Letter from Turabi to Mansur Escadero, Spanish Federation of Islamic Societies, January 1999; Gerard Prunier, "Le Soudan au centre d'une guerre regionale," *Le Monde Diplomatique*, February 1997, pp. 8–9.

[2] "Entretien avec le President du Conseil National Federal Soudanais: Hassan at-Tourabi." *La Revue du Liban*, 7–14 September 1996.

response was less than enthusiastic.[3] The government was further isolated by its abysmal human rights record carefully compiled by the many human rights organizations in the West. Khartoum tolerated the traffic in African slaves and remained indifferent to the widespread death and destruction in the southern Sudan that many regarded as nothing less than genocidal. Since the resumption of hostilities in 1983 more than two million southern Sudanese had perished in war, famine, and drought despite heroic efforts by the international aid agencies.[4]

The Sudan deliberately began to end its international isolation. When the United Nations Security Council decided in March 1997 to continue the 1992 embargo of Libyan air, banking, diplomatic, and military activities, President Bashir was the first to support Qaddafi's denunciation of the sanctions. A few days later the Sudan narrowly escaped expulsion from the IMF until it agreed to implement a ten-month stabilization program and strict economic reforms that would reduce the Sudan's $1.3 billion dollar arrearage with the fund. In the past the Sudan had resisted the demands of the IMF for economic reform, but now the Sudanese appeared more willing to accept the privatization of some of its government run companies. Efforts were made to secure the Heglig and Unity oil fields and the "Greater Nile" pipeline project by enlisting Nuer units of the SPLA, dissatisfied with the Dinka leader John Garang, to join the PDF as militia to defend the oil fields in West Nile. It was a bold military stroke, but Dr. Jim Buckee, President of Talisman Energy Inc., who had bought out Arakis and joined the state oil companies of China and Malaysia in the Greater Nile Petroleum Corporation (GNPC), was vociferously criticized by human rights groups in Canada, Britain, and the United States as the militias and the military began a program of "ethnic cleansing" to clear the human population from a vast region surrounding the oilfields. Buckee was accused of permitting the facilities of Talisman to be used for military operations by the PDF, and his company was condemned for providing the revenue for the government to purchase arms,

---

[3] "Knowing the Other Face of the Middle East; Arab Islamist Campaign Against the African Successes in Sudan," *Mideast Newswire*, Vol. 506, Miami, Florida, 4 February 1997.

[4] Millard Burr, "A Working Document: Quantifying Genocide in the Southern Sudan, 1983–1993, U.S. Committee for Refugees, Washington D.C., October 1993.

"exacerbating tribal rivalries and trying to force an Islamic state on the south, where Christianity and tribal religions predominate." Buckee, an oil man, defended his company and its humanitarian work in the Sudan where Talisman was an agency for good not evil. He brushed aside the protests, confident that security was "adequate to protect the pumping stations and pipeline."[5]

During a visit to Paris in the summer of 1999 the Sudanese energy minister, Awad Ahmad al-Jaz, met with TotalFina Oil executives to apprise them of petroleum developments in the Sudan and hopefully to convince them to return to their Sudan concession. Al-Jaz was no longer the unwelcome Arab diplomat. The discovery of oil in great quantity and the construction of a pipeline from the oilfields to the Red Sea had dramatically altered the continued prospect of an economically stagnant northern Sudan. Oil was the instrument that would free the Sudan from its traditional dependence on the largesse of wealthy Arab and Muslim states. It could immeasurably improve both the Sudanese economy and the ability to wage war against its African insurgents. It emboldened Bashir to marginalize Turabi and give the surviving members of the RCC freedom of action internationally they did not have in the past. TotalFina was a new company created by the merger of Total of France and Fina of Belgium that inherited the original Total Oil/Marathon Oil/Kuwait Oil Exploration Company concession. Its Block B comprised some 170,000 square kilometers located south of Malakal in the Bor Basin. TotalFina demonstrated interest to return to the Upper Nile after al-Jaz offered it a portion of the productive Block 5, but the company was cautious. The French remembered the loss of the Jonglei Canal after the SPLA had destroyed the Sobat base camp of CCI, and since 1984 security in their concession was precarious. The company expressed interest but deferred any direct investment for the future.

In August 1999 at Port Bashir, formerly Marsa Numayri, the oil terminal fifteen miles south of Port Sudan, President Bashir presided over a ceremony celebrating the launching of oil exports from the Sudan. A Panamanian tanker was being loaded with 600,000 barrels of Sudan crude to sail for Singapore. A second vessel, a South

---

[5] Susan Sevareid, "Start of oil exports brings hope and fear to war-weary Sudanese," Associated Press, Heglig, Sudan, 22 August 1999.

Korean tanker, was ready to load oil bound for a refinery in South Korea. Port Bashir had a storage capacity of two million barrels, which was expected to increase to 3.2 million, while the billion dollar pipeline would be expanded to 450,000 bopd in four to seven years. Sudan had become a major oil producer and a member of the Organization of Petroleum Exporting Countries (OPEC).

Ruling the Sudan

Omar Hasan Ahmad al-Bashir was elected president for four years in April 1997 to begin his struggle between him as the leader of the executive branch of government and Hasan al-Turabi, the speaker of the National Assembly, the *Majlis Watani*. After years in the shadow of this charismatic and international Islamist, Bashir was determined to regain control of Sudanese foreign policy as he had dominated the Sudanese military. Turabi was still welcomed by friends like Emir Shaykh Hamad al-Thani of Qatar who had begun to introduce some of Turabi's Islamic institutions in the emirate including the creation of a consultative *Majlis al-Shura* and the election of municipal councils in towns and villages. At the invitation of the Qatar Center for Future Studies, Turabi arrived in Doha in November 1998 to deliver a series of lectures and was warmly welcomed by local Islamists.

Meanwhile Bashir had been actively courting Mubarak, Qaddafi, the Algerian military, and the Tunisian political leadership and used the opportunity of the death of the First Vice President General Zubeir Muhammad Salah in a plane crash at Nasir in southern Sudan in March 1998 to make major changes in his cabinet. Ali Osman Muhammad Taha replaced Zubeir as first vice president to become Bashir's "right hand man." Other NIF stalwarts, disenchanted with Turabi, were promoted including the Islamists, Dr. Ghazi Salah al-Din Atabani to minister of culture and information, Ali Muhammad Osman Yassin to minister of justice, and Ahmad Ibrahim al-Tahir to minister of federal affairs. Almost unnoticed, Bashir moved stealthily to reduce Turabi's influence throughout the government and to modify its controversial and revolutionary Islamist past. Turabi might preside over an Islamic *shura* whose meetings offered an outlet for domestic expression, but its international political influence was still very limited. He remained the dominant politician in the National

Assembly, particularly after the creation of the Popular National Congress (PNC) in 1998 that appeared, too, many, to be the resuscitation mirror image of NIF. By the autumn of 1998 the struggle between Turabi and Bashir was no longer a secret.

The Stigma of Terrorism

Despite the removal of Osama bin Laden and most of his Al Qaeda followers from the Sudan, the Khartoum government seemed determined to continue the Islamist course that Hasan al-Turabi had established after the 30 June Revolution. It refused to heed UN Security Council Resolutions 1044, 1054, and 1070 that called for the extradition to Ethiopia of the three suspects in the attempted assassination of Hosni Mubarak, and the United States had prohibited trade and other sanctions with the Sudan. In May 1997 Kenneth R. McCune, the Acting Coordinator for Counter-Terrorism in the State Department, indicated there was every reason to support the sanctions imposed on the Sudan in August 1993 because its government provided support "to groups engaged in acts of international terrorism." The Sudan continued to harbor terrorist groups, including the Abu Nidal Organization, Hamas, Lebanese Hizbollah, the Palestinian Islamic Jihad, and Egypt's *Al-Jama'at al-Islamiyah*. Yasser Arafat maintained a training camp in Sudan, as did Abu Nidal's Fatah Revolutionary Council. At Kadru, located north of Khartoum, "Iranian experts trained terrorists, including Fatah forces headed by Jaber Amer."[6] In the United Nations the Human Rights Committee condemned the Sudan for serious human rights violations "including the crucifixion of convicts, slavery, and the press-ganging of children into the army." The committee chairwoman, Christine Chanet, stressed that "Sudan's failure to respect international human rights agreements could not 'be excused by custom or domestic laws.'"[7]

---

[6] Kenneth R. McCune, "Statement before the Subcommittee on Africa, Senate Foreign Relations Committee," Washington D.C., 15 May 1997; "MK claims Arafat knew of World Trade Center bomb," *Jewish Bulletin of Northern California*, Jerusalem Post Service, Israel, 28 March 1997.

[7] "UN condemns crucifixions and slavery in Sudan," AFP, Geneva, 1 November 1997.

Turabi brushed aside all claims of human rights violations as did his Islamist friends. He welcomed Shaykh Ahmed Yassin, the founder of Hamas, to Khartoum declaring the infirm cleric represented "the pulse of the Islamic Jihad [holy war] for restoration of the rights of the Palestinian people."[8] Yassin, having returned to Gaza in October 1997 from an Israeli jail, was unalterably opposed to the Clinton peace effort that involved Yasser Arafat and the Palestine Authority and had signed an agreement with the radical Popular Front for the Liberation of Palestine to oppose the Oslo accords. On 30 May 1998 Yassin met with Bashir and because of his "contribution to reviving the jihad, championing Islamic rights, and defending the religious sanctuaries," Hamas had been given office space, land, and farms to support the "Palestine struggle." He attended the Friday prayers at the Khartoum University mosque where the Imam Mutesim Abdel Rahim proclaimed that "Mohammad's army has begun to move. The vanguards of this army are now assembling in Sudan." Much of this was rhetoric, but four days after the Shaykh's departure a perturbed Yasser Arafat arrived in Khartoum to talk with Bashir. Neither Bashir nor Turabi would reduce their support for Hamas, but in October Arafat placed Yassin under house arrest.[9]

Sudan's neighbors had no more reason to trust Khartoum now than in the past. Eritrea, which had broken diplomatic relations with Khartoum in December 1994, complained that Khartoum continued "to infiltrate armed agents" into the country, and "three separate anti-Eritrean stations" were believed "to use the same transmitter in Sudan." The Eritrean Islamic Jihad, which changed its name to the Islamic Salvation Movement (*Harakat al-Khalas al-Islami*) in September 1998, led by Shaykh Muhammad Amer and the ELF of Abdallah Idris continued to operate from Khartoum. By 1998 Ethiopia, which had sought on various occasions a rapprochement with Khartoum after the attempt to assassinate Mubarak, had given up convinced that Khartoum's call "for the imposition of the *Shari'a* throughout the Horn of Africa" would continue to cause trouble for Ethiopia so long as the Bashir-Turabi government survived in

---

[8] "HAMAS chief in Sudan on latest leg of tour," AFP, Khartoum, 29 May 1998.
[9] "Hamas founder holds talks with Sudan's president," Reuters, Khartoum, 30 May 1998; "Hamas given office, land in Sudan," AFP, Khartoum, 2 June 1998.

Khartoum.[10] Chad President Idriss Deby, a Muslim and ethnic Zaghawa with close personal ties to Hasan al-Turabi, was outraged by the lack of concern in Khartoum for the devastating drought that struck Darfur in 1998 that had caused thousands of Sudanese Arabs to flee to Chad bringing with them disorder and ethnic violence. In Libya, Muammar Qaddafi managed to create a schism within the PAIC General Assembly that led a number of Sahelian states to break with Turabi.[11]

The Embassy Bombings and the Al Shifa Reaction

In January 1998 the Council of Arab Interior Ministers (CAIM) after "five years of formal discussions" had finally agreed on a program to combat terrorism in Arab League states. The resolution had been given added urgency by recent terrorist attacks in Egypt and Algeria. There would be increased judicial security and intelligence cooperation, the extradition of individuals charged with and convicted of terrorist crimes, and "denying shelter to terrorists or terrorist groups." Special efforts would be made to "curb" access to the media by terrorist organizations. Sudanese participation indicated that Bashir would no longer ignore the unrestrained activity of Islamist terrorists but would continue to support those who opposed Israel and Zionism such as Hamas and Hizbollah. It was, however, this dichotomy that was criticized in the West. "By lending legal validity to some forms of terrorism and remaining silent on the role of state-sponsoring of terrorism within the Arab world itself, the accord sends the wrong message and marks an important opportunity lost." It was not learned until much later that the Sudan external security bureau chief, Qutbi al-Mahdi, had written to the United States Federal Bureau of Investigation (FBI) just a few weeks later indicating "a desire to start contacts and cooperation." He invited the FBI to visit Khartoum,

---

[10] "Eritrea says Sudan continues to infiltrate agents," AFP, Cairo, 25 March 1998; "Media warfare in the Horn of Africa," BBC World Mediawatch, 2 March 1999; "Countries of the Horn Urged To Apply Sharia," IPS, Khartoum, 15 April 1998.

[11] "Gadafi en N'djamena (Chad), al inaugurar el Tercer Congreso del Liderazgo Popular Islamico Mundial," WebIslam (digital publication of Muslims in Spain), No. 81, 9 February 2000.

but the overture was rejected.[12] Khartoum felt further isolated when the Entebbe Summit for Peace and Prosperity held in late March 1998 and attended by President Bill Clinton did not include the Sudan.

Many American legislators and those in the intelligence community were convinced that the Bashir government was incapable of reform given its execrable human rights violations and that terrorism was still present on the African continent even after the departure of Osama bin Laden, al-Zawahiri, and the Al Qaeda leadership from the Sudan. On 7 August 1998 two huge explosions destroyed the United States embassies in Nairobi, Kenya, and Dar es Salaam, Tanzania. Some 224 people were killed, including twelve Americans, and more than 4,000 wounded. The truck bombings were carried out by an Al Qaeda cell led by the "sleeper" Wadih el Hage. When one suspect was captured within hours after the bombing, members of the Al Qaeda cell that operated in Nairobi and Mombasa were arrested and extradited to the United States including one Saudi, one Tanzanian, a naturalized American citizen born in Lebanon, and a Jordanian, Muhammad Sadik Odeh all charged with planning and implementing the bombing.[13] The Nairobi cell responsible for planning and carrying out the bombings had its beginnings with Al Qaeda in Somalia between 1992 and 1994. Twenty-two others were later indicted, including Osama bin Laden and a Muslim from the Comoro Islands.

Many of the men involved in the bombings had moved freely in and out of the Sudan. Others had Sudanese passports, and the cell had operated with the support of Bin Laden before and after he had left Khartoum in March 1996. In 1994 he had personally sent a member of Al Qaeda from Khartoum to reconnoiter the U.S. embassy in Nairobi. Shocked by the carnage, the Clinton administration immediately sought revenge for the embassy bombings. On 20 August 1998, three weeks after the destruction of the embassies, thirteen Tomahawk cruise missiles were launched from United States ships operating in the Red Sea that demolished the Al-Shifa phar-

---

[12] "Arab Anti-Terror Efforts: Assessing an Arab League Initiative," *Policy Watch*, No. 294, January 13, 1998, The Washington Institute for Near East Policy, Washington D.C.; "US rejected Sudanese files on al-Qaeda," *Financial Times*, p. 1, 30 November 2001.

[13] For a precis of the charges see, "Going on Trial: U.S. Accusations of a Global Plot," *The New York Times*, 4 February 2001, p. 27A.

maceutical factory in Khartoum North.[14] Although the plant manager had rented a home in the Khartoum suburb of Riyadh to Bin
Laden shortly after his arrival in Khartoum, the Al Shifa plant
seemed a curious target. It was suspected of manufacturing EMPTA,
one of four virulent chemicals used in the manufacture of VX nerve
gas. The United States claimed it had acted in self-defense allowed
in Article 51 of the UN Charter after efforts had failed to convince
the government of the Sudan and the Taliban government in
Afghanistan to close their terrorist activities and cease to cooperate
with Osama bin Laden's Al Qaeda. Only after the attack did
Washington discover that the plant's owner was Salah Idris and
promptly froze his extensive assets.[15] The United States National
Security Adviser Samuel Berger insisted that the Al-Shifa plant produced EMPTA, but later investigations were unable to prove that
it did.

If the attack on the Sudan, combined with a cruise missile attack
on Al Qaeda bases in Afghanistan, were a signal that the United
States was prepared to halt terrorist activity wherever Al Qaeda operated, it failed. Critics were more inclined to argue that the attacks
were designed to distract the American public from a scandal in the
White House involving the President of the United States and a
young female intern. Others like General Mirza Aslam Beg of Pakistan,
commander-in-chief of Pakistan's military forces between 1988 and
1991, a member of the PAIC General Assembly in 1993, and who
had founded the *Awami Qiadat* (People's Leadership) Party of Pakistan
in March 1995, supported the Taliban in Afghanistan and maintained contact with Osama bin Laden. Beg criticized the United
States and the government of Pakistan for allowing American cruise
missiles to cross Pakistani air space.[16] On his part President Bashir
denied any Sudanese involvement with the terrorists and had written personally to President Clinton in February 1997 offering American
intelligence and counter-terrorism experts access to Sudanese intelligence files. He did not receive a response.[17] *The New York Times*

[14] "U.S. Wasn't Sure Plant Had Nerve Gas Role Before Sudan Strike, CIA Urged
More Tests," *The Washington Post*, 21 August 1999; p. A01.
[15] Michael Barletta, "Chemical Weapons in the Sudan: Allegations and Evidence,"
The Nonproliferation Review, Vol. VI, No. 1, Fall 1998.
[16] "Sharif Assisted U.S. Attack-General Beg," Pakistan News Service, from *InfoTimes*,
Karachi, August 1998.
[17] "Frontline: Interview Omar Hassan Ahmed al-Bashir," Archive, PBS, Washington
D.C., http://pbs.org/frontline/, 2001.

and *The New Republic*, liberal media who generally supported President Clinton, were equally critical of the missile attack.[18] During the final years of the president's second term his foreign policy advisers continued to justify the destruction of the Shifa plant despite that fact it was based on faulty intelligence and Al Qaeda was not involved.

The Search for Peace

In 1997 President Daniel Arap Moi of Kenya urged Bashir to resume negotiations on the civil war in the Sudan through the moribund Intergovernmental Authority on Development (IGAD) ministerial subcommittee. Although Eritrea and Ethiopia were once again at war and both continued to support the NDA opposition against Khartoum, they had not forgotten the IGAD peace initiative. IGAD had been very active in 1993 and 1994 when the first round of peace talks were held. Thereafter, the NIF government of Bashir had sought a military solution to the war by mobilizing the PDF, purchasing arms from abroad, and exploiting the differences among southern Sudanese ethnic groups. Thus, when negotiations were reopened in Nairobi in October 1997 Khartoum was seeking to restore friendly relations with its neighbors. Neither Bashir nor Moi were sanguine that much could be achieved, but there was considerable international pressure for IGAD to meet with the representatives of the GOS and the SPLA. John Garang sent his close aide, Salva Kiir, to the conference. Dr. Mustafa Osman Ismail announced that his government "would participate with all the sincerity required for achieving peace." President Bashir, however, confirmed that his government "would never deviate from the Islamic trend it had opted for, whatever the price."[19] The Islamic Republic of the Sudan would remain at whatever cost. Although the talks resolved nothing, the military activity remained sporadic. A second round of negotiations was held in Nairobi in May 1998 followed by a third meeting in Addis Ababa in August where Bashir agreed to take as the basis for negotiations

---

[18] J. Risen and D. Johnston, "Experts Find No Arms at Bombed Sudan Plant," *The New York Times*, 9 February 1999, p. 1.

[19] "Sudanese government set for peace talks with southern rebels," AFP, Khartoum, 25 October 1999.

the 1994 Declaration of Principles, which provided for self-determination for the South and the right to secede should there be no
agreement on the future of the southern Sudan. Bashir was prepared
to use IGAD to begin direct bilateral negotiations with the SPLA.
Not to be out-maneuvered by Bashir's acceptance of the Declaration
of Principles, Hasan al-Turabi announced he would meet with the
country's exiled opposition parties "for the first time" since the revolution of 30 June 1989. He met with his brother-in law, Sadiq al-
Mahdi at the World Intellectual Property Organization in Geneva
in May 1999 ostensibly to make peace between old political enemies challenged by the Bashir initiative in Kenya. For many in the
northern Sudan the Turabi-Sadiq reunion was seen as the revival of
a national dialogue that Bashir had terminated by the coup d'état
of June 1989 and a first step toward political reconciliation that would
lead to the demise of the military dictatorship.[20] Characteristically,
Sadiq al-Mahdi remained ambiguous, for he regarded that the peace
negotiations with IGAD were "going to be a long draw-out process"
despite the growing "sense of urgency within the government and
within the [southern] region" for peace. Sadiq and Turabi might
differ on the meaning and morphology of an Islamist state and
neither really supported Bashir, but the concept of a secular Sudan
or the prospect of an independent southern Sudan raised by the concession of self-determination for the South in the Declaration of
Principles was anathema to both of them. Without these principles
the members of the NDA were not about to be seduced into accepting the Geneva agreement.

The impression that the government was serious in its negotiations and secure in Khartoum gathered momentum when Bashir
agreed that the former president of the Sudan, Jaafar Numayri, could
return to his country after fourteen years of exile in Cairo. Vice
President Ali Osman Muhammad Taha met with Muhamed Osman
al-Mirghani in Cairo, the leader of NDA, the coalition of Sudanese
opposition parties. None of these Sudanese Arabs participating in
these mutual negotiations trusted one another, and the closer Bashir
moved toward a resolution of the civil war, the more distrustful they
became. Bashir postponed a new round of IGAD talks that were

---

[20] "Leader: Sudan to meet opposition," UPI, Cairo, 13 May 1999.

scheduled to be held in Nairobi from April to July 1999. The Sudan
government offered proposals for a comprehensive cease-fire that
differed little from those tabled at the "First Round," but the Foreign
Minister Dr. Mustafa Osman Ismail "reaffirmed" his government
commitment to the IGAD initiative. More talks were planned.[21] Those
IGAD partners, Kenya, Ethiopia, Eritrea, and Uganda, were more
active in promoting the negotiations, and the Europeans agreed to
provide funds for the IGAD secretariat to organize the peace process
in Nairobi. The IGAD ministerial sub-committee dealing with the
Sudan conflict was expanded to include a partner forum compris-
ing fourteen European states and Canada, Japan, and the United
States.

In October 1999 the United States Secretary of State Madeleine
Albright began a six-nation tour of Africa, during which she met
with Kenya President Moi and SPLA leader John Garang. She and
Moi were convinced that the IGAD process offered the best prospect
for peace in the Sudan for the IGAD Declaration of Principles would
permit self-determination for the southern Sudan and possible secession if the two sides could not agree to a democratic, secular Sudanese
state. The following day Albright met with Garang, whom she labeled
"sophisticated, dedicated, and determined". Direct U.S. humanitarian aid to the southern Sudan was increased from two to three million dollars a year. She expressed concern about the support of
Talisman Energy for Khartoum and was "definitely going to talk to
the Canadians about this."[22] Albright did not reject the Egypt-Libya
peace process, but she did little to encourage it. Mustafa Osman
Ismail reacted angrily, particularly when Harry Johnston, President
Clinton's special envoy to Sudan, arrived in Cairo in October where
he met with the NDA opposition. Johnston made no effort to smooth
over the differences that existed between Khartoum and Washington.
Secretary of State Albright announced that United States policy was
to "isolate" Khartoum while working through IGAD to bring peace
to the Sudan.

---

[21] "Press Release, Sudan Government Delegation, Fourth Round IGAD Peace
Talks," Government of the Sudan, Nairobi, 23 July, 1999.
[22] "Albright angered by difficulty of ending Sudan conflict," AP, Nairobi, 23
October 1999.

Bashir, Turabi and the Struggle for Power

In 1999 a new law was introduced and maneuvered through the National Assembly by Speaker Hasan al-Turabi that permitted political parties (*hizb*) to organize under the guise of political alliances (*tawali al-sayasi*). The concept of *tawali* appears to have been the inspiration of Turabi when in November 1998 he urged many former Sudanese parties to become involved in the political process. Party leaders were confused, however, for the root of *tawali* was derived from the verb "to adjoin" or "to follow" and had no meaning in Islamic jurisprudence. Whatever its origins the Umma Party of Sadiq al-Mahdi and the DUP of the Mirghani family were able to emerge from a decade of hibernation. Other splinter *tawali* immediately appeared in Sudanese politics including the Communists, the Nile Basin Unity Party, and a plethora of southern "alliance" parties. Turabi still controlled the National Congress through his own *tawali* (party), the Popular National Congress (PNC). This new political initiative by Turabi and his PNC was an unexpected democratization of the *shura* to reduce the power of the presidency and bring the military under civilian control. The months of 1999 were spent in political maneuvers between President Bashir, on the one hand, and the speaker of the National Assembly and secretary-general of the PNC, Hasan al-Turabi on the other. In August in Tripoli the leaders of the NDA met to accept the offer of Muammar Qaddafi to mediated in the Sudanese civil war, and a joint Egypt-Libya delegation left Cairo for Khartoum with a plan for a national reconciliation conference that would bring the government and insurgents together.[23]

Turabi had never held Qaddafi or Mubarak in high regard, but he supported the Egypt-Libya peace effort and, as in the past, welcomed Egyptian immigration to the Sudan. "The gates to Sudan will be open to the Egyptian brothers to an extent that the Sudanese and Egyptian identities are legally unified and ultimately removed altogether." This was almost as bizarre as his earlier expressed desire to see a million Chinese come to Sudan to intermarry with Sudanese in order to "bring forth a hard-working people. . . . If I am looking for people in China, why shouldn't I long for such a people from

---

[23] "Egyptians Fly to Sudan to Mediate Between Government, Rebels," Xinhua News Agency, Cairo, 18 August 1999.

Egypt, an overpopulated country?"[24] The northern Sudanese and most certainly the southern Sudanese did not want to see Egyptians, let alone Chinese, immigrants flooding into the Sudan. The United States State Department was adamantly opposed to the Egypt-Libya peace initiative. It had learned to discount much of what Turabi said to journalists including his recent solutions. "We want to Islamize America and Arabize Africa," a task easily accomplished because of America's growing spiritual poverty.[25] When it came to peace, Washington strongly supported the IGAD initiative so that the Egyptian Foreign Minister Amr Musa complained. "You cannot say that the Sudanese problem is some private concern in which no one else should get involved or that it's a problem that should be dealt with by just some of Sudan's neighbours and not others.... Egypt has an important role and interests [in Sudan] which cannot be ignored."[26]

In September 1999 the peace process came to a halt when President Bashir was challenged by Hasan al-Turabi and his political followers in the National Assembly and the PNC. Bashir could not compete with Turabi as a politician, learned Islamist, or charismatic Muslim leader who sought to reduce the powers of the president by his position as speaker. When Turabi sought to use the National Congress to consolidate his position, he had the support of a half dozen ministers including Ghazi Salah al-Din Atabani and the Minister of Higher Education Ibrahim Ahmad Omar. They were no match for Bashir, his allies, and the military. A new constitution drafted by a presidential committee was approved in June 1998 by a national referendum that significantly increased the powers of the president, specifically President Bashir. By December 1998 Turabi had been outmaneuvered. Ten of his former disciples in NIF supported legislation that severely limited the power of the speaker in the National Assembly that inversely granted greater powers to President Bashir.

Turabi sought to regain his authority through the Sudanese National Council, the national *shura* commission, a national consultative body of 600 members, most of whom were loyal to him. His aim was to

---

[21] "Sudanese-Egyptian dialogue should forge strong links: Turabi," AFP, Khartoum, 16 September 1999.

[25] *Cairo Times*, 7 January 1999.

[26] "Egypt steps up criticism of US position on Sudan peace process, AFP, Cairo, 12 November 1999.

gain the presidency of the *shura* general commission composed of sixty members. Once that was achieved he would reorganize the National Congress including the Leadership Office of thirty members and the Leadership Council of 110 members both of which were under the control of Bashir. The Leadership Council ratified all nominations for vice presidents, ministers, and senior officials before their names were submitted to the National Assembly for approval. On 17 December 1999 Turabi proposed to abolish both the Leadership Office and the Leadership Council. Their powers would be assumed by Hasan al-Turabi that set the stage for a major confrontation between the two political leaders of the Sudan. The general assembly of the PNC elected Turabi its party chief and then voted to eliminate the Leadership Office and the Leadership Council that were controlled by supporters of President Bashir. Mohammad al-Hassan al-Amin, a Turabi ally in the PNC, claimed that the changes were approved, "in an almost unanimous vote."[27] The Leadership Office and the Leadership Council would now be replaced by a sixty member Leadership Authority loyal to Turabi. The new authority would have the power to approve the nomination of vice presidents, ministers, and senior government officials before the nominations were submitted to the National Assembly for ratification giving Turabi control of the civil administration of government.

Although Bashir defiantly opposed these constitutional amendments that would drastically limit his presidential authority, there was little he could legally do to divert or obstruct the the legislative challenge by Hasan al-Turabi despite the fact he had few followers among the majority of the Sudanese. They who regarded him as an Islamic intellectual representing the educated elite from the bureaucracy, wealthy businessmen, and professionals in the three cities at the confluence of the Nile. In a popular election he would "not get much more" than the five percent of the votes he had received "in the last free multi-party contest, in 1986."[28] Nevertheless, Turabi succeeded. He had spent months touring the country contacting old allies and former members of NIF. Bashir's political base was limited to the military, and Turabi's offer to institute constitutional

---

[27] "Sudan's Secretary General Has Power," AP, Khartoum, 18 September 1999.
[28] "Sudan: Through the Looking Glass," *The Economist*, 30 October–5 November 1999.

reforms and expand the powers of the Sudanese *shura* was politically popular. A majority of congress members gave Turabi a victory even though the Islamist triumph was seen by outsiders "to be more destabilizing than the Pan-Arab option" embodied by Bashir and his military members of the former RCC.[29]

At a meeting of a "mediatory committee" held on 9 October Bashir agreed to serve as chairman of the PNC, an honorific position of no substance. Real power resided with Turabi who would serve as the secretary-general and chairman of the Leadership Authority of the National Congress. In addition, the Leadership Authority created a committee of seven people chaired by Turabi to make immediate changes in government. As a sop to Bashir he would be the National Congress candidate for president in the elections to be held in 2001. If the congress expected Bashir to quietly acquiesce, they were mistaken. In an address to the PDF Defenders of the Fatherland Brigade (*Liwa Humat al-Watan*) in Khartoum, he reminded the men that "he would continue in the path of jihad and martyrdom," for the RCC "came to unify the Sudanese people and save them from disintegration and disunity. . . . [for] "We are calling for freedom in Sudan but those who think that freedom is a call to anarchy" are mistaken.[30]

In Cairo Mohamed Osman al-Mirghani, president of the NDA, supported the Egypt-Libya peace initiative launched in May 1999. The SPLA demanded that any agreement must be negotiated in the context of the Declaration of Principles of IGAD. The frustrated foreign ministers of Egypt, Amr Musa, and the Sudan, Mustafa Osman Ismail, did not seem sanguine that a peace conference was possible in the near future, but President Bashir traveled to Cairo to seek reconciliation with the NDA that deeply disturbed Turabi in Khartoum. Bashir had created an executive commission that pledged in November 1999 to return all the private property that belonged to the leaders of the Umma and DUP parties confiscated after 30 June 1989 and to discuss peace with the NDA.[31] After Cairo Bashir traveled to

---

[29] "Islam and Democracy: The 1999 Palace Coup in Sudan," *Middle East Policy*, Vol. 7, No. 3, 1 June 2000.

[30] "Sudan: President pledges to continue 'jihad', warns against anarchy," Radio Omdurman in Arabic, 1300 GMT, 18 October 1999.

[31] "Sudan to return confiscated property to appease opposition," AFP, Khartoum, 14 November 1999.

Tripoli to meet with the leaders of neighboring states—Libya, Eritrea, Uganda, and the Democratic Republic of Congo—all of whom gave unconditional support for his leadership in Sudan. At the same time John Garang and the seven opposition groups that comprised the NDA began talks at Asmara to discuss a conciliatory letter sent by Hasan al-Turabi "on the future of Sudan."[32] Turabi agreed to open negotiations with the NDA, in all places Mecca despite the fact that the military forces of the NDA were southern Christians or those who practiced traditional religions. The president of the NDA, Mohamed Osman al-Mirghani of the DUP, dismissed Turabi's offer, for it "reveals the dubious purpose behind this scheme."[33]

Upon his return to Khartoum Bashir and Turabi publicly and vigorously disagreed over the constitutional amendments that would limit the powers of the president. Turabi wanted a prime minister who would answer to parliament, and a parliament that could call for direct elections of the governors of the twenty-six federal states of the Sudan which hitherto had been appointed by the president. In a contentious four hour meeting nothing was resolved.[34] Beshir immediately invited more than 100 deputies to a dinner at his home to discuss the constitutional amendments that would weaken his authority as president. The confused political situation was further complicated when Sadiq al-Mahdi and Bashir met at Djibouti for the first time since Sadiq was overthrown in 1989 and where the Sudanese Foreign Minister Osman Ismail meeting with Mubarak al-Fadl al-Mahdi, Sadiq's nephew and confidant, arranged for Sadiq to return to Khartoum. Bashir sought to use Sadiq as a counter-poise to the growing political powers of Hasan al-Turabi, but the return of Sadiq to Khartoum compromised the "exiled opposition alliance." The NDA denounced Sadiq's unilateral action to return as treachery, and in Nairobi the SPLA called the agreement between Sadiq and Bashir "an ill-conceived public relations stunt" that was destined to fail.[35] The SPLA predicted that the agreement between

[32] "Sudanese rebel chief in Asmara to meet allies," AFP, Asmara, 16 November 1999.
[33] "Bashir-Turabi showdown deemed imminent," *Mideast Mirror*, 17 November 1999.
[34] "Sudan's President Beshir in widening rift with speaker Turabi," AFP, Khartoum, 15 November 1999.
[35] "Bashir-Mahdi 'deal' or a step toward a solution in Sudan?" *Mideast Mirror*,

Bashir and Sadiq would only escalate the war in the South and perhaps postpone the referendum for self-determination by which the
South would choose a federal system of government or a separate
state. Although Sadiq claimed that the agreement he and Bashir had
signed would "pave the way towards a comprehensive settlement to
the Sudanese conflict," no one believed him. Many feared that he
had struck a deal that would "allow him to return to a position of
power in Sudan while enabling Khartoum to improve its international image." In Djibouti Sadiq had proposed a national conference to decide the future of Sudan, "voices calling for peace and
democracy—both inside Sudan and abroad—have been gaining in
strength."[36]

In December 1999 Turabi continued his struggle with Bashir by
using parliamentary stratagems that would increase his authority and
the powers of the PNC, but Bashir refused to tolerate any longer
the erosion of his personal authority and particularly that of the
army. Turabi's policy for direct elections in the twenty-six state governments would have eliminated Bashir's predominant role in the
selection of governors. His appeal to "democratize" the National
Assembly called for a change in the constitution that would permit
a two-thirds vote of parliament to depose the president. Bashir, still
the military man, was not about to surrender to Turabi or a National
Congress dominated by him as the personification of the Islamist
state that would marginalize the president. Ideologically less committed to the Islamist ideal and certainly concerned with its fuzzy
economic policy, the military were overwhelmingly opposed to Turabi's
attempts to achieve power through the legislature at the expense of
its president. As prime minister Turabi would not only threaten
Bashir's preeminence, but the historic and traditional power of the
Sudanese military. In the ensuing internecine struggle, a frustrated
Omar Hassan Ahmad al-Bashir abruptly used force to remove Hasan
al-Turabi as speaker of the National Assembly. On 12 December,
two days before the National Assembly was to vote on curbing the
powers of the presidency, soldiers and tanks surrounded the legisla-

---

20 November 1999; "Sudan rejects reconciliation accord," AP, Nairobi, 29 November
1999.
   [36] "Sudan opposition criticizes peace accord", BBC World Service, 18:18 GMT,
28 November, 1999.

tive building. Bashir peremptorily dismissed Turabi as speaker and dissolved the assembly.[37]

Bashir immediately declared a state of emergency and announced new elections to the National Assembly in December 2000. During his ten years as ruler of the Sudan Bashir had assiduously cultivated his popularity with the military that was the decisive factor in his conflict with Turabi. He never lost this base of his power, and he never forgot that he was a soldier first and a politician second. The decade-long effort by NIF to infiltrate the military and to ensure the promotion of dependable Islamists had succeeded, but the senior officers never trusted Turabi and Taha, and they were determined not to permit the rabble of the PDF to supersede their authority in the SPAF. The fall of Turabi was welcomed by Sudan's neighbors as an end to the Islamist experiment. Although he was approaching seventy and his charisma diminished, he still had a large following among the urban elite who venerated him and his message for the primacy of Islam. A committee of reconciliation was hastily organized in which Turabi was represented by his close associate and banker, Mutasim Abd al-Rahim, but it failed to heal the breach between the president and former speaker. His downfall for some was a "loss not just for him personally but for the Islamist movement and the regime too." It was Turabi "and no one else, who led the process of political liberalization and gradual transition toward constitutionalism and institutionalized democracy that Sudan has witnessed over the past two years."[38] During his visits to Saudi Arabia, Bahrain, Qatar, and the United Arab Emirates President Hosni Mubarak of Egypt strongly supported Bashir. Even the Emir Shaykh Hamad al-Thani of Qatar, who admired Turabi, failed to mediate a reconciliation and urged him to relinquish his position as secretary-general of the ruling PNC. Turabi refused.

He argued that the struggle between the Muslim and non-Muslim worlds had little to do with personalities. It was a "conflict between two contrasting visions of political action." Where the nation had been moving toward "a free and Islamic Sudan," it had entered a period of stagnation that required curbing the powers of the president

---

[37] Stefano Bellucci, "Islam and Democracy: The 1999 Palace Coup in Sudan," *Middle East Policy*, 1 June 2000.

[38] "Sudan's Turabi" "One of the world's best Islamist thinkers, and worst politicians," *Mideast Mirror*, 20 December 1999.

and bring to fruition the powers of the *shura* that would be the beginning, the "breakthrough," of a new stage of political development.[39] The Sudan Minister of Defense Abd al-Rahman Sir al-Khatim flew to Cairo to assure Hosni Mubarak that Turabi was not "staging a comeback" despite the fact that Bashir had included some of Turabi's men in the new cabinet.[40] Even Dr. Mustafa Osman Ismail, the Sudan foreign minister and a former protégé of Turabi in NIF, announced that the government would no longer provide facilities for the PAIC General Assembly. The last significant action taken by the PAIC occurred in late October 1999 when it denounced Russia for its genocidal "bombing campaign" in Chechnya which it considered akin to "ethnic cleansing."[41] The Russians were delighted to see the last of Turabi and his PAIC General Assembly, for he and the PAIC had supported the Dudayev element of the Chechyna mujahideen for nearly a decade.[42] The PAIC General Assembly had "helped African leaders win presidential elections" and had "financed elections which were won by African Muslim presidents while the stupid [people] of the West were not aware that those presidents were Muslim and that their electoral campaigns had been financed from Sudan." On 10 February 2000 the Bashir government shut down the PAIC; its building was confiscated. Its Secretary-General Ibrahim al-Sanoussi announced that the PAIC would look "for a substitute outside Sudan" to "continue with its activities of backing Muslim causes worldwide, including the Chechens."[43]

President Omar Hasan Ahmad al-Bashir made it quite clear that "the rule by two heads in Sudan was over." Bashir publicly urged friends and enemies, including the United States, to judge the Sudan by its present and future, and not its past.[44] In January 2000 he

---

[39] "Turabi: Why Qatar broke off its mediation in Sudan," *Mideast Mirror*,6 January 2000.

[40] "Sudanese assure Egypt that Torabi has been cut out of power," *Deutsche Presse-Agentur*, 29 January 2000.

[41] "Sudan-based Islamists denounce war in Chechnya," AFP, Khartoum, 31 October 1999;

[42] "Moscow welcomes Sudanese drive against militants's supporters," ITAR-TASS news agency, Moscow, 18 February 2000.

[43] "Khartoum drops support for Turabi's international Islamic movement," AFP, Khartoum, 11 February 2000; Mohammad Ali Saeed, "Khartoum closes Turabi's international organization," *Middle East Times*, 18 February 2000.

[44] "Sudan woos world after shooing Turabi aside," *The Middle East Times*, 17 March 2000; "Sudan Getting Down to Business," Robert Lowry, *Okaz* interview in *Arabies Trends*, 1 April 2000.

reorganized his cabinet, firing nine ministers close to Turabi. The pragmatic Islamist Mustafa Osman Ismail retained his post at foreign affairs and Qutbi al-Mahdi at social welfare, and even First Vice-President Ali Osman Muhammad Taha made the transition from a determined Islamist to a pragmatic Islamic politician. Taha had supervised the internal security apparatus, and he had proved his worth. When Turabi turned to the security services for support, he found to his dismay that the apparatus was loyal to Taha, and Taha was loyal to Bashir. In the months following the downfall of Turabi, Bashir sought to repair the Sudan's tattered relations with its neighbors. He sent his cabinet adviser and old friend, Major General Bakri Hassan Salih, to make peace with Eritrea, and overtures were made to Algeria, Egypt, Ethiopia, and Saudi Arabia.[45] Bashir, however, made little impression on the United States Secretary of State Madeline Albright. When questioned at a Senate hearing she remarked that while the United States wanted peace in the Sudan and supported the IGAD process, she denigrated his efforts to change the image of the Sudan Government and its international relations. "I hate to say this, but you can't believe everything you read in the newspapers," but she approved a special envoy to the Sudan to review relations with Khartoum.[46]

In March the Sudanese Constitutional Court appointed by Bashir ruled that the state of emergency, which had confined Turabi and his followers, had been legally imposed by the government. Bashir began to circumscribe the Turabi family business interests and cutoff all government funds that had hitherto been the principal source by which Turabi had been able to attract followers to NIF, pursue his political activity, and subsidize the PAIC General Assembly. By the spring of 2000 Turabi was finished. His energetic efforts to secure the support of the military and security forces, crucial to his survival, had failed. Even the two creations of NIF, the PDF and the more radical paramilitary forces, the *dababeen*, refused to rescue Turabi from his growing political isolation. There were rumors that a shadowy "third force" led by officials from the intelligence services might attempt tp exploit the situation to seize power, but they could not

---

[45] "Bashir Appoints New Cabinet," PANA, Khartoum, 25 January 2000; "Sudan woos world after Turabi sidelined," Reuters, Khartoum, 12 March 2000.
[46] "Sudan Albright Warns "Don't Believe Everything You Read," Senate Foreign Relations Committee Hearing, testimony, Washington D.C., 8 February 2000.

prevail against the loyalty of the Sudanese military to Bashir.[47] Two months later Bashir sought to bury the former ruling Popular National Congress by rejecting its demand for an extraordinary general assembly to reconsider the nomination of Bashir as the lone candidate for president in the parliamentary and presidential elections scheduled for October. The party was now divided between Bashir and Turabi supporters and the role, if any, of Hasan al-Turabi.

Oil Again

In 1997 the Arakis Energy Corporation announced a "major project milestone" by awarding contracts for a 1610 kilometer twenty-eight inch pipeline from Heglig to the Red Sea. The China Petroleum Technology and Development Corporation would be responsible for 1,100 kilometers of pipe and Mannesman Handel AG of Germany for 500. Pumps were manufactured by the Weir Pumps Company of Glasgow.[48] The pipeline would have a capacity of 250,000 bopd, and CNPC, with a forty percent interest in the concession, was determined to begin work and to provide security for the pipeline "and engaged in very significant grading and engineering efforts," all of which would require heavy military vehicles, including tanks, trucks and heavy armaments that enabled Sudan armed forces to launch offensives against the SPLA.[49] Hasan al-Turabi had predicted that oil revenue would be used "to finance the factories" to produce tanks and missiles.[50] The pipeline was opened in August 1999 as a "conduit to respectability in a hostile world." The SPLA considered the pipeline a "weapon of war" and launched an unsuccessful attack to disable it in September.[51]

---

[47] "Sudan: Will the spooks take over?" *Mideast Mirror*, 15 May 2000.
[48] "Arakis Energy Corp.," *Business Wire*, Calgary, Alberta, 15 October 1997; "Letter from Khartoum," *Private Eye*, United Kingdom, 12 November 1999.
[49] "News from the Oil Fields in Sudan (Unity, Heglig, and the Regions South of Bentiu," Personal correspondence from Eric Reeves, Smith College, Northampton, Massachusetts, 4 February 2000.
[50] AFP, Khartoum, 30 April 1999.
[51] "Pipeline offers Sudan veneer of respectability," *The Independent*, London, 3 February 2000.

With the new oil revenues the ministry of defense began to purchase arms, but the Khartoum Islamists could not buy trust. Although France "promised to side with Sudan" in the European Union and United Kingdom diplomats returned to Khartoum, there was widespread criticism against Talisman of Canada as a major partner in the GNPC when the Sudan government forced thousands of villagers to flee from the oil fields where Talisman operated. Unfortunately, "if it were not for this oil-inspired softness on Sudan, an end to the country's murderous civil war might just be conceivable," but any prospects for peace now seemed buried by the revenue from oil estimated at a billion dollars a year when it reached full production.[52] By January 2000 the pipeline from Heglig to the Red Sea was in full operation. Arakis had been bought out by Talisman Energy Corporation of Canada, and the threat of SPLA disrupting the flow of oil proved ephemeral. Plans were underway to construct a Red Sea Free Trade Zone that stretched from Port Sudan to Suakin, and a joint agreement had been signed with the Jiddah Free Trade Zone of Saudi Arabia that would create trade advantages for both countries. During his visit to Saudi Arabia in February 2000, Bashir for the first time gave special attention to the Gulf States. Even Qatar who had thought of mediating the dispute between Bashir and Turabi appeared willing to forgive the Sudan for its support of Iraq in the Gulf War.[53] The political demise of Hasan al-Turabi and the emergence of the Sudan as an oil producer and OPEC member had gone a long way to mollify former enemies. The Sudan still bore the burden of a crushing external debt, but at the beginning of 2000 fifteen million barrels of oil had already been exported, and for the first time in a decade Sudanese exports exceeded imports. Having repaired relations in the Arabian peninsula Bashir sought the more difficult task of restoring diplomatic normalcy with Washington and to lift American sanctions against the Sudan.

---

[52] "Exploiting Sudan's Agony," *The Washington Post*, 15 November 1999.
[53] "Sudanese president says relations with Gulf Arab states improving," *Deutsche Presse-Agentur*, Dubai, 21 February 2000.

The Clinton administration was wary. The Congress had been adamantly hostile to the Sudan for a decade because of its human rights violations. Secretary of State Albright remained convinced that Khartoum offered terrorists a safe-haven, especially for anti-Israeli and pro-Iranian organizations. Iranian military activity in Sudan had decreased significantly since the election of President Muhammad Khatami in 1997, but the Iranian military firmly supported Bashir. The deputy commander of Iran's notorious Revolutionary Guard, Brigadier Zolqadr, was welcome in Khartoum as the invited guest of Sudan Chief of the General Staff Lt. General Abbas Arabi Abdallah.[54] In May 1999 Khartoum had informed Washington it was prepared to sign the U.N. conventions on the suppression of terrorism and related conventions.[55] Intentions were admirable, but as long as the Iranian Revolutionary Guards continued their support of Lebanon's Hizbollah and other terrorist organizations, the United States was not interested in making deals with the Sudan or reopening the American embassy in Khartoum particularly when there was much agitation in the Congress and humanitarian agencies over slavery and human rights.

Despite a mountain of evidence Khartoum adamantly denied that slavery existed in the Sudan, but in 1999 it did acknowledge that "abductions" were carried out by "outlawed militia groups." It was an admission that defied reality. The Sudan government continued to arm and train the Baggara Arab *murahileen* on the frontier of Islam across the Bahr al-Arab (Kiir) from the southern Sudan and gave them legitimacy by enlisting them in the PDF.[56] Washington sent a chargé d'affaires and then a diplomatic team from Cairo to Khartoum in April with a request to freeze Bin Laden's business assets which the Sudanese claimed he had sold before leaving in 1996. There was, however, the issue of human rights abuse. Amnesty International had documented "massive human rights violations by Sudanese security forces, various government allied militias and armed opposition

---

[54] BBC Worldwide Monitoring, "Iranian Guards commander in Sudan, inspects USA-bombed Shifa factory," IRNA, Tehran, in Persian, 10:21 GMT, 12 February 2000.

[55] See Kenneth Katzman, "Terrorism: Middle Eastern Groups and State Sponsors, 2000," Congressional Research Service, Washington D.C., 17 August 2000.

[56] "Sudanese hope for U.S. policy change," AP, Khartoum 16 May 2001; On previous activity of the *murahileen* see J. Millard Burr and Robert O. Collins, *Requiem for the Sudan: War Drought and Disaster Relief on the Nile*, Boulder: Westview Press, 1995.

groups."[57] Linking the depredations to foreign oil company operations, the report confirmed the mood of the Congress of the United
States not to press for a rapprochement with the Sudan. Four months
later, on the second anniversary of the attack on the Shifa pharmaceutical factory in Khartoum, the Sudan made another effort to
open relations with the United States when seeking compensation
for the physical damage done to the factory and for the "injustice"
the nation had sustained. At the same time the Sudan foreign ministry called for a dialogue with the United States "as the best way
to resolve all issues of dispute between the two sides."[58] Having no
credibility in Washington, its fragile overtures were ignored by the
Clinton administration.

Turabi's Last Hurrah

In May 2000 Hasan al-Turabi made his last public statement at the
popular Arabic Al Jazeera television station in Qatar on his seventy-
third and last appearance. He predicted that the Sudanese authorities would soon place him under arrest. He exhorted the Sudanese
people to take to the streets, as in the past, to defend his Islamist
revolution and to free the Sudanese from a resurgent military dictatorship. Bashir was a "power-hungry" dictator. Bashir acted quickly
to defuse Turabi's challenge accusing him of "meeting secretly with
army officers to overthrow his government." Turabi, his NIF followers, and Muslim Brothers were banned from participating in political activity.[59] On 6 May Hasan al-Turabi himself was removed as
secretary-general of the PNC in what the military hoped would end
two years of petulant squabbling. Within a month Khartoum had
restored relations with Tunisia. A Yemeni-sponsored mediation begun
by Turabi's friend and Islamic fundamentalist, Shaykh Abd al-Majid
al-Zandani and sponsored by more than sixty eminent Islamists, was
held in Cairo in June and failed miserably. No common ground
could be found on which both Bashir and Turabi would stand
together.

---

[57] "The Human Price of Oil," *Amnesty International News Service*, AI Index: AFR
54/04/00, London, 3 May 2000.
[58] BBC, Summary of World Broadcasts, *The Middle East: Sudan*, 21 August 2000.
[59] "Marginalizing Al-Turabi," *Al-Ahram Weekly*, Issue No. 481, 11–17 May 2000.

Bashir also moved rapidly to marginalize Turabi's men in the National Congress, and he cleaned out some of the most intransigent *mujahideen* of NIF in the Sudanese intelligence services and the government bureaucracy.[59] Turabi, however, was not about to be repressed nor marginalized, and historically he had always had his say despite attempts to silence him. He ceased to call the civil war a jihad and began to talk of peace with the SPLA and John Garang. Some thought his fall had actually rejuvenated him. He still had a following in the universities, and a generation of young professionals considered him their mentor. In November 2000 Hasan al-Turabi appeared at the Inter-Religious Diagoue Conference sponsored by the CIPF and the Sudan Council of Churches. He presented a paper on "Shar'ia, Democracy and Human Rights." His arguments were given with great cogency and humor, and although he was approaching seventy and the government had restricted his activities, no one familiar with the Sudan's perpetual survivor was prepared to write Turabi's political obituary.

The response of the Islamists to the downfall of Hasan al-Turabi was electric. On 24 May 2000 ninety Islamist leaders representing themselves and organizations from Malaysia to Morocco protested the arrest of the *za'im* [leader] Hasan al-Turabi. It symbolized the failure of the "Islamic Application," the wisdom of the *shura*, and the rule of the *umma* in the Sudan. The *khilaf* [dispute between Bashir and Turabi] was "a source of happiness to the enemies of Islam and regimes of suppression," the end result of which would lead to the destruction of the "Islamic Project." These leaders of the *Haraka Islamaya* (Islamic movement) urged the rift in Sudanese leadership to be mended as soon as possible.[61] In fact the "Islamic Project" in the Sudan was over. Turabi's party headquarters were closed and guarded by the Sudan army, but even President Bashir could not isolate him politically. Hasan al-Turabi founded his own Popular National Congress (PNC) in August 2000 to recover the Islamist momentum that he and his allies had achieved over the past decade. His *Rai al-Shaab* newspaper published political broadsides. The indomitable politician appeared to have survived his demotion until February of the following year when, in the name of his PNC, he

[59] "Failure of Islamist mediation," *The Indian Ocean Newsletter*, 10 June 2000.

[61] Mahgoub El-Tigani, "The Crisis of Religious Faith and Ruling Politics, "The Legal Research Center for Human Rights, Cairo, Egypt, 6 July 2000.

signed a "memorandum of understanding" in Geneva with the SPLA, his life-long enemies, by which he sought a final resolution of the eighteen year old Sudanese civil war by accepting a democratic system and a federal government. This was a mistake, for the Islamist to become the ally of the African insurgents was treason. Turabi was arrested, jailed, and threatened with criminal charges for "communicating with the enemy."[62] Thirty of his associates were imprisoned the following day.

There had always been the latent tensions between the Islamist movement of Hasan al-Turabi and the Sudanese military that would in time erupt into open conflict when the army realized that it was in their best interest to divest themselves of the "Islamist Pope." After the successful coup d'état of 30 June 1989, Bashir had the choice to follow the Islamist path of Hasan al-Turabi or those of the secular Arab nationalists like Qaddafi and Mubarak. By the year 2000, in an ironic twist of fate, events had come full circle. Turabi was once again imprisoned, just as he had been jailed by Bashir's men following the 30 June coup d'état. The PAIC General Assembly that had burned so brightly in 1991 had been extinguished, and the Afghan-Arabs had left the Sudan. The monopoly on power by NIF, Turabi's own political creation, had eventually led to a schism within its ranks and no resolution to the debilitating civil war. Nor had the government found a dependable solution to the nation's economic problems despite the bonanza of oil.

---

[62] "Sudan's Beshir says jailed opposition leader will face criminal charges," AP, Abu Dhabi, 20 March 2001.

CHAPTER THIRTEEN

THE MURSHID FORSAKEN

During the decade following the 30 June Revolution, there were various occasions when President Omar al-Bashir might have chosen to terminate the political career of Hasan al-Turabi. Instead, Bashir always chose discretion. Even when it appeared that the Sudanese military, his power base, was being relegated to an inferior role in the government bureaucracy, he chose patience over revenge. Thus, ever since being named assembly speaker in 1996, Turabi was in ascendance. The elections of that year were held on a "non-party" basis, but Turabi and his "interest group" easily dominated the 400-seat parliament. Within two years, however, all was not well within Turabi's National Congress. In 1999, Bashir was an interested observer as Turabi blocked the efforts of his associates, the so-called "group of ten," to reduce the powers of the secretary-general—and by extension those of Hasan al-Turabi himself. The rebels, including Foreign Minister Mustafa Osman Ismail, Presidential Adviser for Peace Affairs Nafi Ali Nafi, and Minister of State for Information Amin Hassan Omar, were all former Turabi devotees. They had urged the murshid to retire from Parliament and devote himself full time to building the party, something that they felt was badly needed. Their break with Turabi and Turabi's break with them was irrevocable.

In the aftermath of that political shock, Turabi's nerve was put to the test. He worked in concert with only his most trusted associates and plotted revenge on the insurgents and on Bashir himself. In January 1998, Turabi had been responsible for a bit of political legerdemain when he introduced controversial legislation that avoided the use of the word "party" but still provided room for its creation. In the months that followed, Turabi traveled through much of northern Sudan reigniting his NIF base while remolding the Islamist block found within the National Congress itself. Together they transformed a political "association" into the Popular National Congress (PNC), a political party beholden to Turabi, and one that replicated the National Islamic Front, Turabi's former creation. If anyone, it was President Bashir who needed to guard his flanks.

Turabi had no time for extraneous matters, not even for his Popular Arab and Islamic Conference (renamed the Popular Islamic Conference in deference to the many non-Arab members). In January 1999, its secretariat announced that an international conference scheduled for February would be canceled. Although invitees from more than fifty countries had said they would attend, the Sudanese government reportedly halted the meeting because of unexplained "security considerations." The Popular Islamic Conference administration explained that there was a lack of financing for the event. In truth, neither Turabi nor the government had the time for a major conclave. Both were consumed by the intense political activity that followed the promulgation of the controversial 1998 constitution, and the legislation that allowed on 1 January 1999 the revival of "political associations."

The new constitution, endorsed in a 1998 referendum and signed into law by President Bashir that June, allowed the reemergence of political movements beginning in 1999. This would be accomplished through the registration of political associations. Although the opposition in exile rejected the legislation, Turabi appeared determined to end the polarization that had characterized political affairs since the NSRCC seized power. Turabi would prove that he could coexist peacefully with other Sudanese parties, and in April he admitted that he had just entered into "secret talks" with the "northern opposition." It was unclear until a month later who or what was meant. Then, in a move that surprised nearly everyone, Hasan al-Turabi and Sadiq al-Mahdi met clandestinely in Geneva. Aspects of their discussion, which was to have remained a secret, almost immediately leaked to the public. When questioned about the meeting, Turabi stated that he expected the former prime minister to return soon. Abroad, Sadiq said he had no immediate plans to do so; still, he did acknowledge that the meeting itself had "opened a door for political dialogue between the opposition and the Sudanese government." When asked if the event heralded an end to the armed struggle, Mahdi replied in the negative. The war for Khartoum would continue.

Following the disclosure of the secret meeting, a disgusted President Bashir acknowledged that his administration had agreed to a Geneva meeting "covering basic issues," but that he had expected it to be kept a secret. Sadiq was blamed for violating the pledge of confidentiality, but Turabi was hardly disappointed with an outcome that gave the appearance of his assuming the roles of chief of state and minister of foreign affairs, both at one time. A few days after returning from Geneva, Turabi appeared on a Khartoum radio station and announced that he was prepared to conclude peace agreements with "all parties" who were in opposition to the government.[1]

To those experienced politicians who had followed the long career of Hasan al-Turabi, it was just possible that the relapsed Muslim Brother had finally awakened to the fact that it was the military that was supposed to join the Ikhwan and not vice versa. Turabi, the consummate opportunist and political pragmatist, had long believed that more could be accomplished within government than by viewing events from the sidelines. He had done just that when he joined the Numayri government and had lost stature within the Ikhwan movement. Later, the International Muslim Brotherhood, with its headquarters in Egypt, persisted in its mistrust after the Sudanese murshid joined Bashir and the military-dominated NSRCC. Historically, it was the military that had crushed the Islamist movements; it happened first in Egypt under Nasser, and history was later repeated in Libya, Jordan, Iraq, and Algeria. It was past time for Turabi, a man who had never disguised his distaste for military dictatorship, to make a clean break with the past; it was past time to put into practice the Islam prescribed by such modern polemicists as al-Afghani, Amir Shakib Arslan, Muhammad Rida, Seyyed Qutb, and even Hasan al-Turabi himself.

Accustomed to working in the background, Turabi generally limited his personal reflections and political conclusions to the occasional interview with journalists and foreigners. He was aware that in much of the Sudanese community at large he still remained an unpopular political figure. He could do little about that, but when the founding conference of his PNC party met in October, Turabi was ready. In less than a year he had regained the political command snatched from him in December 1998, and the inevitable clash with Bashir was nearing a flashpoint. A mediation committee had recommended Turabi serve as both National Congress secretary-general and chairman of the powerful National Congress Leadership

---

[1] Agence France Press news report, 30 April 1999, with news derived from *Akhbar al-Youm*, Khartoum, of the same date; http://www.sudan.net/www.board/news/71623.html; "Sudan Opposition Leader Meets Egypt's Moussa," Reuters, Khartoum, 13 May 1999.

Authority. Once that had been accomplished, Bashir, who did not face reelection for a second five-year term as president until 2001, was effectively minimized. In order to achieve Bashir's total diminution, Turabi next sought to amend the constitution to ensure the predominance of the prime minister over the president.[2] If Turabi had his way, Bashir would survive only as a political figurehead.

Ironically, after years of playing the game of primus inter pares, when Turabi finally moved to take power he was very easily confounded by Omar al-Bashir, a man of no great military or political distinction. Bashir did not wait to be steamrollered, and in December 1999 he dissolved Parliament and declared a three-month state of emergency. The move was unexpected and shrewd, and with one blow Turabi was deprived of his political base and his political voice. Ruling the Sudan by fiat, Bashir could depend on both the military and intelligence services. And with Turabi mired in a politician's limbo, Bashir took charge of both domestic and foreign policy. In doing so he gave comfort to leaders in the surrounding Arab and African states, receiving the immediate backing of Mubarak, Qaddafi, and Ethiopian Prime Minister Meles Zenawi. Even Saudi Arabia and the rulers of other Gulf states responded favorably. It seemed that all were tired of Turabi's waspish tongue and his decade-long association with a congeries of revolutionaries, terrorists, and radical clerics.

As Bashir became more secure it was noted that "several Arab countries expressed support for Bashir in various ways over the past month or so, and Egypt was reported to be trying to broker a thaw between Khartoum and Washington." It was a daunting task. Among many other reasons, Washington could not forget that Turabi and Bashir had provided Hamas a permanent base in Khartoum in advance of a June 1998 visit by its founder and spiritual guide, Shaykh Ahmed Yassin. In recognition of its "motivating Moslems for Jihad," office space and farmland had been donated to support the "Palestinian struggle." Also, the 20 August 1998 bombing of the Al Shifa pharmaceutical plant in Khartoum by American cruise missiles was still a barbed issue.[3]

---

[2] "Sudan's President Bashir in Widening Rift with Speaker Turabi," Agence France Press, 15 November 1999.

[3] "Sudan: Turabi Bounces Back as Bashir Unveils Reshuffled Cabinet," *Mideast Mirror*, Vol. 14, No. 16, 25 January 2000. On Washington, see "CIA Chief: Bombing Sudan Pharmaceutical Plant No Mistake," AP, Washington, D.C., 18 October 1999. On Hamas, see AFP and DPA news reports, dateline Khartoum, 2 June 1998.

With Parliament dissolved, Turabi reacted by working assiduously to keep his base solid within the NC. Bashir was also busy, and in January he formed a new government featuring many former Turabi faithful who had switched sides. In all, ten new ministers were appointed, and governors were named for the twenty-six states. Seemingly in the blink of an eye, the Khartoum media turned on Turabi and attacked him in an unexpectedly vicious fashion. Turabi could only respond weakly that if he was to be cast to the political wilderness, Bashir should be treated similarly. In public, Bashir appeared perfectly at ease and would have none of Turabi's mischief. Indeed, taking a page from Turabi's book, he initiated a campaign of reconciliation with the Sudanese political opposition in exile. The opposition, which initially wondered if Bashir and Turabi were playing a new game in an old set, was pleasantly surprised by Turabi's diminution. It was especially pleased that the military had moved expeditiously to disarm the Popular Defense Force, long deemed the NIF's private army.

Having marginalized Turabi, and occupying stage center, it was up to Bashir to solidify his own power base. Bashir had some initial success in winning over his political opponents and in constructing a government of national reconciliation. As one report from Khartoum viewed the situation, if his unity government were to succeed, it "would definitely spell the end of any role in government by Turabi." And if that were to occur, one source suggested that the Sudanese people "would not miss the most powerful man of yesterday if left in the cold political winter of the Sudanese desert."[4]

The New Millennium

As the Sudan entered the new millennium, the fog that had enveloped the Bashir-Turabi clash of wills began to clear. Both Turabi and his ruling PNC were sidelined, but although Turabi labeled Bashir's action a "coup d'état," the Sudanese voter generally welcomed Bashir's move to clip the Speaker's wings. The power struggle continued through January 2000, during which time Turabi accused

---

[4] "Bashir Clips Turabi's Political Role in Sudan," PANA (Panafrican News Agency), Khartoum, 18 January 2000.

Bashir of repudiating the constitution and instituting dictatorial rule. A mediation undertaken that month by Qatar Foreign Minister Sheikh Hamad Bin Jaber al-Thani, an old friend of Turabi, came to nothing. And when Turabi and his diminishing number of political allies used the Constitutional Court to challenge both the closure of Parliament and the state of emergency imposed by Bashir, nothing came of that either. The Court members, most of whom were thought to be favorable to Turabi, held their first hearing in February 2000, but the result was inconclusive.

In the same month, Turabi appeared before thousands of Islamists at the Kuranic University in Omdurman and warned that the escalation of the existing political crisis could eventually lead to the disintegration of the Islamic state. At one point in the address he offered the interesting aside that the collapse would be a setback to "Islamists abroad." He then asserted that during his tenure, the Islamist movement had expanded from the Sudan to include neighboring African nations. The beneficiaries of the Islamist largesse were not otherwise identified, but in a surprising admission Turabi said he was pleased that while Khartoum financed such elections, the "stupid" people in the West had not recognized what Khartoum was up to.

As the Bashir-Turabi struggle continued through mid-2000, Turabi was the loser at every turn. At 72, he was finally showing his age. He fought back weakly as his businesses were sequestered and his movement's funds were threatened. Still, even as the president's supporters formed the National Congress Party (NCP), Turabi fought back, and a new political movement emerged as the Popular Congress Party (PCP). Yet, no sooner was the party formed than his Islamist coalition began to fracture. In contrast, the military, the senior bureaucracy, the security services, and a large number of political opportunists were solidly behind Bashir. Working from a position of power, the president signaled that he was ready to open discussions with the United States, and his fellow military officers did not object when he began to consider opening the stalled peace talks with the SPLA.

Although Turabi's Islamist movement was forced to yield ground, the foreign media from time to time questioned whether Bashir himself was losing control of his power base. It was obvious to all that should the military and intelligence agencies coalesce in opposition to Bashir, the president's days were numbered. However, such an event was only wishful thinking, and there was no general unhappiness with his one-man rule.[5] Instead, in assessing the man the *Mideast Mirror* wondered: "What is the extent of Bashir's aspirations? Or will circumstances and regional and international pressures turn him into a Sudanese version of Nigeria's late Gen. Sani Abacha, ruling by brute force with the approval of neighboring countries?" With Bashir firmly seated in Khartoum, only time would tell.

In August 2000, Turabi's London-based biographer, Abdelwhahab al-Effendi, argued, "There's no way he can return to power now, and he should retire from political life if he is to have any chance of playing an indirect role in future." As Effendi saw it, once Turabi's power had been reduced, he had embarked on a suicidal political campaign that could lead only to his political humiliation. Effendi visualized that should Turabi get his way and the Bashir regime fall, the result would be "mayhem." Either the Sudan would "become the next Somalia, or else the armed opposition will seize power-with bloody consequences for Turabi and his supporters."[6]

Turabi Counters and Is Countered

Effendi was correct. Turabi had begun a process of self-destruction. Seeking to revenge slights and diminish his enemies both domestic and foreign, Turabi began to reveal state secrets. Among other things Turabi openly discussed aspects of Sudanese diplomacy in Africa south of the Sahara. He revealed the role Iraq had played in assisting in the Sudanese Islamist revolution—something that was already fairly well known. His revelations of Egyptian counter-Islamist activity outraged Cairo (if that were possible), and he told tales and some lies involving the exploration and exploitation of Sudanese oil fields. In sum, Turabi jettisoned political associates left and right as secrets were revealed to an astonished public. In playing the role of tabloid journalist, Turabi admitted to certain activities in the early years of the 30 June Revolution that he previously had denied. He claimed

---

[5] "Will the Spooks Take Over?" *Mideast Mirror,* 15 May 2000. Based on a report by Mu'awiya Yassin that appeared in that week's edition of *Al-Wasat.*
[6] "Sudan's Turabi 'on a Politically Suicidal Course,'" *Mideast Mirror,* Vol. 14, No. 149, 4 August 2000. Effendi quotes were derived from the pan-Arab *Al-Quds alArabi.*

that it was he who planned the 30 June Revolution, something that most Sudanese knew but a fact he had denied for more than a decade. And in the unfolding of political activity during that decade, he sought to place himself at the apex of the revolutionary pyramid. In describing the Bashir regime as a corrupt, oppressive, and un-Islamist dictatorship, he was belaboring the obvious and denouncing a state of affairs that he himself had enjoyed since the early days of the 30 June Revolution. When he complained in the year 2000 that the army had utterly failed to make progress in the South, the conditions in that region at that point were little different from those that existed during the years when Turabi was top dog in Khartoum. He launched unseemly attacks on NIF party members who had left the fold. And in excoriating the present, he sounded like a man who had picked a bushel of sour grapes and was determined to inform the world that he had a bellyache. As Effendi put it, "peddling secrets and gossip is an abhorrent practice even if such practices do indeed damage your enemies, because it is such a gross abuse of trust."It would certainly "destroy the chances of any leader ever trusting Turabi again," Effendi continued. In revealing the past, Turabi exposed himself as a serial liar. He validated his enemies who had characterized him for years as a man unworthy of political leadership or trust.

When Parliament finally reopened in 2000, Turabi still served as Speaker of Parliament, and his nascent PNC seemingly had enough strength to ensure his survival. Nonetheless, Bashir with his ruling NCP easily eclipsed Turabi. In national elections held in December 2000, Bashir was reelected president for a second (and legally his last) five-year term. The opposition led by Hasan al-Turabi boycotted an election in which Bashir received 86.6 percent of the vote, and his NCP won 97 percent of the seats in parliament.

Turabi would have to wait for another day to make a political comeback, but, as ever, he remained unpredictable. Cast aside by old friends and forced to confront a strong political movement, Turabi initiated a new political campaign and sought new allies among the political leaders who inhabited the periphery of eastern, southern, and western Sudan. In the west, where he had long cultivated ties with both Arab and African tribes, he began to expand the reach of his PCP. In addition, he began to make overtures to the SPLA. This change in tactics angered Bashir, who knew such moves could be potentially dangerous, especially in Darfur, an underdeveloped and lightly populated region the size of France, where conflict between the tribes and government-armed militias was rapidly spinning out of control.

When the Bashir government learned in early December 2000 that the leaders of the National Democratic Alliance (NDA) had met "secretly" with Glenn Warren, an American diplomat, Bashir responded furiously. The NDA, an umbrella organization uniting the opposition to Khartoum, had been established in October 1990 by exiled Umma and Democratic Unionist Party (DUP) political leaders and their military allies. It had expanded over the years to include in its membership the SPLM/A, the Union of Sudanese African Parties, the Communist Party, and opposition trade union and professional leaders. In the 1990s, the NDA leadership council had welcomed the inclusion of dissident leaders of an incipient political opposition in Darfur. That region had become increasingly insecure during the course of 1999. Warren was charged with "holding talks with an unregistered opposition party," and the NDA leaders were jailed after being accused of passing information to the rebel SPLA. Apparently soon convinced that he had acted rashly, at least with regard to the American diplomat, Bashir was calling within a month for closer relations and a meeting with the newly elected president of the United States, George W. Bush. He even urged United States oil companies to consider investment in the Sudan.

In a move that few would have expected given Turabi's historic antipathy for John Garang and the Southern Sudanese in general, Turabi's PCP signed an agreement with the SPLA in February 2001 that was little less than a call to overthrow the Bashir regime, albeit "by peaceful means." While Khartoum observers waited for the next shoe to drop, it was suggested that Turabi was forming an alliance of increasingly dissatisfied ethnic minorities found in the periphery of the Sudanese state. That included everyone from the Nubians of the North to the Hadendowa and Beja of the East. In Darfur, it was rumored that disaffected Zaghawa were on the prowl and had formed an alliance with Turabi's PCP. Some observers anticipated that Turabi would use the Sudan's ethnic minorities as the fulcrum needed to return him to power in Khartoum and end the rule of Bashir's National Congress Party.[7]

---

[7] "The Darfur Conflict—The Sudan," *White Fathers—White Sisters*, October-November 2004, p. 3.

A potential Turabi-Garang alliance was, however, more than Bashir could bear. And once again the president moved swiftly. The government banned all PCP activity, and it jailed its leaders, most particularly Hasan al-Turabi. They were charged with subverting the constitution and "waging war on the state." In effect, the incarcerated Turabi was back where he started when as a younger man he had suffered arrest during the tenure of Sudanese President Jaafar Numayri.

Darfur Aflame

In the Darfur region, many students and the regional Islamist party leadership had followed Turabi into political exile. Just how crucial the Darfur students would be to Turabi's political future was explained by one observer who claimed that the murshid had "target[ed] the upwardly mobile students of western Sudan," and it was "something he did with extraordinary dedication and adroitness."It was argued that "the Islamic Front would never have been able to conquer power without the critical input of dedicated and creative fanatics from Western Sudan."[8]

In retrospect, it is evident that personal security had been tenuous to nonexistent throughout Darfur well in advance of the 30 June 1989 Revolution.[9] The situation was later exacerbated by the Revolutionary Front's acquiescence to a wide-reaching 1994 constitutional decree that permitted a regional administrative reorganization. The Sudan was redivided into twenty-six states from the existing nine, and in the West the states of North, South, and West Darfur were created where the two provinces of North and South Darfur had previously existed. Originally proposed by members of Hasan al-Turabi's National Islamic Front, the move, some observers believed, resulted from the need to divide the region into more manageable political units. Unfortunately, the reorganization was promulgated without any effort to obtain input from Darfur or from the large ethnic Fur community active in Khartoum. The state of West Darfur, although

---

[8] Mutasim [pseud?], "Season of Migration from Allah to Race," SecularSudan.net, 28 June 2003.

[9] See J. Millard Burr and Robert O. Collins, *Darfur: The Long Road to Disaster*, (Princeton, NJ: Markus Wiener Publishers, 2008).

dominated by Fur and Masalit populations, accommodated a mélange of ethnicities. Yet, despite the predominance of Fur and Masalit, ethnic Arabs were allowed to assume powerful roles in local government both there and throughout all of Darfur. Some thirty new leadership positions (emirs) were created in the Dar Masalit region alone, and most of the positions were filled by the Arab Umm Jallul tribe. Not surprisingly, the Fur, Masalit, Zaghawa, Berti, and other African tribes feared the usurpation of their historic leadership roles and thus their political diminution. Most of all, they feared attacks by increasingly well-armed Arab militias.[10]

In March 1995, the weekly *Darfur al-Jadidah* (New Darfur) was banned after an article criticized government policy in the region. Inexplicably, the magazine was closed down, although it was reportedly owned by NIF members and thought to be pro-Government.[11] While Turabi remained silent on the issue, Darfur's Fur and Masalit leadership would thereafter claim that not only was there no press freedom in Darfur, there was no indigenous press.

In May 1996, when Bashir addressed the security situation in Darfur he asked, "What is a human being's life without security?" He answered his own question with a pat on the back: "That is what the Salvation Front provided, security, and it broke the back of the mutiny and liberated very vast areas in the south and even in the north in Darfur."[12] Only a few months later, however, the government was finally forced to admit publicly that a series of bloody inter-ethnic clashes had continued to imperil Darfur. Minister of the Interior Bakri Hassan Salih informed the national parliament that the government had taken "precautionary measures to enforce law in western Sudan." Already some 92 persons had been killed and 14 wounded (an obviously bogus count) in recent fighting. Only weeks later it was announced that some 100 people had been killed and 15,000 displaced before life could be said to return to "normal."And

---

[10] See Dawud Ibrahim Salih et al., Representatives of the Massaleit Community in Exile, "The Hidden Slaughter and Ethnic Cleansing in Western Sudan," http://www.massaleit.info/open_letter.html, Cairo, 8 April 1999; Korwa G. Adar, "Theocracy and State Reconstruction in the Civil War-Ravaged Sudan: In Pursuit of an Illusive National Consensus," http://www.kas.org.za/Publications/Seminar Reports, 2002.

[11] *Sudan News and Views*, No. 6, 16 March 1995.

[12] Sa'id Muhammad al-Hasan, "An Interview with President Lt. General Umar al-Bashir," *Al-Sharq al-Awsat*, 29 May 1996.

in October 1996, clashes were reported less than two months after Masalit and Arab tribes had signed a truce sponsored by Khartoum.[13] In April the following year, the Arab militias burned some one hundred Masalit villages east of Geneina, the region's capital; more than five hundred people were killed, thousands were displaced, and livestock losses were massive.[14]

The insecurity continued in western Darfur through January 1999 when once again the region was the locus of Arab nomad attacks on Masalit villages. To halt the incursions, the government reported that it would reinforce the region's Sudanese army units. That action appeared to check the antagonists for a time, but persistent reports on the deterioration of human rights in that vast region continued to reach Khartoum. The peace would not last, and ethnic tensions began to mount once again.[15] In the Masalit homeland, the sedentary villagers and Arab nomads clashed once again. And once again the Masalit were outgunned. In a spate of new killings, the Arab militias left more than 125 villages either totally or partially burned, and hundreds were killed (including a large number of Arabs). The army was then ordered to end the violence, and the region was placed under the administration of a military officer. All-powerful, he was given responsibility for regional security and could overrule any decision made by the West Darfur State governor.

An attempt at ethnic reconciliation was obliterated after the Masalit chief, Yakoub Ahmed, and his wife were assassinated in front of their house in Geneina. The chief had been "a member of the reconciliation committee working to pacify the African Masalit ethnic group and the pastoral Arab tribesmen in western Sudan," and his wife, a schoolteacher, was a member of Parliament in West Darfur State. Ahmed Ishak Yakoub, the spokesman of the western Darfur state government, informed the Khartoum newspaper that "a three-man hit-team used automatic rifles to kill the chief and his wife and

---

[13] *Muslim World Daily News Briefs*, Vol. 1, No. 98, 11 October 1996; *Al-Sudan al-Hadith*, Khartoum, derived from *Muslim World Daily News Briefs*, 27 October 1996; "Tribal Fighting Resurfaces,"derived from *Al-Rai al-Aam*, Reuters, Khartoum, 17 October 1996.

[14] Philippa Coults, "Grounding Food Security Monitoring in an Understanding of the Local Economy," The Food Economy Group, n.d.

[15] Committee on the Elimination of Racial Discrimination, 54th session, Summary Record of the 1,329th Meeting, Palais des Nations, Geneva, 17 March 1999, Ms. McDougall, Country Rapporteur.

escaped in an off-road vehicle." The killers did not seem to care that the Ahmed home was adjacent to the police headquarters and to the office of the state governor. The gunmen were not further identified, but the Masalit were convinced that they were Arabs determined to keep the Darfur pot boiling.[16] Khartoum declared a state of emergency, a commission was ordered to study the problem, and a special representative was sent to Darfur to impose security.

In 2000, the Bashir-Turabi split had its own impact on Darfur. Many Darfur leaders who entered the Islamist movement because of Turabi had begun to leave the government and organize both politically and militarily. In El Fasher, a leadership circle was organized, and in May 2000, something truly unexpected transpired when the Darfur opposition produced their explosive *Black Book* (*al-Kitab al-Aswad*). Subtitled *Imbalance of Power and Wealth in the Sudan,* it was a broadside authored by an unknown group calling itself "The Seekers of Truth and Justice." A ferocious diatribe, it detailed the region's historic disadvantages—with regard to its economy, its political representation, and the general lack of educational opportunity. The book, which illustrated how the riverain Arabs centered in Khartoum had divided the north along racial lines, was an immediate cause célèbre.

The authors had "plucked sensitive records from state archives and, with other information gleaned from open sources, produced a detailed précis of the post-Independence plight of Darfur's African Muslim tribes. In doing so, it provided the rationale for the recent history of political conflict both within the region and against the central government itself. The argument was both simple and unsettling: political Sudan was dominated by a single region—riverain Sudan. Its locus was the Khartoum/Omdurman conurbation. This northern region contained little more than five percent of the nation's population, but its three major Arab dynasties had long monopolized its political, economic, and military power. The *Black Book* was a booklet that documented "Khartoum's neglect and ostracism of the western tribes in the decision-making process; it showed that the great majority of important positions in the country were filled by figures from a northern Arab background." It documented the neg-

---

[16] "Gunmen Kill Chief and His Wife in Western Sudan," DPA, derived from *Al-Rai al-Aam,* Khartoum, 31 October 1999.

lect Darfur had suffered in regard to both political and economic decision making.[17] The book used many tables and a plethora of statistics to make its point: all presidents and prime ministers had come from the northern region, and they controlled key positions in the country ranging from ministerial posts to bank directorships, from leaders of agricultural development schemes to commanders of the army and police.[18]

The authors, writing anonymously, were quietly applauded if for no other reason than that the *Black Book* had managed to skirt the government's seemingly airtight control of the news. As if by magic, hundreds of copies appeared at the University of Khartoum and other schools. President Bashir even "found one on his desk when he returned from his devotions." Most telling, the book was distributed after Friday prayers at major mosques in Khartoum and Omdurman. Eventually, as many as 50,000 copies of this broadside, which "castigated the moral bankruptcy" of Bashir's government—a "regime that had based its legitimacy on Islam"—were disseminated throughout the Sudan. By then, Turabi had already made common cause with the Darfur revolutionaries, and he and his followers were responsible for circulating thousands of copies. Indeed, "the book soon became the most talked about document in the country. It was an envy of any writer, the world over.[19] Eventually, the names of most of the fifteen authors emerged, including its publishers, Khalil Ibrahim Muhammad and Idris Mahmoud Logma, future leaders of an indigenous political movement in Darfur.

The Bolad Uprising

In the *Black Book*, the Darfur rebel Daoud Yahya Bolad was described as a "martyr,"and it was asserted that "Daoud's uprising" (which occurred shortly after the NSRCC took power) had marked "a turning point in many people's consciousness in Darfur."[20] In the

---

[17] Anders Hastrup report, http://www.tharwaproject.com/English/MainSec/Files/Darfur/hastrup.htm.

[18] A Part Two of the *Black Book* appeared in August 2002 on the website Sudanjem.com. Part Two contains more than 200 tables.

[19] William Wallis, "The Black Book History[,] or Darfur's Darkest Chapter," *The Financial Times*, 21 August 2004.

[20] "The Darfur Conflict: Crimes against Humanity in Sudan," Crimes of War Project, 9 April 2004.

centuries during which ethnic Fur have populated the western region of modern Sudan, a long list of Fur martyrs who died in support of ethnic nationalism and the perpetuation of their Dar can be chronicled. One of the few voices to be raised against Jaafar Numayri had been that of Daoud Yahya Bolad, a Fur born in 1952 near Nyala, South Darfur. The Bolad family had strong ties to the nineteenth-century Mahdi, and to the Ansar religious sect whose leadership would eventually be assumed by his grandson, the Sudanese politician Sadiq al-Mahdi. Indeed, most Fur farmers who cared about politics supported Sadiq's Umma Party. That lasted until the 1980s, when the government began to champion the aims of Arab *jallaba* (merchants), whose involvements in livestock were commercially interlocked with the Arab nomads.

While still a youth, Bolad learned Arabic by memorizing the Koran, and he considered it a second language. Educated in local schools, he showed great talent and was one of the few students of western Sudan to enter the University of Khartoum. He was already politically active and was familiar with the Muslim Brotherhood movement. The movement had very shallow roots in Darfur; the Ikhwan had established the *al-Balagh* newspaper, but a series of articles it published led the military dictatorship to force its closure in June 1958. In the decade that followed, the Ikhwan found it "more and more difficult to maintain contact with the provinces," and thus a decline in membership resulted. [21]

It was during his early years as an engineering student at the University of Khartoum (1971-1978) that Bolad finally joined the Muslim Brotherhood. In doing so, he rejected the siren call of Dr. Ali al-Haj, the leader of the Darfur Development Front (who would one day become Hasan al-Turabi's trusted aide); likewise, he spurned the Sudanese Communists and the Baath Party Socialists. Finally, he rejected his youthful flirtation with Sufi mysticism and the Ansar political movement led by Sadiq al-Mahdi. In the end, Bolad joined Turabi because he respected the latter's Islamist militancy. Bolad believed as Turabi did that the Sudan should be ruled by an Islamist government, and that the Sudan itself should be in the forefront of *da'awa*, the projection of Islam throughout Africa.

---

[21] Susanne Wolf, "The Muslim Brotherhood in the Sudan," M.A. thesis, University of Hamburg, 1990.

The adept Bolad was elected chairman of the Khartoum University Students Union in his final year at school. It was no small achievement, as President Numayri had forced the Muslim Brotherhood underground and would not effect a reconciliation with Turabi until 1978. In that year, Bolad returned to Nyala, Darfur, where, with the help of an Islamic bank, he founded a carpentry company. Bolad would then serve as an important link between the Darfur region and the Muslim Brotherhood. He worked closely with Turabi, and with Turabi's right-hand man and potential Iago, Ali Osman Muhammad Taha, to expand the Ikhwan in the West. Bolad was said to be responsible for much of the growth of the Muslim Brotherhood in Darfur, and in representing the West, he became an important figure in Turabi's National Islamic Front and in the national elections held in 1986. Ironically, in 1985, SPLA policy began to focus on gaining allies and exploiting new fronts where ethnic minorities had profound grievances against the government. In Darfur, the SPLA effort converged on Jebel Marra and the burgeoning Fur concerns prompted by constant Arab nomad incursions onto their farmland and pasture. This effort had little success during the tenure of Sadiq al-Mahdi, but the SPLA alliance with the Fur advanced rapidly after Bolad turned on the NSRCC government. In the months following the 30 June 1989 Revolution, Bolad had a falling-out with Hasan al-Turabi. It is argued that Bolad and Turabi diverged politically, but it is not clear why. The rupture seems to have occurred while Turabi was spending the latter half of 1989 in comfortable confinement in Kobar prison. It is quite possible that the break resulted not from personal or theological differences; rather, Bolad was obviously dismayed by a series of inconclusive government-sponsored meetings held in Darfur that were designed to end the years of internecine tribal warfare that pitted African ethnicities against Muslim cattle (*baqqara*) and camel (*abbala*) nomads. Regionally, the African ethnicities argued that the NSRCC favored the Arabs and had imposed a peace that was detrimental. The Arabs were threatening further deprivations as the long regional drought persisted. Arable land became yearly more scarce and population pressures more intense. In response, Bolad activated rebel cells in Darfur, and the Peoples Movement was revived.

Engineer Bolad went underground, and when he emerged it was in southern Sudan where in 1990 he was involved in talks with SPLA commander John Garang. In a break with his past, Bolad came to the conclusion that the Fur had more in common with the southern tribes than he had ever been willing to admit. It is likely that he was attracted to an SPLA that, from its inception, "called for the restructuring of power, the equitable distribution of wealth, religious tolerance, a democratic dialogue between the different ethnic and cultural groups in Sudan, and the creation of a new sociopolitical, economic, and cultural dispensation," which was called "the New Sudan."[22] The SPLA and its predecessor southern rebel organizations had for decades opposed the riverain Arabs, whose power was centered in Khartoum, and who had dominated the Sudan from the moment of its independence in 1955.

Following a meeting with SPLA/SPLM leadership, Bolad would serve as "Garang's entree in Darfur." Labeled the personal representative of Jebel Marra insurgents and chief of the SPLA's Darfur Division, in August 1991 Bolad led the small unit of "local activists" into Darfur. They marched through a drought-impacted region where the search for water brought the unit ever closer to springs and water holes controlled by Arab militias friendly to Khartoum. They surfaced at Khor Gimbal, south of Jebel Marra. The Darfur Division, never much more than company size, had been tracked by the Beni Halba, a vicious Arab militia armed by the Sudan Army. Weakened by weeks of marching that began in Bahr al-Ghazal, Bolad's unit was attacked and easily overrun. Bolad was captured and then interrogated by Sikha Khair, the NSRCC's satrap for Darfur. Ironically, Khair himself had formerly been the "bodyguard to the leader of the Khartoum University Islamists, Daoud Bolad." Shortly afterward, Bolad appeared on television, "a battered but composed prisoner, and was accused of treason." He died a mysterious death a week before he was to come to trial.[23] With his capture and death, the Peoples Movement faded away. Garang sought without success to keep the insurgency alive in Jebel Marra, and next turned to Darfur's two best-known political exiles, Ahmed Ibrahim Diraige and Dr. Sharif Harir. During meetings held in Europe, the parties agreed to form the Revolutionary Army for western Sudan. However, neither

22 "SPLM Position on Developments in Darfur," Press Statement, SPLM/A News Agency, 20 March 2003.
23 See Minority Rights Group, http://www.sudanupdate.org/REPORTS/PEOPLES/darf.htm, 1995.

Diraige nor Harir had an effective military force that could be used to attack the Khartoum government.[24]

Turabi and Darfur

That Turabi would choose to enter the fray in Darfur was hardly surprising. His involvement there can be traced to the late 1950s, when he and his Muslim Brother associates began to support Muhammad al-Baghalani, an ethnic Zaghawa and leader of the ulcan Force that operated in the Chad-Sudan borderland. Baghalani represented the "traditionalist" strain of Muslim chiefs, and he was one part of a cabal determined to rid Chad of its Christian and animist African rulers and replace them with Muslims. Little was known of Baghalani aside from the fact that he was Muslim and perhaps educated in Darfur and Khartoum. The Zaghawa were noted for their business acumen, and their Dar Zaghawa straddled both sides of the northern border between Chad and the Sudan.

In the following decades, Turabi's interest in the Zaghawa never waned. Nearly thirty years later, Idris Deby, the Chad rebel and Zaghawa leader, overthrew the government of Hissene Habre. Calling Hasan al-Turabi "his spiritual father," he would remain on friendly terms with Khartoum as long as Turabi remained a powerful figure in the government.[25] Since 1990, when Deby had been a staunch supporter of the Khartoum government, he had maintained good relations with Khartoum, and in recent years had been determined to keep the Darfur conflict from spreading into Chad. As a Zaghawa warlord himself, he was perfectly aware that if an attack by Arab militia on the Zaghawa in the Sudan was not met by a determined Sudan Army action, the Zaghawa of Chad would soon join the fray and the fighting would likely spill over into his country. After Turabi was ousted from the government, and when Arab militia began to attack Zaghawa villages in 2001, Chadian Zaghawa joined their brothers in Darfur, and Deby's relationship with Bashir and the Khartoum leadership was irrevocably damaged. In Darfur, it was said

---

[24] "Movements and Organizations of Political Protest in Darfur," Sudan Online Inc., http://www.sol-sd.com/darfur_dos/militias.htm.
[25] "Chad: Operation Rezzou," *Africa Confidential*, 4 May 1990, p. 4.

that Turabi had sought alliances with the sheikhs and religious leaders of the Fur, Masalit, and other minorities. In that move he was far from successful. As one of the most powerful men in the Sudan, if not the most powerful, Turabi did little to halt the growing gangsterism in Darfur. The Fur had been the first to suffer. The Masalit, a major tribe found in central Darfur, dated the Arab invasion of and attacks within their traditional homeland from August 1995. The Darfur Arabs, armed during the succession of governments that began in the 1980s, clashed repeatedly with the various minorities inhabiting Darfur. Neither the parliament nor the military could be counted on to bring an end to an ominous situation that was spreading from the very north to the far south. Given the conflict in southern Sudan, it still seemed of little consequence. The government-sponsored November 1996 reconciliation agreement involving the Masalit and the Arab tribes solved nothing.

Turabi played no important role as peacemaker in Darfur. His inaction was surprising because over the decades he had made a real effort to attract Arab, Fur, and other ethnicities to his Islamist political movements. Although Turabi had absolutely no concern for the southern Sudanese, he had a history of supporting the African Muslim communities of central and western Sudan. In the 1970s, he had championed the Fallata, the West Africans who while on pilgrimage to Makka had found a home and settled in Sudanese agricultural complexes. It had been Turabi's mission to ensure that all Muslim residents of the Sudan be extended citizenship, and for years thereafter he supported the recognition of more than a million Fallata. Composed in the main of ethnic Hausa and Fulani, the group as a whole was very religious, and in time very Islamist. Following the 30 June Revolution they were finally granted citizenship, and Turabi, who had helped empower their sheikhs, was easily able to merge the Fallata aspirations with his own.

Also in the 1970s, Turabi began a political outreach program designed to spur Darfur youth to gain a university education in Khartoum and to join the Muslim Brotherhood and, eventually, Turabi's political movements. "That the new armed rebels of Darfur have called themselves the Boladis of Darfur is pregnant with meanings over and above revealing their roots in political Islam. For Bolad was one of the most prominent Darfurian Islamic leaders the University of Khartoum has ever seen." Daoud Bolad, Khalil Ibrahim, and Ali

Al-Haj were counted among the leading Islamists from Darfur and were labeled "key figures in the movement and government that caused the death of hundreds of thousands of southerners and Nuba before opportunistically discovering their brotherhood with the races they murdered."[26]

It was in early 1998 that Abd al-Rahim Muhammad Hussein, the Sudan's interior minister "told the media that 'fifth columnists' had killed all the Arab chieftains in West Darfur. This untrue and inflammatory remark provoked many more Arab tribesmen in the region to join in the conflict than might otherwise have done so."[27] It followed that chances for regional peace were greatly diminished after a failed Arab militia attack on Masalit villages of Mount Junun in late January 1999. As both sides armed and awaited their opportunity to attack, the government response was little less than criminal. The Masalit in general were labeled rebels. Westerners claimed that, "with the official encouragement of the NIF government in Khartoum, and through the agency of the NIF officials in the state of Western Darfur, the way was clear for the Arab militias to begin a full and final assault on the Masalit." Armed by the government with weapons, Toyota Land Cruisers ("desert chariots"), and communications gear, "the government also sealed off the Dar Masalit area and prevented Masalit people from fleeing."[28]

Armed militias then attacked in force, and it was claimed that Sudanese military helicopters were used to support them. More than two thousand Masalit were killed, thousands were wounded, and tens of thousands fled to Chad, where they joined other thousands who had fled previously. Following reports in mid-March 1999 that more than one hundred Masalit had been killed in yet another Arab militia attack, the "People from Darfur" living in Khartoum warned the government in a petition that the "bloody tribal confrontation" in Darfur was a "looming danger" to the Bashir government itself. They decried the recent deadly events in that region and the proliferation

---

[26] "Season of Migration from Allah to Race," SecularSudan.net, 28 June 2003.

[27] The Massaleit date the Arab invasion from August 1995. Note "Sudan: People from Darfur Warn of Danger Following Bloody Tribal Confrontation," Radio Voice of Sudan, Voice of the National Democratic Alliance, in Arabic 1600 GMT, 21 March 1999.

[28] Mohamed Adam Yahiya, Spokesman of the Massaleit Representatives in Exile, "More Massaleit Civilians Die in Arab Militia Attacks in Western Sudan," Cairo, Egypt, 25 April 2000.

of firearms among its citizens. The petition urged the Sudanese "to assist in the relief of thousands of families" who had fled a "hellish death in the Junaynah area."The displaced had formed camps along the Chad-Sudan border, where they survived without services and were soon battered by a meningitis epidemic. The petition was signed "by 10,000 people who hail from Darfur State, among them politicians, chiefs, and local administrators," and the protesters were continuing the work of collecting even more signatures from "citizens from Darfur, living in Khartoum."[29]

A month later, on 8 April 1999, the Masalit political community in exile in Egypt issued an open letter from Cairo to the international community denouncing "the hidden slaughter and ethnic cleansing in western Sudan." They claimed the existence of "wide-spread and systematic abuses of human rights carried out by the current National Islamic Front (NIF) government," and that these abuses had spread from the southern Sudan and the Nuba Mountains into westernmost West Darfur. The Masalit leaders, a Muslim tribe whose leaders speak their own dialect as well as Arabic, claimed that their people were under a systematic attack of "ethnic cleansing"—just "like other non-Arab ethnic groups in the regions such as the Fur and Zaghawa"— by Khartoum-armed Arab paramilitary militias. These *janjaweed* (the name has many derivations, including the G3 automatic weapon; the *jawad*, or horse; and, reportedly a word from a Darfur dialect signifying an outlaw band) militias massacred civilians, burned villages, "and caused a massive flight of whole non-Arab communities from their ancestral lands."[30]

Faced with a revolt that exceeded the capacity of the country's overstretched army, Bashir's military leadership knew exactly what to do. Several times during the war in the South they had mounted counter-insurgency on the cheap, with famine and scorched earth being their weapons of choice. Where it was possible, they sought out a local militia or disaffected military leader, provided supplies and armaments, and declared the area of operations an ethics-free zone. Thus, the Beni Halba *fursan* (mounted cavalry) used against Bolad in 1991 was revived in the center and the south, as were the

---

[29] Dawud Ibrahim Salih et al., Representatives of the Massaleit Community in Exile, "Genocide of the Massaleit in Western Sudan," Cairo, Egypt, 28 March 2000.
[30] "The Hidden Slaughter and Ethnic Cleansing in Western Sudan," http://www.massaleit.info/open_letter.html, 24 December 1999.

abbala in the north, and the retired Qaddafi-armed Arab Islamic Legionnaires. When the government maintained that it was ignorant of the aims and abilities of the Arab militias—elements of which it had armed and officered—its denials were soon seen as a duplicitous attempt to cloak the activities of Bashir and his cohorts in their support of an Arab jihad.

Eventually, a reconciliation conference was held that eventually agreed on the payment of compensation for Masalit and Arab losses. It was, however, a palliative and not a solution to the crisis. By then the Minority Rights Group estimated that 5,000 Fur and 400 Arabs had been killed, tens of thousands had been displaced, and 40,000 homes destroyed. This time the Masalit were dragged into the internecine maelstrom, and the horrific warfare that emerged in 2001 was the result. In mid-1999 there were more than 25,000 western Sudanese living in deplorable conditions in refugee camps in Chad. Despite the efforts of refugee organizations, the Masalit would not move "for fear of tribal clashes at home."[31] Anti-government forces reported that the peace was fragile. Indeed, improvement in security would not last the year, and conditions immediately deteriorated after the Masalit chief Yakoub Ahmed and his wife were assassinated in front of their house in Geneina town. [32]

The Masalit leadership noted that the NIF used the term "jihad" to describe its war against the southern Sudanese rebels, but in Muslim western Sudan, it had become apparent "that the discourse of Islamization is a code word for something else. Behind the banner of Islamization in Northern Sudan is a deeply racist policy of Arabization, and it is a part of the logic of this policy that the non-Arab ethnic groups of Western Sudan have come under attack." These attacks were occurring either despite or because of the region's "deep roots in Islam" and the "traditional loyalty to the Umma Party," and because the Khartoum government considered non-Arabs "to be potential fifth-columnists in the civil war because of their 'African' identity and cultural heritage." And although Khartoum has claimed that the violence that has plagued western Sudan in the 1990s "is the

---

[31] "Thousands of Sudanese Refugees in Chad Reportedly Refuse to Return Home," AP, Khartoum, 14 August 1999, with information derived from *Al Bayan* newspaper, Khartoum.

[32] "Gunmen Kill Chief and His Wife in Western Sudan," DPA, derived from *Al-Rai al-Aam*, Khartoum, 31 October 1999.

result of tribal conflicts which have always existed in the area," it has
not been the case until recently that such clashes became commonplace. [33]

The Agony of Darfur

After Hasan al-Turabi returned to power in Khartoum in 1990, he
spent little energy on Darfur—or for that matter on conditions in
the North and East. In contrast, he had sponsored the jihad in southern Sudan and, impelled by the NIF, sustained a genocidal war that
claimed over two million lives. Little thought and even less action
was devoted to bettering the livelihood of the Sudan's ethnic minorities. Like his nemesis, Sadiq al-Mahdi, Turabi appeared content
to permit the military to use Darfur as a playground in which to work
out its prejudices and proclivities. It was a policy as old as the
Republic of the Sudan itself.

The military element within the NIF government—which brooked
little civilian interference in its military affairs—continued to arm
Arab militias in Darfur. And the parliament sitting in Khartoum was
content to sit back and watch as the competition for land between the
sedentary non-Arabs and the semi-nomadic pastoral Arab tribes spun
out of control. In doing nothing, and in actually approving the dis-
arming of the non-Arab tribes in Darfur, the Khartoum government—and Turabi himself—seemed to be endorsing racial conflict
and ethnic cleansing.

Yet, in a curious juxtaposition of political forces that could only
occur in the Sudan, the appearance of the *Black Book* in May 2000
marked "a symbolic rapprochement" between Turabi and his
Islamists and the "secular radicals of Darfur." That unity of opposites
coincided with the formation of the Darfur Liberation Front, which
would soon attack government forces throughout Darfur.[34] It was a
signal moment, because it was clear that the Bashir-Turabi split was
having a pernicious effect in Darfur, and that many of the region's
political rebels who had joined Turabi and his Islamist movement

---

[33] Samantha Power, "Dying in Darfur," *The New Yorker*, 30 August 2004.
[34] Alex de Waal, "Counter-Insurgency on the Cheap," *London Review of Books*,
Vol. 26, No. 15, 5 August 2004.

were now moving to organize on their own. In July, the nascent Popular Congress Party formed by Turabi entered into formal opposition to Bashir and his National Congress. Yet, despite Turabi's urging that nothing less than a jihad was required to overthrow President Bashir, it was soon seen that the PCP hardly dented the solidarity of the ruling regime's political coalition. In November, the parliamentary elections were boycotted by Turabi and his party. By then, Khartoum had received a warning that the Islamists beholden to Turabi had made common cause with the secular opposition. Together they were primed to join the NDA and an alliance with the SPLA's John Garang, and that could mean nothing but trouble for Bashir.

In what was to be the first significant public disturbance in Darfur since the NSRCC took power, three days of rioting in Darfur erupted in mid-September 2000 and shook the Khartoum government to its foundation. Seemingly from nowhere, an opposition appeared in the streets of El Fasher. The demonstration had begun when government teachers protested the constant delay in the payment of salaries, and their pupils joined in. A mob had formed, and buildings, vehicles, the radio station, and other symbols of government were attacked. Order was only slowly restored and only after a female student was killed and a score of protesters injured. Ominously, an amorphous opposition threatened even more anti-government protests if its demands were not met.

The Bashir government was unable to hide what had occurred and chose to blame the outbreak on the People's Congress. Turabi, the speaker of the country's discharged parliament, would receive special attention, and the government soon announced: "Leaders in the North Darfur State legislative council, known for their loyalty to the People's Congress, have instigated the riots." In Khartoum, Turabi responded with a press conference held in front of his party office; he warned that the political climate was "ripe" for demonstrations. He asserted that "the government is ignoring the rights of teachers and taking money from the pupils." He also denounced the rising cost of living in the Sudan and opposed the conscription of young men for compulsory military service, something that he had long championed in the war with the southern Sudanese.[35]

---

[35] "Sudan: Anti-Government Riots Blamed On Opposition," PANA (Panafrican News Agency), Khartoum, at allAfrica.com, 15 September 2000.

The attacks on the Masalit continued with increasing savagery, and as Darfur's Arab nomads continued their invasion of tribal lands, an alliance involving the Islamists in Khartoum and Darfur's African Muslims were busy cobbling together a loose alliance of military forces. The secular rebel forces were building the Darfur Liberation Front (renamed in early 2003 the Sudan Liberation Movement/ Army, or SLM/A); beginning as a small and vulnerable armed militia, its roots were traced to the unrest that resulted from the terrible famines that befell Darfur in the late 1980s. It was joined by ethnic Zaghawa, angry because the government had failed to enforce the terms of a spate of peace agreements that had followed attacks on Zaghawa villages and the murder of "prominent tribal leaders." Many ethnic Zaghawa who had been bloodied in previous battles in Darfur and Chad were already well armed.

In contrast, the PCP supported the Justice and Equality Movement (JEM) with its leavening of Islamists. Of the two rebel groups that participated in the Darfur revolt, the JEM was the smaller fraction of the rebel whole, and it was said by both friends and enemies to be an arm of the Popular Congress Party. Because Turabi had sponsored a program that for the first time allowed African Muslims to enter the officer corps in large numbers, his enemies claimed that he had personally chosen the JEM leadership from a circle of military friendly to him and his political movement. [36] Officially founded in November 2002, the JEM was led by Turabi ally Dr. Khalil Ibrahim, an ethnic Zaghawa of the important Kubie tribe, whose numerous villages were located in northeastern Chad. Dr. Ibrahim had previously served as minister for Darfur, and in the early 1990s he had also ingratiated himself with Zaghawa and other Darfur minorities active in military service.

When the Darfur opposition threatened even more anti-overnment protests, the Bashir government responded furiously. It issued more statements accusing Turabi and his People's (or Popular) Congress of instigating trouble. Turabi's enemies explained what was happening in Darfur by drawing the analogy between nineteenth-century Mahdism, a movement whose power was grounded in the

---

[36] "Darfur Governor Links Khartoum Plot with Rebels," Reuters, 26 September 2004; "What Kind of Intervention Will Work in Darfur," News from Africa, Nairobi, August 2004; "Power Struggle," *Time*, 31 October 2004.

West, and a nascent twenty-first century "Turabism," with the deposed speaker of parliament having long ties to Darfur's Arab and ethnic minorities. When Turabi and his PCP followers refused to join the new parliament later that year, the leader and his movement were treading on dangerous ground.

In juxtaposition, the government was arming and providing military leadership to the local Arab militias. Coalesced as the janjaweed, their attacks (and atrocities) were directed at the region's ethnic Fur, Tunjur, Masalit, and Zaghawa. They would degenerate into a massacre that observers argued was nothing less than genocide. Given the history of the region since the independence of the Sudan, the rebellion should have taken no one by surprise. The only wonder was why the gestation period had lasted so long.[37] Unfortunately for Turabi, for his PCP, and for the growing opposition in Darfur, the cabal of military and security officers that had been running the wars in the Sudan since 1983, and that served as the central pillar of the Sudanese state, was still solidly in place.

To make matters worse, the drought in 2000 was almost universal throughout Sudan, and for those affected in Darfur there was only limited employment opportunity in Central and riverain Sudan. In October, a regional study, confirmed by U.N. FAO and World Food Program investigations, discerned that crop production in two thirds of North Darfur's villages had been greatly reduced. The vast majority of Darfur's families soon had no food reserves left, and nearly ninety percent were dependent on food purchased at local markets. Even worse, some 400,000 people were soon "critically short of water." Thus, to prevent widespread famine in 2001, the United Nations began to plan for the provision of at least 25,000 tons of grain. Khartoum was forewarned that severe famine threatened the country in 2001 if nothing were done to overcome food shortages in Darfur.[38]

Using the deteriorating situation in Darfur as a hammer with which to beat an indifferent Bashir regime, a physically and mentally revived Turabi worked tirelessly in opposition until February 2001.

---

[37] For a history of the region, see J. Millard Burr and Robert O. Collins, *Darfur: The Long Road to Disaster* (Princeton, NJ: Markus Wiener Publishers, 2008).

[38] Steve Collins, "How Bad Does It Have to Get? The Nutritional Status in N. Darfur in the Spring of 2001," Save the Children, United Kingdom/El Fasher, 2001, pp. 2-4.

He was arrested a day after holding a rabble-rousing news conference, during which "he called on Sudanese to rise against President
Omar al-Bashir's government, [and] announced that he was in
contact with the U.S. government." In noting talks with the Americans he stated, "Of course they want to know what Islamists think and
how they think." Turabi did not further elaborate but managed to
lob another symbolic grenade at Bashir, claiming he had "reached
an understanding with rebels fighting successive Khartoum governments in the south of Sudan since 1983."[39]

That blatant move, one unlike anything Turabi had tried before,
was too much for Bashir to take. Turabi was arrested at his Khartoum
home on 21 February and was charged with conspiring with the SPLA
"to topple the government." The SPLA wasted no time confirming
that a "breakthrough" memorandum of understanding had been
reached. It substantiated Turabi's claim that there existed "no gap"
between the two parties with respect to "the question of religion,"
but the SPLA declined to be more specific. Then, with Turabi under
arrest, the Bashir regime seized the moment to overwhelm his followers, and in March 2001 it placed on trial the eight PCP politicians,
who, as noted above, were arrested in December 2000.

The United States: Sudan on Trial

In February 2001, four members of the Al Qaeda organization were
put on trial in New York for the bombing of U.S. embassies in Kenya
and Tanzania in 1998. Jamal Ahmad al-Fadl, a former Bin Laden aide
and paymaster turned FBI informant, was a star witness. He had
previously pleaded guilty, at a secret hearing held in federal court in
New York City, to a charge of terrorism, and he described in detail the
early years of Al Qaeda, including its formative period in the Sudan.[40]
Al-Fadl recounted the activity that occurred at the Bin Laden headquarters in Khartoum, where he managed the Al Qaeda payroll. He
was an intriguing witness, having had access to the files on Al Qaeda

---

[39] Mohamad Osman, "Former Parliament Speaker in Sudan Is Arrested after
Calling for Uprising against Government," AP, Khartoum, 21 February 2001.
   [40] Peter Grier, "A Terrorist Version of NATO?" *The Christian Science Monitor*,
date unknown, 2001; A. Brownfeld, "Bin Ladin's Activities Exposed in New York
Trial," *Jane's Terrorism and Security Monitor*, 14 March 2001.

members, and he was aware of the intricacies involved in the purchase of clandestine passports and the efforts undertaken to purchase uranium and chemical weapons. He outlined in great detail the Bin Laden banking apparatus in the Sudan, as well as the Al Qaeda leader's investments in the country. He also detailed the role played by Hasan al-Turabi as protector and inspiration for Osama Bin Laden and his organization.

In the United States, the trial was the precursor to a CNN report on the Khartoum/Bin Laden connection, which aired on 14 February 2001. It provided startling material on the interrelationship of the "National Islamic Front" regime and Al Qaeda. In May, the *Washington Post* reported that despite Bashir's claim that he wanted better relations with Washington, the State Department's annual report on terrorism claimed: "Sudan remains a safe haven for members of several terrorist groups, including Osama bin Laden's Al Qaeda organization, and has not fully complied with U.N. Security Council resolutions demanding that it end assistance to terrorists." The report noted that even though the Bashir government's policies had improved, the Sudan still "continued to be used as a safe-haven" by members of Al Qaeda, the Gamaat al-Islamiya, Egypt Islamic Jihad, Palestine Islamic Jihad, and Hamas. [41]

The State Department warned that the worldwide threat from terrorism was not over, and on the release of its annual report on the status of international terrorism, Secretary of State Colin Powell averred, "The fight goes on."He added that even as the government acknowledged some successes, the future would offer both new challenges and setbacks: "But we continue to reduce our vulnerability and above all to renew our determination to combat an ever-present danger to international peace and innocent lives."[42] The very uneasy relationship between the Sudan and the United States would continue until later that year. It was the September 11 terrorist attacks in the United States that changed the calculus in the Sudan-United States equation, and both sides were immediately forced to review in some detail their policies toward one another.

---

[41] Alan Sipress reporting, *The Washington Post*, 1 May 2001; "Sudan, Osama bin Laden, and Terrorism," *The Washington Post*, 21 August 2001.
[42] As reported in the *Los Angeles Times*, 1 May 2001, and other American newspapers.

The attack on the United States placed intense pressure on the Bush administration to expand the war on terrorism from its focus on individual cells to broader campaigns against nations that harbored terrorist organizations. President Bush informed the nation that a shift in emphasis in the War on Terror was underway. In an address to the nation from the White House, he stated: "We will make no distinction between the terrorists who committed these acts and those who harbor them." News articles noted that intelligence agencies argued that Afghanistan, Iran, Iraq, and the Sudan continued to provide safe haven for terrorist groups. [43]

By October, Washington had decided to lift at least some of the sanctions it had imposed on the Sudan in 1996. The decision resulted from Khartoum's increased efforts to cooperate with the United States in what was being called "its global anti-terrorism campaign." In a propaganda effort to show a new face to the world, forty-eight hours after the United Nations lifted its sanctions on the Sudan on 1 October, Bashir ordered the release of opposition leaders who had been charged with plotting an uprising backed by the United States and were now facing trial. Sudanese diplomat Al-Fatih Urwah then asserted that the process of lifting sanctions and the discussions with United States officials had involved "counter-terrorist experts in the Sudan," and they were able "to meet the concerns that the U.S. government had." [44]

The whirlwind attack on Afghanistan and the success of that invasion provided the obvious signal that it would not be wise for Khartoum to antagonize Washington. Still, if anything, the 9/11 attacks strengthened Bashir's political position at home. And cynics argued that his rapprochement with the United States was prompted more by domestic politics than by any commitment to liberal democracy or the jettisoning of the Islamic Civilization project. Many Sudanese, including some in Bashir's circle, were convinced that the Sudan had avoided a United States invasion of southern Sudan in the early 1990s only through the fortuitous election of President Bill Clinton. Fortunately for Khartoum, Clinton had found conditions in Somalia more demanding of his time than U.S. concerns involving the Sudan.

---

[43] Esther Shrader et al., "America Attacked; World Reaction," *The Los Angeles Times*, 12 September 2001.

[44] "Sudan Frees Turabi and Leaders Accused of U.S.-backed Plot," 2 October 2001, www.islamonline.net/english/news/2001-10/02/article4.shtml.

Turabi in Jail, Bashir in Charge

For his part, 9/11 or not, the incarcerated Turabi was determined to make trouble. Under no circumstance, however, would he be allowed to make a political comeback. In October, a day after the foreign press reported that Khartoum sought to open a dialogue with Washington, the Sudanese security forces arrested seven members of Turabi's PCP. The action took place after members provoked the police who were "guarding" the party headquarters, which the government had closed. When members tried to enter the compound, the police roughed up a number of the protestors, including Ibrahim al-Sanoussi. The event at PCP headquarters was a portent of government attacks to come.

The government was determined to minimize PCP activity, and in so doing it used propaganda to good effect. In one instance, Bashir discontinued the court case that had been brought against six NDA members. It was announced that these individuals were no longer considered a threat to national security, but that Hasan al-Turabi would remain under house arrest. In effect, the move to free politicians while holding Turabi ransom was seen locally as a transparent effort to improve the regime's image, curry favor with the United States, and "protect the president's power base at home." In releasing "some members but keeping Turabi under arrest, the government could maintain pressure on its most threatening opposition."[45] Despite the fact that the Constitutional Court had already ruled in favor of Turabi and ordered his release from arrest, the government would keep him in indefinite confinement. As one political analyst explained: "Freeing Turabi, who has been associated with terrorism and Osama bin Laden, would send the wrong signal to the U.S. That's why he's still in custody." The PCP was warned by the Minister of Interior, Abd al-Rahim Muhammad Hussein, that although the regime would release jailed politicians, it would also act swiftly to arrest those regarded as a menace to good order.[46]

Turabi began the year 2002 in jail, and though he maintained a significant and vociferous public following, the extremist image that the

---

[45] Alfred Taban, "Sudan Seeks to Boost Foreign Ties, Keep Power Base," Reuters, 3 October 2001.

[46] BBC Monitoring Service, United Kingdom, 4 October 2001; text of report by Sudanese newspaper Al-Ra'y al-Amm web site, 3 October 2001.

Sudan sought to dispel ensured his confinement. In keeping Turabi locked up while maintaining pressure on the PCP, the Bashir regime managed to kill two birds with one stone. In June, a spokesman for the PCP condemned the continuing arrest of Hasan al-Turabi after the leader underwent his fourth eye surgery in seventeen months. Calling his incarceration a "huge injustice," the PCP sought his release on both ethical and humanitarian grounds. Instead, in August 2002, an additional twenty-six PCP members were arrested on charges that they had stored arms and explosives and were planning to spring Turabi from detention. In a late 2002 interview with the editor of *Al Sharq Al Awsat*, Turabi, by then under house arrest outside Khartoum, was his customary confident and defiantly Islamist self in his interpretation of recent historical events. He was as convinced as ever that men like Bashir would fail, and "policies inspired by the readiness to appease America, practiced by dictatorial regimes intent on repulsing Islam in the name of fighting terrorism, will be of little use in subjugating the Islamic movements."[47]

President Bashir ignored the jibes thrown his way, and despite all indications to the contrary, he declared that 2002 would be the "year of peace" in war-torn Sudan. Indeed, the quest for peace in southern Sudan gained momentum following 9/11 when, in January 2002, a cease-fire was agreed to in the Nuba Mountains. The SPLA, left for dead on numerous occasions, was not finished and in June captured Kapoeta, the important South Sudan garrison town. It was the SPLA's most important victory in two years. Almost on cue, rumors of peace talks abounded. With Turabi sidelined, Bashir and his military friends were no longer convinced that the interminable conflict in South Sudan was worth the jihad. The conflict of nineteen years' duration had caused at least two million deaths in southern Sudan, and it had exhausted the nation. Nonetheless, Bashir warned that while his government was committed to negotiations with the SPLM/A, it would not shy away from the "military option," if that were the only means to achieve peace.

As for the SPLA, it was primed to continue the battle, claiming that the government had used a pause in fighting to further secure the oil pipeline, and in doing so had carried out continuous attacks

---

[47] Hasan al-Turabi, "America Will Not Tolerate Islamic Movements, Even if They Are Peaceful," *New Perspective Quarterly*, Vol. 19, No. 2, pp. 59-64.

on civilian targets. And if the war in the South seemed endless, in the West internecine warfare between African and Arab Muslims was spiraling out of control. Even worse for the military, the situation in Darfur had begun to attract attention in Europe and the United States. It was a mounting headache that would somehow have to be contained. The janjaweed had already uprooted thousands of villagers, and the displaced sought safety wherever they could– whether in Darfur or in neighboring Chad.

In Washington, the Bush administration seized on Bashir's peace initiative, and the Sudan Peace Act (H.R. 5631) was signed into law by President Bush on 21 October 2002. This legislation continued the effort begun in Washington to bring the long civil war in southern Sudan to a close. In July, a success had been recorded when the Machakos Protocol resolved "critical issues of state, religion and the right of Sudan's south to self-determination." It was a slow process, but the efforts of former Senator John Danforth, the United States Special Envoy for Peace in Sudan, would eventually have their effect on the war in the South. It would not be easy. In Khartoum, Bashir vowed that his administration would never accept a secular system of government in Khartoum and rejected the SPLA demand that the federal capital city should be given secular status.

The End of an Islamist Experiment

In early 2003, while Turabi remained under arrest, the violence in Darfur increased exponentially. Many observers, including the authors of the *Black Book* who had joined the "Darfur Conflict," reported on the strife. By then the world was aware that the conflict had resulted in an additional tens of thousands killed and hundreds of thousands of residents displaced. Reporters issued accounts of the deplorable conditions suffered by more than a hundred thousand refugees crowded together in Chad.[48] And as the horrific janjaweed attacks increased in number and ferocity, the claims of genocide began to spread in the Western media. After years of deadly warfare, Darfur had at last captured the attention of the world.

---

[48] "Thousands of Sudanese Refugees in Chad Reportedly Refuse to Return Home," AP, Khartoum, 14 August 1999, with information derived from *Al Bayan* newspaper, Khartoum.

As for the Popular Congress Party, Turabi's associates labored to keep the movement alive while Turabi still sought to play a role in Darfur. He supported the SLM/A insurgency launched in early 2003, but the JEM, which had ties to Turabi and the PCP, was still operating on its own. And while Darfur deteriorated, in the shadow play of Sudan politics, Dr. Ali Al-Haj, PCP Deputy Secretary-General, met with Commander Nhial Deng, member of the SPLA leadership in June 2003, and together they continued the process of political agreement that had begun with the Memorandum of Understanding signed in February 2001. A working paper was distributed concerning "the issues of Peace and Democratic Transition." In it, the two parties urged the end of "arbitrary detention, persecution and torture and the release of all political detainees—most notably Dr. Hasan al-Turabi, the Secretary-General of the Popular Congress."[49]

In southern Sudan, United States special envoy John Danforth and Assistant Secretary of State Walter Kansteiner continued in their efforts to advance the peace talks between Khartoum and the SPLM/SPLA. In September 2003, the Navaisha Agreement began to unknot the seemingly intractable security issues that had divided Khartoum and the rebels of South Sudan. The following month the two sides agreed to cooperate in providing humanitarian access to all areas of the Sudan. Unfortunately, even as the effort to bring peace to southern Sudan was making slow progress, the normalization of Khartoum-Washington relations was being blocked by a number of obstacles. President George W. Bush responded predictably after the Sudan refused to meet Washington demands that it close the Hamas and Islamic Jihad offices in Khartoum. As far as Washington was concerned, the War on Terror trumped any progress made in the wars in the Sudan, and the policies pursued by Khartoum were still seen as a potential threat to the national security of the United States.

Although it was perfectly clear that Turabi remained a dangerous antagonist, his release was scheduled for mid-August 2003 (according to the "emergency law" that then governed the Sudan). However, the day for his discharge came and went, and when Turabi's PCP lawyers urged Justice Minister Ali Othman Ismael to free their client, they were told that only Bashir himself could take that step. Bashir had already offered to release Turabi, but he was in no hurry to do so.

---

[49] Translation in the authors' possession.

When his release finally came on 13 October 2003, the Khartoum media reported that it was the result of ongoing peace talks with southern Sudanese during which Khartoum had promised to free a number of political detainees. With Turabi's release, all restrictions against the PCP were lifted.

Still, Turabi's freedom was tenuous. Within days, Sudanese Vice President Ali Osman Taha, the determined politician bound to assume the leadership of the Sudan's Islamist movement, accused his old mentor of abetting sedition in Darfur. Indeed, the government argued that Turabi and his party members were manipulating events in the West, and that the JEM rebels were in actuality an arm of the PCP itself. Taha observed events in Darfur with great concern as Turabi began a personal effort to involve European countries, the United Nations, and international aid agencies in Darfur peace talks. That effort was visualized as Turabi's first move in a new chess match whose endgame would be the fall of the Bashir government. In effect, Darfur would serve as the stage on which the Taha-Turabi rivalry for control of the Islamist movement would be played out. And Taha was determined to win at all costs.

President Bashir could hardly have been pleased when, only days after being freed, Turabi announced that he would soon meet with John Garang—although neither the date for the meeting nor "its venue" was set. Likewise, he could not have been pleased when Turabi offered his own solution to the wars in the Sudan; Turabi formulated a peace that would include revenue sharing with sixty percent of the budget going to the central government and forty percent to the states. After spending nearly three years under arrest, and after only a month of freedom, Turabi was again on the march. He accepted the invitation of Al Jazeera Television to appear as a featured guest on a religious program, and on his arrival at Doha, the Islamist emissary would be received with the honors a *murshid* might expect.[50]

Demonstrating that it was not finished with Turabi, in December the government arrested twenty-three PCP members. The event was explained by *Al Jazeera,* which noted that, "According to diplomatic sources, one of the Darfur rebel groups, the Movement for Justice and Equality, has been expanding with support from Turabi."[51]

---

[50] "Turabi Meets with Garang Shortly," ArabicNews.com, 31 October 2003; "Turabi Is Permitted to travel to Doha," ArabicNews.com, 14 November 2003.

[51] "Al-Turabi Denies Starting Darfur Conflict," Al Jazeera.net, 31 December 2003.

Obviously under threat, in February 2004 Turabi held a press conference that was designed to cause trouble. He stated that the PCP
"was unapologetic about its solidarity with [the] rebels' cause." He
then promised that he would use his influence, "not to ask them to
lay down their arms, but to ensure they will get their full rights." Nat-
urally, it was only a matter of time after Turabi asserted that the revolt
in the West was a "just cause" that he would be arrested once again.
It finally happened in late March 2004, and, as the Interior Ministry
explained the situation, the arrest followed "an attempted coup led
by senior army officers of Darfur origin."[52]

The arrest came only hours after the arrest of twenty-seven army
officers of Darfur birth (and who had been placed under surveillance
since 2002). According to government press releases, Turabi's arrest
resulted from his plotting with ten military officers to end the
Machakos peace process, and because he supported the rebel agenda
in Darfur. On 1 April 2004, Turabi was officially charged with dam-
aging Sudan's security; the party newspaper was closed, and the PCP
headquarters and the party's state offices were once again shuttered.
And this time, the Interior Ministry vowed that Turabi would not get
off so easily; he would be put on trial for "instigating tribal and regional sedition and harming security." In July, thirty-six PCP leaders
were also charged in the alleged coup, and two months later another
seventy PCP members were detained and charged with assisting the
subversive JEM movement. Ultimately, scores of PCP members arrested in connection with the alleged coup were held until December 2004 when the government dropped charges against Turabi of
plotting a coup. The government did not offer an explanation or
clarification, but Turabi remained in official custody.

Turabi was still under arrest when the Comprehensive Peace
Agreement was signed by the SPLM/A and government on 9 January
2005, and thus his comments on the agreement were stifled by government censorship. With that signing the civil war of more than
twenty years' duration was finally ended. Turabi was held for fifteen
months in detention, and when he was released the date was chosen
with some care. It took place as the government celebrated the fifteenth anniversary of the 30 June 1989 revolution. Once again Turabi

---

[52] Anders Hastrup, "Sudan's Black Book," The Tharwa Project, July 2004,
http://www.tharwaproject.com/English/Main-Sec/Files/Darfur/hastrup.htm.

and his party were permitted freedom to operate, the PCP headquarters was reopened, and the party newspaper was allowed to publish. Undaunted, Turabi immediately went on the attack against
Bashir. The situation in Darfur was intolerable, and as far as he was
concerned, anti-democratic elements had hijacked the nation's
interim constitution.[53] As Turabi continued his drumbeat of criticism,
few observers expected that he would remain free for long.

Conclusion

The Islamic Project of Hasan al-Turabi had failed. It had little appeal
for the mass of Sudanese in the countryside. It had never diminished
the allegiance of those Sudanese loyal to the Mahdiyya and Khatmiyya Brotherhoods, leaving Turabi the leader of a small minority
movement in the urban communities where the Blue and the White
Nile meet. Although many Sudanese on the periphery of the Sudan
in the south, west, and east were devout Muslims, they were never
attracted to the Islamists, who demanded conformity at the price of
others'deep attachment to their traditional cultures, Sufi Islam, and
ethnic identity. Despite his learning, charisma, and oratory, his
energy and panache, and his vision of the new Islamic society that
stimulated and excited the new Sudanese and Islamists abroad,
Hasan al-Turabi was a flawed revolutionary.

In 1989, Turabi recognized the opportunity to create the brave
new Islamist world, the Islamic renaissance, to which he had devoted
his talents throughout his life, but he never conceived the necessary
means to achieve it. He sincerely believed that his PAIC General
Assembly would be the convocation where Islamists of the world
could meet to discuss, define, and demonstrate their allegiance to
the revival of the Faith that would transcend its historic divisions
through its universal global appeal. Here in the sanctuary of the
Sudan on the frontier of Islam, the Islamists under Turabi's guidance
and direction could explore the means to achieve the Islamic renaissance. He perceived that his mission was to define the ideology

---

[53] The Darfur story is continued in the authors' "Epilogue" in *Darfur: The Long
Road to Disaster* (Princeton, NJ: Markus Wiener Publishers, 2008), pp. 305-317.
Turabi was next arrested on 12 May 2008 and charged with "aiding a Darfur rebel
attack on the capital." AP, Khartoum dateline, 12 May 2008.

and the goal, not to physically lead the Islamist jihad against Muslim and non-Muslim unbelievers. When confronted by supporters and critics, his words were more a rhetorical call to arms without the marching orders to achieve the objective. His leadership may have been inspirational, but the contradictions and ambiguities of his thought and speech obscured the path to a utopian world of peace and fellowship governed by a beneficent Islam. His leadership may have been inspirational, but when his followers required instructions on the methods for building his vision of a universal Islamic society, he had no practical answers except his rhetoric, the example of the Sudan as the new Islamic model, and his association with a network of unsavory terrorists. The more he employed his oratorical skills to rally his followers, the more he exposed the contradictions in his message. The more he held up the revolutionary government of the Sudan as the model for the Islamic renaissance, the more he became the prisoner of his own hubris. The more dependent he became on terrorism as the means to overthrow secular Islamic states and ultimately the West, the more he fell into denial.

To his supporters, Hasan al-Turabi remains the one who provided the vision for a new society to arise from the corruption of the old. To his critics, Hasan al-Turabi remains the charming salesman of a dysfunctional mission—a mission that was exposed on 19 February 2001 by his signature on the memorandum of understanding with the SPLA. It appeared to all but the faithful a desperate, if not cynical, "last hurrah" of a disillusioned man seeking a place in history.

When Omar Hassan Ahmad al-Bashir realized that the Sudan was no longer to be the center for the resurrection of the Islamic world, there was no longer any place for an old and failing Hasan al-Turabi and his Islamist experiment.

RECENT DEVELOPMENTS IN SUDAN

In memoriam,
by Robert O. Collins's former graduate student
Ahmad A. Sikainga

For about ten years, Hasan al-Turabi was considered the prime mover behind Sudan's Islamicist regime, which seized power through a military coup in 1989. During this period, he helped consolidate the regime's control of the country and firmly established a strong political and economic base for his Islamicist organization, which was transformed from the National Islamic Front to the National Congress. At the same time, Turabi embarked on an ambitious project to create a kind of "universal" Islamic movement throughout the Muslim world. However, Turabi's status and fortunes drastically changed when the power struggle between him and President Bashir reached a peak in 1999. This conflict, which was known in Sudanese political circles as the struggle between "the Palace and Al-Manshiyyah," a reference to the location of Bashir's office in the Republican Palace and the house of Turabi in the suburb of Al-Manshiyyah, was brewing for some time. At its core were Turabi's systematic efforts to marginalize Bashir and concentrate power in his own hands. This led to the alienation of Bashir and the military establishment, as well as some of the leading figures in the Islamicist movement, such as Ali Osman Taha, Turabi's protégé and deputy. The situation exploded in November 1999 when, as a parliament speaker, Turabi introduced a bill to reduce the president's powers. Bashir responded swiftly by dissolving the parliament, suspending Turabi as National Congress chairman, and declaring a state of emergency.

The Islamicist movement, which Turabi had worked so hard to create, split right in the middle. Having lost all his partisan and official positions, Turabi was forced to form an opposition party, called the Popular Congress Party. However, the bulk of the Islamicist movement and most of its leading figures, such as Taha, joined the Bashir camp. Ultimately, Turabi–the man who was once considered the "godfather" of the regime—was accused of plotting to overthrow it and was consequently detained from February 2001 to October 2003.

The split between Bashir and Turabi had profound ramifications both within and outside Sudan. To end the crippling isolation that resulted from his earlier radical policies, Bashir took steps to improve relations with Sudan's neighbors such as Egypt, Uganda, Kenya, and Eritrea. Under intense international pressure and George Bush's war on terror, he finally caved in and resumed peace talks with the Sudan People's Liberation Movement (SPLM) to end the debilitating civil war in the South. The negotiations culminated in the signing in 2005 of the Comprehensive Peace Agreement (CPA). In addition to splitting oil revenues with the South, the accord provided for a six-year period of interim rule headed by a government of national unity. At the end of the interim period, the South would hold a referendum to decide whether to remain part of a united Sudan or to break away. The agreement was met with jubilation throughout the country and was seen by many as Sudan's last chance to achieve peace and stability. However, these hopes were dashed quickly with the tragic death of John Garang, the leader of the SPLM, in July 2005, three weeks after he arrived in Khartoum as the first vice president in the government of national unity. His mysterious death in a helicopter crash near the Sudan-Uganda border led to deadly riots in Khartoum and northern Sudanese towns, increased southerners' suspicions of the North, and drastically diminished the possibility of unity. Compounding the problem was the continuing haggling between the ruling National Congress and the SPLM over the implementation of the provisions of the CPA.

As the conflict in the South was coming to an end, a new one erupted in the western province of Darfur in early 2003. As was the case in the South, the Darfur conflict was a consequence of the political and economic marginalization the region had suffered for many decades. In response to the outbreak of the rebellion, the Bashir regime pursued relentless scorched earth warfare by creating and then providing military and financial support to the Janjaweed militias, who have been accused of gross human rights violations. The death and the displacement of millions of people triggered a huge reaction from the international community, prompting the United Nations to call the situation the world's worst humanitarian crisis and leading the United States to accuse the Sudanese government of committing genocide. Despite the deployment of U.N./African Union peacekeeping troops in the region and the signing of a number of ceasefire agreements, the conflict has continued to rage with no end in sight.

Bashir and his supporters often accused Turabi of being the mastermind of the Darfur conflict, in view of the fact that some of the rebel leaders were former members of his political organization. As a result, Turabi was frequently detained and harassed by the regime's security forces. The Sudanese government also blamed Chad for supporting the Darfur rebels, which became a major source of tension between the two countries. The matter was finally referred to the International Court of Criminal Justice (ICC), which charged Bashir with crimes against humanity and issued a warrant for his arrest in March 2009. Only days later, Turabi, who had been detained in January 2009 following his call to Bashir to surrender himself to the ICC for the sake of the country, was released yet again.

As a result of the Bashir-Turabi split, the Islamicist regime lost its ideological cohesion and splintered into several factions that are vying for power and the control of economic resources. The collapse of the regime's so-called "cultural project" and the flow of money from the recently discovered oil have intensified factional competition and led to the emergence of a class of nouveau riche that has used the state institutions to amass considerable wealth. The internal power struggle seemed to be narrowing to one between Bashir and Taha, his vice president, who was considered the mastermind of Turabi's removal. However, recent developments, such as the removal of Salah Abdalla (Ghosh), the head of the powerful Public Security Agency, is a clear indication that Bashir is tightening his grip on power despite the ICC indictment.

Sudan's future may well be decided by two important events: the general elections that are scheduled for April 2010 and the referendum in the South in 2011, the outcome of which will determine whether Sudan will remain a unified country or disintegrate into two or more entities.

BIBLIOGRAPHY

Armstrong, Karen. *The Battle for God*, New York: Ballentine Books, 2001.

Bechtold, Peter. *Politics in Sudan: Parliamentary and Military Rule in an Emerging African Nation*, New York: Praeger, 1976.

Bodansky, Yossef. *Offensive in the Balkans*, Alexandria, Virginia: International Strategic Studies Association, 1995.

———. *Bin Ladin: The Man Who Declared War on America*, Roseville, California: Prima Publishing, 1999.

Burgat, Francois and William Dowell. *The Islamic Movement in North Africa*, Austin, University of Texas Press, 1993.

Burr, J. Millard and Robert O. Collins. *Requiem for the Sudan: War Drought and Disaster Relief on the Nile*, Boulder, Colorado: Westview Press, Boulder, 1995.

———. *Africa's Thirty Years' War: Chad, Libya, and the Sudan, 1963–1993*, Boulder, Colorado: Westview Press, 1999.

Chevalerias, Alain. *Hassan al-Tourabi: Islam, avenir du monde*, Paris: J.C. Lattes, Paris, 1997.

Cohen, Herman J. *Intervening in Africa: Superpower Peacemaking in a Troubled Continent*, New York: Palgrave, 2000.

Deng, F.M., and P. Gifford. *The Search for Peace and Unity in Sudan*, Washington D.C.: Wilson Center Press, 1987.

Esposito, John L. and John O. Voll. *Islam and Democracy*, New York: Oxford University Press, 1996.

El-Affendi, Abdelwahab. *Turabi's Revolution: Islam and Power in Sudan*, London: Grey Seal, 1991.

Hamdi, Mohamed Elhachmi Hamdi. *The Making of a Political Leader: Conversations with Hasan al-Turabi*, Boulder, Colorado: Westview Press, 1998.

Hoffman, Bruce. *Holy Terror: The Implication of Terrorism Motivated by a Religious Imperative*, Santa Monica: RAND Corp., 1993.

Holt, P.M. and M.W. Daly. *A History of the Sudan: From the Coming of Islam to the Present Day*, London: Longman, 1988.

Huntington, Samuel J. *The Clash of Civilizations*, New York: Simon and Schuster, 1996.

Ibrahim Ali, Hayder. *Al-Jabha al-islamiyya al-qawmiyya fi al-Sudan numudhajan* (The Crisis of political Islam: the example of the National Islamic Front in the Sudan), Uzmat al-Islam al-siyasi, Cairo: Center of Sudanese Studies, 1991.

Jacquard, Roland. *In the Name of Osama Bin Laden: Global Terrorism & the Bin Laden Brotherhood*, trans. George Holoch, Durham, NC: Durham University Press, 2002.

Johnson, Douglas H. *The Root Causes of Sudan's Civil Wars*, The International African Institute in association with Oxford: James Currey; Bloomington: Indian University Press; Kampala: Fountain Publishers, 2003.

Khalid, Mansour. *War and Peace in the Sudan: A Tale of Two Countries*, London: Kegan Paul, 2003.

Kobayashi, M. *The Islamist Movement in Sudan: The Imapact of Dr. Hassan al-Turabi's Personality on the Movement*, University of Durham, United Kingdom, Doctoral Dissertation OCLC #48469721, 1996.

Lesch, Ann Mosely. *The Sudan: Contested National Identities*, Bloomington: Indiana Univeristy Press, 1999.

Mitchell, Richard P. *The Society of the Muslim Brothers*, London: Oxford University Press, 1969.

Niblock, Tim. *Pariah States and Sanctions in the Middle East: Iraq, Libya, Sudan.* Boulder, Colorado: Lynne Rienner Publishers, 2002.

Petterson, Donald. *Inside Sudan: Political Islam, Conflict and Catastrophe,* Boulder, Colorado: Westview Press, 1999.

Prendergast, John. *Frontline Diplomacy: Humanitarian Aid and Conflict in Africa,* Boulder, Colorado: Lynne Rienner Publishers, 1996.

Roy, Oliver. *L'echec de l'islam politique,* Paris: Le Seuil, 1994.

Simone, T. Abdou M. *In Whose Image? Political Islam and Urban Practices in Sudan,* Chicago: University of Chicago Press, 1994.

Turabi, Hasan al-. "Hiwar al-Din wa al-Fau" (Dialogue on Religion and Art), Majallat al-Fikr al-Islami, No. 1, pp. 41–64, Khartoum: The Islamic Culture Group, 1983.

———. "Principles of Governance, Freedom and Responsibility in Islam," *American Journal of Islamic Social Sciences,* Vol. 4, No. 1, September 1987.

———. *Al-Harakah al-Islamiyah fi al-Sudan: al-Tatwer wa-al-Kasb wa-al-Manhaj,* Call No. BP64. S73T87, 1991.

———. "Islam, Democracy, the State, and the West," *Middle East Policy,* Vol. 1, No. 3, 1992.

———. "Women in Islam and Muslim Society," *The American Muslim,* Vol. 2, No. 6, April–June 1993.

———. "The Islamic Awakening's New Wave," *New Perspectives Quarterly,* Vol. 10, No. 3, Summer 1993.

———. "Islam as a Pan National Movement and Nation-States: An Islamic Doctrine of Human Association," Lecture, Royal Society for the Encouragement of Arts, Manufactures, and Commerce, London, 27 April 1992, London: The Sudan Foundation, 1997.

U.S. Department of State. *Patterns of Global Terrorism,* Washington D.C.: Office of the Office of the Coordinator for Counterterrorism, U.S. Department of State, 1991 and annually.

Violet, Bernard. *Carlos: les reseaux secrets du terrorisme international,* Paris: Le Seuil, 1996.

Weaver, Mary Anne. *A Portrait of Egypt,* New York: Farrar, Straus and Giroux, 2000.

Wöndu, Steven and Ann Lesch, *Battle for Peace in Sudan,* Lantham, MD: University Press of America, 2000.

Wright, Lawrence. "The Man Behind bin Laden: *How Ayman al-Zawahiri, an Egyptian doctor, became Al Qaeda's guiding force," The New Yorker,* 16 September 2002.

Wright, Robin. *Sacred Rage,* New York: Touchstone Books, 1986.

GENERAL INDEX

The central character of this book is Dr Hasan al-Turabi. References to him can be found throughout the entire book. The references to him in this index have been limited to those that are most crucial to the main arguments of the book.